TROUBLESOME PRESENCE

TROUBLESOME PRESENCE

Democracy and Black Americans

Eli Ginzberg and Alfred S. Eichner

*With a New Introduction and
Postscript by Eli Ginzberg*

Transaction Publishers
New Brunswick (U.S.A.) and London (U.K.)

Library of Congress Catalog Number: 93-16163
ISBN: 1-56000-695-1
Printed in the United States of America

Library of Congress Cataloging-in-Publication Data

Ginzberg, Eli, 1911-
    Troublesome   presence: democracy   and   Black Americans/Eli Ginzberg and Alfred S. Eichner; with a new introduction and postscript by Eli Ginzberg.
        p.   cm.
    Includes bibliographical references.
    ISBN 1-56000-695-1 (pbk.)
    1.   Afro-Americans—History.   2.   United   States—Race relations. I. Eichner, Alfred S. II. Title.
E185.G52   1993
973'.0496—dc20   93-16163
                                                                       CIP

To Ruth

A prudent wife is from the Lord.

Contents

Introduction to the
Transaction Edition

W HEN MY FRIEND AND PUBLISHER, Irving Louis
Horowitz, asked whether I would write a new introductory
and a concluding chapter to *Troublesome Presence* if he agreed
to bring out a new edition, I quickly said yes, since both the
hardback and paperback editions had been out of print for
some time and I believed that my earlier analysis and
interpretation of black experience in white America had
stood the test of time.

I had at least one important confirmation of that
conclusion. I had repeatedly offered one dollar to
anybody—scholar, writer, politician, or member of the
public—who could identify the origins of the title with the
help of two clues: it was a phrase that Lincoln had used, and
he had used it in talking about Henry Clay. I never had to
pay the dollar, which confirmed my belief that both white
and black Americans know less than they should about the
racial relations that have dominated their respective histories.

The answer to the origin of the title is simple and direct.
Henry Clay was a founding member of the African
colonization movement that encouraged free Negroes to
emigrate to Africa in order to assist their black brethren
improve the quality of their lives. In eulogizing Clay, Lincoln
stated that white America had always encountered major
difficulties in accommodating "the troublesome presence of
the free Negro."

Since I delivered the lectures on which the book was based in 1961 at Morris Brown College at Atlanta University and I am writing this new introduction in 1992, the book falls just mid-way in my active working life. The passage of three decades since the book was first published (1964) coincided with the most tumultuous era in the changing relations of black and white Americans since the Civil War and the early years of Reconstruction. How tumultuous is suggested by the anachronism of my original subtitle: "American Democracy and the Negro." In the early 1960s no one talked of blacks, even less of Afro-Americans; today it is significant that no writer or speaker would use the term "Negro."

To stay with matters of language a little longer. I have changed the subtitle from Negro to black Americans but I have let the term Negro stand in the text because the basic analysis dates from the era when "Negro" was the designation that blacks used to describe themselves.

It is more difficult to assess some of the more important developments of the last thirty years that have altered the lives of blacks and whites, the relationship between them and such complicating factors as the large recent inflows of immigrants from abroad. The probability that by 2010, or shortly thereafter, Hispanics will outnumber blacks as the nation's largest minority, was obscure when this book was first published.

The less one knows about the history of small or large groups and their relations to each other—the Census reported in 1990 that the United States had a black population of 30 million and 200 million non-Hispanic whites—the more likely it is that personal experiences will prove misleading as a basis for generalization. There are few whites or blacks who have had an ongoing close relationship with as many as ten members of other racial groups, a fact which makes it difficult to arrive at even the most tentative generalizations. It is not surprising therefore that the strength of opinion on matters of race is so much greater than supportable propositions.

But after acknowledging this critical handicapping element, attention must still be paid to some of the more important developments that have affected both whites and blacks during the past three decades and that have contributed to both continuities and changes in the relations between them.

With major assistance from each of the three branches of the federal government, especially under Lyndon B. Johnson, and with further support from many state and local governments and important private sector interests, from corporations to religious bodies, most of the legal structure supporting segregation was leveled in the decade between the Brown decision in 1954 and the passage of the Civil Rights Act in 1964. The momentum for change emerged from the decision of a large number of Southern blacks who, with some support from northern whites, took to the streets, using nonviolent tactics to capture the attention of the vast majority who to that time were on the sidelines of the racial struggle. It is easy, especially for those who had no personal experience with the momentous decade of struggle, to minimize what was accomplished. The simplest way to correct this misconception is to point out that (the Reconstruction period aside) for the first time in 345 years after a few blacks had first been deposited by a Dutch trading vessel on the shores of Virginia, blacks were free to enjoy their full rights of citizenship, defined as the use of public accommodations, the right to vote, and to be protected against overt discrimination in the job market.

One hears the cynical and hostile comments of many young blacks, especially those who are trapped in poverty and are exposed to crime, drugs, and stray bullets, questioning the significance of the demolition of the political and legal structures supporting segregation. Many of them are quick to add that since whites continue to control jobs, income, financial assets, and political power, the black minority can be suppressed without the formal apparatus of segregation. True, but overstated.

The overstatement derives in part from an exaggerated view of the depth of racism among the white population, powerful as such prejudices continue to be. Another source of error is to assume that the struggle of people for upward mobility is determined solely or largely by considerations of race, as if ability, education, effort, and values are of little or no importance in the pursuit of opportunities and the distribution of rewards.

While no sensible person will argue that the child of a single-parent household on public assistance, living in a deteriorated urban area will have the same, or even approximately the same, opportunities to "make it" as will a suburban youngster with college-educated parents growing up in a stable, middle-class community. But this gross difference in opportunity must not obscure the fact that over the past three decades a much larger number of blacks—although still a minority—have succeeded in becoming well-educated and obtaining good jobs, and have been able to obtain living quarters in nonsegregated neighborhoods. These, and still other accomplishments, are not to be interpreted as meaning that substantial equality of opportunity or achievement characterize this successful segment of the black community, but only to point out that the last several decades have seen many black families join the dominant middle class despite the many overt and insidious forms of racism that continue to pervade almost every sector of American life.

This latter development is not to be minimized or brushed aside in favor of a preoccupation with blacks in poverty, characterized by the cumulative pathologies of many inner-city black neighborhoods with their high incidence of out-of-wedlock births, large numbers of high school dropouts, widespread involvement with drugs, the persistence of crime, high unemployment, and exposure to many more social pathologies. The term "underclass" which I have never used, was unknown when this book was first published. But some if not all of these same conditións afflicted many urban blacks of an earlier generation.

As is so often the case in social investigations, the analyst is free to focus on what is of personal interest, and the reader in turn is free to accept or reject the interpretations and the conclusions of the analyst. The more emotionally loaded the subject, the more likely that even cautious and balanced analyses are likely to confuse the part with the whole.

It has, in fact, been difficult to select a limited number of themes of black-white relationships during the last three decades which can both illuminate some of the more important developments since my original analysis of the early 1960s and connect it to more recent events. The order in which I deal with these developments neither adds to nor subtracts from their importance.

The overwhelming electoral victory of Lyndon Baines Johnson in November 1964 and the depth of his commitment to improving the status of black Americans represented a unique change from the earlier commitments of chief executives, with the exception of Harry Truman. But, as Martin Luther King, Jr. recognized and feared, the nation's deepening involvement in Vietnam foreshadowed a reduction of both presidential and national attention to the unsolved problems of race. I can offer personal testimony to this shift in presidential priorities. In 1965 President Johnson established a "secret" White House Task Force (of which I was a member) under the chairmanship of George Shultz to review the conditions in urban ghettos and to design remedial policies and programs. As we approached the end of our mission in 1966 with a proposal that carried with it an annual expenditure of around $14 billion, the president's assistant, Joseph Califano, came to our meeting and confiscated all the copies of our draft report. With expenditures in Vietnam putting increasing pressure on the federal budget, Johnson was in no position to pursue a program of both guns and butter. The program to revitalize the ghetto was one of the many casualties of the nation's deepening involvement in Vietnam.

The positions taken by Johnson's successors varied with their political preferences. Nixon did his best to curry favor with northern blacks as well as with southern whites. And he succeeded in bringing a number of southern states into the Republican electoral column, a trend that was strengthened under Reagan and Bush as they played the race theme with little shame and much success. Carter as Democratic candidate, and as president, repeatedly reaffirmed his long-term commitment to racial equality.

Shrewd politician that he was, Johnson realized that his aggressive leadership in racial reforms held risks for the continued dominance of the Democratic Party in future presidential elections in the south, but it is doubtful that he foresaw the extent to which the Republicans would successfully play the racial card in these elections. But they did and with great success, reminding us that racism can continue to thrive after its legal scaffolding has been demolished.

When Martin Luther King, Jr. sought to bring his southern nonviolent public demonstration model to Chicago he found a largely nonresponsive and hostile environment. This model was attractive neither to the blacks whom he sought to engage, nor to whites whose sympathies he needed to mobilize. The model that had succeeded in Birmingham, Selma, Atlanta and in many other cities of the south, was not readily transferable to Chicago or other centers of black concentrations in the North. In retrospect, the moral is clear. Politicians and the law were able to eliminate segregated practices that had earlier been protected by an entrenched legal system. But in the North where the excrescences of formal segregation had never existed, or had been removed decades earlier, there was relatively little that political action could accomplish in the near term, for the large numbers of blacks who were living on the fringes of the white society and who needed better education, more jobs, more and better housing, more income.

Another observation: some of the most potent instruments that the federal government used to advance the integration of blacks into our mainline society, such as court orders to speed school integration, affirmative action policies and quotas to increase the number of blacks who were hired and promoted; set-asides for minorities bidding on public programs, special scholarships and fellowships restricted to blacks and still other measures newly designed to help blacks led to grumbling, opposition, and legal and political counter-attacks by aggrieved whites. They argued that the "favoritism" shown blacks was improper and illegal and they insisted that present-day whites should not be forced to pay for wrongs that had been committed by other whites decades or centuries earlier. The longer the new remedies were in use and the more successful they proved to be in helping the formerly excluded blacks to enjoy expanded opportunities and rewards, the more the opposition gained strength. Eventually President Bush became the leading opponent of the use of "quotas" to right old wrongs.

Few of the early enthusiasts for integrated schooling and integrated housing considered the relative strength of public versus private decision-making in the areas of race relations, especially where the white majority holds strong views about where they want to live and the schools that their children should attend. The courts could order landlords to rent or sell to blacks but the courts were unable to stop the flight of many whites to new suburban locations where blacks could not readily follow. And as white families moved, the proportion of minority children attending urban schools, particularly in the north, grew to a point where many became more, not less, segregated.

Two additional developments of recent decades can help illuminate how the early 1990s differ from the early 1960s. Making use of the title of the last chapter of my 1964 book, the first challenge is to trace what happned as the racial struggle shifted "from freedom to equality." The key challenge is to assess the important changes in the labor market, including educational preparation for work. The second requires focusing on the changing structures in the black community, including the old and new leadership.

On the job front, the nation's record must be judged to have been good during the two decades of the 1970s and the

1980s with each showing close to 20 million additional jobs, a rate of growth far greater than any of our principal competitors in Europe or Asia. On the other hand, there were several substantial recessions that had differentially large and unfavorable effects on blacks. In addition, the number of well-paying blue-collar jobs declined; the number of "knowledge jobs" requiring at a minimum a community college degree increased; and a large number of inner-city jobs previously available to the urban black population had been shifted to the suburbs and beyond. These developments made it much more difficult for young blacks who had dropped out of high school to get and hold a regular job with a potential for advancement. A significant number of young black men and women who had found school oppressive to the point of dropping out were unable to establish a link with the job market and led marginal existences without jobs, regular incomes, or hopes for a better future.

Although the number of young black urbanites who fall through the cracks of the preparatory cycle is disturbingly large, they fortunately represent a diminishing minority. The majority of young blacks have been able to stay the educational course, at least to the point of obtaining a high school diploma and many pursue some college or earn a college or higher degree. With this level of competence, most of them have been able to find a place for themselves in the world of work. But once the civil rights movement lost its momentum the earlier high hopes of the black community for rapid progress toward full equality of opportunity and parity of rewards faded.

The loss of momentum had many causes, including the inability of the black leadership after King's murder to define, once the political and legal supports for segregation had been eliminated, its next set of objectives. The problems confronting the black leadership were compounded by the much reduced growth of U.S. productivity; the growing disillusion with government programs; the repeated victories in the successive presidential races of the Republicans (except for Carter); and the growing concerns of less affluent white

Americans with their growing precarious future, which left them less interested and less concerned about helping to improve the status of blacks.

While blacks made considerable gains in local politics and more modest advances in state politics, their needs, desires, and expectations for full citizenship and economic justice no longer held the attention and support of the White House, the Congress or the Supreme Court. Even a strongly engaged federal government would have encountered difficulties and disappointments in accelerating the progress of the black minority from freedom to equality, to the extent that black progress largely depends on the goodwill of whites, a commodity that has always been in short supply. The best that can be said for the post-Civil Rights era is that most of the earlier gains were maintained and strengthened. But we must quickly add that additional gains have been disappointingly slow.

The presidential campaign and election of 1992 provide an opportunity for further reflections on the changing role of white-black relationships. Although it will be months, in fact years, before the principal racial dimensions of the campaign and election are probed in depth a few highlights stand out.

The racial issue did not keep all of the southern states in the Republican column but neither was the Clinton-Gore ticket, despite its southern roots, able to recapture most, and surely not all, of the South for the Democrats.

The fact that voters in the State of Illinois chose a black female, Carol Braun, as their new U.S. Senator is a striking development since Illinois has long manifested negative attitudes and behavior toward its black minority. The election of 39 blacks to the House of Representatives reinforces the gains that blacks have been able to make in the political arena.

But impressive as these recent political gains are, they cannot obscure the fact that the quarter of a century since the assassination of Martin Luther King has witnessed a deceleration in the struggle for equality for blacks.

Racism remains a potent force in American life and politics. However disappointing the post-King era has been to most blacks, as well as to many whites, the Civil Rights gains of the 1950s and 1960s have been secured and reinforced and new gains achieved. Dr. King once remarked that he hoped that all vestiges of discrimination against blacks in the labor market could be eradicated by 2005. This is a target that should command our attention and guide our action.

1 America and the Negro

In February, 1832, a distinguished young Frenchman sailed for home after an extensive nine-month tour of the United States. Though he was no longer as sure as he had once been that democracy would prove suitable for his native land, he returned to France with a genuine appreciation of the way it worked in the land he had visited. The prospects for the new nation, he concluded, were bright. He saw only one dark cloud on the horizon. "The most formidable of all the ills that threaten the future of the Union," Alexis de Tocqueville wrote, "arises from the presence of a black population upon its territory." The two races, European and Negro, he pointed out, "are attached to each other without intermingling; and they are alike unable entirely to separate or to combine."[1] Today, 132 years and a civil war later, the United States still has not found a satisfactory way to integrate its Negro population into the general society, although it has tried almost every conceivable approach.

The counterpoint between American democracy and the Negro can be illustrated by reconstructing the major episodes in our history of race relations and delineating the major themes that underlay this history. The friendly and informed foreigner who first studied our racial problem, Gunnar Myrdal, saw it as a dilemma resulting from the lack of consistency between the basic democratic ideals that Americans profess and the undemocratic way in which they have dealt with the Negro minority. Myrdal's suggestive formulation is the starting point of our inquiry. We have addressed ourselves to the question of why this nation, which has contributed so much to extending the frontiers of freedom and broadening the opportunities for equality, did not include the Negro within the province of its democratic dream. The answers must be sought in a series of strands which are woven through our experience, strands containing the central conflicts that American democracy encountered and the manner in which it resolved them. What happened, or failed to happen, to the Negro minority can be explained by the way in which the white majority read its past, responded to its present, and sought to shape its future.

The first theme is the unique experience of the Negro compared with the many different ethnic groups that came to the American shores. The Negro was not the only one to arrive in the English settlements as a bondsman; yet while the others eventually became free, the Negro became a slave. Why? When we review the historical record, it seems clear that an immense gulf separated the early colonists from the Africans whom they had purchased. Physically and culturally, the Negro was different, and the settlers believed it would be impossible to incorporate him into their community as a free and equal member. They were convinced he was inherently inferior and that only corruption and evil would result from mixing his race with theirs. In a certain important sense, then, slavery was the means by which the early Americans hoped to regulate their relations with the black strangers in their midst.

Slavery, once established, created a wide gulf between the colonists and the Negro. The Negro became a slave because he was a Negro. And because he was a Negro, he had no place in American society. This was the conviction of the illiterate farmer. It was also the conviction of most of this country's great leaders.

Only the conception of the Negro as a substandard species can explain the roster of statesmen who, seeking no prospect of a solution which would enable the two races to live together in harmony, sought to remove the Negro from these shores. From the earliest days of the Republic its leaders, including Washington, Jefferson and Madison, favored this approach, while in the early nineteenth century such luminaries as John Marshall and Henry Clay were among the sponsors of the colonization movement. Lincoln repeatedly advocated colonization; he eulogized Clay for seeking to remove the "troublesome presence of free negroes"[2] from this country. Even in the midst of the Civil War, when the North was straining to defeat the rebellious Southern states, Lincoln cajoled Congress into providing funds for the resettlement of the freedmen in Central America.

The same reason played a part in the determined, if unsuccessful, efforts of President Grant to annex the island of Santo Domingo which he hoped to turn into a haven for former slaves. Only this approach, which so many of our leaders continued to espouse, even though its efficacy had been repeatedly denied, explains the later position of President William Howard Taft, who early in this century told a group of Negro college students that they would be better off if they emigrated to Africa.

Another facet of the deeply ingrained belief in the fundamental incompatability of the races is revealed by the attitudes of the white community concerning intimate personal relations between the races. Concern about mongrelization, about racial defilement in its most primitive form, lies at the root of the Negro issue. The first law case on record dealing with a Negro in this country involved the punishment of a white man and a Negro woman in Jamestown for having had sexual relations. In the 334 years of history since then, this motif has never dropped far below the surface. All discussions about race soon touch on the question of intermarriage.

The first theme is social, the second, political. In a democracy a minority can be effective only if it can accumulate sufficient power to force a change in its status. Today the Negro stands on the threshold of full emancipation. The question that we will attempt to answer is how, despite his difficult lot and the injustice visited upon him, he has been able to make even this much progress. How did this minority, with no rights or power, unloose its shackles and come slowly but surely to the perimeter of American democracy, only steps away from the inner ring?

The reason for this almost miraculous achievement is again to be found in the story of the white majority. Throughout its history our nation has not been so monolithic, so bound together by overriding commitments that innovation and change were impossible. It was out of the periodic struggles of one white group with another over the basis of representation in Congress, over the conditions for settlement of the West, over the rights of states to secede, over the terms of Reconstruction, over the use of Federal power to advance the general welfare—out of these searing conflicts that the Negro was able to make important gains. Each step was modest, but they were cumulative and the Negro, who started with nothing, gradually acquired many of the rights and privileges of citizenship.

Many groups are content to struggle long and hard simply to hold or increase their political power, but some of them are moved by ideas and ideals. From this nation's earliest beginnings, from the protest of the Germantown Quakers in 1688 against the injustice of holding human beings as slaves, through the efforts of some of the founding fathers, such as Benjamin Franklin, John Jay, Benjamin Rush, and their spiritual descendants, the abolitionists, to today's efforts by that large group which supports the current civil rights movement, a moral voice denouncing abuse of the Negro has been heard throughout the land. From Anthony Benezet, the eighteenth-century Quaker leader, to William L. Moore, the recently martyred Baltimore postman, there have always been men of conscience so that the Negro never stood completely alone.

However, even when religious and lay leaders spoke out against the inhumanity of slavery, few were concerned about the place of the free Negro in American democracy. White men were not asked to accept the Negro as their brother. The colonial religious leaders early agreed that baptism did not alter the status of a slave, and most of their successors found no incongruity between accepting the biblical injunction to love one's neighbor and actions that placed the Negro beyond the pale of the community. Most spiritual and ethical leaders of America never spoke out even against that most heinous of crimes, lynching. It was the white women of the South who finally were able to achieve its elimination.

A regional theme pervades our history. Most Americans who live outside of the South believe that the South alone has been responsible for the plight of the Negro. But this places too great a burden on a single section of the country. Even before the Civil War, the South was not a dominant region, and after the war its influence dwindled as the North and West expanded more rapidly.

The Negro was robbed of his Constitutional rights after the end of the war because the North and West actually shared the basic prejudices of the South. For a very few years after the Civil War these two regions made a half-hearted attempt to better the Negro's circumstances but they soon lost interest, leaving him to his fate at the hands of the Southern white leadership. After emancipation, the Negro's freedom could have been made secure only by major programs aimed at raising his educational and economic level, and only the federal government had the resources for such programs. But neither the North nor the West was prepared to devote to this end the substantial resources that would have been necessary. Thaddeus Stevens alone understood the situation and its remedy, but he was unable to persuade the nation's leaders.

In the years following the end of Reconstruction, the vast majority of northerners and westerners were concerned primarily with the pursuit of their own interests. There were frequent evidences of their indifference to the Negro's plight. The Force Bill, which in 1890 proposed to use federal power to protect the Negro's right to vote was defeated because western Republicans deserted their leadership and made a deal with the Democrats. They were more interested in maintaining the price of silver than in securing for the Negro his right to vote.

In 1921, and again during the New Deal, another piece of legislation seeking to protect the rights of Negroes, this time the right to life itself, went down to defeat because of indifference in the North and West. When Congressmen, friendly to the Negro, sought to achieve passage of an anti-lynching bill, they were met by a Southern filibuster. Because many leading Democrats were racists, and, more importantly, because many Republicans were more concerned about other legislation, the filibuster could not be overridden. In fact, the continuing efforts by Republicans, from Rutherford B. Hayes and Chester Arthur to Herbert Hoover and Dwight D. Eisenhower, to curry favor with Southern conservatives, form a subordinate theme in the history of American race relations.

An economic motif has also been threaded through the nation's attitude toward the Negro. For many years his labor was essential to the cotton culture of the South, and one of the reasons that the North did not intervene in the Negro's behalf —either before or after the Civil War—was the desire of its merchants and businessmen to maintain their commercial relations with the South. Even Northerners without such narrow interests were aware of the importance of the export of cotton, not just to the economy of the South, but to the economy of the nation as a whole. And for this reason Northerners were reluctant to interfere with the system of tenant farming which replaced slavery after the Civil War. Based on credit and buttressed by various social controls the system of farm tenancy enabled many plantation owners systematically to exploit the Negro so that he was unable to turn the need for his labor into an asset for himself.

It was not until after World War I and, more dramatically, World War II that the needs of the white community began to run congruent with those of the Negro minority. For the first time, American industry needed Negro manpower on a large scale. Suddenly many Negroes had access to jobs in mass production, unionized industries outside of the South, and were enabled thus to earn more than they could ever have hoped to earn as farmers. Suddenly they had access to the much better public services of the North and West and were able to provide their children with a better start in life. Paralleling these gains on the civilian front were increased opportunities in the armed forces, opportunities to improve their education, their skills, and their income. However, since these improved job opportunities have been available to Negroes for such a short time, they have not yet quite succeeded in solidifying their position. This is what makes the upward drift in unemployment during the past decade, especially among Negroes, ominous. The freedom that the Negro has almost won will profit him little unless he has a job that yields him an income sufficient to support himself and his family. Whether he will have that job will depend, to a large extent, on the performance of the American economy. But it will also depend on his own educational and social achievements.

This brings us to the next theme, that of educational and social deprivation. The slave owner was prohibited by law from teaching his slaves to read and write. In the first years after the Civil War, when schools first were opened to Negro adults and children alike, hundreds of thousands, even millions, took advantage of them. But the southern states and localities, with very little money to spend on all public services, allocated only the bare minimum for Negro schools. Therefore, although the ex-slaves made substantial progress, they still lagged far behind most white men. Blocked by discrimination from social advancement, many Negroes fell into despondency and despair. Why learn a skill if there were no opportunities to use it? Why learn to read if the only jobs were janitorial? Many Negroes once more began living only for the present with no thought for the future. This typified their reactions to work, family, and community. They had little interest and less pride. A great many drifted in and out of work and in and out of personal relationships.

These all-too-common facets of Negro life were a legacy of slavery's dehumanizing character, whereby marriage was not known and slaves frequently bred like cattle. Even after slavery had been abolished, segregation and discrimination operated in much the same way to rob a man of his pride and a sense of responsibility for himself and his family. Many Negroes learned that it was better to enjoy the present than work toward a better future that might never come. They might be robbed, beaten or, even worse, lynched.

The hard-headed majority of whites saw the poor performance of the Negro as evidence of his inherent inferiority,
while a sentimental minority saw it as the result of an unfavorable environment. But a search for an explanation is less
important than a search for an effective remedy. We know that
remedies are not easy to find or to apply. Millions of seriously
handicapped Negroes in the rural South, the urban South, and
the metropolitan centers of the North and West live outside
the mainstream of American life. Not all handicapped citizens
are Negroes, and not all Negroes are seriously handicapped.
But a great many Negroes do need major help, not just for the
moment, but over a long period of time, if the freedom which
will soon be theirs is to be more than an empty shell.

One more theme relates to the Negro's own role in his
emancipation. While Negro resistance to oppression by the
white community has characterized his experience from his
earliest days in the colonies, his scope for independent action
has been severely restricted. The vast majority of Negroes
were forced to acquiesce first to slavery and then to segregation. Since they could not alter the major terms of their relationship with the white majority, they devoted what energy
they had left to making their lives a little more tolerable.

Today, at the threshold of full emancipation the Negro no
longer needs to rely on conflicts among whites for his gains. He
has accumulated sufficient power to affect the outcome of his
struggle for full equality. In 1948 it was the northern Negro
vote which helped elect Harry Truman president and in 1960
it was the same Negro vote which helped elect John F. Kennedy. Negroes have played a crucial role in state and local
elections in the South as well as in the North, and will become
even more potent in the future as the drive to register Negro
voters gathers momentum.

The Negroes' second source of power is their market
strength. As consumers, they have control over billions of dollars of disposable income and this now represents an effective
economic force.

But the Negroes' most important source of power is the
protest movement itself. Large numbers of disciplined Ne-

groes in all parts of the country are increasingly resorting to peaceful assembly to bring their just demands to the attention of government and community leaders and to petition for redress of wrongs long endured. For the first time in American history the Negro has taken the initiative, forcing the pace of his own emancipation. Any white community that refuses to grant him his rights and privileges must pay an increasingly high price in terms of disorder, disturbance, and discontent, forces which weaken the entire community. In the background, the threat of federal intervention is ever present.

The white majority was able to hold the Negro minority in bondage and then in subservience for almost three and a half centuries by institutional arrangements that were relatively easy to introduce and maintain. But these are now being undermined by a vast array of forces, the most important of which is the growing power of the Negro minority, the willingness to use that power and the readiness to face whatever must be faced—including injury or even death.

Lincoln talked of granting freedom to the free. But freedom cannot be granted. It must be fought for and won. The Negro is at last in a position where he himself can fight for his freedom. He cannot fight alone, nor need he now fight alone. Today the President, the Supreme Court, the Congress, and many others in the white community—including businesses, trade unions, universities, foundations, and the press—are his allies. But once his freedom has been secured, he will face the even more difficult task of transmuting this freedom into equality. White efforts and white resources can help. In fact, without white assistance, equality for the Negro will long remain elusive. But the Negro, now that he is becoming free, holds for the first time the key to his own salvation. He, and he alone, can take the necessary actions himself, within his family, and within his own community that will enable him to develop the values, obtain the education, and acquire the skills which alone can provide the foundation for true equality within the American system.

These, then, are the major themes that have underlain the counterpoint between American democracy and the Negro:

the racial atavism of the white man; the conviction that Negroes could not be integrated into American society as equals; the search for alternative solutions to slavery short of integration; the slow but steady progress of the Negro as a result of conflict among whites; the drag on his progress exerted by prejudice and discrimination in the North as well as the South; the weak economic position of the Negro until very recently, due to the lack of an industrial demand for his labor; his continuing vulnerability because of a lag in his educational and social advancement; his increasing political power following his migration out of the South; and his growing ability to take the initiative to secure his rights.

America originally excluded the Negro from the promise of its democracy, and until recently only a small minority advocated his inclusion. No longer is it true as George W. Cable, the distinguished Southern journalist, wrote in 1884 that "we may reach the moon some day, not social equality" of white and Negro citizens.[3] However we Americans are a pragmatic people. Since each of the alternatives we have tried has failed, we are left with very little choice.

If our democracy is to survive, it must make a place for the Negro as an equal. Some of us will favor it as an act of justice; others will accept it out of necessity. But now, after 345 years, America is well on the road toward establishing the first biracial democracy in history—an accomplishment that will be the equal of its earlier contribution to mankind, a democracy white men.

NOTES

1. De Tocqueville, Alexis, *Democracy in America*, Schocken Books, New York, 1961, Vol. I, p. 424.

2. *Abraham Lincoln, Selected Speeches, Messages, and Letters,* T. Harry Williams, ed., Rinehart, New York, 1958, p. 37.

3. Cable, George W., *The Negro Question*, Doubleday, New York, 1958, p. 71.

2 Colonist and Slave

OF THE SEVERAL MILLION PERSONS who reached Great Britain's North American colonies before 1776, it is conservatively estimated that close to 80 per cent arrived under some form of servitude. The conditions of servitude, of course, varied considerably. Helen Catterall, in her study of colonial judicial cases, found nine or ten distinct degrees of bondage, ranging from the redemptioner, who bound himself out to serve for a period of years in return for his passage to America, to the man who was sold as a slave by some captor to a master who owned him for life.

Yet in most cases the fact of prior servitude proved no handicap to social or economic advancement. At one time, it is estimated, over half the lower chamber of the Virginia House of Burgesses consisted of former indentured servants. They and other one-time bondsmen had become substantial landowners and respected citizens in the King's plantations across the sea. Even when rapid social and economic advancement was not possible within a single generation, the children of one-time bondsmen often were able to accomplish it. Thus did America earn its reputation as the land of opportunity.

There was, however, one great exception to this general rule. The African Negro found, not the chance to advance his general condition, but the cruel alternative of lifelong hard labor and irreducible social status. For him the American dream proved to be a bitter illusion. Why was it that the Negro alone, of the many peoples who came to these shores, failed to win the full rights and privileges of citizenship?

Certainly there was nothing in British history to suggest that her colonies would adopt the institution of slavery. In England itself, prior to colonial expansion, slavery was sanctioned neither by law nor custom. Anglo-Saxon slavery had been abolished at the time of the Norman conquest in 1066, and villeinage, a form of serfdom, had rapidly died out after Henry VIII confiscated the church estates. When, in 1569, a man named Cartwright was brought into court for beating a slave he had purchased in Russia, the judges declared "that England was too pure an Air for Slaves to breath in."[1] This was the only recorded case concerning slavery in England before 1670. When, in 1620, an English sea captain trading for gold and ivory off Africa's west coast was offered slaves, he answered with truth that the English "were a people who did not deale in any such commodities, neither did wee buy or sell one another, or any that had our owne shapes."[2]

Even the first Negroes in the colonies, who happened to land in Virginia, were not treated as slaves, though they had been purchased from a Dutch man-of-war that had taken them off a captured Portuguese slaver. Possibly because English law did not cover slavery, possibly because they were Christians, these twenty Negroes appear to have enjoyed a status similar to that of indentured servants. Moreover, many of the other Negroes in Virginia during the next several decades had a similar status. After a stipulated number of years of service, they received their freedom as well as land and a few implements. Some even became masters of other men, even white men. Yet these early years of the Virginia colony were, in reality, a transition period. For social, religious, and economic factors were at work, stamping the Negro indelibly with the status of slave property to be bought and sold.

The growth of Virginia's Negro population was slow. In 1625, six years after the first Africans arrived in the colony, there were still only twenty-five Negroes among a total population of approximately 2,500; by mid-century the number of Negroes had increased to only 300. By 1670 they constituted but 5 per cent of the colony's 40,000 inhabitants. Negroes were not, as yet, essential to Virginia's economy. Tobacco, already an important crop, could be grown profitably on small holdings, without numerous field hands. Large plantations were, in fact, almost unknown; when a man cultivated more land than he himself could care for, he generally employed one or two white indentured servants. White servants were far more important to the colony's economy, and before 1670 their number increased six times as rapidly as did the number of Negroes. African labor was, in fact, quite casual during these early years. Negro slaves were usually transported directly to the West Indies, where the demand was greater and the prices higher. Only the backwash, those Negroes considered unfit for plantation labor, reached the continental colonies. Yet, in this first half-century of the Negro's life in what was later to become the United States, the colonists were developing certain special attitudes toward him.

In the first place, the Negro was physically different. Not only was his skin black, but other parts of his anatomy, such as his lips and nose, were noticeably peculiar. Certainly the Negro was unlike any person most colonists had known; since the English had not had several centuries' close contact with the Moors, as had the Spanish. These physical differences then became the basis for asserting other differences. Even Morgan Godwyn, a seventeenth-century minister otherwise disposed to take the Negro's side, contended that the African was inherently inferior. He argued, "methinks the consideration of the shape and figure of our negroes' Bodies, their Limbs and Members, their Voice and Countenance in all things according with other Mens; together with their Risibility and Discourse (Man's *peculiar* Faculties) should be a sufficient Conviction."[3]

This conception of the Negro as inherently inferior was reinforced by the condition of most Negroes by the time they reached the Virginia colony. African slaves generally came from the interior tribes; many had been captured during one of the frequent wars between neighboring tribes. A few were criminals condemned to slavery as punishment. The captives were sold to the coastal tribes in exchange for iron bars, fire-

arms, liquor, beads, cloth, and other European products.
Once the terms of trade were agreed upon, the slaves were
tied together by the neck and started on the long, misery-
filled trek to the sea. Before that journey was over, about a
third who had set out had died from thirst, starvation, or
other hardships encountered along the way. For those who
survived this initial leg of the journey to America, the terror
had only begun, for the passage between Africa and the West
Indies still remained.

In order to derive the maximum profit from each voyage,
ship captains packed as many slaves as possible into the holds
of their vessels. Death was frequent, either from sickness,
harsh punishment, or simply severe depression. Despite efforts
to keep them alive, many Africans chose death to the unknown hardships that lay ahead. If the slaves were fortunate,
the voyage was short and lasted only two months.

Before a year in the New World was over, another third
of the slaves who had started out from the interior of Africa
died. And those who survived had been drastically transformed. Daniel Mannix has remarked that "the communal
life of many tribes was so highly organized by a system of customs, relationships, taboos and religious ceremonies that
there was practically nothing a man or a woman could do
that was not prescribed by tribal law. To separate an individual from this complex system of interrelationships and suddenly place him, naked and friendless, in a completely hostile
environment was in some respects a greater shock than any
amount of physical brutality."[4] As Stanley Elkins has pointed
out, the Negro slave, like the twentieth-century concentration
camp inmate, had been, in effect, brutalized and decultural-
ized. With his past obliterated by successive shock and terror,
he began to take on the only character that would enable him
to survive in his new surroundings—that is, the character of a
docile beast. This was the character which his white masters,
holding absolute power over him, demanded. Little wonder
that the Virginia colonists found it difficult to think of these
creatures as fellow human beings.

The Negroes in bondage were treated, in general, like

other servile classes in Virginia. But as the number of Negroes increased and some gained their freedom, white Virginians became increasingly concerned about these people who they felt were aliens in their midst. Could the colony assimilate these strange-looking, strange-speaking, strange-acting creatures? Could they be integrated into the community and share the privileges and responsibilities of citizenship? The answer, as more and more Negroes came to the colony and as more and more of their children were born, was no. In the minds of the Virginians and the other English colonists, Negroes were not simply different; they comprised a lower order of human beings. As early as 1630 in Virginia, Hugh Davis was ordered "soundly whipt before an assembly of negroes and others for abusing himself to the dishonor of God and shame of Christianity by defiling his body in lying with a negro. . . ."[5] And an English minister, when he sought to baptize Negro slaves, was asked incredulously, "What, such as they? What, those black dogs be made Christians? What, shall they be like us?"[6]

If the Negro was not an equal, if he was not accepted as a free man, what was to become of him? The question was not consciously faced; it was decided as the issue arose, and by many different groups. In various ways, the Negro's length of servitude was extended: he was a stranger without friends in a culture he did not understand; he had been brought to the colony as a captive and offered for sale. Unlike the Indian, he had no fellow Africans nearby to offer him shelter if he should escape, nor were the whites dissuaded from enslaving him for fear of reprisals by other Africans. In such a hostile environment he could not long survive without the help of a white master, and this made it easier for the master to keep him permanently.

Some Negroes, having no knowledge of the law, simply continued working for their masters beyond the conventional required time. Others, even when they knew the law, found it difficult to achieve the status of a free man when challenged by former masters in courts dominated by white men. At first a distinction was made between Negroes who were Christians

and Negroes who were not. The former were freed like any
indentured servants; the latter were forced to serve for life.
But soon even this distinction broke down. It became more
and more difficult for the Negro to win his freedom, whether
he had been baptized or not. In 1640, for example, when
three escaped servants were apprehended and brought back
to Virginia, the two whites among them were ordered to
serve an extra year with their former masters, plus an additional three years as servants of the colony. However, the
third escaped servant, a Negro, was ordered to serve his former master for the rest of his life.

The colonists, concerned with increasing the flow of immigrants from England, acted with relative liberality toward
their countrymen, but they did not shy away from severity in
dealing with the Negro. According to Lewis Gray, the historian of southern agriculture, "For two decades before the beginnings of legislative definition and regulation of slavery in
Virginia, there was a tendency to reduce Negroes to a state
of slavery, partly by undue influence to compel Negro servants to agree to indentures for life, partly through lack of
formal contract, and partly through importation of those held
to be already in a state of slavery."[7] Nevertheless, a significant
number of Negroes, taking advantage of ambiguities in the
law, were able to win their freedom. But the white settlers
were so determined to prevent the growth of free Negro
communities within their midst that they soon turned to the
law for assistance.

Although English common law before 1620 did not recognize human slavery, neither did it prohibit it. The American colonists, then, were free to develop their own law; this
was made easier by their distance from the mother country
and a judicial ruling that the colonies, since they were the
king's plantations, did not come under the English common
law. The first colony to sanction lifelong slavery was not
Virginia, but Massachusetts. In 1641 its Body of Liberties
provided, ironically, that "lawful captives taken in just wars,
and such strangers as willingly sell themselves or are sold to
us"[8] might be made slaves. The use of the word "strangers,"

however, was ambiguous. It seemed to exclude the children
of slave parents, born in the colony, from those who might be
enslaved, and a number of Negroes gained their freedom in
this way. In 1670 this loophole was closed when the word
"stranger" was eliminated.

Maryland did not make a similar mistake when it sanctioned slavery in 1663. A law enacted that year specifically
provided that "all negroes or other slaves . . . shall serve
durante vita."[9] Virginia never specifically sanctioned Negro
slavery in the seventeenth century, though a law enacted in
1661 assumed its legality. The statute held that "negroes are
incapable of making satisfaction [for the time lost in running
away] by addition of time,"[10] implying that Negroes were already slaves for life.

Baptism had been, at the beginning, a protection against
enslavement. It was for this reason, some historians believe,
that the first Negroes brought to Virginia were not made slaves,
since from their names it appears they were Christians. This
created a problem for the owners of slaves. If they did their
Christian duty and had their slaves baptized, they might not
be allowed to keep them as slaves. Most owners solved the
dilemma by refusing to allow their slaves to be baptized; this
was particularly prevalent in Massachusetts, where slavery had
originally been justified as a means of extending Christianity
to the heathen.

In other colonies, however, the law was gradually modified to eliminate any protection which Christianity might
offer the Negro. In Virginia, for example, the Assembly declared in 1667 that "Baptisme doth not alter the condition of
the person as to his bondage or freedom; that divers masters,
freed from this doubt, may more carefully endeavor the
propagation of christianity."[11] Not satisfied with just this
declaration, the Assembly three years later enacted a law providing that only those Negroes baptized before being shipped
to the colony would be protected against enslavement. This,
however, cut off the importation of slaves from Christian
lands and so, in 1682, the Assembly passed a law that thereafter all Negroes, whether Christian or not, might be brought

in as slaves. All the other southern colonies enacted similar statutes.

Miscegenation seemed to offer yet another way out of slavery. Under English common law, the status of the child depended on the status of the father. But in a land where Negro slave women frequently bore children fathered by white masters, to confer on a child his father's status threatened to produce within a short time, a large class of free, independent mulattoes. To the seventeenth-century American colonists, this was unthinkable. Therefore, from the very beginning, intimate relations between whites and Negroes were resolutely discouraged. Numerous court cases, in which the parties to such unions were severely punished, as well as continued legislative enactments, attest to this taboo.

Yet the law could not prevent sexual intercourse between the races, particularly in a country where there were many more white men than white women. Very early, therefore, the colonists recognized the need to clarify the status of the mulatto. To solve this threat to the existing order, Virginia (in 1662) enacted into law a bill providing that the status of the mulatto was determined by the status of the mother, not the father. The same rule was then adopted by the other colonies. Maryland unwittingly incorporated into its 1663 slave code the English custom of accepting the father's status for the child. But before long Maryland reversed itself and adopted the Virginia statute. Even in Massachusetts, where no legislation on this point was ever enacted, the custom was that the mulatto acquired the status of the mother.

Of course, a child might have a Negro father and a white mother. Such cases were not unknown even in the seventeenth century, when the number of white women was so few. The discovery of such relationships brought immediate, stern punishment. The woman was usually whipped, separated from her mulatto offspring, and either sold into servitude for a number of years or transported out of the colony.

Thus, by the close of the seventeenth century, the English colonists had made it virtually impossible for a Negro to rise above his slave status. Neither baptism nor a white father gave him the status of a free man. Some Negroes were already free, but all others thereafter arriving in the colonies—an ever-increasing number—were doomed to lifelong slavery, they and their children. The only exception were those few slaves manumitted by their masters, but even here the law was constantly being tightened, particularly in the southern colonies. Virginia in 1691 forbade manumission unless the owner agreed to transport the freed slaves out of the colony; and in 1723 it prohibited manumission altogether except in cases of exceptionally meritorious conduct.

The other southern colonies soon followed Virginia's example. While these limitations on manumission were inspired to a large extent by fears that free Negroes might instigate slave rebellions, raise the crime rate, or become public charges, they also reflected the white colonists' belief that the Negro could not be integrated into their society except as a slave. This belief was also reflected in the growing hardships under which the free Negro labored. In various ways his rights were gradually curtailed until finally, except that he was not another man's property, he enjoyed a status not much higher than that of a slave.

At the same time, there was a growing tendency to equate the Negro with the slave. As we have seen, the Maryland law of 1663, as well as the later laws of South Carolina, Georgia, and Mississippi defined the Negro as a slave. If free, the burden of proof rested with the Negro: ". . . It shall always be presumed," the 1740 South Carolina slave code declared, "that every negro, Indian, mulatto and mustezo is a slave, unless the contrary can be made to appear."[12] The southern white colonist, according to Stanley M. Elkins, proceeded on the basis of "a simple syllogism. . . . All slaves are black; slaves are degraded and contemptible; therefore all blacks are degraded and contemptible and should be kept in a state of slavery. . . . This [syllogism] took on a life of its own in the attitudes of the people, and the very thought of such a creature existing outside the pale of their so aptly devised system filled the most reasonable of Southerners with fear and loathing."[13]

This growing tendency to make and maintain the Negro a slave has not been the result of economic factors alone. The Negro suffered the same fate in Massachusets, where he never became important economically, as he did in Virginia, where his labor was essential. Moreover, in the Spanish and Portuguese colonies in Central and South America, where the Negro was essential as a source of cheap labor, his fate was more fortunate. As Frank Tannenbaum has pointed out, in these colonies every effort was made and every benefit of the doubt given to assure the Negro his freedom. "The law in Spanish and Portuguese America," says Tannenbaum, "facilitated manumission, the tax-gatherer did not oppose it [manumission was the only transaction not taxed by the government], and the church ranked it among the works singularly agreeable to God. A hundred social devices narrowed the gap between bondage and liberty. . . ."[14]

One reason that the Spanish and Portuguese colonies took a more liberal attitude toward freeing the slave, according to Tannenbaum and Elkins, was the greater power which the church exercised in those lands. The church insisted that "Slavery is not to be understood as conferring on one man the same power over another that men have over cattle. . . . For slavery does not abolish the natural equality of man. . . ."[15] And in fact, while not specifically banning human slavery, it consistently condemned the slave trade. On the issue of whether the Negro ought to be baptized, the Catholic Church insisted without exception that once a Negro was sufficiently instructed in the Christian religion, he could not be prevented from becoming baptized. The fact that the Spaniards were exploiters, not settlers, enabled them at least initially to avoid many of the troublesome problems of social integration.

In contrast, the various Protestant churches in the English colonies were unable to induce the colonists to baptize their slaves. Morgan Godwyn's experience in Barbados and in Virginia was probably typical. His efforts to spread the Christian religion among the Negroes in these two colonies were met with derision, anger and outright hostility. ". . . it was told

me with no small Passion and Vehemency," Godwyn later
wrote, "and that by a Religious Person (for so in all things
else she appeared), that I might as well Baptize a Puppy, as a
certain young Negro, the Mother whereof was a Christian. . . ."
Most of the English colonists, according to Godwyn, thought
"Negro's were Beasts, and had no more souls than Beasts, and
that Religion did not concern them."[16] Since the English
ministers were dependent on the colonists for financial support, they were far less able to press their claims than the
Spanish padres who were able to draw on the powerful church
in the home country for support. Not even Cotton Mather,
perhaps the greatest preacher in colonial America, could
persuade his fellow Puritans that they ought to see that their
Negro slaves were baptized. In vain did he argue that the
Negro was not a beast, that he had a soul capable of reason.
For in New England church membership led most directly to
political and social equality.

Not only the church but the crown was less influential in
the English colonies. The Spanish and Portuguese kings themselves had put up the money to finance their countries' colonial adventures in the hope of finding gold and converting
the heathen. From the very beginning both rulers had established powerful bureaucracies to administer their overseas
possessions. They were in a preferred position to set limits on
what their subjects could and could not do. The English colonies, on the other hand, were often private enterprise companies, organized for profit. Even when the colonies later
passed into the hands of the crown, the settlers retained considerable independence. While a royal governor often resided
in the colony to safeguard the king's interests, his salary, like
that of the ministers, was paid by the local citizens. Moreover,
England in the seventeenth century was often racked by civil
wars, which preempted the attention of the crown. This left
the English colonists essentially free to pursue their own
policies.

Yet neither the lesser influence of the church nor the
greater weakness of the crown is sufficient to explain why the
Negro found it so much more difficult to secure his freedom

in the English colonies than in the Spanish and Portuguese colonies. A more fundamental explanation is the greater race consciousness of the British people. As we have seen, this reflected in part their lack of previous contact with peoples of darker skins and in part the degraded state of those Negroes with whom they first came in contact. Soon, however, it came to have an existence all its own, firmly embedded in the attitudes and habits of the British colonials. According to Philip Bruce, the historian of seventeenth-century Virginia, "the belief was held by many, even in England, that the Negro was not a man but a wild beast, marked by an intelligence hardly superior to that of a monkey, and with instincts and habits far more debased."[17] Lorenzo Greene noted that the same attitudes were prevalent in New England. Rhode Island slaveholders regarded the Negroes "as creatures of another species," and Cotton Mather referred to them as "miserable children of Adam and Noah," enslaved because they had sinned against God.[18]

As long as the number of Negroes was insignificant, the consequences of American slavery were not too serious. But after 1680, when the Negro slave came to acquire increasing importance as a source of cheap labor in the southern colonies, this racism, which had already removed virtually all hope of the Negro's ever becoming a free man, was to lead to a system of chattel slavery unique in the history of Western civilization for the degree to which it deprived its victims of human rights and personality.

The great economic problem facing the Virginia colonists, once they discovered that tobacco could be grown profitably, was the lack of adequate cheap labor. By raising tobacco a man could comfortably sustain himself and his family through his own labor, and if he added the labor of others he might rapidly grow rich. All around him stretched miles and miles of virgin land, virtually free for the asking. It was to help cultivate this land that the system of indentured servitude was designed. By paying a man's passage to the New World, a colonist might have the benefit of his labor for a period of up to seven years. Moreover, under the "headright" system, for each indentured servant whose passage to America he paid, the colonist was entitled to an additional grant of land. But the indentured servant had a number of disadvantages as far as the colonial planters were concerned. He had to be clothed and fed according to a certain standard, his period of servitude was limited, and he was apt to run away before his period of service was over.

The planters soon found that with Negro slaves these disadvantages were to a large extent eliminated. The Negro could be clothed and fed more cheaply, his period of servitude lasted for life, and escape was more difficult, given the surrounding community's hostility toward him. As an added windfall, if the slave bore children, they too would one day labor for the planter. Benjamin Franklin, writing in 1751, while admitting that slave labor was expensive if all the costs were properly calculated, put his finger on the crux of the matter. "Why then will *Americans* purchase slaves?" he asked. "Because Slaves may be kept as long as a Man pleases, or has Occasion for his Labour; while hired Men are continually leaving their Masters (often in the midst of his Business) and setting up for themselves."[19]

By 1680 the advantage of Negro slaves over white indentured servants was already evident. Only thus could a man build up an estate; and only thus could he live as a gentleman.

This fact was widely recognized not only in Virginia but also in the newly established colony of Carolina, rapidly being settled by colonists from the overcrowded West Indies. "A rational man will certainly inquire," wrote one South Carolinian, "When I have Land, what shall I doe with it? What commoditys shall I be able to produce that will yield me money in other countrys, that I may be enabled to buy Negro-slaves (without which a planter can never doe any great matter) ?"[20] And nearly half a century later, when the philanthropist James Oglethorpe tried on moral and religious grounds to prevent the introduction of slavery into the colony of Georgia which he had founded, he was told by the colonists, "In Spite of all Endeavors to disguise this Point, it is as clear as Light itself, that Negroes are as essentially necessary to the Cultivation of Georgia, as Axes, Hoes, or any other Utensil of Agriculture."[21]

However, in 1680 only a few wealthy planters had accumulated sufficient capital to begin buying Negro slaves. First, the demand for the Africans was insatiable, particularly in the West Indies. Second, the high price of slaves was maintained by chartered monopolies, which saw to it that only a limited number of Africans reached the New World each year. While interlopers added to this number somewhat, the supply still fell far short of what the colonists considered adequate. In such a market, the Virginians, Marylanders, and Carolinians were ill equipped to bid. In 1698, however, Parliament threw the slave trade open to all English subjects, and New England sea captains gained lawful entry into the African trade. Soon it became the backbone of the New England economy. The familiar triangular trade enabled the hardy New Englanders to exchange beans, corn and rum for slaves in Africa, slaves for sugar in the West Indies and sugar for rum in New England. "Slaves, costing the equivalent of £4 to £5 in rum and bar iron in Africa," notes Lorenzo Greene, "were sold in the West Indies in 1746 at prices ranging from £30 to £88."[22] Even allowing for the cost of slaves lost in passage and the cost of the passage, the business was quite profitable. And the New Englanders were constantly finding ways to make it even more profitable; they reduced the size of their crews and crowded even more slaves onto their ships. Upon this trade rose the first great New England fortunes. Leading citizens of their communities, the slave merchants included the Cabots, Waldos, and Fanueils of Boston, the Ellerys of Newport, and the Browns of Providence.

For the first time, then, England's North American colonies were assured of an adequate supply of slaves. Between June, 1699, and October, 1708, more than 6,600 Negroes were shipped to Virginia, of whom all but 236 came directly from Africa. This nearly doubled that colony's slave population. During approximately the same period almost 2,300 slaves were shipped to Maryland. At the same time the first generation of Negroes born under slavery was coming of working age. Not surprisingly, the inflow of white indentured servants soon slowed to a trickle.

Southern agriculture soon began to take on an increasingly capitalistic complexion. A planter immediately invested his profits in Negro slaves. Additional slaves not only enabled him to cultivate a larger area, but, under the "headright" system, he could secure additional land. Thus extensive plantations were built up; some were as large as 100,000 acres. Loose administration of the generous land laws, moreover, aided the engrossment of the land by a small group of wealthy planters. On these estates all efforts were concentrated on growing a single crop—tobacco in Virginia and Maryland, rice or indigo in the Carolinas. Every effort was made to increase the profits, so that still more slaves could be purchased. Against this aggressive rationalized system of agriculture the yeoman farmer found it difficult to hold his own for, as Gray pointed out, "the small farmers found themselves unable to resist the competitive power of slave labor, organized under the plantation system. Gradually they were compelled either to become great planters—and many did not possess sufficient ability and command over capital to accomplish this—or to reestablish a regime of rude self-sufficing economy in a region less favorable to commercial agriculture."[23]

The result was not simply the growth of a powerful planter class, soon to give the region its dominant tone, but also an increasing disposition to treat the Negro as merely another commodity, "no otherwise as Horses and Cattle." Just as New England slave captains tried to squeeze another Negro on their ships, southern planters tried to wring another hour's work from their Negro slaves. This growing tendency to consider the Negro strictly as an economic commodity added to the already existing racial attitudes and led to a steady deterioration in the Negro's status. In the eyes of the law he was an article of property, not a person.

A Virginia law enacted in 1705 made explicit the customary procedure of treating the Negro slave as real property. For the next seventy years Virginians argued this question of whether the slave ought to be considered as real or chattel property, whether he descended to heirs with the land or could be seized as payment for debts. If the Negro were attached to the land, his status would have been more secure and he might eventually have evolved into a serf. But the debate never hinged on the Negro's best interests. It hinged instead on the white man's best interests, and so the Negro developed a status which was that of half chattel and half real property. He could not be seized as payment for debt but neither was he legally tied to the land.

From this conception of the Negro various conclusions followed. If his master's economic interests so dictated, a slave might be sold without restriction to whoever stood ready to pay the highest price. Neither marriage nor blood ties could interfere. Husband or wife, parent or child, might be separated from each other through inheritance or sale. "The relation between slaves," a North Carolina judge ruled on the eve of the Civil War, expressing a long-held view, "is essentially different from that of man and wife joined in lawful wedlock. . . . [for] with slaves it may be dissolved at the pleasure of either party, or by the sale of one or both, depending on the caprice or necessity of the owners."[24] To hold otherwise would have led to a lowering of slave prices, since requiring the sale of entire families intact would have made it difficult to find buyers.

In fact, the law did not even recognize the Negro family. A Kentucky court held that "the father of a slave is unknown to our law."[25] And a Virginia court, ruling on the status of three Negro children, declared that "the apprentices in question are bastards, their father being a slave, and therefore incapable of contracting matrimony. . . ."[26] From this it followed that the Negro slave had no rights as a spouse. According to the Attorney General of Maryland, "A slave has never maintained an action against the violator of his bed. A slave is not admonished for incontinence, or punished for fornication or adultery. . . ."[27] The slave could not protect himself against the violator of his marriage bed, particularly if the violator was his master. More important, however, since slave marriages were not recognized, the practice gradually developed of breeding Negroes for market. In offering several Negroes for sale, an advertisement in a Charleston, South Carolina, newspaper in 1796 stated that "They were purchased for stock and breeding . . . , and to any Planter who particularly wanted them for that purpose, they are a very choice and desirable gang."[28] This practice seemed logically to follow if one accepted the view that the Negro was a subhuman form of property. As a Maryland judge later reasoned, "Suppose a *brood mare* be hired for five years, *the foals* belong to him who has a part of the *use* of the dam. The *slave in Maryland, in this respect, is placed on no higher or different grounds.*"[29]

The law also refused to recognize any other type of contract which the Negro might enter. The 1705 Virginia code, for example, declared that "Contracts of masters with their servants [are] void, unless approved in court."[30] Thus, the slave had no legal right to hold property, no matter how he had acquired it, whether through labor, purchase, charity or inheritance. The law in all the colonies and later in all the southern states was the same. "A slave," an Alabama court held, "is in absolute bondage; he has no civil right, and can hold no property, except at the will and pleasure of his master."[31] Under the South Carolina slave code, enacted in 1740, he was not even allowed to buy or sell articles, keep a boat or raise horses and cattle. Moreover, when Georgia later adopted the same restriction, it provided that the slave's master would be fined for even permitting him to carry on such activities. This prohibition, too, logically followed. "If the slave could possess property," the abolitionist William Goodell pointed out, "he could dispose of it; he could make contracts; he might contract marriage; he might become a man, and becoming such, cease to be a slave. The safety of the entire fabric required that not one stone in the edifice should be missing."[32]

The law in regard to slavery, as with property, was designed to protect the owner's interest. However, since the Negro was withal a human being, the law had to cope with

unique problems. Thus it was even expanded to take care of
the special threat to property ownership resulting from attempts of slaves to run away. To discourage such attempts, the
1705 Virginia code adumbrated punishment proper for a recaptured runaway slave, "for the reclaiming of any such
incorrigible slave and terrifying others from the practice."[33]
Any white or free Negro who helped a slave escape was subject
to even harsher punishment, especially since this would in-
flict no loss on an owner.

The slave owner was also protected by law against third
parties' injuring his property. Anyone who seriously crippled
or killed a slave was required to compensate the owner—even
if the colonial authorities, in punishing a slave for some
crime, caused his death. Few legal penalties, however, attached themselves to the master who seriously crippled or
killed his own slave. In Virginia, if a master could prove that
he had killed a slave while the latter was resisting correction,
he went free "since it cannot be presumed that prepensed
malice (which alone makes murder a felony) should induce
any man to destroy his own estate."[34] Since slave testimony
was barred from the courts, it was usually impossible to prove
that the master had killed his slave under any other circumstances. Under the South Carolina code, a master who will-
fully killed his slave was forced to pay a fine of £700—but
only half that amount if the murder was committed "on sudden heat and passion." In effect, the slave was forced to rely
entirely on his master's recognition of his own self-interest
for protection. "The power of the master must be absolute,"
a North Carolina judge later said, "to render the submission
of the slave perfect. I most freely confess my sense of the
harshness of the proposition. I feel it as deeply as any man
can. . . . But it is inherent in the relation of master and
slave."[35]

In the Spanish American colonies, in contrast, where economic motives were at least equally powerful, the Negro slave
suffered few of these restrictions on his personal and civil
liberties. The marriage contract was recognized by law, families could not be separated by sale or inheritance, slaves were

allowed to own property and were permitted to work for themselves on certain days, and masters could not mistreat them.

There were also important differences between the way Negroes were treated in the southern colonies and in the North. To a large extent these differences reflected the lesser importance of slave labor in the New England economy. A marriage contract between two Negro slaves in New England was treated with almost the same solemnity as one between a white man and woman. The couple was required to publish wedding banns, and not infrequently one of the region's leading ministers performed the ceremony. Once married, each was expected to remain faithful to the other. If either violated his marriage vows, he might be punished for adultery and the spouse granted a divorce. To some extent this sharper legal recognition of marriage between Negro slaves in New England reflected the particular religious views of the Puritans, their overwhelming concern with sexual morality. But in fact such marriages were often disrupted by the sale of husband or wife to owners in different towns. Children were frequently separated from parents. Nevertheless, since the New England economy was based on the slave trade and not slave labor, marriage between bond servants was not treated cavalierly. And breeding slaves for market was virtually unknown.

Another difference between the regions was that the slave in New England had the right to own property. If his master tried to appropriate the property, the slave could take his master to court, where he had the same right to testify as a white man. Records exist of numerous court cases in which the testimony of a slave proved conclusive. In addition, unlike the custom in the southern states, the wife of a slave could not testify against her husband. Finally, a master did not have the right to take the life of his slave. While he might punish the slave for disobedience, he was guilty of murder if the punishment resulted in the slave's death. According to the summary of colonial law in 1771 by Massachusetts' Chief Justice, "Slavery by the Provincial laws gives no rights to the life of the servant; and a slave here is considered as a servant would be who bound himself for a period of years exceeding the ordinary term of human life. . . ."[36]

This, then, was the heritage of the new nation which would be conceived in 1776 from colonial America. In all thirteen colonies the Negro was viewed as inherently inferior, a low order of the human species, who could not be integrated into the larger community as a citizen. This applied even to those Negroes who were free—and one-tenth were. In all thirteen colonies free Negroes suffered from various handicaps. Yet the two regions differed in their stance and outlook. The North had no deep commitments to slavery; the South could not seriously contemplate its abolition. But in this one regard they agreed: North and South alike believed the Negro to be an inferior human being and could not contemplate his being absorbed as an equal into the American community.

NOTES

1. Catterall, Helen T., *Judicial Cases Concerning American Slavery and the Negro,* Carnegie Institute, Washington, D.C., 1929, Vol. I, p. 9.

2. Davies, K. G., *The Royal African Company,* Longmans, Green, New York, 1957, p. 15.

3. Godwyn, Morgan, *The Negro's and Indian's Advocate,* London, 1680, p. 64.

4. Mannix, Daniel P., *Black Cargoes, A History of the Atlantic Slave Trade, 1518–1865,* Viking, New York, 1962, pp. 120–1.

5. Catterall, *op. cit.,* p. 77.

6. Godwyn, *op. cit.,* p. 61.

7. Gray, Lewis C., *History of Agriculture in the Southern United States to 1860,* Peter Smith, New York, 1941, Vol. I, p. 360.

8. Greene, Lorenzo Johnston, *The Negro in Colonial New England, 1620–1770,* Columbia University Press, New York, 1942, p. 63.

9. Tannenbaum, Frank, *Slave and Citizen, The Negro in America,* Knopf, New York, 1947, p. 67.

10. Ballagh, James Curtis, *White Servitude in the Colony of Virginia, A Study of the System of Indentured Labor in the American Colonies,* Johns Hopkins Press, Baltimore, 1895, p. 58.

11. Hurd, John Codman, *The Law of Freedom and Bondage in the United States,* Little, Brown, Boston, 1858, Vol. I, p. 232.

12. *Ibid.,* p. 304.

13. Elkins, Stanley M., *Slavery, A Problem in American Institutional and Intellectual Life,* University of Chicago Press, Chicago, 1959, p. 61.

14. Tannenbaum, *op. cit.,* p. 53.

15. Elkins, *op. cit.,* pp. 68–70.

16. Godwyn, *op. cit.,* pp. 38–9.

17. Bruce, Philip A., *Economic*

History of Virginia in the 17th Century, Macmillan, New York, 1896, Vol. II, p. 64.

18. Greene, *op. cit.,* pp. 260, 288.

19. *The Papers of Benjamin Franklin,* Leonard W. Labaree, ed., Yale University Press, New Haven, Conn., 1959, Vol. IV, p. 230.

20. Gray, *op. cit.,* p. 352.

21. Du Bois, W. E. Burghardt, *The Suppression of the African Slave-Trade to the United States of America, 1638–1870,* Longmans, Green, New York, 1904, p. 8.

22. Greene, *op. cit.,* pp. 22–32.

23. Gray, *op. cit.,* p. 444.

24. Catterall, *op. cit.,* Vol. II, p. 221.

25. *Ibid.,* Vol. I, p. 287.

26. *Ibid.,* p. 216.

27. Goodell, William, *The American Slave Code,* American and Foreign Anti-Slavery Society, New York, 1853, p. 106.

28. Tannenbaum, *op. cit.,* p. 80.

29. Goodell, *op. cit.,* p. 30.

30. Hurd, *op. cit.,* p. 240.

31. Goodell, *op. cit.,* p. 92.

32. *Ibid.,* p. 96.

33. Ballagh, *op. cit.,* pp. 78–9.

34. Hurd, *op. cit.,* p. 232.

35. Goodell, *op. cit.,* p. 172–3.

36. Greene, *op. cit.,* p. 177.

3 The Founding Fathers

THE YEARS PRECEDING THE OUTBREAK of armed conflict between the colonists and the mother country were indeed a revolutionary period in American history. Popular assemblies, newspapers, and pamphlets denounced each Parliamentary scheme for taxing the colonies. There were torchlight parades and blood-rousing speeches. In Boston a stamp distributor was hanged in effigy, and in Newport a revenue cutter was set ablaze.

These were times not simply of deeds but of words as well, as the revolutionaries sought to justify their actions. At the heart of the quarrel lay the question of which body was to rule the thirteen colonies, the English Parliament or the colonists' own selected representatives. The colonists feared that if they were subordinated to the will of Parliament, in which they were not and could not be represented, their own economic interests would thereafter be sacrificed to those of the mother country, particularly the interests of the English landlords and merchants.

From the standpoint of contemporary English constitutional law, however, the colonists did not have a strong case. "What Parliament doth," said William Blackstone in his *Commentaries,* "no power on earth can undo."[1] Even William Pitt, a champion of the colonial cause, warned his American friends that Parliament possessed "an authority they ought not to question."[2]

Denied the aid of positive law, the colonists were forced to rely on natural law to justify their defiance of Parliament.

Ironically, these were the very same arguments that Englishmen a century before had used to assert the supremacy of Parliament over the Crown. In defending this earlier revolution, John Locke had declared that man possesses certain natural rights, including the right of private property, which no sovereign can subvert and which governments are formed to protect. If the natural rights of its citizens are violated, the social contract establishing the state is dissolved. "Whenever, therefore, the legislative shall transgress this fundamental rule of society, and either by ambition, fear, folly, or corruption, endeavor to grasp themselves, or put into the hands of any other, an absolute power over the lives, liberties, and estates of the people, by this breach of trust they forfeit the power the people had put into their hands. . . ."[3] Locke's writings were well known to the Americans. "The natural rights of the colonists," Samuel Adams declared in 1762 in the name of the Massachusetts legislature, "we humbly conceive to be the same with those of all other British subjects and indeed of all mankind. The principle of these rights is to be 'free from any superior power on earth and not to be under the will or legislative authority of man, but to have only the law of nature for his rule.' " Christopher Gadsden, a South Carolina merchant and planter, referred to those "latent though inherent rights of society, which no climate, no time, no constitution, no contract can ever destroy or diminish"[4] and Thomas Jefferson, drafting the resolutions of the Albemarle County freeholders in 1774, spoke of the "privileges [men] hold as the common rights of mankind, confirmed by the political constitutions they have respectively assumed. . . ."[5] In 1774 the First Continental Congress asserted "That the inhabitants of the English Colonies in North America, by the immutable laws of nature . . . are entitled to life, liberty, and property. . . ."[6]

Thus the doctrine of natural rights, first elaborated to oppose the prerogatives of the English Crown, was now used to oppose the sovereignty of Parliament. It was not long, in fact, before the great mass of Americans were demanding the equality which the doctrine of natural rights implied. What had begun as a political protest was soon transformed into a social revolution. Before it was over, most of the props supporting special class privileges had been destroyed. The landed estates were broken up, entail and primogeniture were abolished, universal male suffrage adopted, the churches disestablished, imprisonment for debt ended, the criminal codes liberalized, the sumptuary laws overthrown, and knee breeches and silk stockings replaced by pantaloons. Thomas Jefferson aptly expressed the prevailing mood. "We hold these truths to be self-evident," he wrote in the Declaration of Independence, "that all men are created equal; that they are endowed by their creator with certain inalienable rights; that among these are Life, Liberty and the pursuit of Happiness."[7]

But was the Negro included when the Virginia Convention adopted a Bill of Rights which declared, "That all men are by nature equally free and independent, and have certain inherent rights, . . . namely, the enjoyment of life and liberty"?[8] On the eve of the Revolutionary War there were approximately 500,000 Negroes in the thirteen colonies, nearly a fifth of the total population. Less than one in twenty was free. In the colonies below the Mason-Dixon line, where over three-fourths of the Negroes were concentrated, the ratio of black to white was even higher and the ratio of free Negro to slave lower. Negroes comprised nearly half of Virginia's population, and in South Carolina they vastly outnumbered the whites.

Even in certain areas of the North the same situation prevailed. On the Narragansett peninsula and in the Hudson Valley, where large estates predominated, Negro slaves were the basis of the labor force. While less dependent on Negro labor than the South, the economy of New England was deeply caught up in the slave trade. Earlier, when London suddenly sought to enforce the Navigation Acts which would have favored trade in British-owned colonial bottoms, Massachusetts merchants warned that such a policy would beach 700 ships and throw 5,000 seamen out of work. Such was the importance of the trade with the foreign-held West Indies which exchanged slaves for sugar. The Rhode Island merchants would also be affected. "Two-thirds of our vessels will become useless and perish upon our hands," they prophesied; "our merchants and those who depend upon the merchant for employment must seek for subsistence elsewhere; and . . . a nursery of seamen, at this time consisting of twenty-two hundred, in this colony only, will be . . . destroyed."[9]

Here was a crisis in conscience, a conflict between the prevailing mood of the times and the practical necessities of everyday life. When the South Carolina patriot, Henry Laurens, wrote to his son John, an aide-de-camp of General George Washington, in August, 1776, that he wished to manumit his slaves, worth £20,000, he added, "Great powers oppose me—the law and customs of my country, my own and the avarice of my countrymen. What will my children say if I deprive them of so much estate? These are difficulties. . . ."[10] It was a conflict which the Americans of that generation, even the most liberal-minded, never completely resolved. Eventually they were forced to fall back on compromise. But the Revolutionary period did raise the issue in a significant way for the first time. In formulating the doctrine of the inherent equality of all mankind it provided a touchstone for later generations as they sought direction for the evolving democracy.

Even before the Revolutionary era, the colonial conscience had been occasionally twinged by the existence of Negro slavery. As early as 1688 the Quaker community at Germantown, Pennsylvania, had protested against the institution. "Now though they are black," the Monthly Meeting resolved on the issue of the Negro, "we cannot conceive there is more liberty to have them slaves, as it is to have other white ones. There is a saying, that we should do to all men like as we will be done ourselves; making no difference of what generation, descent, or colour they are. And those who steal or rob men, and those who buy or purchase them, are they not all alike?"[11] This was the first such protest in the American colonies, and it marked the beginning of the Quakers' long efforts to eliminate slavery in English-speaking America.

The campaign was initially led by a handful of radicals among the Quakers, against the opposition of the conservative, slaveholding leadership. Though some of the radicals were ousted from the group for their outspoken views, the remainder, insisting on the inherent evil of slavery, eventually won over the majority. In 1730 the Philadelphia Yearly Meeting warned its members against purchasing slaves, "it being disagreeable to the sense of this Meeting."[12] Those Quakers who persisted in the practice were to be gently admonished. Later the Friends took a much more forceful step. They resolved to expel any member who bought or sold Negroes, and to encourage those who already owned slaves to set them free. In urging this stand, John Woolman who, along with Anthony Benezet, had led the fight against slavery within the Quaker group said: "Many slaves on this continent are oppressed, and their cries have reached the ears of the Most High. In infinite love and goodness He hath opened our understanding from one time to another concerning our duty toward this people, and it is not time for delay."[13]

Except for the Quakers, however, practically no one raised his voice in protest against slavery on religious grounds. Judge Samuel Sewall of the Massachusetts Superior Court was one exception. He argued that "it is most certain that all Men, as they are the Sons of *Adam,* are Co-heirs, and have equal Rights unto Liberty, and all other outward Comforts of Life."[14] This opinion, however, did not endear him to his neighbors, and he found himself socially shunned.

Some opposed slavery on other grounds. The lower-class whites disliked having to compete against slave labor. In nearly every important colonial city, at one time or another, they voiced their protests against this competition. In 1722, several of the laboring white population complained in a petition to the Pennsylvania legislature that "the keeping of *Negroes,* to be hired out to do all or most of the servile work in and about the City of Philadelphia, debars the Petitioners from being employed, to the utter Ruin of themselves and Families."[15] In that same city eighteen years later, in the midst of an economic recession, the white artisans petitioned against the employment of Negro slaves on public works "instead of imploying the Common People or Poor Laborers . . . and Circulating Money for their Support, as all good Common Wealths in erecting Public Edifices have required."[16] Meanwhile, New York City's white artisans had protested against the "pernicious custom of breeding slaves to trade."[17] John Adams, explaining why slavery had finally been abolished in Massachusetts, said "the real cause was the multiplication of laboring white people, who would no longer suffer . . . the labor, by which alone they could obtain a subsistence, to be done by slaves."[18]

Opposition to slavery among the rural lower-class whites was not as vocal, but nevertheless, it was strong. In the South every farmer forced to migrate west because he could not compete against a slaveholding neighbor became an enemy of the institution, unless he dreamed of one day owning slaves himself. Even in the North, where Negroes were seldom employed in agriculture, the yeoman farmer recognized the danger which the institution of slave labor posed to his way of life. He, too, on emigrating to the West, carried with him a deep antipathy to the system.

While antipathy to slavery for economic reasons was confined mainly to the lower classes, the wealthier members of society had other reasons for opposing the institution. Some felt that the existence of an alien race within their midst endangered the safety of the colonies. Others felt that slavery sapped the vitality of the white population and retarded its growth. "I am sensible of many consequences of multiplying these Ethiopians among us," wrote Colonel William Byrd, a leading Virginia plantation owner. "They blow up the pride, and ruin the Industry of our White People, who seeing a Rank of Poor Creatures below them, detest work for fear it should make them look like slaves." He wrote further, "We have already at least 10,000 Men of these descendants of Ham fit to bear Arms, and their Numbers increase every day as well by birth as Importation. And in case there shoud arise a Man of desperate courage amongst us, exasperated by a desperate fortune, he might with more advantage than Catiline kindle a Servile War."[19]

In thus explaining Virginia's efforts to limit the importation of Negroes into the colony, Byrd expressed the fears held by many of his fellow Americans. Even those who opposed slavery on religious grounds shared these fears. The German-town Friends had wondered what would happen "If once these slaves (which they say are so wicked and stubborn men,) should join themselves—fight for their freedom, and handel their masters, as they did handel them before. . . ."[20]

These fears accounted in great part for the colonists' persistent efforts to limit the slave trade. In the years prior to the Revolutionary War, Virginia enacted at least thirty-five laws, and South Carolina thirteen, that either restricted or taxed the importation of Negro slaves. Although many of these laws were later vetoed by the king's Privy Council, acting to protect the English merchants' commercial interests, they reflected the attitudes of the colony's leading citizens. "We must therefore beg leave to inform your Majesty," a group of South Carolinians petitioned the king in 1734, "that, amidst our other perilous circumstances, we are subject to many intestine dangers from the great number of negroes that are now among us, who amount at least to twenty-two thousand persons, and are three to one of all your Majesty's white subjects in this province. Insurrections against us have been often attempted."[21]

Six years later, after a slave named Cato had led an unsuccessful Negro uprising, South Carolina placed the prohibitive duty of £100 on the importation of a Negro slave. A similar fear of insurrection held the North. Pennsylvania, after hearing rumors of an attempted Negro revolt in New York City, hurriedly passed a law levying a duty of £10 on each imported slave, only to have the crown disallow the tax the following year. New York and Massachusetts, motivated by the same fear, also tried to limit the importation of Negro slaves, but with the same lack of success.

Of course, not all those who sought to restrict the importation of slaves did so because they feared an insurrection. Some desired the restrictions because of their opposition to slavery on moral and religious grounds. Others hoped to limit the supply of Negroes in order to raise the price of slaves. Many merely wished to keep slavery within manageable proportions. A substantial group of citizens felt that the dangers of having such an alien race within their midst far outweighed the benefits which might accrue. As many Americans then and later realized, limiting the slave trade was the first step toward eliminating the institution itself.

As the eighteenth century entered its second half, these strands in the opposition to slavery were joined by those American colonists who had come under the influence of the French Enlightenment. Although it was not a large group, it included many men who would later play a leading role in the founding of the United States: George Mason and Thomas Jefferson of Virginia, Charles Carroll of Maryland, Benjamin Franklin and Benjamin Rush of Pennsylvania, John Jay of New York, and James Otis of Massachusetts. Believing in the essential rationality of all human beings, they began to view slavery as one of the social institutions which perverted man's inherent nature. "Slavery," Dr. Rush wrote, "is so foreign to the human mind, that the moral faculties, as well as those of the understanding are debased, and rendered torpid by it. All the vices which are charged upon the Negroes in the southern colonies and the West-Indies, such as Idleness, Treachery, Theft, and the like, are the genuine offspring of slavery, and serve as an argument to prove that they were not intended, by Providence for it."[22] Some, such as Tucker and Pinckney, quoted Montesquieu on the evils and dangers of slavery. Others, although less directly influenced by French thought, concurred that slavery had no place in a rational, progressive society.

No individual combined these various strands of opposition to slavery in his own person as completely as did Benjamin Franklin, the colonies' most noted citizen. In the early years of his life, Franklin differed little from his Philadelphia neighbors in his attitude toward the Negro. As a leading printer in that city, he frequently acted as the agent in the sale and purchase of slaves, although he himself refused to own any. He wrote his mother in 1750 that he and his wife were about to sell a house servant who had come into their possession, "for we do not like Negro Servants."[23]

Thereafter Franklin often warned of slavery's harmful effects. "The Northern colonies," he wrote in his *Observations Concerning the Increase of Mankind,* "having few Slaves increase in Whites." The Southern colonies, on the other hand, found it difficult to attract white settlers. "The Whites who have Slaves, not labouring, are enfeebled, and therefore not so generally prolific; . . . Slaves also pejorate the Families that use them; the white Children become proud, disgusted with Labour, and being educated in Idleness, are rendered unfit to get a Living by Industry."[24] To Franklin slavery also represented a danger to the peace and security of a country. Later, when a South Carolina delegate to the Continental Congress argued that slaves should not be counted as part of the population for purposes of taxation, that they should be counted as were sheep, Franklin replied that "there is some difference between them and sheep; sheep will never make any insurrections."[25] Finally, Franklin felt that slave labor was economically unsound, that the colonists used it only because there was no other kind of labor. "Reckon then," he said in his *Observations,* "the Interest of the first Purchase of a Slave, the Insurance on Risque on his Life, his Cloathing and Diet, Expences in his Sickness and Loss of Time, Loss by his Neglect of Business (Neglect is natural to the Man who is not to be benefited by his own Care of Diligence), Expence of a Driver to keep him at Work, and his Pilfering from Time to Time, almost every Slave being *by Nature* a Thief."[26]

Between 1757 and 1775 Franklin was in London much of the time, representing the interests of the various colonies abroad. There, coming into contact with the most advanced and liberal thinkers of Europe, his own attitudes toward slavery began to change perceptibly. By 1772 he wrote Benezet, the Quaker antislavery leader, "I am glad to hear that the disposition against keeping negroes grows more general in North America."[27] And a year later he wrote to Dr.

Rush, "I hope that in time the endeavors of the friends to liberty and humanity will get the better of a practice, that has so long disgraced our nation and religion." To Condorcet he admitted that the free Negroes of Pennsylvania were generally "improvident and poor," but he blamed this on their lack of education. "I think they are not deficient in natural understanding. . . . They make good musicians."[28]

At the same time as the colonies' quarrel with the mother country deepened, Franklin became increasingly critical of Great Britain's role in promoting the slave trade. He pointed out the "hypocrisy" of Great Britain, "which encourages such a detestable commerce by laws for promoting the Guinea trade; while it piqued itself on its virtue, love of liberty, and the equity of its courts, in setting free a single Negro."[29] Like many other Americans, he realized that the existence of slavery damaged the colonies' own case for freedom in the eyes of the world. As a Boston Tory wrote in 1775: "Negro slaves in Boston! It cannot be! It is nevertheless very true. For though the Bostonians . . . have resolved in their Town Meeting, that 'It is the first principle in civil society, founded in nature and reason, that no law of society can be binding on any individual, without his consent . . .' they actually have in town two thousand Negro slaves, who neither by themselves in person, nor by representation of their own free election, ever gave consent to their present state of bondage."[30]

Franklin had written for a London newspaper what was purported to be a conversation between an Englishman and a Scotsman and an American. "As to the Share England has in these Enormities of America," Franklin has his American say, "remember, Sir, that she began the slave trade; that her merchants of London, Bristol, Liverpool, and Glasgow, send their Ships to Africa for the Purpose of purchasing slaves. . . . This [her merchants] have not only done and continue to do, but several Laws heretofore made in our colonies, to discourage the Importation of Slaves, by laying a heavy Duty, payable by the Importer, have been disapproved and repealed by your Government here, as being prejudicial, forsooth, to the Interest of the African Company."[31]

But some Americans found Franklin's position too disingenuous. "Is it not amazing," Patrick Henry asked in 1773, "that . . . in a Country above all others fond of Liberty, that in such an Age, and in such a Country we find Men . . . adopting a principle as repugnant to humanity as [slavery]?"[32] This conflict between the colonists' professed ideals and their sanction of slavery became an added argument against the institution of human bondage, one that grew in importance as the Revolutionary ferment increased. Rhode Island, from whose ports many a slave ship had sailed, acted in 1774 to restrict the slave trade, since "the inhabitants of America are generally engaged in the preservation of their own rights and liberties, among which, that of personal freedom must be considered as the greatest; . . . those who are desirous of enjoying all the advantages of liberty themselves, should be willing to extend personal liberty to others."[33]

In the first flush of outright rebellion, it actually seemed that slavery might be abolished. Indeed, some persons in Europe thought that the Declaration of Independence, with its affirmation of inalienable rights and universal equality, had actually set the slaves free. Those at the scene knew better, but they could not ignore Jefferson's words. In Boston, only a few months after the Declaration of Independence was proclaimed, public indignation was aroused when Negroes aboard a British ship which had been captured were offered for sale at public auction. In voting to forbid their sale, the Massachusetts House of Representatives declared that "the selling and enslaving the human species is a direct violation of the natural rights alike vested in all men by their Creator, and utterly inconsistent with the avowed principles on which this and other United States have carried their struggle for liberty. . . ."[34]

A year later, when the settlers of Vermont announced that they were severing their ties with both Great Britain and New York, they drew up a constitution expressly outlawing slavery, the first state to do so. Meanwhile, the Quakers in Pennsylvania took the final step on the road which had begun with the resolutions of the Germantown Friends in 1688. At their 1776 Annual Meeting they forbade their members from owning slaves in the future, while some of the more radical Quakers immediately set about the task of freeing the Negroes still held in bondage throughout the newly independent state. Even in Virginia, where the radicals were in control, a committee appointed to rewrite the colony's statutes prepared a bill that would have provided for gradual emancipation of the slaves.

But the first flush was deceiving. The Massachusetts legislature was unable to forbid the sale of the two Negroes captured from the British until the Senate had forced deletion of the clause calling slavery "a direct violation of the natural rights vested in all men by their Creator." In Vermont there were so few Negroes that its abolition of slavery had very little practical effect, while in Pennsylvania the Quakers could make no progress in extending the prohibition of slavery to the rest of the state. In Virginia the radicals decided that the bill to emancipate the slaves would never be enacted and would only stir up bitter opposition.

The final form of the Declaration of Independence did not even include all that Thomas Jefferson had drafted. His original version had included a paragraph condemning the King for his role in the slave trade. When the delegates from South Carolina protested that they did not want to see the slave trade ended, the Continental Congress voted to strike out the offending passage. "Our northern brethren, also, I believe," Jefferson later wrote, "felt a little tender under those censures; for though their people had very few slaves themselves, yet they had been pretty considerable carriers of them to others."[35] Among the many rights for which the Revolution was being fought was the right to own property, and for many of the colonists this included Negro slaves. Since the Revolution needed all the support it could muster, the Declaration could not insist that the Negro slave had rights too. Therefore, as the colonists threw themselves wholeheartedly into the struggle forcibly to eject the British from the continent, the question of slavery was quietly put aside.

Yet the exigencies of war soon raised the issue anew,

though on a somewhat different plane. As many had long warned, the presence of a large servile population made the colonists particularly vulnerable to military attack. As Virginia's Governor Robert Dinwiddie had explained during one of the innumerable colonial wars with the French, "We dare not venture to part with our white men any distance, as we must have a watchful eye over our Negro slaves who are upwards of 100,000."[36] This was even more important when the British themselves became the enemy. As early as 1768 the citizens of Boston had demanded the arrest of Captain John Wilson, commanding officer of His Majesty's 59th Regiment, for urging the slaves to rise up against their masters and "drive the Liberty Boys to the Devil." Later Abigail Adams wrote her husband, John, about rumors that the Negroes had petitioned the royal Governor, "telling him they would fight for him provided he would arm them, and engage to liberate them if he conquered."[37] In Virginia, where the slave population was much larger, the inhabitants had even more reason to fear a Negro insurrection which might be instigated by the British.

It is not surprising, then, that the colonists were noticeably reluctant to enlist Negroes in their cause. Although Crispus Attucks, a runaway slave, had been killed as a revolutionary during the Boston "Massacre," and Peter Salem, an ex-slave from Framingham, was soon to distinguish himself in the Battle of Bunker Hill, the Committee of Safety, which then exercised effective control over Massachusetts, resolved in May 1775, to admit no slaves into its army, it being "inconsistent with the principles that are to be supported."[38] When General George Washington arrived to take command of the Continental Army after the Battle of Bunker Hill, this policy was made even more stringent. Soon after convening a council of war, Washington issued orders not to enlist "any deserter from the ministerial army, nor any stroller, negro, or vagabond, or person suspected of being an enemy to the liberty of America. . . ."[39]

Although Negroes could not thereafter enlist, the Continental Army contained many Negroes. Their depressed social and economic status made them eager recruits, while the enlistment of whites in sufficient numbers was difficult to procure. Thus Negroes were found in all the New England regiments. This situation soon aroused the concern of the southern delegates to the Continental Congress, and in September, 1775, Edward Rutledge of South Carolina moved that all Negroes serving in the revolutionary armies be discharged. Whether Washington himself had a hand in this is not known, but the motion was readily defeated. Four days later, however, Congress dispatched a committee "to confer with General Washington and others on the most effectual method of continuing, supporting and regulating a Continental Army."[40] But before this committee was due to arrive, Washington again convened a Council of War. The officers present voted unanimously to reject all slaves as enlistees and by a large majority to reject all Negroes. The congressional committee, which included Benjamin Franklin, had little choice but to go along with the wishes of Washington and his officers. Later one of the dissenters, General John Thomas of Massachusetts, wrote, "I am sorry that any prejudices should take place . . . with respect to the troops raised. . . . We have some Negroes; but I look on them in general, equally serviceable with other men for fatigue; and, in action many of them have proved themselves brave."[41]

Washington's attitude is not surprising. He was a substantial slaveholder, and he had been trained to believe in the inherent inferiority of all Negroes. Not once had he had reason to question this assumption, for all the Negroes with whom he was likely to come in contact were, in fact, inferior —outwardly if not basically. Like most Virginia slaveholders, Washington demanded absolute obedience from his Negroes and rewarded those who gave him this obedience with kindness and consideration. When he hired an overseer for one of his outlying plantations, he bade him "take all necessary and proper care of the Negroes committed to his management using them with proper humanity and discretion."[42] His diary contains frequent references to caring for sick slaves, but it also notes the case of an unruly slave, a "fellow [who] is

both a rogue and a runaway (tho' he was by no means re-
markable for the former, and never practiced the latter till
of late),"[43] whom he ordered sold in the West Indies. Like
most Virginians, he keenly felt the danger of allowing Negroes
to arm themselves, to assemble in large numbers or to roam
the countryside. Yet under the press of wartime conditions,
Washington's attitude toward the Negro was to undergo a
significant change.

Hardly had Washington reaffirmed his intention of permitting no more Negroes to enlist in the Continental Army
than the Royal Governor of Virginia, Lord Dunmore, provoked by the first actual physical resistance to British authority in that colony, declared that all rebels were slaves and
all indentured servants were free. His proclamation, issued
November 7, 1775, threw the Virginia plantation owners into
a panic. If Dunmore were not crushed before spring, George
Washington wrote from Cambridge, he would become
America's most formidable enemy; his strength would increase "as the snowball by rolling; and faster, if some expedient cannot be hit upon to convince the slaves and servants
of the impotency of his design."[44] But such an expedient was
difficult to find. Often it was necessary to promise the slaves
eventual freedom to win their loyalty, and this the colonists
were reluctant to do. At the same time, the slaves' uncertain
allegiance precluded the military victories which would have
dissuaded them from fleeing to the British. For most Virginians in the Tidewater region were too worried about what
the Negroes might do in their absence to take up arms against
the British. Similar fears hampered the revolutionary cause
in the other southern colonies, particularly in Georgia and
South Carolina.

Meanwhile, in Massachusetts, Washington was faced with
a similar problem. If the Negroes were not permitted to join
the Continental Army, they would find a welcome in the
British battalions. Indeed, many were already doing so.
Alarmed by this situation, Washington was forced to reconsider his previous position, since "the free negroes, who have
served in this army, are very much dissatisfied at being dis-

carded [and] it is to be apprehended, that they may seek employ in the ministerial army. . . ."[45] Two weeks later, a committee of Congress formally approved Washington's recommendation "that the free negroes who have served faithfully in the army at Cambridge, may be re-inlisted therein, but no others."[46]

But even this less stringent restriction on Negro enlistment broke down in the face of the continuing difficulty in raising sufficient troops from other sources. Therefore, in 1777 Connecticut promised its slaves their freedom if they would enlist in the state militia for three years. Their masters, of course, were to be compensated for their loss. And in the dark winter of 1777–1778, when the revolutionary armies were reduced to a ragged, half-starved remnant, Washington agreed to Rhode Island's plan for raising an entire battalion from among its Negro slaves. New York and other New England states soon followed this example. Massachusetts agreed to raise a battalion from among its Negro population, and New Hampshire offered the same bounties to Negroes as the whites for enrolling in its forces. Before the war was over, each of these states had enlisted Negroes in its armies, with the understanding that they would be given their freedom upon completing their term of service. Washington had no choice but to give his unofficial approval to these developments. The unsettling conditions of the war were pushing men along paths they had previously wished to avoid.

In the South the revolutionary cause continued to fare badly, and at the heart of the problem lay the Negro. Without his loyalty it was impossible for the colonists to confront the British with sustained and determined resistance. John Laurens of South Carolina suggested to Washington that the southern states raise a body of soldiers from among the blacks, just as the northern states were doing. "I am aware," he said, "of [the] monstrous popular prejudice . . . against . . . undertaking to transform beings almost irrational into well disciplined soldiers." Yet he was convinced it could be done. "The hope that will spring in each man's breast respecting his own escape will prevent his being miserable. Those who fall in battle will not lose much; those who survive will obtain their reward. Habits of subordination, patience under fatigue, sufferings and privations of every kind are soldierly qualifications, which these possess in an eminent degree. . . ."[47] Such an army, he felt, would presently drive the British from the Carolinas. His proposal was warmly endorsed by another young member of Washington's staff, a man born in the West Indies but then a citizen of New York. Writing to John Jay in support of Laurens' plan, Alexander Hamilton said, "This will secure [the slaves'] fidelity, animate their courage and, I believe, will have a good influence upon those who remain, by opening the door to their emancipation."[48]

These arguments convinced the Continental Congress; a vote taken on March 29, 1779, authorized South Carolina and Georgia "to take measures immediately for raising three thousand able-bodied negroes."[49] The masters of these men were to be paid up to $1,000 for each slave enlisted, while the slaves themselves were to receive $50 and their freedom at the end of the war. The proposal met with bitter opposition in the two states themselves, however—particularly in South Carolina, where the revolutionary council threatened to make peace with Britain. The Congress consequently did not press its proposal. "The policy of our arming the slaves," Washington wrote to Laurens' father, "is in my opinion a moot point, unless the enemy set the example. For, should we begin to form Battalions of them, I have not the smallest doubt, if the war be prosecuted, of [the British] following us in it, and justifying the measure upon our own ground. The upshot then must be, who can arm fastest. . . . Besides, I am not clear that a discrimination will not render slavery more irksome to those who remain in it."[50] No longer, it seems, was Washington opposed in principle to employing Negro soldiers; it was the practical disadvantage that cautioned him.

Young Laurens continued to press for implementation of his proposal, but with no success. In 1781, he was again turned down by South Carolina; he was, he said, "opposed by a triple-headed monster, that shed the baneful influence of avarice, prejudice, and pusillanimity. . . ."[51] A year later, he wrote General Washington reporting failure to win over the Georgia legislature. "I must confess," Washington wrote back, "that I am not at all astonished at the failure of your plan. That spirit of freedom which at the commencement of this contest would have gladly sacrificed everything to the attainment of its object, has long since subsided, and every selfish passion has taken its place. It is not the public, but private interest, which influences the generality of mankind, nor can the Americans any longer boast an exception."[52] Washington was by that time wholly in favor of using Negro troops.

This letter indicates his own changed attitude toward Negroes, probably because he had seen so many of them fight valiantly for the cause to which he had committed his life and fortune. While he never publicly stated his feelings on the subject, Washington's attitude in his later years is clear. He warmly welcomed his friend Lafayette's "laudable" plan to buy a small estate in the West Indies, free its slaves, and employ them as tenants, though characteristically he avoided taking an active role in the project. To a neighbor, Alexander Spottswood, he confided, "Were it not then, that I am principled against selling negroes, as you would cattle at a market, I would not in twelve months from this date, be possessed of one as a slave." Then he warned, "I shall be happily mistaken, if they are not found to be a very troublesome species of property ere many years pass over our heads."[53] And he provided in his will for the freeing of his slaves upon the death of his wife.

The South's reluctance to enlist Negroes in the revolutionary cause led large numbers of them to desert to the British. The British, however, frequently treated them no better than had the Americans. Nevertheless, some even took up arms in the Loyalist cause. Others took advantage of the unsettled times to run away. Virginians, according to Thomas Jefferson, lost 30,000 of their slaves in 1778 alone. The citizens of South Carolina were reported to have lost at least 25,000 slaves between 1775 and 1783, while the citizens of Georgia lost approximately 11,000 during this same period, representing 75 per cent of their total slave population. The losses were not confined to the South. When Sir Guy Carleton, the British commander, evacuated New York at the end of the war, he insisted on taking with him all those Negroes who had come into his possession. When Washington protested that this would be a violation of the peace treaty clause prohibiting the British from "carrying away any Negroes, or other property of the American inhabitants,"[54] Carleton replied that he had found the Negroes free when he took command of New York. He pointed out that any slaveowner deprived of his property could later claim compensation from the British government, but, he added, "restoration, where inseparable from breach of public faith, is utterly impracticable."[55] Settlement of the compensation for these and the other Negroes carried away by the British was to exacerbate relations between the new nation and its former rulers for many years to come.

Although a large number of Negroes had gone over to the British side, an even larger number gave their allegiance to the revolutionary cause. Of the 300,000 men who served in the Continental forces, approximately 5,000 were Negroes. The North, which had the fewest Negroes, had enlisted by far the great majority. When the war was finally concluded, they were rewarded in a number of ways. Almost all who fought, either in the Army or in the Navy, were given their freedom, swelling the ranks of the new nation's free Negro population. Many also received the various bounties voted the revolutionary soldiers by the several states. Even Virginia voted to set free all slaves "who served in the late war," and to grant them western lands.

Thus the newly freed states paid off their debt to Negroes who had fought in their behalf. But what about their debt to Negroes in general? Now that the war had been won, the Americans were free, if so disposed, to turn their attention to the conflict between advancing the rights of men and the institution of slavery. Here, as peace returned to the one-time colonies, two distinct regional patterns began to emerge.

In the North state after state abolished first the slave trade, then slavery itself. Vermont led the way in 1777, when its constitution declared that no person "ought to be holden by law, to serve any person, as a servant, slave, or apprentice"[56] without his or her consent. This was followed in 1786 by a law imposing stiff penalties on anyone who tried to kidnap or otherwise interfere with the liberty of a free Negro. Pennsylvania acted while the war was still in progress. Its legislature, in 1773, had already taxed the slave trade out of existence. In 1780, "in grateful commemoration of our own happy deliverance from that state of unconditional submission, to which we were doomed by the tyranny of Britain,"[57] it provided for the complete, though gradual, abolition of Negro slavery. No child thereafter born in Pennsylvania was to be held as a slave, though he might be kept as a servant until the age of twenty-eight if his mother had been a slave. A handful of Friends, most notably Benezet, had lobbied strenuously for this measure, but it owed surprisingly little to the efforts of the Quakers as a whole, who because of the war had largely withdrawn from politics. As one of those responsible for the law remarked, "Our bill astonishes and pleases the Quakers. They looked for no such benevolent issue of our new government exercised by Presbyterians."[58] Other states followed the Pennsylvania example, Rhode Island and Connecticut enacting similar measures in 1784.

Massachusetts adopted a new constitution with a clause patterned after George Mason's Declaration of Rights, which asserted that "all men are born free and equal." Another constitution, which had been proposed earlier but which did not contain such a clause, had been rejected by the voters. Three years later Chief Justice William Cushing, in *Commonwealth v Jennison*, held that this clause had abolished slavery in the Bay State. "The idea of slavery," he said, "is inconsistent with our own conduct and Constitution; and there can be no such thing as perpetual servitude of a rational creature, unless his liberty is forfeited by some criminal conduct or given up by personal consent of contract."[59] A similar clause in the New Hampshire Constitution was later interpreted in the same manner. Thus judicial interpretation was sometimes a substitute for legislative enactment.

In New York and New Jersey efforts to abolish slavery were met with determined resistance by the large slaveholders. In the immediate postwar period the antislavery forces were able only to push through the passage of laws ending the slave trade and facilitating manumission. Once these were enacted, Societies for Promoting the Manumission of Slaves were organized in both states. John Jay was president of the New York Society. These Societies, which the Quakers were instrumental in founding, worked assiduously for abolition of slavery itself, and finally New York and New Jersey passed laws providing for gradual emancipation.

By the time the Continental Convention prepared to convene in Philadelphia in 1787, almost all the states in the North had either abolished slavery or were headed in that direction. However, in many instances the laws did not benefit the Negroes. Since they generally called for gradual abolition, a master could easily avoid their effect by either moving to another state himself or by selling his slaves to a buyer in another state. Many masters did, in fact, take advantage of the loopholes in the various abolition laws. Nevertheless, these laws did produce a moral climate which induced a great many masters to free their slaves voluntarily. Most important, these laws removed slavery's moral opprobrium from the North and ended the contradiction, at least in that region, between the expressed rights of man and the actual practice of slavery.

In the South, however, the situation was quite different. There, too, the leaders of the newly formed governments, those who had taken the most active roles in asserting the rights of the colonists against the encroachments of Parliament, were troubled by the continued existence of slavery. Notable among these leaders were Charles Carroll, a signer of the Declaration of Independence and a distinguished citizen of Maryland; Thomas Jefferson and George Mason of Virginia; and Henry Laurens of South Carolina, whose son John had been killed in the closing days of the war. Their concern about slavery was shared by certain religious sects, particularly the Society of Friends and the Methodists. The first required its members to divest themselves of all their slaves on penalty of expulsion from the Society; and many Quakers, in complying with this rule, were forced to resettle in the west, across the Appalachians. The Methodists, after resolving that "slavery is contrary to the laws of God, man, and nature, and . . . contrary to the dictates of conscience and pure religion"[60] also put pressure on their members not to own slaves.

Yet the most that these groups could accomplish in the political sphere was to persuade the Virginia legislature in 1782 to make it easier for masters to free their slaves. Previously the various restrictions on voluntary manumission had discouraged many Quakers and Methodists, as well as others, from obeying their moral scruples. When these restrictions were removed, the number of free Negroes in Virginia, for example, more than doubled in two years. But when these same groups tried to persuade the Virginia legislature to pass an act providing for gradual compulsory abolition, they met complete defeat. While the majority of Virginians were willing to sanction, and even to encourage, voluntary manumission, they balked at forcing all slaveholders to free their slaves.

In Maryland the same forces could not achieve even these very limited successes. When the House of Delegates received petitions from some of the western countries for the abolition of slavery, it voted thirty-two to twenty-two not even to consider them. Later a bill to make it easier for masters to manumit their slaves was cleared by a House committee and vigorously supported by William Pinckney. But when it became entwined with a measure to abolish slavery completely, both bills were killed, never to be resurrected again. In South Carolina and Georgia the issue of abolition did not even arise.

Thus a distinct regional response emerged in the attitude toward slavery. Both in the North and in the South slavery was considered a blemish on the body politic. But in the North the institution was not so deeply embedded that it could not be rooted out, while in the South even enlightened men, who saw its pernicious effects and wished that it could be abolished, were afraid to tamper with it. Slavery was too closely interwoven into the region's economic and social fabric.

No one realized better how great an evil slavery was, yet how difficult to uproot, than Thomas Jefferson, one of the South's most learned and cultivated men. Educated at William and Mary, Jefferson had early come under the influence of liberal British and French thought, and took what for his day and locale was an advanced stand on the issue of slavery. As a young legislator he introduced a bill giving masters the right to manumit their slaves. His attitude toward slavery is clear from a case he argued in 1770, when he unsuccessfully defended a third-generation mulatto in a suit for freedom. In drafting the Declaration of Independence, he declared that "all men are created equal." He helped draft the laws for the new state of Virginia, including one that provided for the gradual abolition of slavery. This was never submitted to the legislature for approval, however, since it "was found that the public mind would not bear the proposition."[61] As Richard Hofstadter has pointed out, he was always noticeably circumspect about attacking slavery in his own state. Yet he was instrumental in securing the legislation by which his state banned the further importation of slaves and which made it easier for slaveholders to manumit their slaves, and in 1784 he proposed the abolition of slavery in all of the territories.

When he had completed his second term as Governor of Virginia, Jefferson found at last the leisure he needed to answer certain questions about his native state which had been put to him by the Marquis de Barbe-Marbois. Jefferson's reply, published anonymously in Paris as *Notes on Virginia*, reflected his views on a number of issues, including that of slavery. "The whole commerce between master and slave," he wrote, "is a perpetual exercise of the most boisterous passions, the most unremitting despotism on the one part, and degrading submissions on the other." However, he pointed out, these habits are transmitted from parent to child. "The parent storms, the child looks on, catches the lineaments of wrath, puts on the same airs in the circle of smaller slaves, gives a loose to the worst of passions, and thus nursed, educated, and daily exercised in tyranny, cannot but be stamped by it with odious peculiarities. The man must be a prodigy who can retain his manners and morals undepraved by such circumstances."[62]

Under a system of slavery, Jefferson pointed out, half the population is forced to trample on the rights of the other half, destroying their own sense of righteousness in the process. "With the morals of the people, their industry is also destroyed. For in a warm climate, no man will labour for himself who can make another labour for him." By all rights, according to Jefferson, such a system is doomed. "Indeed," he said, "I tremble for my country when I reflect that God is just; that his justice cannot sleep forever; that considering numbers, nature and natural means only, a revolution of the wheel of fortune, an exchange of situation, is among possible events . . ."[63]

Yet Jefferson did not foresee that the Negroes would ever be set free and allowed to live at peace with their white neighbors. He wrote: "Deep-rooted prejudices entertained by the whites; ten thousand recollections, by the blacks, of the injuries they have sustained; new provocations; the real distinctions which nature has made; and many other circumstances, will divide us into parties, and produce convulsions, which will probably never end but in the extermination of the one or the other race. To these objections, which are political, may be added others, which are physical and moral."[64] Jefferson elaborated on this last point. The Quakers who have freed their slaves, he wrote, must "plan their crops for them . . . direct all of their operations . . . watch them . . . almost constantly to make them work and even to whip them. A man's moral sense must be unusually strong if slavery does not make him a thief."[65] In another letter Jefferson observed that "the blacks . . . are inferior to the whites in the endowments both of mind and body. . . . This unfortunate difference of colour, and perhaps of faculty, is a powerful obstacle to the emancipation of these people."[66]

Since Jefferson did not believe Negroes could ever be

peacefully integrated into the American community as free
men, he proposed in his *Notes on Virginia* that they be re-
settled elsewhere. He maintained that first, however, it was
necessary to prevent the further importation of slaves and to
train those already here in the various arts and sciences.
Recognizing that the economy of Virginia, like that of the
other southern states, was dependent on Negro labor, Jefferson proposed that Negroes transported out of the country be
replaced by an equal number of white inhabitants from other
parts of the world.

These, then, were the studied reflections of an American
statesman and philosopher on the question which troubled
his own conscience and that of his country. He could see no
end to slavery. His efforts, before and later, to ban the further
importation of Negroes into Virginia, to abolish slavery in
the Northwest Territory, and to promote the colonization of
Negroes in Africa flowed from his analysis of the situation.
Much as he detested slavery, he saw no way of abolishing it
short of transporting the Negro back to Africa.

Jefferson was in Paris, serving as ambassador to France,
when delegates from twelve states—Rhode Island refused to
take part—assembled in Philadelphia in 1787 to consider the
question of how the Articles of Confederation might be improved. The delegates soon voted to cast aside the Articles and
to institute an entirely new government. These men were of a
different temper from those who had assembled in the same
city eleven years before to draw up the Declaration of Independence. Although some of the delegates had been present
on that earlier occasion, experience and the caution that
comes with success had softened their revolutionary ardor.
They had won their war of independence. What they now
feared most was social upheaval such as Shay's Rebellion in
Massachusetts portended. At one time they had sought to
loosen the ties of government; now they wished to tighten
them. Above all, they hoped to create a stronger central government.

To the delegates assembled in Philadelphia, the issue of
slavery was peripheral, although it concerned them all. In-

deed, at one point, Gouveneur Morris of Pennsylvania referred to slavery as "a nefarious institution— . . . the curse of heaven on the States where it prevailed."[67] And Rufus King of Massachusetts, Roger Sherman of Connecticut, and Luther Martin of Maryland expressed similar views. On the other hand, such men as Charles Pinckney of South Carolina were equally adamant in their defense of the institution. But the delegates were determined not to let their personal feelings about slavery interfere with the work at hand. As Roger Sherman said, in explaining why he would not press for abolition of the slave trade, "it was expedient to have as few objections as possible to the proposed scheme of Government."[68]

Still, try as they might, the founding fathers could not avoid touching on the question of slavery. It affected too many aspects of the daily life in their respective states, and it lurked in the background of too many important issues which the delegates at Philadelphia had to resolve. As James Madison slowly came to realize, the important division was not between the large states and the small, but between those states which permitted slavery and those which did not. When the Convention finally took up the question of import duties, an impasse arose and threatened to deadlock the convention. The New England states objected to the proposal that the passage of any navigation act require a two-thirds vote in both houses of Congress, fearing that this restriction would make it too difficult to secure the tariffs they felt their region needed to protect its infant industries. South Carolina and Georgia, on the other hand, said they could not accept the constitution "unless their right to import slaves be untouched." The right to tax, as they well knew, was the right to prohibit. Thus despite the hopes of avoiding it, the issue of slavery had arisen.

As already noted, numerous attempts had been made during the colonial period to restrict the slave trade, but with little success. As soon as the colonies gained their independence, many of them immediately prohibited the further importation of Negroes. These prohibitions were prompted on the one hand by a dislike of the institution of slavery and on the other by the fear that the Negro population was growing too rapidly for the welfare and safety of the whites. But larger interests were also involved. Virginia and Maryland had long produced more slaves than their economies could absorb, and they had turned to exporting the surplus to their southern neighbors. In effect, Virginia and Maryland had become nurseries for South Carolina, where the unsalutary working conditions on the rice and indigo plantations used up slaves more rapidly than they could be replaced by natural increase, and Georgia, which had only recently been opened up to slavery.

One of the most vociferous opponents of the slave trade at the Convention was Maryland's Luther Martin, an advocate of cheap money, a friend of debtors, and himself the owner of six Negroes. In urging that slaves be taxed along with other imported goods, Martin declared "it was inconsistent with the principles of the revolution and dishonorable to the American character to have such a feature [as slavery] in the Constitution."[69] He was seconded by George Mason of Virginia, who pointed out that Virginia had made numerous attempts before to abolish the "infernal traffic" originating "in the avarice of British merchants." Mason, who himself owned 300 slaves, said: "The present question concerns not the importing States alone but the whole Union. . . . Slavery discourages arts and manufactures. The poor despise labor performed by slaves. They prevent the immigration of Whites, who really enrich and strengthen a Country."[70]

The other southern delegates were quick to point out Maryland and Virginia's interest in the question. "As to Virginia," said General Pinckney of South Carolina, "she will gain by stopping the importations. Her slaves will rise in value, and she has more than she wants. It would be unequal to require S.C. and Georgia to confederate on such unequal terms." Besides, he argued, it was in the interests of all the states to encourage the slave trade. "The more slaves, the more produce to employ the carrying trade," he said. "The more consumption also, and the more of this, the more of revenue for the common treasury."[71] His fellow delegate John

Rutledge shifted the argument to a different plane. "Religion and humanity have nothing to do with this question," he said. "Interest alone is the governing principle with Nations —The true question at present is whether the South (n.) States shall or shall not be parties to the Union. If the Northern states consult their interest, they will not oppose the increase of Slaves . . ."[72]

The New England delegates quickly picked up the hint. "Let every State import what it pleases," said Oliver Ellsworth of Connecticut, a wealthy lawyer who was intimately connected with the leading commercial interests in his state. He added: "The morality or wisdom of slavery are considerations belonging to the States themselves. What enriches a part enriches the whole, and the States are the best judges of their particular interest."[73] Besides, the New England states needed South Carolina's and Georgia's support if they were to win for Congress the right to impose tariffs by majority vote.

But there were still other political factors. As Rufus King pointed out, the North would never consent to exempting slaves from import duties while other commodities were taxed. The South demanded protection against runaway slaves, which it did not have under the Articles of Confederation. So a compromise was worked out. Slaves might be taxed, it was agreed, along with all other imported goods, by a majority vote of Congress, but by no more than $10 a head. In addition, slaveowners were given the right to repossess slaves who fled to neighboring states. Finally, Congress would be given the power to abolish the slave trade, but only after twenty years—sufficient time, it was felt, to enable South Carolina and Georgia to acquire adequate numbers.

With the Deep South and New England united on the issue, the compromise was readily approved by the Convention. Only four states—New Jersey, Delaware, Pennsylvania, and Virginia—voted against the plan. Still, one matter remained to be settled: some of the delegates objected to the use of the word "slave" in the Constitution. By clever use of language, the Convention finally succeeded in eliminating those expressions "which might be odious in the ears of Americans."[74]

The question of slavery cropped up in only one other connection during the Constitutional Convention. Here humanitarian considerations were even less an issue. It involved the question of whether a slave was a person or an article of property. No academic point, the answer vitally affected the power relationships between the slave and nonslaveholding states. If considered a person, the slave would be counted in determining the number of representatives a state would have in the lower chamber of the proposed new Congress. But if considered property, he could not be counted. At stake, then, was the power which the two regions would wield in the new national government. Quite naturally, the South supported the first view and the North the second. Through the long hours of debate each region clung stubbornly to its own interpretation of the Negro slave's status. As in the many similar situations during the Convention, the need was for some acceptable compromise. The prospects for achieving one were greatly enhanced when it was pointed out to the South that if slaves were to be considered as persons for purposes of determining representation, then they should also be considered as persons in the levying of taxes. Soon thereafter the two sides reached agreement and accepted a compromise. For purposes both of representation and of taxation, the slave would be considered equal to three-fifths of a free man. This was the "Federal ratio," already embodied in previous legislation under the Articles of Confederation. Aside from its invidious evaluation of the Negro, however, the importance of this compromise was in its definition of the power relationship between the North and the South. It touched the institution of slavery not at all.

Their work accomplished, the delegates returned home, most of them convinced that under the circumstances they had drawn up the best plan of government possible. Almost all of them would admit in private that the proposed constitution contained certain defects, even if they could not agree what they were. Some of these defects, such as the absence of a bill of rights, could be corrected by later amendment. Many felt that others, such as the failure to limit the slave trade for at least twenty years, could be overlooked in favor of the greater benefits that would derive from a stronger central government. "Great as the evil is," James Madison argued in the Virginia convention called to consider whether the proposed constitution ought to be adopted, "a dismemberment of the union would be worse."[75] For South Carolina and Georgia had clearly indicated their unwillingness to become a part of the new nation unless this twenty-year clause were included in the constitution.

Truly slavery itself had not been an overwhelming issue in the Constitutional Convention. The delegates tacitly agreed that the question was best left to the individual states to solve for themselves. The existence of large Negro populations presented the southern states with many problems for which there were no easy solutions, while even in the North slavery had not been completely eliminated. The proposed Constitution at least took the first step toward abolishing slavery in that it gave the new Congress the right to forbid the importation of Negro slaves in the future. While it could not exercise this power for twenty years, its predecessor, the Continental Congress, had not been able to do even that much.

Although many delegates were troubled by the new Constitution's failure to deal more forthrightly with the institution of slavery, they thought that perhaps it would soon die of its own accord, as it had already done in most of New England. Oliver Ellsworth of Connecticut had said during the constitutional debates: "Let us not intermeddle. As population increases, poor laborers will be so plenty as to render slaves useless. Slavery in time will not be a speck in our Country."[76] His fellow delegate, Roger Sherman, added that "the abolition of slavery seemed to be going on in the U.S. and that the good sense of the several States would probably by degrees compleate it."[77]

A few of the delegates refused to accept these contentions. When Luther Martin went before the Maryland legislature to outline his arguments against the proposed Constitution, he criticized, among other things, its failure to abolish the slave trade at once. A nation that has appealed to God to grant it freedom, he argued, should not fail to take the first step toward granting the Africans their freedom, too. In Virginia, George Mason opposed ratification of the Constitution on similar grounds. "As much as I value an union of all the States," he said, "I would not admit the Southern States into the union, unless they agreed to the discontinuance of this disgraceful trade, because it would bring weakness and not strength to the union. Such a trade," he added, "is diabolical in itself and disgraceful to mankind."[78] But Ellsworth, answering Mason's objections, expressed the view of most of the delegates to the Philadelphia Convention when he said, "I readily agree, and all good men wish the entire abolition of slavery, as soon as it can take place with safety to the public, and for the lasting good of the present wretched race of slaves. The only possible step that could be taken towards it by the convention [,however,] was to fix a period after which they should not be imported . . ."[79]

These, then, were the compromises on the issue of slavery upon which the United States was founded. Some delegates to the Convention wished to see importation cease at once, others to keep it unrestricted. As a compromise, they agreed to allow it to continue for at least twenty years. Some desired the abolition of slavery; others were determined to use federal power to strengthen the institution. Again a compromise was worked out: the control of slavery was left to the individual states, and the federal government had the right to intervene only by returning runaway slaves to their owners.

The South warned that only with these compromises would union be possible. And since it was far more concerned about other matters, the North readily agreed to them. Moreover, the North had no more real understanding of or feeling for the Negro as a person than did the South. Nor did the North have any effective answer to the question of the future of the freed slave. Jefferson, observing these events from

Paris, was at first critical of the proposed constitution. Soon, however, he was an enthusiastic supporter, believing that the good it contained more than compensated for its defects.

NOTES

1. Van Tyne, Claude H. *The Causes of the War of Independence,* Houghton Mifflin, Boston, 1922, p. 226.

2. *Idem.*

3. *Introduction to Contemporary Civilization in the West;* A Source Book Prepared by the Contemporary Civilization Staff of Columbia College, Columbia University Press, New York, 1954, Vol. I, p. 979.

4. Van Tyne, *op. cit.,* pp. 236–7.

5. *Documents of American History,* Henry Steele Commager, ed., F. S. Crofts, New York, 1947, Vol. I, p. 78.

6. *Ibid.,* Vol. I, p. 83.

7. *Ibid.,* Vol. I, p. 100.

8. *Ibid.,* Vol. I, p. 103.

9. *Records of the Colony of Rhode Island and Providence Plantations in New England,* John R. Bartlett, ed., A. Crawford Greene, Providence, 1862, Vol. VI, p. 381.

10. Mazyck, Walter H., *George Washington and the Negro,* Associated Publishers, Washington, D.C., 1932, pp. 64–5.

11. Commager, *op. cit.,* Vol. I, p. 37.

12. Drake, Thomas E., *Quakers and Slavery in America,* Yale University Press, New Haven, Conn., 1950, p. 42.

13. *Ibid.,* p. 61.

14. Moore, George H., *Notes on the History of Slavery in Massachusetts,* Appleton, New York, 1866, p. 83.

15. Herrick, Cheesman A., *White Servitude in Pennsylvania,* J. J. McVey, Philadelphia, 1926, p. 88.

16. *Idem.*

17. Olson, Edwin, *Negro Slavery in New York,* William Frederick Press, New York, 1947.

18. John Adams to Jeremy Belknap in 1795 in "Belknap Papers," Massachusetts Historical Society, *Collections,* 5th Series, Vol. III, p. 402.

19. "Documents" in *American Historical Review,* Vol. I, p. 89.

20. Commager, *op. cit.,* Vol. I, p. 37.

21. Du Bois, W. E. Burghart, *The Suppression of the African Slave-Trade to the United States of America,* Longmans, Green, New York, 1904, p. 10.

22. *The Selected Writings of Benjamin Rush,* Dagobert D. Runes, ed., Philosophical Library, New York, 1947, p. 4.

23. *The Writings of Benjamin Franklin,* Albert H. Smyth, ed., Macmillan, New York, 1905, Vol. III, pp. 3–4.

24. *Ibid.,* p. 68.

25. Van Doren, Carl, *Benjamin Franklin,* Viking, New York, 1938, p. 557.

26. The Writings of Benjamin Franklin, *op. cit.,* Vol. III, pp. 66–7.

27. *Ibid.,* Vol. V, pp. 431–2.

28. *Ibid.,* Vol. VI, p. 100; Van Doren, *op. cit.,* p. 479.

29. *The Writings of Benjamin Franklin, op. cit.,* Vol. V, p. 431.

30. Moore, *op. cit.,* pp. 145–6.

31. Crane, Verner W., "Benjamin Franklin on Slavery and American Liberties," *The Penn-

sylvania Magazine of History and Biography, Vol. LXII, No. 1, January 1938, p. 7.

32. Meade, Robert D., *Patrick Henry, Patriot in the Making,* Lippincott, Philadelphia, 1957, p. 299.

33. *Records of the Colony of Rhode Island and Providence Plantations in New England, op. cit.,* Vol. VII, p. 251.

34. Moore, *op. cit.,* p. 150.

35. *The Writings of Thomas Jefferson,* H. A. Washington, ed., Derby and Jackson, New York, 1959, p. 19.

36. Mazyck, *op. cit.,* p. 24.

37. Moore, *op. cit.,* p. 129.

38. Franklin, John Hope, *From Slavery to Freedom, A History of American Negroes,* Knopf, New York, 1961, p. 130.

39. *Ibid.,* p. 131.

40. Mazyck, *op. cit.,* p 37.

41. *Ibid.,* p. 41.

42. *Ibid.,* p. 14.

43. *Ibid.,* p. 13.

44. Franklin, John Hope, *op. cit.,* p. 132.

45. *The Writings of George Washington,* Jared Sparks, ed., American Stationers *et al., 1833–1839,* Vol. III, p. 218.

46. *Journals of the Continental Congress,* U.S. Government Printing Office, Washington, D.C., 1909, Vol. IV, p. 60.

47. Mazyck, *op. cit.,* p. 66.

48. *Ibid.,* p. 70.

49. *Journals of the Continental Congress, op. cit.,* Vol. XIII, p. 385.

50. *The Writings of Washington,* Worthington Chauncey Ford, ed., Putnam's, New York, 1890, Vol. VII, p. 371.

51. Mazyck, *op. cit.,* pp. 76–7.

52. *Idem.*

53. Weyl, Nathanial, *The Negro in American Civilization,* Public Affairs Press, Washington, D.C., 1960, p. 26.

54. Mazyck, *op. cit.,* p. 85.

55. *Ibid.,* p. 86.

56. *The Federal and State Constitutions and Colonial Charters,* Frances Newton Thorpe, ed., U.S. Government Printing Office, Washington, D.C., 1909, Vol. VI, p. 3740.

57. *Laws of the Commonwealth of Pennsylvania,* M. Carey and J. Brown, Philadelphia, 1803, Vol. II, p. 246.

58. Drake, *op. cit.,* pp. 90–1.

59. Dumond, Dwight Lowell, *Antislavery, the Crusade for Freedom in America,* University of Michigan Press, Ann Arbor, 1961, p. 31.

60. Russell, John H., *The Free Negro in Virginia 1619–1865,* Johns Hopkins Press, Baltimore, 1913, p. 58.

61. Malone, Dumas, *Jefferson, The Virginian,* Little, Brown, Boston, 1948, Vol. I, p. 264.

62. *The Life and Selected Writings of Thomas Jefferson,* Adrienne Koch and William Peden, eds., Modern Library, New York, 1944, p. 279.

63. Malone, *op. cit.,* p. 265.

64. *The Life and Selected Writings of Thomas Jefferson, op. cit.,* p. 256.

65. *A Jefferson Profile, As Revealed in His Letters,* Saul K. Padover, ed., John Day, New York, 1956, pp. 61–2.

66. Malone, *op. cit.,* pp. 267–8.

67. *The Records of the Federal Convention of 1787,* Max Farrand, ed., Yale University Press, New Haven, Conn., 1937, Vol. II, p. 221.

68. *Ibid.,* Vol. II, p. 369.

69. *Ibid.,* Vol. II, p. 364.

70. *Ibid.,* Vol. II, p. 370.

71. *Ibid.,* Vol. II, p. 371.

72. *Ibid.,* Vol. II, p. 364.

73. *Idem.*

74. *Ibid.,* Vol. III, p. 210.

75. *Ibid.*, Vol. III, p. 325.
76. *Ibid.*, Vol. II, p. 369.
77. *Ibid.*, Vol. II, pp. 369–70.
78. Hill, Helen, *George Mason, Constitutionalist*, Harvard University Press, Cambridge, 1938, p. 230.

79. *The Records of the Federal Convention of 1787, op. cit.,* Vol. III, p. 165.

4 The Great Silence

On February 12, 1790, at the first Congress, a petition was read bearing the signature of the semiretired but still venerated Benjamin Franklin. It came from him as president of the Pennsylvania Society for Promoting the Abolition of Slavery, and it called on the assembled representatives to give their "serious attention to the subject of slavery; . . . that you will devise means for removing this inconsistency from the character of the American people; that you will promote mercy and justice towards this distressed race; and that you will step to the very verge of the power vested in you for discouraging every species of traffic in the persons of our fellow men."[1]

The petition, along with two others presented the day before, brought the work of the House to an abrupt halt as southern members protested strenuously against referring the memorials to committee. Such a move, a South Carolina representative warned, "would sound an alarm and blow the trumpet of sedition in the Southern states." A colleague from the same state called the Franklin petition "mischievous," arguing that it "contained an unconstitutional request." He was surprised, he said, to see such a request "signed by a man who ought to have known the Constitution better."[2]

The leaders of the new government were equally distressed by this unexpected turn of events. John Adams, presiding over the Senate, was annoyed; he thought Franklin's petition "silly." James Madison, a leader of the Administration forces in the House, was disgusted. The southern representatives, he felt, had committed a tactical error in opposing referral of the petitions to committee. "The true policy of the Southern members," he wrote Edmund Randolph, "was to have let the affair proceed with as little noise as possible, and to have made use of the occasion to obtain along with the assertion of the powers of Congress a recognition of the restraints imposed by the Constitution."[3] Both Adams and Madison were deeply disturbed by the possible consequences of the sudden eruption of the issue of slavery. It came in the midst of a campaign to have the federal government assume the debts contracted by the states during the Revolutionary War, and consequently threatened the enactment of that measure, which was considered important to the success of the new government. But the Franklin memorial had an even more ominous aspect: it seemed to call into question the basis on which the North and South had agreed to join together in union.

The *quid pro quo*, although only set forth in scattered clauses of the Constitution, was nevertheless well understood by the leaders of the Federalist era. Charles C. Pinckney had already spelled it out for his fellow southerners during the convention called by South Carolina to ratify the proposed constitution. Questioned sharply as to why he and the other southern delegates had agreed to give Congress the power to limit the importation of slaves after 1808, Pinckney replied that this had been necessary to elicit other promises from the New Englanders. "Show some period," the New England delegates had said, "when it may be in our power to put a stop, if we please, to the importation of this weakness, and we will endeavor, for your convenience, to restrain the religious and political prejudices of our people on this subject." The result was the compromise that was then worked out. "By this settlement," Pinckney declared, "we have secured an unlimited importation of negroes for twenty years. Nor is it declared that the importation shall be then stopped. It may be continued." On the other hand, he said, "we have a security that the General Government can never emancipate [our slaves], for no such authority is granted and it is admitted on all hands, that the General Government has no powers but what are expressly granted by the Constitution; and that all rights not expressed [are] reserved by the several states."[4]

Pinckney then enumerated the positive points gained by the South. First, three-fifths of its slave population were to be counted for purposes of representation in the proposed national legislature's lower chamber. "I confess," Pinckney said, "I did not expect that we had conceded too much to the Eastern States, when they allowed us a representation for a species of property which they have not among them." Equally important, Pinckney pointed out, "We have obtained a right to recover our slaves in whatever part of America they may take refuge, which is a right we had not before. In short," he concluded, "considering all circumstances, we have made the best terms, for the security of this species of property, it was in our power to make."[5]

The North's leaders were less candid in acknowledging their agreement with the South. It remained for John Quincy Adams, many years later in a speech to his Massachusetts constituents, to spell out its exact terms to the people of the North. The South, he said, had not been content merely with the general benefits that would ensue from establishing a national government, such as increased protection against foreign enemies, restoration of the nation's credit, and the revival of commerce. Its representatives, he said, had "prescribed, as a condition of their assent to the Constitution, three special provisions to secure the perpetuity of their dominion over their slaves. The first was the immunity for twenty years of preserving the African slave trade; the second was the stipulation to surrender fugitive slaves . . . ; and thirdly, the exaction fatal to the principles of popular representation for slaves—for articles of merchandise, under the name of persons." The northern delegates, Adams said, were reluctant to grant these demands, but, "reduced to the alternative of departing from the vital principle of their liberty, or of forfeiting the Union itself, [they] averted their faces, and with trembling hand subscribed the bond."[6] Although

Adams may have exaggerated the nothern delegates' uneasiness, he accurately described the tacit bargain they made.

It was this bargain at which Franklin's memorial struck. Although many of the Georgia and South Carolina delegates continued to spurn Madison's counsel either to ignore the petition or to use it as the occasion of reaffirming the constitutional *quid pro quo* over slavery, the majority of the House decided on the second alternative. By a vote of forty-three to eleven, the memorial was submitted to a specially appointed committee which, since the Georgians and South Carolinians refused to serve on it, was dominated by northern representatives. This committee reported to the House that under the Constitution Congress did not have the power to prohibit the importation of Negro slaves into America before 1808. Nor did it have the power to emancipate those slaves already in this country or otherwise to interfere with the way in which the several states regulated their condition. Though the Deep South's representatives forced the House, meeting as a Committee of the Whole, to make certain changes, the House substantially adopted the views of the special committee as its own. Then, to discourage the issue from being raised again, it ordered both reports printed as part of the official record. The House of Representatives, had, in effect, reaffirmed the *quid pro quo* on which the union was based. Thus, on the issue of slavery, began "The Great Silence" that was to last half a century, a silence punctuated only by the momentary flare-up over Missouri.

In the years that followed, it was within the context of that North-South understanding that any dialogue over the issue of slavery took place. For the most part Congress studiously avoided the subject, refusing recognition to the memorials from the various abolition societies that now began to pour into its halls in ever-growing numbers. In fact, to discourage such memorials, it even considered censuring a Quaker petitioner.

In 1793 Congress enacted a fugitive slave law, giving substance to the promise made to the South that it would be allowed to recover those of its slaves who fled to other states.

Ironically, this legislation stemmed from an attempt made by the Pennsylvania governor two years earlier to extradite for trial two men from Virginia who had kidnapped a free Negro. When the Virginia governor refused to hand them over, citing the lack of any state or federal statute empowering him to do so, the Pennsylvania governor appealed to George Washington for his aid in resolving the interstate jurisdictional conflict. The President tried to persuade the two governors to settle the matter quietly between themselves, but when these efforts failed, he reluctantly submitted the dispute to Congress, with a request that it put into law the pertinent provisions of the Constitution. Still, it was almost a year and a half before Congress passed the requested legislation. Twice, committees were appointed—once in the House and once in the Senate—but each time the bills they reported failed to win approval. Finally, a second Senate committee was named, and the measure that it reported was passed by both houses of Congress and signed by Washington.

Unfortunately, Congress chose not to publish its debates on these measures, and we therefore know very little about them. Since the bill which was enacted simply gave substance to the provisions already contained in the Constitution, however, study of the debate that took place over these clauses at the Philadelphia Convention is revealing.

At that time, the delegates from South Carolina had suggested that runaway slaves be treated no differently from fugitive criminals. To this James Wilson of Pennsylvania had objected that, as the clause relative to fugitive criminals then stood, "this would oblige the executive of the state to [deliver up runaway slaves] at the public expense." Roger Sherman of Connecticut added that he could see "no more propriety in the public seizing and surrendering a slave or servant than a horse."[7] In face of these objections, Pinckney and Pierce agreed to drop their proposal and to insert instead an additional clause simply requiring the return of runaway slaves and servants without specifying who was to perform the task. The legislation that Congress enacted in 1793 preserved that distinction. The sheltering state was legally bound to apprehend and return the fugitive criminal but not the runaway slave. The slave could be recaptured by his master or his master's agent and then taken to the nearest judge and certified as having fled from legal bondage.

In addition to converting the merely declaratory constitutional provisions into positive law, the 1793 statute provided a $500 fine and a year in prison for anyone who interfered with the return of a fugitive criminal or runaway slave. After it had honored this part of the North-South understanding, Congress passed no further laws on the subject until 1850.

With regard to the slave trade the unwritten agreement was also duly observed. Even in the Constitutional Convention the majority of delegates had wished to see an end to the further importation of Negroes. Virginia and Maryland, with a surplus of slaves, had special reasons for wishing it ended, but even the delegates from other states—in fact, all except those from South Carolina and Georgia—saw danger in adding still larger numbers of that alien and seemingly unassimilable race to the American stock. In addition, they were of course concerned with the contradiction that a nation professing the ideals of freedom should countenance the involuntary bondage of its own inhabitants. Slavery itself could not be challenged if the hopes of establishing a stronger central government were to be realized. But the slave trade was different; because of its notorious barbarity, it had always been strongly condemned. The Convention delegates were able to separate the issue of the slave trade from the issue of slavery itself. Only the strong opposition of South Carolina and Georgia, which insisted that they still lacked sufficient slaves for their needs, prevented the Convention from giving Congress the power to prohibit the slave trade outright.

Yet in the decade that followed Franklin's petition, the issue of the foreign slave trade remained dormant. This was partly because the Constitution barred the abolition of the trade until the year 1808, but, even more important, by 1793, all thirteen of the seaboard states, including both South Carolina and Georgia, had enacted legislation to forbid the importation of Negro slaves. While these laws were seldom enforced, they seemed to soothe the nation's conscience. In fact, the situation was ideal: South Carolina and Georgia, as a result of the illegal importations, had all the slaves they needed, and the other states had all the laws they desired.

This equilibrium was upset in December, 1803, when South Carolina's legislature voted to end its abolition of the slave trade. The approach of the year 1808, when Congress would almost certainly prohibit further importations plus the recent purchase of Louisiana, which would present a far greater demand for slaves than the current illegal operations could hope to supply, had led the South Carolina legislature to end all pretense. "Such a combination of advantages," W. E. B. Du Bois has written, "which meant fortunes to planters and Charleston slave-merchants, could no longer be withheld from them; the prohibition was repealed, and the United States became again, for the first time in [many] years, a legal slave mart." With the Haitian uprising only a recent specter, Du Bois adds, "this action shocked the nation, frightening Southern States with visions of an influx of untrained barbarians and servile insurrections, and arousing and intensifying the anti-slavery feeling of the North, which had long since come to think of the trade, so far as legal enactment went, as a thing of the past."[8] Yet, because of the constitutional provision, there was little that Congress could do directly for another five years. A $10 tax, as authorized by the Constitution, was considered; but as in the past, it was rejected on grounds of expediency. Such a tax, it was thought, could not possibly discourage the trade, but if the federal government became dependent on it for revenue, it might hamper its later abolition. However, there was no doubt what action Congress would take once those five years had passed.

As early as 1806 Thomas Jefferson, who was then president of the United States, urged Congress to begin carrying out this last remaining item of the North-South understanding. In a message to Congress he said, "I congratulate you, fellow-citizens, on the approach of the period at which you may interpose your authority, Constitutionally, to withdraw the citizens of the United States from all further participation in those violations of human rights which have been so long continued on the unoffending inhabitants of Africa, and which the morality, the reputation, and the best interests of our country, have long been eager to proscribe. Although no law you may pass can take prohibitory effect till the day of the year one thousand eight hundred and eight, yet the intervening period is not too long to prevent, by timely notice, expeditions which cannot be completed before that day."[9] Within exactly three months this message was translated into a law that prohibited for all time the importation of slaves into the United States.

The bill elicited virtually no opposition. Those most immediately affected, southern slave traders and New England sea captains, knew that its provisions, like those of the state laws already on the books, could be easily evaded. The north was primarily concerned about what should be done with those illegally imported slaves who fell into the hands of the federal government. The bill, as originally drafted, would have had the government sell them at public auction. To this, several northern congressmen objected, pointing out that this would put the federal government in the business of selling human beings. "By the same law," they said, "we condemn the man-stealer and become the receivers of his stolen goods. We punish the criminal, and then step into his place, and complete the crime."[10] These congressmen proposed instead that any slaves illegally imported be set free.

Such an amendment, the southern Representatives declared, would make the law unenforceable, since no person in the South would give information about an illegal importation if they knew that the Negroes involved would be given their freedom as a result. "It is a principle in legislation, as correct as any which has ever prevailed," Peter Early of Georgia pointed out, "that to give effect to laws, you must not make them repugnant to the passions and wishes of the people among whom they are to operate. How, then, in this instance stands the fact? Do not gentlemen from every quarter of the Union prove, on the discussion of every question that has ever arisen in the House, having the most remote

bearing on the giving freedom to the Africans in the bosom
of our country, that it has excited the deepest sensibility in
the breasts of those where slavery exists?" Nathan Macon of
North Carolina, Speaker of the House, also questioned the
wisdom of giving the Negro slaves their freedom. "What is
to become of the cargoes of those persons," he asked, "when
thus turned loose in any State? By what means are they, understanding nothing about the country, to be supported?"[11]

These arguments elicited sympathy from many of the
northern representatives. Josiah Quincy of Massachusetts
asked what was to prevent the Legislature of Georgia, after
Congress "declared these people shall be free, [from] considering them as vagabonds, and selling them as vagabonds, and
selling them for a term of years, or for life, to the highest
bidder."[12] And Orchard Cook, also from Massachusetts, declared that to set them free would be to "let loose a set of
banditti, in hostility to the whole country."[13] For this reason,
many of the northern representatives joined with their southern brethren in opposing the amendment to free the illegally
imported slaves. Nevertheless, they were not willing to see
the federal government become involved in the sale of human
beings. Under the compromise finally accepted, the states
themselves were to dispose of any confiscated slave cargoes as
they should see fit.

Actually, there were many points on which the North and
South could find common ground in their attitude toward the
Negro. Few persons in the North, for example, would have
disputed the prevailing view in the South that the Negro was
inherently inferior. "There is no doubt," said Massachusetts'
James Sullivan, "of a great disparity in the natural abilities of
mankind, and we have great reason to believe that the organization of the Africans is such as prevents their receiving the
more fine and sublime impressions equally with the white
people."[14] Sullivan, who as a judge of the state Supreme Judicial Court, had participated in the decision declaring slavery
illegal in Massachusetts, was more generous toward the Negro
than most men in the North. With equal education and other

opportunities, he felt, the Negro might become the equal of the white within three generations.

Most northerners would have agreed that emancipation had not improved the Negroes' lot. "If a comparison be made between the former and present condition of this class of people in the New-England states," Jeremy Belknap wrote, "it may be said that unless *liberty* be reckoned as a compensation for many inconveniences and hardships, the former condition of most of them was preferable to the present."[15] "Their condition," said Dr. E. A. Holyoke, first president of the Massachusetts Medical Society, "is, in general, pretty miserable . . . many are not industrious, and frugality [they] seem to be utterly unacquainted with . . ."[16] Foreign visitors generally agreed with this assessment of the free Negro's condition, though they saw other factors at work. "Nearly all colored people are poor and unhappy, and obliged to work as servants," Moreau de St. Méry, an exiled Frenchman, wrote in his diary. "Workmen do not want to accept them, or to let them be apprentices."[17] The same prejudice barred them from other occupations. "The Whites," said his fellow countryman, J. P. Brissot de Warville, "though they treat them with humanity, like not to give them credit to enable them to undertake any extensive commerce, nor even to give them the means of a common education, by receiving them into their counting-houses."[18]

The North had given the Negro his personal freedom, but it balked at giving him his political and civil freedom. In an age of limited franchise, the Negro's generally depressed economic condition effectively barred him from any participation in the North's political life. Meanwhile, popular prejudice closed the door to any social intercourse with his white neighbors. The schools, the churches, the cemeteries— in fact, nearly every social institution—either segregated the Negro or denied him admission. The lower classes of white people, often finding themselves reduced to the same economic circumstances as the Negro, went to great pains to assert their social superiority. "A white servant," Moreau wrote from Philadelphia, "no matter who, would consider it

a dishonor to eat with colored people."[19] This was true even
among the white convicts condemned to Philadelphia's Wal-
nut Street prison. "The lowest of the people sometimes asso-
ciate with [the Negroes]," Dr. Holyoke reported from Salem,
"but I believe they generally consider it as an act of con-
descension."[20]

In the North the upper and lower classes shared a common dislike for the free Negro. To the wealthier members of
society it seemed that he served only to swell the relief rolls
and increase the crime rate. To the laboring man it seemed
that he served mainly to force down wages. If they could have
found a way, both classes would gladly have got rid of their
Negro neighbors, free men though they were. Massachusetts
had already gone as far as it legally could when in 1800 it
ordered the expulsion of 240 Negroes who were not citizens
of the state. Ohio, meanwhile, attempted to prevent the immigration of others. In 1807 it forbade any Negro from entering the state without first posting bond guaranteeing good
behavior. This was as near as Ohio could come to outright
prohibition.

The South was equally hostile toward the free Negro, but
for another reason. As we have seen, southerners feared that
the free Negro might one day provide the spark for a slave
revolt. Since the successful Haitian uprising and the unsuccessful Gabriel conspiracy involving several thousand Negroes in
Virginia in 1800, these fears had grown even stronger. As a result, the black codes were made even more stringent; free Negroes were forbidden to assemble, carry firearms, or even worship together. Any free Negro convicted of inciting his enslaved
brethren to rise up against their masters was to be put to
death. With the specter of a general slave insurrection continually haunting it, the South readily joined with the North
to welcome the plan of a New Jersey minister for dealing
with the nation's free Negro population.

Robert Finley, a Princeton graduate, had been pastor of
the Baskingridge, New Jersey, Presbyterian church for twenty
years. At the end of that time, he had built the small congregation into one of the largest and most powerful churches in

the New Brunswick presbytery. "The Great Awakening"—
that tidal wave of mass religious feeling which had recently
swept over the former colonies—had left in its wake a host of
newly organized benevolent and ameliorative organizations,
such as the American Sunday School Union, the American
Tract Society, the American Temperance Union, the American Education Society, the American Home Missionary Society, and the American Seamen's Friend Society. The Reverend Mr. Finley wished to become a part of this growing
movement and to demonstrate, as one intellectual leader of
this religious phenomenon had put it, a selfless or "disinterested" love for his fellow human beings.

For some time Finley had been aware of the condition of
the free Negroes living near Baskingridge. "Their number
increases greatly," he noted, "and their wretchedness, too. . . .
Every thing connected with their condition, including their
colour is against them."[21] He said that he thought that there
was not much prospect that their state could be greatly
ameliorated while they continued in this country. Only in
Africa could they and the other free Negroes living in the
United States escape the prejudice and feeling of inferiority
which prevented them from realizing their true capabilities.
Their removal to Africa, Finley believed, would also promote
the general good. It would make possible an end to slavery
and eliminate its "injurious effect on the morals and habits of
[the] country where it exists." In the process, society would
"be saved many a pang which now is felt, and must in course
of time be much more sensibly felt from the intermixture of
the different colors, and at the same time be relieved from a
heavy burden, in supporting that large portion of this people
which falls into poverty and must be maintained by others."[22]
Moreover, the removal of the free Negroes would carry
Christianity and civilization to Africa. With these aims in
mind, Finley resolved to organize a benevolent society whose
aim it would be to colonize free Negroes in Africa.

Finley had an influential friend in Washington; his
brother-in-law, Elias Boudinot Caldwell, was Clerk of the
Supreme Court. Finley succeeded in winning his support for

the scheme, and Caldwell in turn persuaded his friend, Francis Scott Key, a prominent Washington attorney—and, incidentally, the author of "The Star Spangled Banner"—to join with them. Caldwell and Key approached other influential men in Washington and urged them to attend a meeting for the purpose of organizing a colonization society. Henry Clay, speaker of the House, was at first unimpressed with the idea but, at Key's urging, agreed to chair the meeting. Bushrod Washington, a Supreme Court Justice and the heir of the first President, and William Crawford, Secretary of the Treasury, were more easily won over. Many other leading citizens of Washington, including congressmen and clergymen, agreed to attend. Meanwhile, Finley published his *Thoughts on Colonization* in the widely read *National Intelligencer*. Thus a distinguished group of about twenty prominent persons was on hand when the American Colonization Society was formally organized in December, 1816.

The new organization seemed to meet a deeply felt need as men from all sections of the country joined its ranks. Its members included, at one time or another, James Madison, Andrew Jackson, Daniel Webster, Stephen Douglas, William Seward, John Marshall, Roger Taney, Matthew Carey, and General Winfield Scott. Even William Lloyd Garrison at first endorsed its aims. "Men of all parties," wrote abolitionist William Jay, "and of all religions, and of no religion have zealously espoused its cause. . . . The Legislatures of fourteen States have passed resolutions in its favor . . . Politicians have declaimed, ministers have preached, and Christians have prayed in its behalf."[23] Of course, there were those opposed to colonization. Some in the North feared it was a diabolical scheme to divert attention from the evils of slavery itself. Some in the South feared it was the first step toward compulsory emancipation. But most Americans, as even the critical American Convention of Abolition Societies admitted, welcomed colonization as the only solution to the racial problem.

Finley had deliberately chosen Washington as the base of his operations, for if his scheme of transporting the free Negroes to Africa were ever to be successful, the assistance of the federal government was crucial. Only the national treasury could provide the resources and protection that such a move would require. At first the Colonization Society's request for federal assistance was rebuffed, but in 1819 Congress turned over to the President the responsibility for disposing of Negro slaves illegally brought into this country. Appropriating $100,000 for this purpose, Congress authorized President James Monroe to "make such regulations and arrangements, as he may deem expedient, for the safeguarding, support and removal"[24] of the Africans. Though the measure failed to mention colonization, the Society's friends in Congress hoped it would be the first step toward making substantial federal aid available for their project.

In the Administration itself, however, there was opposition. Monroe, cautious in temperament, asked his cabinet whether under the Constitution he could use the recently enacted law to launch a colony in Africa. John Quincy Adams, his Secretary of State, demurred. Such a step, he argued, would unconstitutionally augment federal powers. After a prolonged debate within the Administration, the President agreed to send two agents designated by the Colonization Society to Africa to set up a colony. But from that time on, Monroe and his successors were grudging in their support, financial and otherwise, of the project.

The Colonization Society soon encountered more fundamental problems than the reluctant backing of the federal government. There was, first of all, the difficulty involved in actually planting a colony on Africa's west coast. The soil and climate proved inhospitable, and most of the early colonists sent out were killed by fever. Though a tiny settlement known as Liberia managed to sustain itself, the expense involved in maintaining it soon drove the Colonization Society to the verge of bankruptcy. It seemed that the contributions to remove the free Negroes from America were far more generous than those to support the Negroes once they had arrived in Africa.

But an even greater weakness was the lack of enthusiasm, even outright hostility, for the scheme among the free Negroes in the United States. Only a month after it was founded, the American Colonization Society was denounced by the free Negroes of Philadelphia for failing to condemn slavery and for even helping to perpetuate it by seeking to remove from the country its most persistent critics. These attacks were echoed by other Negro organizations. The notion of returning to Africa was deprecated. "This is our home," the free Negroes declared, "and this is our country. Beneath its sod lie the bones of our fathers; for it some of them fought, bled, and died. Here we were born, and here we will die." The Negroes wanted, not a return to "the burning sun, the arid plains, and barbarous customs of Africa,"[25] but the abolition of slavery in America and political recognition for the Negro. The Colonization Society's consistently unflattering remarks about the free blacks' inherent nature and present condition certainly did not help to earn it the Negroes' good will. As a director of the Society sadly concluded, "the free people of color, taken as a community, look on our undertaking with disaffection."[26]

With the free Negroes almost unanimous in their opposition, their white friends in the North began to examine the Colonization Society more critically. And they discovered that it was dominated by men from the Upper South. It had, in fact, been dominated by them from its very inception. Clay and the others from that region had made it a condition of their support that the Society avoid the "delicate question" of emancipation. Colonization was intended for free Negroes, not slaves. Consequently, the Colonization Society necessarily appeared, as the friends of the Negro in the North were wont to complain, as having "originated in the bosom of the Slave States," as a scheme of the slaveholders to get rid of the free blacks and their surplus slaves.[27]

Though these criticisms were partly valid, they came with increasing frequency and growing venom in the years that followed. In 1821 the American Convention of Abolition Societies declared that colonization was "incompatible with the principles of our government, and with the temporal and spiritual interests of the blacks."[28] In 1831 it condemned colonization *per se.* Soon Garrison denounced the advocates of colonization. "They can love and benefit [the Negro] four thousand miles off," he wrote, "but not at home. They profess to be, and really believe that they are, actuated by the most philanthropic motives, and yet are cherishing the most unmanly and unchristian prejudices."[29]

Actually, the colonization movement was the last attempt to carry out the *quid pro quo* reached at the Constitutional Convention over the issue of Negro slavery. While agreeing not to interfere in any way with the institution as it then existed, many of the delegates to that gathering had looked forward to the day when slavery would die of its own accord. This was particularly true of the delegates from the Upper South. The major obstacle to the realization of these hopes in the years that followed was the question of what to do with the Negroes who had been slaves. To let them loose on the countryside, where they might either incite insurrection or prey upon the white inhabitants, was such a foreboding vision that many southerners were dissuaded from manumitting their slaves, even when they found them to be economically unprofitable. Colonization seemed to offer a solution to this problem, and it was not surprising that many southerners grasped at it. If colonization were successful, manumission might be facilitated, slavery might cease to be an issue, and the wisdom of the founding fathers would be vindicated. It was for this reason that many men from the North gave their support to the scheme.

But the plan for colonization was too late. Though the federal government was grudging in its support, the settlement of Africa's west coast did prove difficult, and the free Negroes were opposed to the scheme, all these obstacles might have been overcome in time. But changing political and economic conditions were undermining the basis on which the North and South had reached an understanding on slavery. It was this, more than any other factor, which doomed the colonization movement. The American Colonization Society itself was to continue its almost desperate struggle to resettle Africa's west coast with free Negroes from the United

States for another forty years. But its efforts, no matter how valiant, were overshadowed by the repercussions of the vast political and economic changes that had become increasingly apparent since 1820.

The most important of these changes stemmed from the invention of the cotton gin by a New England school teacher, Eli Whitney. Cotton had been grown in the southern colonies almost from their very beginning. It had become quite popular as a fiber for domestic use, the back country of South Carolina and Georgia producing two to three million pounds of the short staple variety as early as 1793. But commercial exploitation of the crop was thwarted by the difficulty of separating the seeds from the fiber. The fact that cotton could be grown much faster in the warm southern climate than it could be cleaned by hand severely limited the amount that reached the market. This was unfortunate, since that market was growing rapidly.

Whitney's technological breakthrough came just at the time when there were indications that the plantation system was weakening. Tobacco, the great southern staple, was no longer profitable. In Tidewater, Virginia, the soil was exhausted, while the newer agricultural regions found it more profitable to grow wheat and other cereals for which the market was greater. These crops were better raised by white yeoman farmers than by Negro slave labor, and the years immediately before and after the Revolutionary War had witnessed the steady migration of northern farm families into Virginia's Shenandoah Valley and Piedmont region. Rice and indigo, the other two southern staples, had also become unprofitable. The price of slaves, that sensitive economic barometer of the plantation system, reflected the general decline. In some parts of the South prices were so low that plantation owners would gladly have given away their slaves. Many did just that by taking advantage of the various manumission laws enacted during this period. Consequently, from 1790 to 1820 the number of free Negroes in the South increased more than threefold. The new unprofitability of slavery explained, in part, the South's willingness to countenance the end of the slave trade and even gradual emancipation. The founding fathers had foreseen the possibility of this development.

The cotton gin, however, changed all this. With commercial production of cotton possible and indeed highly profitable as a result of England's industrial revolution, the plantation system took on new life. It expanded into new areas, carrying its distinctive way of life to the South Carolina and Georgia uplands, the Nashville basin of Tennessee, and the lower Mississippi valley. Many a younger son and many a man of humble origins found that with hard work, intelligence, craft and luck, he could have a white-columned mansion surrounded by downy fields of cotton tended by ebony-hued field hands. Even in the older regions cotton revived many a family's fortunes.

With its renewed prosperity, the South once more became increasingly sensitive to criticisms of the "peculiar institution" that underlay the plantation system. It even began to drive from its midst those of its leading citizens who had openly condemned slavery. The Reverend George Bourne, for example, after serving seven years as pastor to a Virginia congregation, was forced to leave the state in 1816 for publishing *The Book and Slavery Irreconcilable*. Others with similar views, many of them natives of the South, found it expedient to pack their belongings and head North. In 1827 there were still 106 antislavery societies, small and weak though they were, throughout the South, but within a decade all had been dissolved.

As the years went by, it became increasingly dangerous for the casual traveler in the South to openly criticize slavery. In 1832 an English traveling salesman was whipped and driven out of Petersburg, Virginia, for saying that Negroes "ought to be emancipated." Three years later an Ohio seminary student found in Nashville with a Bible wrapped in an antislavery newspaper received the same treatment. Abolitionist propaganda particularly created furor. In 1835 the citizens of Charleston, South Carolina, learning that several packages of anti-slavery tracts had just arrived by mail steamer, broke into the post office building, seized the suspect packages and burned them in the street. The state Governor, after violently denouncing the abolitionist literature, demanded that such interference be punishable by death without benefit of clergy.

The South, heretofore defensive about slavery, now began openly to proclaim the positive virtues of the institution. In the 1820's the first of many pamphlets describing slavery's beneficial aspects began to flow from southern presses. "Slavery has ever been the stepping ladder by which countries have passed from barbarism to civilization," one declared. "History, both ancient and modern, fully confirms this position."[30] The widely respected Dr. Thomas Cooper of South Carolina College asserted that the southern slave was no worse off than the poor in other parts of the world.

As the South began to rediscover the benefits that redounded to the economy from slavery, the understanding it had once reached with the North was no longer sufficient for resolving the intersectional conflict. Implicit in that understanding was the assumption that slavery would not expand. The founding fathers had believed that if humanitarian considerations did not suffice, the increase in the white population, which would make Negro labor redundant, would eventually lead to its abolition. But now, with slavery once more remarkably profitable, the South was no longer willing to contemplate its demise.

Nevertheless, the North might have been willing to reach a new accommodation. After all, except for moral qualms, the North had little interest in demanding an end to slavery. The Northern attitude toward the Negro was basically the same as prevailed in the South; moreover, its leading businessmen realized that the rapidly expanding cotton industry was laying the foundation for their own fortunes as well as for those of their Southern friends. But a new development, the nation's westward expansion, was making a permanent accommodation impossible.

The plantation system, like all economic systems, had to expand in order to retain its dynamism. And since it was an agricultural system, it had to expand geographically. Based on the extensive cultivation of large holdings, the plantation system soon led to the engrossment of the best land. "As one man grows wealthy and thereby increases his stock of Negroes," a contemporary observer of the expanding South noted, "he wants more land to employ them on; and being fully able, he bids a large price for his . . . neighbor's plantation, who by selling advantageously can raise enough money to go into the back country. . . ." In addition, the cultivation of cotton exhausted all but the richest soils within a few years. "Our small planters," an Alabama senator wrote, "after taking the cream off their lands, are going further west and south in search of other virgin lands which they . . . will despoil in like manner."[31]

In their own way, the planters from the older regions of the South were as dependent on the frontier as the men who actually settled there. Many an eastern slaveholder was able to hold on to his plantation only because he could sell or otherwise dispose of his surplus slaves in the West. "The cultivators of Eastern Virginia," said a contemporary observer, "derive a portion of their income from a source quite distinct from their tillage. . . . This source of income is the breeding and selling of slaves. . . . No man is so inhuman as to breed and raise slaves, to sell off a certain proportion similarly as a western driver does with his herds of cattle. But sooner or later the general result is the same. Sales may be made voluntarily, or by the sheriff—they may be made by the first owner, or delayed until the succession of his heirs—or the misfortune of being sold may fall on one parcel of slaves, instead of another; but all these are but different ways of arriving at the same . . . inevitable result."[32] Thomas Jefferson Randolph said that Virginia had become "one grand menagerie, where men were reared for the market like oxen for the shambles."[33] In the 1830's the Old Dominion state exported 118,000 slaves to the West, while Kentucky and South Carolina together exported another 91,000.

Just as the West proved to have an irresistible appeal for the displaced southerner, it attracted his northern counterpart, who also needed new lands as old ones were either worn out or pre-empted. But the northern immigrant, if he did not already have a prejudice against slave labor, soon acquired one as he was forced to compete against a slaveowning neighbor in the West. The small yeoman farmers from the North, then, and many from the South, refused to settle in those western areas where slavery flourished. The Northwest Ordinance had reserved for free men the entire territory lying between the Ohio and Mississippi rivers, but it was not long before the line of settlement had passed beyond the Mississippi into the Louisiana Territory, where the legal status of slavery was still unclear. Here the seeds of conflict were sown.

In the North the economic link between the man who went west and the man who stayed behind was not quite as close as in the South. In fact, the leading men of the North, striving to build up that region's mining and manufacturing industries, would have preferred to see the western migration slowed if not halted. The more persons remaining in the East, the lower wages would be in the infant industries. However, these northerners soon realized that they, too, had a stake in the West. As the trans-Appalachian territories filled up, were admitted to the Union as states, and sent representatives to Washington, they came to hold the balance of power in determining national policy. Their votes determined whether tariffs would be raised, internal improvements supported, or a national bank rechartered. In order to insure passage of these measures, which were so important to the development of manufacturing and mining, the North had to have the support of the new western states. Thus, in order to insure sufficient national political power, the North had to wage a battle to make certain that slavery was barred from those areas of the Louisiana Territory where the issue was still undetermined—not only to prevent the forging of a common bond between those areas and the South, but also to make it attractive for northerners to settle there.

The controversy erupted in 1819 over Missouri's admission into the Union. This future state was crucial for several reasons. Louisiana had already been carved from the vast expanse purchased from France in 1803, but it so clearly lay in the South, where slavery had for so long been permitted, that the North made only a feeble attempt to prohibit the institution when that territory applied for statehood. Missouri, however, was considerably farther to the North; it lay astride the meridian that had previously marked the boundary between the slave and free regions of the nation. If slavery were permitted within its borders, a precedent might be set for the states yet to be carved from the Louisiana Territory. At that time the number of states where slavery was prohibited exactly equaled the number of states where it was permitted. If Missouri came into the Union as a slave state, as it appeared it might if the question were left to the determination of its own people, the balance of power in the Senate, where representation was equally apportioned among the states, would be tipped to the South. Then the various measures which the North desired would be jeopardized.

The Missouri question burst upon the national scene with a suddenness that caught the leaders of both sections almost totally unprepared. In February, 1819, the House of Representatives routinely resolved itself into a Committee of the Whole to consider the question of Missouri's admission to the Union. During the debate Representative Tallmadge of New York offered an amendment prohibiting the further introduction of slavery into the Missouri territory and freeing those slaves already there. Similar amendments seeking to bar slavery in states to be admitted had been introduced before. In fact, only the year before Tallmadge had opposed the Illinois constitution for not specifically outlawing slavery. In the past such antislavery amendments had always been defeated. This time, however, after a lengthy and bitter debate, the House adopted the Tallmadge amendment. When the Senate, more in sympathy with the South, refused to approve the Missouri statehood bill with the Tallmadge amendment, the Missouri controversy erupted.

In the debates that took place over the Tallmadge amendment and in those that followed in the next two years over this same question, the growing gap between the attitudes of the North and South was clearly revealed. To many of the

representatives from the North who took part in those debates, slavery was morally abhorrent. This was seldom their
only consideration, but it colored their whole outlook. Representative Arthur Livermore of New Hampshire declared:
"In those states where it is tolerated, laws are enacted, making
it penal to instruct slaves in the art of reading, and they are
not permitted to attend public worship, or to hear the Gospel
preached. Thus the light of science and of religion is utterly
excluded from the mind, that the body may be more easily
bowed down to servitude." Referring to the frequent forced
division of families, he said, "The sympathies of nature in
slaves are disregarded; mothers and children are sold and
separated; the children wring their little hands and expire in
agonies of grief while the bereft mothers commit suicide in
despair. How long," he asked, "will the desire of wealth render us blind to the sin of holding both the bodies and souls
of our fellow men in chains!"[34]

Tallmadge admitted that perhaps slavery could not be
prohibited in those areas where it already existed without endangering the white population. "But," he said, "all these
reasons cease when we cross the banks of the Mississippi." His
colleague from New York, John Taylor, continued this argument. "If the few citizens who now inhabit the Territory of
Missouri were alone interested in . . . this question," he said,
"it would be one thing. But the fact is far otherwise. . . . Cast
your eyes on that majestic river which gives name to the
Territory . . . ; trace its meanderings through fertile regions
for more than two thousand miles; cross the stony mountains,
and descend the navigable waters which empty into the Western ocean; contemplate the States hereafter to unfurl their
banners over this fair portion of America, the successive generations of freemen who there shall adorn the arts, enlarge
the circle of science, and improve the condition of our species.
Having taken this survey, you will be able, in some measure,
to appreciate the importance of the subject before us. Our
votes this day will determine whether the high destinies of this
region, and of these generations, shall be fulfilled, or whether
we shall defeat them by permitting slavery, with all its baleful

consequences, to inherit the land."[35] The people of the North, he hinted, would not settle where slavery was permitted. Rufus King, New York's veteran Senator added during the debate in that chamber, "The existence of slavery impairs the industry and the power of a nation; and it does so in proportion to the multiplication of its slaves: where the manual labor of a country is performed by slaves, labor dishonors the hands of freemen."[36]

For the South, Representative Philip Barbour denied that permitting slavery in Missouri would discourage northern migration. "The Northern hive," he said, "is continually pouring forth its swarms of emigrants, and many of them, especially of the mercantile class, alight and settle amongst us; they soon become familiar with our habits and modes of life, prosper in an eminent degree, far beyond our own people, and, indeed, . . . [are] entirely satisfied and happy." Nor would the Northern yeoman farmer, forced to migrate West, be degraded by having to labor. "We, too, have some of our citizens who are unable to purchase slaves, and who, therefore, till the ground with their own hands. But, sir, notwithstanding this, they have all that erectness of character which belongs to them as freemen . . . and he who should dare to treat them with disrespect, because fortune has not poured as much wealth into their laps as into his, would draw down upon him the execration of all good men." However, he went on, failure to permit slavery in Missouri would close that entire territory to the southern migrant, for he was inseparably attached to his slaves by prejudice, education, and habit. If a master were to emigrate, Barbour stated, he would carry his slaves with him, not only for these reasons, but also because he would be going into a wilderness and would need their labor to clear the land. "Under these circumstances," he said, "a prohibition of the importation of slaves would, in almost every instance, be tantamount to a prohibition of the emigration of the Southern people to the State of Missouri." Would it be fair, Barbour asked, to "open an illimitable tract of the most fertile land to the Northern part of the United

States, and, in effect, entirely shut out the whole Southern
people?"[37]

At stake here was the question of which of two diamet-
rically opposed conceptions of the good society—one based on
free labor and the other based on slave labor—would prevail
in the new western territories. But there was a more immediate concern. Tallmadge asked, "Are the numerous slaves in
extensive countries, which we may acquire by purchase, and
admit as States into the Union, at once to be represented on
this floor, under a clause of the Constitution, granted as a
compromise and a benefit to the Southern States which had
borne part in the Revolution?" And he noted, "Such an expansion of that clause in the Constitution would be unjust in its
operations, unequal in its results, and a violation of its original intention."[38]

King, in a later speech in the Senate, was more explicit on
this point. One of the few delegates to the 1787 Constitutional Convention still active in politics, he had remained an
ardent Federalist though the country, and particularly his
own state of New York, had turned overwhelmingly anti-
Federalist. Yet so adequately did he reflect the feelings of the
North on slavery that the Democratic-controlled New York
legislature hesitated to deprive him of his senatorial seat in
1819. "To secure to the owners of property in slaves," King
said, "greater political power than is allowed to the owners
of other and equivalent property seems to be contrary to our
theory of the equality of personal rights. . . ." Of the 181 men
then sitting in the House, he pointed out, twenty owed their
election to the fact that slaves were counted for purposes of
representation. "Thus, while 35,000 free persons are requisite
to elect one representative in a state where slavery is prohibited, 25,559 free persons in Virginia may, and do, elect a
representative—so that five free persons in Virginia have as
much power in the choice of representatives to Congress, and
in the appointment of presidential electors, as seven free persons in any of the states where slavery does not exist." While
the three-fifths provision of the Constitution gave the slaveholding states a disproportionate share of power, "it is an

ancient settlement, and faith and honor stand pledged not to disturb it. But the extension of this disproportionate power to the new states," King declared, "would be unjust and odious. The states whose power would be abridged, and whose burdens would be increased by the measure, cannot be expected to consent to it; and we may hope that the other states are too magnanimous to insist on it."[39]

King's hopes, however, were unfounded. The South did insist that slavery be extended to Missouri. It, too, understood the importance of the West in determining control of the national government. The North, by virtue of its more rapidly growing population, already dominated the House of Representatives. If Missouri were admitted to the union as a free state, and, more importantly, if the remaining parts of the Louisiana Territory were also admitted as free states, control of the Senate as well as the House would pass to the North.

With this in mind, the southern representatives openly threatened that if slavery were prohibited in Missouri, dissolution of the union or civil war would shortly follow. To these threats, Representative Tallmadge had a ready reply: "If a dissolution of the Union must take place, let it be so! If civil war, which gentlemen so much threaten, must come, I can only say, let it come!"[40] But men of more moderate views were genuinely alarmed. And as the debate resumed with the reconvening of a new Congress in the winter of 1819–1820, their alarm grew. For the recent elections, instead of weakening the more extreme forces in both sections, had reinforced their position. In the North, particularly, many of the congressmen who had voted against the Tallmadge amendment were replaced by men firmly opposed to permitting slavery in Missouri. The moderates were aware that the increasingly bitter debate was threatening to rend the union asunder. Led by Henry Clay, they groped for some compromise.

Eventually a compromise was hammered out. Missouri was permitted to enter the union free of any restriction on slavery. But in the territory both to the north and to the west, the instituiton was to be forever barred. Meanwhile, Maine was to be detached from Massachusetts and allowed to enter the union as a separate state, thus once again balancing the number of free and slaveholding states. The compromise was not warmly greeted by either the North, which controlled the House, or the South, which still controlled the Senate. Only with patience and parliamentary skill was it pushed through both houses of Congress. Even so, when the time came for Congress to approve the Missouri state constitution, a group of northern congressmen succeeded in reopening the issue. Ultimately, however, the compromise worked out by Clay and the other moderates was accepted by both sections of the country.

In this way, the Missouri question was finally laid to rest. But "The Great Silence" had at last been broken. The aging Jefferson and many of his fellow Democrats were convinced that the Missouri controversy had been precipitated by the Federalists in the hope of regaining their political power. In any case, the Federalists had touched upon a sensitive northern nerve, one that within a generation would enable their political heirs to drive the Democrats from office. In the contest for national political power the Federalists and those Democrats who supported them had succeeded in interweaving the moral issue of human slavery with ballots.

Jefferson did not believe that the issue would be relegated to permanent silence again. "This momentous question," he wrote from Monticello, "like a fire bell in the night, awakened and filled me with terror. I considered it at once as the knell of the Union. It is hushed, indeed, for the moment. But this is a reprieve only, not a final sentence."[41] Earlier he had written to John Adams, "I thank God that I shall not live to witness its issue."[42] Nevertheless, Jefferson himself was preparing against that eventual day. Believing that the large number of southern youths who were being educated in the North were being inculcated with "lessons in Anti-Missourianism," he redoubled his efforts to establish a University of Virginia where his conception of the proper doctrine of states rights would be taught. "All the States but our own," he wrote, "are sensible that knowledge is power. The Missouri question is for power. The efforts [of] . . . the States to advance their science, is for power; while we are sinking into the barbarism of our Indian aborigines, and expect, like them, to oppose by ignorance the overwhelming mass of light and science by which we shall be surrounded."[43] Jefferson, the great apostle of the French Enlightenment in America, had become caught up in narrow southern sectionalism.

John Adams' son, John Quincy, was also expecting the death of the union. "If slavery be the destined sword in the hand of the destroying angel which is to sever the ties of this Union," he wrote in his diary, "the same sword will cut in sunder the bonds of slavery itself." A dissolution of the union, he felt, could only lead to civil war, with the abolition of slavery the ultimate result: ". . . calamitous and desolating as this course of events . . . might be, so glorious would be its final issue, that, as God shall judge me, I dare not say that it is not to be desired."[44] At the time, however, Adams did not publicize these views, since he still nourished presidential ambitions.

In 1836, the abolitionists petitioned the national legislature, as they had done ever since the very first Congress. This time they demanded an end to slavery in the District of Columbia. The South, more sensitive than ever to abolitionist propaganda, was no longer content merely to refer the memorials to committee for quiet burial. Its representatives now demanded that Congress not only voice its approval of slavery in the nation's capital, but also agree not even to consider any further antislavery petitions. At this point Adams rose to speak out, but he was silenced on a point of order. The majority in the House, hoping to maintain "The Great Silence," which had redescended after the Missouri Compromise, went along with the South: first they issued a statement sanctioning slavery in the District of Columbia and then they enacted a gag rule prohibiting consideration of any future antislavery petitions.

Adams, then seventy-one years old, with the Presidency behind him, was undaunted. At the beginning of the next congressional session and thereafter at the beginning of every session until he fell dead in the Capitol cloakroom in 1848, he

sought to introduce, in defiance of the House gag rule, petitions from his constituents protesting against slavery. Each
time the House refused to consider them. Yet he persisted,
declaring that the repeated refusals to accept these petitions
were "outrages on the constitution of the country and on the
freedom of the people." They were part, he added, of a much
larger campaign to stifle debate on the subject. "It was, indeed, true," he said in 1837, "that all discussion, all freedom
of speech, all freedom of the press on the subject had within
the last twelve months, been violently assailed; and assailed,
too, in every form in which the liberties of the people could
be assailed."[45] In protesting, Adams hoped to awaken the
nation to the essential evil of slavery. Thus Adams added a
new thread to the antislavery fabric: the principle of free
speech and the right of peaceful petition now had to be considered along with the question of national political power
and the moral issue of human bondage.

In all these years, Adams' was a voice virtually alone. But
it was becoming apparent to many throughout the country
that, despite Congress' will, "The Great Silence" could be
maintained no longer, that Jefferson had been correct when
he trembled at the "fire bell in the night" and warned during
the Missouri debate, "We have kindled a fire which all the
waters of the ocean cannot put out, which seas of blood can
only extinguish."[46]

NOTES

1. *Annals of the Congress of
the United States,* 1st Congress,
2nd session, 1834. Gales & Seaton,
Washington, D.C., Vol. II, pp.
1186–7.

2. *Idem.*

3. *The Writings of James
Madison,* Gaillard Hunt, ed., Putnam's, New York, 1906, Vol. VI,
pp. 8–9.

4. Elliot, Jonathan, ed., *Debates on the Adoption of the Federal Constitution in the Conven-*

tion held at Philadelphia in 1787,
Lippincott, Philadelphia, 1876,
Vol. IV, p. 277.

5. *Idem.*

6. Phillips, Wendell, ed., *The
Constitution; A Pro-slavery Compact,* American Anti-Slavery Society, New York, 1856, pp. 181–3.

7. Elliot, *op. cit.,* Vol. V, p.
487.

8. Du Bois, W. E. Burghardt,
*The Suppression of the African
Slave-Trade to the United States*

of America, 1638–1870, Longmans, Green, New York, 1904, pp. 86–7.

9. Annals of the Congress of the United States, op. cit., 9th Congress, 2nd session, Vol. XVI, p. 14.

10. Ibid., p. 201.

11. Ibid., pp. 173–4.

12. Ibid., p. 176.

13. Ibid., p. 177.

14. Massachusetts Historical Society, Collections, 5th Series, Boston, 1877, Vol. III, p. 415.

15. Ibid., 1st Series, Vol. IV, p. 206.

16. Ibid., 5th Series, Vol. III, p. 400.

17. Moreau de St. Méry's American Journey (1793–1798), Kenneth and Anna M. Roberts, eds., Doubleday, Garden City, New York, 1947, pp. 302–3.

18. de Warville, J. P. Brissot, New Travels in the United States of America performed in 1788, J. S. Jordan, London, 1792, pp. 282-3.

19. Moreau de St. Méry's American Journey (1793–1798), op. cit., p. 303.

20. Massachusetts Historical Society, op. cit., 5th Series, Vol. III, p. 401.

21. Staudenraus, P. J., The African Colonization Movement 1816–1865, Columbia University Press, New York, 1961, p. 15.

22. Brown, Isaac V., Biography of Reverend Robert Finley, John Moore, Philadelphia, 1857, pp. 142-3.

23. Jay, William, Miscellaneous Writings on Slavery, John J. Jewett, Boston, 1853, p. 79.

24. Staudenraus, op. cit., p. 50.

25. Litwack, Leon F., North of Slavery, The Negro in the Free States, 1790–1860, University of Chicago Press, Chicago, 1961, p. 25.

26. Ibid., p. 28.

27. Staudenraus, op. cit., p. 33.

28. Litwack, op. cit., pp. 26–7.

29. Idem.

30. Jenkins, William S. Pro-Slavery Thought in the Old South, University of North Carolina Press, Chapel Hill, 1935, p. 73.

31. Cohn, David L., The Life and Times of King Cotton, Oxford University Press, New York, 1956, p. 47.

32. Gray, Lewis C., History of Agriculture in the Southern United States to 1860, Peter Smith, New York, 1942, Vol. II, pp. 661–2.

33. Annals of the Congress of the United States, op. cit., 15th Congress, 2nd Session, Vol. XXXIII, pp. 1170ff.

34. Ibid., pp. 1191–2.

35. Ibid., p. 1170ff.

36. Niles Weekly Register, Vol. XVII, 1819, p. 219.

37. Annals of the Congress of the United States, 15th Congress, 2nd Session, Vol. XXXIII, op. cit., pp. 1188–90.

38. Ibid., p. 1213.

39. Niles Weekly Register, op. cit., p. 219.

40. Annals of the Congress of the United States, 15th Congress, 2nd Session, Vol. XXXIII, p. 1204.

41. The Writings of Jefferson, Paul Leicester Ford, ed., Putnam's, New York, 1899, Vol. X, p. 157.

42. Ibid., p. 152.

43. Moore, Glover, The Missouri Controversy, 1819–1821, University of Kentucky Press, Frankfort, 1953, pp. 254–5.

44. Memoirs of John Quincy Adams, Charles Francis Adams, ed., Lippincott, Philadelphia, 1875, Vol. V, p. 210.

45. Register of Debates in Congress, 24th Congress, 2nd session, Vol. XIII, part I, p. 1314.

46. Annals of the Congress of the United States, 15th Congress, 2nd Session, Vol. XXXIII, op. cit., p. 1204.

5 The Agony of Lincoln

THERE IS IRONY in the fact that the man who would one day lead the North into a great civil war had been born in the South and had family ties to that region. But the life of Abraham Lincoln, the backwoods farmer's son who grew up to becoming a leading corporation lawyer, is replete with such ironies. A devoted constitutionalist, he would, as president, stretch the words of the historic document as they had never been stretched before. An innate pacifist, he would preside over the bloodiest war yet waged. And in prosecuting that war, this man who believed in the sanctity of private property would order one of the largest confiscations of wealth in modern times, without the compensation he had advocated for so long. Most ironic of all, in issuing his Emancipation Proclamation, Lincoln would do what he had always warned against: he would free an entire race, degraded and despised by those who had held them in bondage for so long, without provision for either their removal from the country or their gradual absorption into the surrounding hostile society.

"It would do no good," Lincoln once said, "to go any faster than the country would follow,"[1] and his great political strength lay in the fact that he never lost touch with the mood and feelings of the section he had come to represent. Thus a study of Lincoln's political career, with its twists and turns, is a study of the North itself. But Lincoln was not merely a political follower, a simple barometer of the northern mood. He was in many ways the articulation of that mood, the prophet who showed others where their finest instincts ought to lead them. It was he who, in distilling the essence of the American dream, declared that it had relevance even to the Negro. Like so many in the nation, he believed in America's destiny, but he, almost alone among the political leaders, warned that under slavery that destiny might never be fulfilled. Finally, it was he who, when confronted by demands that the property rights vested in the institution of slavery be protected under the law, replied that human rights were more important.

Yet, despite Lincoln's determination to reflect no more than the mood of the country, albeit its most enlightened tone, events had a way of overtaking him. Even before he was inaugurated as President, the southern states had begun to secede, and he was forced to call his fellow countrymen to arms in order to preserve the Union. As the conflict spread and the casualties mounted, the lines in Lincoln's face deepened, and he found himself impelled more and more by events. Reluctantly, he was forced in turn to suspend the writ of habeas corpus, to enlist Negroes in the northern armies, and finally to issue his Emancipation Proclamation. And each time events forced his hand, Lincoln, a conservative by nature, trembled at the possible future consequences of his acts. The agony of Lincoln was the agony of the nation.

The political life of Abraham Lincoln had three distinct phases. The first, which took place between 1834 and 1854, covered his entry into public life as well as his temporary withdrawal from the political arena in 1849. These were the years when Lincoln and the North itself struggled with the issue of slavery, hoping to keep faith with the nation's democratic tradition and at the same time not destroy the Union. The second phase, covering the years from 1854 to 1861, began with Lincoln's re-entry into politics following the passage of the Kansas-Nebraska Act and ended with his election as President. These were the years when the North finally came to accept Lincoln's view that while slavery should be permitted in those states where it already existed, it should be prevented from spreading to new states. The final phase covers the years when Lincoln was President, when he and the North, having determined to prevent the further spread of slavery, sought to preserve the Union.

Lincoln was serving his second term as a Whig representative to the Illinois state legislature when he faced the slavery issue publicly for the first time. The year was 1837, and the abolitionists had already achieved considerable success in drawing attention to their cause. In the forefront of their ranks was William Lloyd Garrison, editor of the *Liberator* and an indefatigable author of abolitionist tracts. Garrison had first come to public notice in 1829 when he favored what he later referred to as "the popular but pernicious doctrine of *gradual* abolition."[2] His fervor in advocating the Negro's freedom soon attracted many loyal followers, and in a little over two years he was able to found the New England Anti-Slavery Society.

Garrison was only one of many abolitionists then coming into prominence. In New York City Joshua Leavitt, William Jay, and the Tappans, Arthur and Lewis, had organized a rival antislavery society which, by 1837, could claim 274 local affiliates throughout the state. Ohio had nearly as many local societies and, in addition, could claim two antislavery institutions of higher learning, Lane Seminary and Oberlin College. Further west, in Illinois and Missouri, other antislavery groups were springing up.

Meanwhile, a slave uprising led by a slave, Nat Turner, had left the citizens of the South fearful that more insurrections might break out in the future. The South blamed the revolt on abolitionist propaganda, and southern leaders pressed their northern counterparts to suppress the agitation. As a result, the abolitionists came under increasing attack. In many cities of the North their meetings were broken up by mobs encouraged by the leading local citizens.

When these indirect methods failed to halt the steady stream of abolitionist propaganda southward, the South began petitioning northern legislatures to take direct action. It was one of these southern requests, calling on the Illinois legislature to suppress the abolitionists within the state, that gave Lincoln an opportunity to express himself publicly on the slavery question. The joint Senate-House committee appointed to consider the petition had recommended adoption of a series of resolutions reaffirming the right to own slaves under the Constitution, reasserting the exclusive jurisdiction of the states in the matter and denying the power of the federal government to prohibit slavery in the District of Columbia. Along with five other Representatives, Lincoln voted against the resolution.

But when the legislature returned to the subject several weeks later, this time condemning the formation of abolition societies, Lincoln did more than just register his negative vote. He joined with a fellow Sangamon County Representative, an ex-Vermonter named Dan Stone, in filing a formal protest delineating his position "that the institution of slavery is founded on both injustice and bad policy; but that the promulgation of abolition doctrines tends rather to increase than to abate its evils." Lincoln agreed that Congress had no right to interfere with slavery in the states where it already existed, but he believed that by the same token Congress did have the power under the Constitution to abolish slavery in the District of Columbia, although "that power ought not to be exercised unless at the request of the people of said District."[3]

Toward the end of his career in the state legislature, Lincoln outlined his views on slavery in somewhat greater detail in a private letter to an abolitionist. "I hold it a paramount duty of us in the free States," he wrote, "due to the Union of the States, and perhaps to liberty itself (paradox though it may seem), to let the slavery of the other states alone; while, on the other hand, I hold it to be equally clear that we should never knowingly lend ourselves, directly or indirectly, to prevent that slavery from dying a natural death— to find new places for it to live in, when it can not longer exist in the old."[4] These views were to remain substantially unchanged until the exigencies of the Civil War finally pushed him toward a more radical course.

In 1846, after serving four terms in the Illinois legislature, during which he rose to a position of leadership within his party, Lincoln was elected to Congress. Thirty-eight years old at the time, he arrived in Washington just in time to join his fellow Whigs in denouncing the policies of Democratic President James Polk. But Lincoln was far more conspicuous in his opposition to the war against Mexico and in his support of internal improvements than in opposition to the territorial expansion of slavery. Agreeing with Henry Clay, his political idol, that the slavery issue ought not to be further agitated, he remained largely silent during the many debates that took place in the next two years over the question of whether slavery should be permitted in the territories newly acquired from Mexico. He did, however, vote consistently against slavery's further expansion.

On the question of slavery in the District of Columbia, Lincoln was somewhat more forthright. As a lame-duck congressman, he finally made an effort in 1849 to give shape to the views he had expressed twelve years earlier in the Illinois state legislature. He prepared a bill which provided that all children born of slave parents after a certain date were to be given their freedom and placed under apprenticeship, while any masters who manumitted their slaves voluntarily were to be compensated. But when he learned that there was no chance that the bill would be enacted, he refrained from introducing it and supported instead—unsuccessfully, as it developed—a measure prohibiting the slave trade in the District.

Lincoln's opposition to the Mexican War had cost him a great deal of his earlier popularity, and as the new Congress prepared to convene, he found his political power rapidly slipping away. When he failed to win appointment as Federal Land Commissioner, he became convinced that he no longer had a future in politics. He therefore decided to return to Springfield and devote his full energies to his now quite extensive law practice. For the next five years he was to observe political events largely from the outside.

One of the events he must have viewed with elation was the Compromise of 1850, pushed through a reluctant Congress by Clay, with the help of Daniel Webster. Put together with infinite skill, it promised to end forever the bitter strife over slavery's territorial expansion that had so riven Congress. Under the terms of the compromise, California was to be admitted to the Union as a free state, while New Mexico and Utah were to be organized as territories with no specific prohibition of slavery. The slave trade was to be abolished in the nation's capital, but the fugitive slave laws were to be strengthened. On both sides the extremists were dissatisfied. Delegates from nine southern states, meeting in Nashville shortly after the Compromise became law, declared that "the slaveholding states cannot and will not submit to the enactment by Congress of any law imposing onerous conditions or restraints upon the rights of masters to remove with their property into the territories of the United States."[5] In the North, the radicals were unhappy that slavery had not been prohibited unequivocally from the new territories. But most Americans, including Lincoln, were relieved that a compromise had been worked out. "The Country Saved," "Most Glorious News from Washington" read the newspaper headlines.

Two years later Clay, author of the Compromise, was dead. Lincoln delivered the eulogy in Springfield. Clay, he pointed out, "ever was, on principle and in feeling, opposed to slavery. . . . He did not perceive, that on a question of human right, the negroes were to be excepted from the human race." And yet, Clay was himself the owner of slaves. "Cast into life where slavery was already widely spread and deeply seated, he did not perceive, as I think no wise man has perceived, how it could be at *once* eradicated, without producing a greater evil, even to the cause of human liberty itself." For this reason, Lincoln said, Clay stood opposed to both extremes: "Those who would shiver into fragments the Union of these states; tear to tatters its now venerated Constitution; and even burn the last copy of the Bible, rather than slavery should continue a single hour" and those who, "for the sake of perpetuating slavery, are beginning to assail and to ridicule the white man's charter of freedom—the declaration that 'all men are created free and equal.' "[6] There was much of Lincoln himself in this portrait of "The Great Compromiser."

Lincoln dwelt at length on Clay's role in the colonization movement. "If as the friends of colonization hope," he said, "the present and coming generations of our countrymen shall by any means, succeed in freeing our land from the dangerous presence of slavery; and, at the same time, in restoring a captive people to their long-lost fatherland, with bright prospects for the future; and this too, so gradually, that neither race nor individuals shall have suffered by the change, it will indeed be a glorious consummation."[7]

Toward the end of his withdrawal from politics, Lincoln wrote some "Fragments on Slavery." Noting that even the ant "will furiously defend the fruit of his labor" and that even "the most dumb and stupid slave that ever toiled for a master, does constantly *know* that he is wronged," Lincoln disposed of the sophists who held that slavery was a good thing. He pointed out that men do not enslave themselves. Lincoln said that, "while *most governments* have been based, practically, on the denial of equal rights" to all, the United States had started by affirming the equal rights of all.[8]

Lincoln concluded this attempt to put down in writing his thoughts on slavery with a series of syllogisms. "If A. can prove, however conclusively, that he may, of right, enslave B. —why may not B. snatch the same argument, and prove equally, that he may enslave A.?" If color is determining, he said, "By this rule, you are to be slave to the first man you meet, with fairer skin than your own." The same argument would apply if intelligence is the rule. "But, say you, it is a question of *interest;* and, if you can make it your *interest,* you have the right to enslave another. Very well. And if he can make it his interest, he has the right to enslave you."[9]

We now can see that Lincoln's attitude toward slavery had taken shape by the end of this first phase of his political career. He recognized its evil and injustice. Yet he also recognized its legality under the Constitution. He hoped that if slavery were restricted to those areas where it already existed, the institution would slowly die a natural death. Lincoln's eyes were on the future, and he felt that the Compromise worked out by Clay, with its limitation on the spread of slavery, had laid the groundwork for the eventual peaceful solution of the problem.

However, the apparent calm that had descended on the country with the passage of the Compromise ended only four years later. The man who resurrected the bitter intersectional animosities was the Democratic Senator from Lincoln's home state, a man who had launched his political career shortly after Lincoln but who had since advanced much further— the physically undersized but politically powerful Stephen A. Douglas. He pushed through Congress a bill that, in providing for the organization of the Kansas and Nebraska territories, repealed outright the Missouri Compromise of 1820, a compact that in the eyes of the North had become almost sacred.

Douglas, as chairman of the Committee on Territories, had proposed a bill that left unsettled the question of slavery in the two territories. But the South's leaders in the Senate were unwilling to sanction organization of the territories on such a loose basis. They therefore forced Douglas to add to his bill a section specifically providing that the status of slavery in the two territories would be determined by local referendum rather than congressional enactment. This was the "popular sovereignty" doctrine thenceforth championed by Douglas as the most democratic method of resolving the slavery question in the new territories. But some southern Senators were still dissatisfied, even with this tacit repeal of the Missouri Compromise.

Many factors pushed Douglas to go a long way with his southern colleagues. Intensely ambitious, he hoped to become the Democratic presidential nominee in 1856. Already popular in the West, he knew his nomination would be assured if he could cement the support of the South. But his attitude toward slavery transcended even his political aspirations. Unlike Lincoln, he did not entertain a moral repugnance toward the South's "peculiar institution." "Slavery," he said, "may be very essential in one climate, and totally useless in another.

If I were a citizen of Louisiana, I would vote for retaining and maintaining slavery, because I believe the good of that people would require it."[10] As for the Negroes, Douglas felt they had "shown themselves so degraded by ignorance, superstition, cruelty, and barbarism as to be utterly incapable of governing themselves."[11] With this attitude Douglas did not fathom the sense of revulsion and outrage that coursed through the North as news of the Kansas-Nebraska bill began to filter out of Washington. Unlike the great majority in the North, he did not understand the importance of whether the new territories were declared slave or free. He continued to push his measure through Congress, indifferent to the uproar it was creating throughout the North. He honestly believed that he was merely reconciling once more, as the nation's leaders had so often done in the past, the conflicting sectional interests in order to further the national destiny.

Among those deeply moved by the events in Washington was Abraham Lincoln. When news of the final passage of the Kansas-Nebraska bill reached him in Illinois, he was, he later said, roused "as he had never been before."[12] Three months later he had re-entered politics and was stumping in support of the incumbent from his own congressional district. A staunch opponent of the Kansas-Nebraska bill, he himself entered the race for the Illinois state senate.

The years of political retirement had removed much of the partisanship and uncertainty of purpose that had characterized his previous political activity. A new crispness of insight and a new fervor of moral feeling now permeated his speeches. By this time a very skillful orator, he was called upon more and more to state the anti-Nebraska case. When Stephen Douglas returned to Illinois to defend his policies, it was Lincoln who stood up to challenge him.

He began by attacking the bill as a repudiation of the Missouri Compromise, one of the many agreements worked out by the nation to limit and contain slavery. "This *declared* indifference, but as I must think, covert *real* zeal for the spread of slavery," he said, "I cannot but hate. I hate it because of the monstrous injustice of slavery itself. I hate it because it deprives our republican example of its just influence in the world—enables the enemies of free institutions, with plausibility, to taunt us as hypocrites—causes the real friends of freedom to doubt our sincerity, and especially because it forces so many really good men amongst ourselves into an open war with the very fundamental principles of civil liberty—criticizing the Declaration of Independence, and insisting that there is no right principle of action but *self-interest.*"[13]

Lincoln stated that the southerners were no more responsible for slavery than the people of the North. And he admitted his own quandary: "If all earthly power were given me, I should not know what to do. . . . My first impulse would be to free all the slaves and send them to Liberia—to their own native land." But since this was not feasible, except in the long run, what other solutions were there? To "free them all, and keep them among us as underlings?" Possibly, but such a solution was not necessarily desirable. "Free them, and make them politically and socially, our equals? My own feelings will not admit of this; and if mine would, we well know that those of the great mass of white people will not. . . . A universal feeling, whether well or ill founded, cannot be safely disregarded."[14]

Lincoln's speech was the first public expression of these views, some of which he had long held and some of which he had only recently worked out. Even more important was his attack on Douglas' principle of popular sovereignty. Although little could be done to eliminate slavery where it already existed, Lincoln contended this did not by any means furnish an excuse for allowing it to expand into new areas. To the argument that the southerner should be allowed to take his slaves with him to the western lands, just as the northerner was allowed to take his hogs, Lincoln replied, "this is perfectly logical, if there is no difference between hogs and negroes." To the argument that the people of Nebraska should be allowed to determine for themselves whether they shall be allowed to own slaves, he answered; "When the white man governs himself that is self-government; but when he governs himself, and also governs *another* man, that is *more* than self-government—that is despotism. If the negro is a *man,* why then my ancient faith teaches me that 'all men are created equal;' and that there can be no moral right in connection with one man's making a slave of another."[15]

Lincoln denied that the Nebraska question was a local matter. "The whole nation," he said, "is interested that the best use shall be made of these territories. We want them for the homes of free white people. This they cannot be, to any considerable extent, if slavery shall be planted within them."[16] One could repeal the Missouri Compromise and the Declaration of Independence, he said, but one could not repeal human nature; slavery was selfishness and man had a love of justice. "The spirit of seventy-six and the spirit of Nebraska, are utter antagonisms."[17]

Finally, Lincoln insisted that the Kansas-Nebraska act, instead of quieting the controversy over slavery, as Douglas claimed, had raised the issue anew. "Much as I hate slavery," Lincoln said, "I would consent . . . to any *great* evil, to avoid a *greater* one. But when I go to Union saving, I must believe, at least, that the means I employ has some adaptation to the end. To my mind, Nebraska has no such adaptation." Only if the Missouri compromise were restored, he said, would the slavery controversy die down and the Union be preserved. "And what shall we have in lieu of it?" Lincoln asked. "The South flushed with triumph and tempted to excesses; the North, betrayed, as they believed, brooding on wrong and burning for revenge. One side will provoke; the other resent. The one will taunt, the other defy; one aggresses, the other retaliates. . . . But restore the compromise, and what then? We thereby restore the national faith, the national confidence, the national feeling of brotherhood. . . . It would be worth to the nation a hundred years' purchase of peace and prosperity."[18]

This speech made Lincoln the leading spokesman for the anti-Nebraska Whigs in Illinois. The Whigs, however, were only one of several factions opposed to the Nebraska Act. There were, at the one extreme, the antislavery radicals, already organized in Illinois as the Republican Party. At the other extreme were certain of the "know-nothings" who, as the American Party, were opposed to all foreign influences. In the middle were the anti-Nebraska Democrats who had bolted their party on the Nebraska question but remained loyal to its principles on all other issues.

Lincoln turned first to the task of solidifying his support among the radicals. He was unwilling to support their abolitionist program, for he was still a constitutionalist and feared that demands for widespread emancipation would disrupt the Union. At the same time, he felt unable to join with the "know-nothings." "How could I . . . ?" he wrote. "How can any one who abhors the oppression of negroes, be in favor of degrading classes of white people? Our progress in degeneracy appears to me to be pretty rapid. As a nation, we began by declaring that 'all men are created equal.' We now practically read it, 'all men are created equal, *except negroes.*' When the Know-Nothings get control, it will read 'all men are created equal, except negroes, *and foreigners, and catholics.*' When it comes to this I should prefer emigrating to some country where they make no pretence of loving liberty. . . ."[19]

Faced with these narrowing political alternatives, Lincoln agreed in 1856 to attend the state convention at Bloomington called by the antislavery radicals—after the more radical passages were deleted from the announcement of the meeting. In the weeks before the convention was scheduled to meet, northern newspapers were filled with stories of the latest violence in Nebraska, where slaveholders and free-soil men were battling for control of the territory. As a result, the convention was packed by the more conservative anti-Nebraska men who, like Lincoln, were being pushed by events into the Republican Party. An anti-Nebraska Democrat was nominated for governor and a conservative platform drafted, but it was Lincoln who was chosen to deliver the keynote speech.

No full account of the Bloomington address now exists— the reporters were too enthralled to take adequate notes—but through it Lincoln continued to hold his support among the radicals and at the same time to capture the allegiance of the conservatives. By dwelling on the need to bring a halt to the further spread of slavery, to reserve the western lands for the free, white settler, he presented a position on which all factions could unite. "Have we no interest" he was later to ask an audience in Kalamazoo, Michigan, "in the free territories of the United States—that they should be kept open for the homes of free white people?" And his answer: "As our Northern states are growing more and more in wealth and population, we are continually in want of an outlet, through which it may pass out to enrich our country. In this we have an interest—a deep and abiding interest." Lincoln was thus speaking for the northern way of life. Taking note of southern criticisms that the slaves in that region were better off than northern workmen, he told the same Kalamazoo audience: "What a mistaken view do these men have of Northern laborers! They think that men are always to remain laborers here—but there is no such class. The man who labored for another last year, this year labors for himself, and next year he will hire others to labor for him. These men don't understand when they think in this manner of Northern free labor."[20]

When Lincoln finished his Bloomington address, the hall resounded with applause. A new Republican Party was born, and Abraham Lincoln was its spokesman in Illinois. The task of making it dominant in the North was made easier by the continuing train of events: first the unceasing reports of violence in Nebraska and then the very important Supreme Court decision in the Dred Scott case in 1857. Scott, a Negro slave, had, at the instigation of certain abolitionists, sued for his freedom, contending that in carrying him into Illinois and Wisconsin where slavery was forbidden, his master had forfeited ownership. The abolitionists hoped that the suit, if successful, would lead to the freedom of the many Negroes brought North by their masters. But the Supreme Court put an end to this hope. Speaking through its Chief Justice, Roger Taney of Maryland, it asserted that Negroes were not included when the Declaration of Independence said "all men are created equal." The Court stated that, while a Negro may be a citizen of a state, he was not entitled to the rights and privileges of a citizen of any other state. He was not a citizen of the United States itself and had no standing under the Constitution. Under these circumstances, Scott, as a Negro, had no right to sue in a federal court. Taney, however, was not content to rest his case on these grounds. He went on to declare, in a momentous *obiter dictum,* that the Missouri Compromise itself was unconstitutional, since it deprived citizens of their right to hold property. In fact, Taney said, Congress had no right to exclude slavery from any territory.

The Court's decision put Douglas in a difficult position. If Congress had no right to exclude slavery for a territory, Congress also had no right to exclude slavery from a state. What was left of Douglas' "popular sovereignty" doctrine? Was it just an empty phrase, an open invitation for slaveholders to settle with their chattel property wherever in the western territories they might wish? Douglas attempted to reconcile the Dred Scott decision with his position, declaring that the decision was an affirmation of his principle of popular sovereignty. He thereby set a trap for himself that Lincoln was to spring most effectively when the two next met in debate.

When Douglas announced his decision to stand for re-election in 1858, Lincoln was the logical candidate to oppose him. At the very beginning of the campaign Lincoln followed Douglas and spoke to the crowds he had drawn. After several such occasions, Lincoln challenged Douglas to a direct debate. As the incumbent and a nationally known political figure, Douglas had little to gain from a face-to-face confrontation, but since he felt that he could not refuse the challenge, he reluctantly agreed to meet Lincoln on the same platform in seven cities scattered throughout the state.

In the first debate Lincoln fared badly when Douglas put him on the defensive for what were supposedly his abolitionist leanings. But in their second meeting Lincoln attacked. "Can the people of a United States Territory," he asked his opponent, "in any lawful way . . . exclude slavery from its limits prior to the formation of a State Constitution?"[21] Douglas replied with care. Regardless of what the Supreme Court

ruled, he said, "the people have the lawful means to introduce
it or exclude it as they please, for the reason that slavery cannot exist a day or an hour anywhere, unless it is supported by
local police regulations."[22]

But Lincoln felt that even this modified version of the
popular sovereignty doctrine was inconsistent with the Dred
Scott decision, which Douglas, a former judge, continued to
defend vigorously. The Supreme Court had ruled that the
Constitution guarantees to the citizens of the United States
the right to take slaves into the territories. "In the teeth of
this," Lincoln asked, "where can the judge find room for his
unfriendly legislation against their right? The members of a
territorial legislature are sworn to support the Constitution
of the United States. How dare they legislate unfriendly to a
right guaranteed by that Constitution? And if they should,
how quickly would the courts hold their work to be unconstitutional and void!" Moreover, Lincoln argued that slavery
had been originally planted on this continent without the aid
of friendly legislation. Only after the institution had been
firmly established were the necessary supporting laws enacted.
"How futile, then," he said, "is the proposition that the people of a Territory can exclude slavery by simply not legislat-
ing in its favor."[23]

In the debates that followed, Lincoln pressed this point
determinedly, pointing out the further implications of the
Dred Scott decision. If the right to own slaves was guaranteed
by the Constitution, as the Supreme Court had ruled, the
people's representatives in Congress, sworn to uphold that
document, were required to enact positive legislation protecting slavery. If this were done on behalf of the territories,
Douglas' popular sovereignty doctrine would lose all meaning. By the same token, if the right to own slaves was
guaranteed by the Constitution, state laws prohibiting slavery
were unconstitutional. Carried to its ultimate conclusion, the
Dred Scott decision might one day re-establish slavery in the
North. This was the horrifying specter that Lincoln presented
to the assembled crowds.

With little effect, Douglas accused Lincoln of undermining respect for the law and the Constitution by refusing to support the Dred Scott decision. Lincoln insisted that he respected the law and supported the Constitution but that he simply refused to accept the premise upon which the Dred Scott decision was based. "I believe that the Supreme Court and the advocates of that decision," he declared in the fifth debate, "may search in vain for the place in the Constitution where the right of property in a slave is distinctly and expressly affirmed."[24] He said that Douglas was molding public opinion so that it would accept the next Supreme Court decision that would carry the logic of the Dred Scott decision one step further. "In this," Lincoln said, "he is also preparing (Whether purposely or not), the way for making the institution of Slavery national."[25]

This was the nub of Lincoln's plaint against Douglas. In arguing that he did not care whether slavery was voted up or down, Douglas had proven himself unfit to lead the North in its fight against the further extension of slavery to the western territories. He had ignored the moral question involved. "The real issue in this controversy—the one pressing upon every mind," Lincoln said in the seventh and final debate, "—is the sentiment on the part of one class that looks upon the institution of slavery *as a wrong,* and of another class that *does not* look upon it as a wrong. . . . That is the real issue. That is the issue that will continue in this country when these poor tongues of Judge Douglas and myself shall be silent. It is the eternal struggle between these two principles—right and wrong. . . ."[26] Thus, Lincoln raised the political questions of the day to the same moral plane on which the abolitionists had long sought to place them. At the same time, however, he succeeded in avoiding the abolitionists' own radical solutions.

Earlier, before the state Republican convention, Lincoln had delivered his famous "House Divided" speech. "I believe," he had said, "this government cannot endure, permanently half *slave* and half *free.*" Although he had added, "I do not expect the Union to be *dissolved*—I do not expect the house to *fall,*"[27] the speech gave his candidacy a radical tinge, and Douglas in effect said that Lincoln was calling for the dissolution of the Union. Lincoln had not, of course, advocated dissolution or any of the radical solutions put forth by the abolitionists. He simply advocated support of whatever was necessary to prevent the further spread of slavery.

"The Judge alludes very often in the course of his remarks to the exclusive right which the States have to decide the whole thing for themselves," Lincoln told his audience in the final debate. "I agree with him very readily that the different states have that right. He is but fighting a man of straw when he assumes that I am contending [otherwise]. . . . What I insist upon," he said, "is, that the new territories shall be kept free from it while in the territorial condition. . . . Judge Douglas assumes that we have no interest in them—that we have no right whatever to interfere. I think we have some interest. I think that as white men we have. Do we not wish for an outlet for our surplus population . . . ? Do we not feel an interest in getting to that outlet with such institutions as we would like to have prevail there?"[28]

Douglas chided Lincoln for his views on the Negro. Lincoln had exhorted a Chicago audience to "discard all this quibbling about this man and the other man, this race and that race and the other race being inferior. . . . Let us discard all these things, and unite as one people throughout this land, until we shall once more stand up declaring that all men are created equal."[29] Douglas rebuked Lincoln for implying that Negroes were the equal of whites: "I hold that this government was made on the white basis, by white men, for the benefit of white men and their posterity forever, and should be administered by white men and none others."[30] When Lincoln, in their next meeting, said, "I had no thought . . . that I was doing anything to bring about a political and social equality of the black and white races,"[31] Douglas promptly accused him of talking out of both sides of his mouth, of saying one thing in the northern abolitionist section of the state and another in the southern proslavery part.

In the final debate, Lincoln tried once again to establish clearly that he was merely supporting the sentiments expressed in the Declaration of Independence. "I think the authors of that notable instrument," he said, "intended to include *all* men, but they did not mean to say all men were equal in color, size, intellect, moral development or social capacity. . . . They did not mean to assert the obvious untruth, that all were then actually enjoying that equality, not yet, that they were about to confer it immediately upon them. In fact they had no power to confer such a boon. . . . They meant [simply] to set up a standard maxim for free society which should be familiar to all: constantly looked to, constantly approximated and thereby constantly spreading and deepening its influence. . . ."[32]

Thus, for Lincoln, equality for Negroes was an ideal toward which the nation should strive in the future. In the meantime, because of their present inferiority, the nation could deprive the Negro of certain rights without undermining the democratic faith upon which it had been founded. Again, Lincoln was prepared to go so far but no further.

In the election that followed, the Republicans on the state ballot polled several thousand more votes than their opponents, but an outdated apportionment law assured Douglas' re-election by the legislature. The debates with Douglas, however, had been widely reported throughout the country, making Lincoln a national political figure and a leading contender for the Republican presidential nomination in 1860. For the next two years he continued in the public limelight.

In 1859 Lincoln differentiated the Republicans from the Democrats by pointing out that while the latter hold "the *liberty* of one to be absolutely nothing, when in conflict with another man's right of *property*. . . . Republicans, on the contrary, are for both the *man* and the *dollar*; but in cases of conflict, the man *before* the dollar."[33] Six months later, in an address at Milwaukee, Lincoln put his faith in education and free labor as the soundest foundations for national progress, again comparing unfavorably the southern with the northern way of life.

Then, in February, 1860, Lincoln delivered his famous

Cooper Union speech. What does the South demand of the North, he asked his audience. "This, and this only: cease to call slavery *wrong,* and join them in calling it *right.* And this must be done thoroughly—done in *acts* as well as in *words.*" But "wrong as we think slavery is," Lincoln declared, "we can yet afford to let it alone where it is, because that much is due to the necessity arising from its actual presence in the nation; but can we, while our votes will prevent it, allow it to spread into the national territories, and to overrun us here in these free states? . . . If our sense of duty forbids this," Lincoln continued, "then let us stand by our duty, fearlessly and effectively. . . . Let us have faith that right makes might, and in that faith, let us, to the end, dare to do our duty as we understand it."[34] This stirring peroration brought the audience to its feet, and the next morning, when the New York newspapers reprinted the address, much of the rest of the city joined in the applause. Three months later Abraham Lincoln secured the Republican presidential nomination.

He was nominated, according to the Chicago *Press and Tribune,* because "he occupies the happy mean between the alleged radicalism which binds the old anti-slavery men to Mr. Seward and the conservatism which dictates the support of Judge Bates. . . . He is a Southern man by birth and education. He is a man of the people . . . without the stain of Know-Nothingism on his skirts. . . . He is an honest man."[35] Because he occupied this middle position, Lincoln became the candidate of the Republican Party. And because the Republican Party had become the dominant party in the North, and the North, in turn, the dominant section in the country, Lincoln was elected President.

Thus the second phase of Lincoln's political career came to an end. At that time he believed without a doubt that slavery was a great evil, contrary to the laws of God and contrary to the traditions of free men as expressed in the Declaration of Independence. Nevertheless, he held no prejudice against the South, he had no interest in making the Negro the equal of the white man, and he saw no feasible solution to the Negro problem except colonization. He wished to preserve the Union, but even more to halt the further spread of slavery. The territories must be kept free so that white men, through their own labor, could build a better tomorrow for themselves and their children. This was the position of Abraham Lincoln, and it was a position in which a majority in the North concurred.

Lincoln, while duly elected, did not command the support of a majority of his fellow citizens. Of the 303 electoral votes, he had secured 180, well over half, but his share of the popular vote was less than 40 per cent. Since together John Breckenridge, running on a platform of federal protection for slavery in the territories, and Douglas, standing firm on his principle of popular sovereignty, had captured over 47 per cent of the popular vote, Lincoln's mandate with respect to slavery was not clear. But with respect to preserving the Union there was no question. Lincoln did not want war, but he would advocate war if the South attempted to secede.

In the months before his inauguration, Lincoln encouraged North and South in every way to work out their differences peacefully, while refusing to surrender the principle upon which he had been elected. Soon after the election, as the South began moving toward secession, committees were formed in Congress to work out a modus vivendi. Lincoln wrote hastily, and confidentially, to his friends in Congress, "Let there be no compromise on the question of *extending* slavery. . . . Stand firm. The tug has to come, & better now, than any time hereafter."[36] But when conservative southerners, hoping to keep their states in the Union, wrote to Lincoln for assurances that he had no intention of violating southern rights, Lincoln was quick to reply, though again confidentially: "Do the people of the South really entertain fears that a Republican administration would, *directly*, or *indirectly*, interfere with their slaves . . . ? If they do," he wrote his former colleague in the House, Alexander Stephens of Georgia, "I wish to assure you, as once a friend, and still, I hope, not an enemy, that there is no cause for such fears." But he added, "I suppose, however, this does not meet the case. You think slavery is *right* and ought to be extended; while we think it is *wrong* and ought to be restricted. . . ."[37]

In his Inaugural Address, Lincoln tried once more to dissuade the South from its secession course. Quoting from one of his previous speeches, he told its leaders: "I have no purpose directly or indirectly, to interfere with the institution of slavery where it exists. I believe I have no lawful right to do so, and I have no inclination to do so."[38] The only substantial difference between the South and himself, then, was the question of whether slavery should be allowed to expand. Pleading with the southern leaders to place their faith in law, not arms, Lincoln warned that he had taken an oath to "preserve, protect and defend" the government of the United States, and that he did not intend to violate that oath. Nevertheless, the South continued on the path to secession.

The South was unwilling to remain in the Union on Lincoln's terms, because its leaders agreed with him that slavery, if excluded from the western territories, would soon disappear. The dynamics of a slave economy required expansion: without new lands to absorb the surplus slave population, the older regions of the South would soon face an economic decline; and without new lands to draw away the surplus planter class, the younger generations in those older regions would face a blighted future. Even more important, a West where slavery was forbidden would not attract southerners. The new territories would be settled by northerners who, together with their former neighbors in the East, would enact legislation unfavorable to the vital interests of the South until slavery itself, undermined by hostile laws, would disappear and even some day be prohibited. This fear had haunted the South since 1820, and since the last three states had entered the Union as free states, it seemed that the fear was being realized. Lincoln's election confirmed these fears.

The South was thus faced with a Draconian choice. If it remained in the Union, it was certain to lose its property and probably its power. This might take a hundred years or more, as Lincoln estimated, but it would eventually come to pass. The only alternative was a pre-emptive act. If the southern states were to secede, the North might permit them to go in peace. Many in the North were known to favor such a solution. If the North chose to resist, perhaps England, whose textile mills were dependent on southern cotton, might be persuaded to intervene on the South's behalf. At least the second choice offered some hope, a remote one to be sure, but real nevertheless.

The older, conservative leaders in the South were more willing to take their chances with Lincoln. As Stephens pointed out: "The President of the United States is no Emperor, no Dictator—he is clothed with no absolute power. He can do nothing unless he is backed by power in Congress." Pointing out that Lincoln did not have a majority in either House, he appealed for moderation. "Why, then, I say, should we disrupt the ties of this Union, when his hands are tied— when he can do nothing against us?"[39]

But these conservative leaders no longer controlled the situation in the South. A younger, more radical generation, led by William Yancey of Alabama, had brought about a quiet revolution. In the decade before 1860 they had gradually taken over the Democratic Party in the South. While the Republicans in the North were demanding a total prohibition on slavery in the western territories, these new radicals in the South insisted on positive protection. If the next Congress did not enact a slave code for the territories, they were prepared to secede from the Union and turn their attention elsewhere—to Cuba and Santo Domingo, where slavery might still expand. It was this demand that had split the Democrats at their 1860 convention, placing Douglas and his principle of popular sovereignty in an untenable middle position between the Republicans in the North and the Democrats in the South.

Now, to save its "peculiar institution," and the way of life associated with it, the South struck at the North; it opened hostilities by firing on the federal fortress in Charleston harbor. And to preserve the Union, the North struck back.

In his Message to Congress in Special Session on July 4, 1861, Lincoln referred to the hostilities as "essentially a people's contest." The Union, he said, was battling to maintain a government whose principal aim was "to afford all an unfettered start, and a fair chance, in the race of life."[40] He condemned slavery on two counts: It denied the Negro his basic rights, and it denied free white men an equal opportunity in the economic struggle. Still, as before, Lincoln was committed only to preventing the extension of slavery, nothing more.

The outbreak of war had been greeted enthusiastically by the abolitionists, who saw it as the instrument for carrying out God's will and ridding the nation of the curse of slavery. In this spirit, many abolitionists had rushed to don the Union blue. But the great majority of those answering Lincoln's call to arms cared not a whit about slavery, except possibly to prevent its expansion. Asked specifically about this, members of the 128th Illinois Regiment replied that "they would rather be in the woods until the moss grew on their backs than help free the slaves."[41] They were interested only in preserving the Union and punishing the Rebels for their attack on Fort Sumter. Moreover, in several of the border states which had so far remained loyal to the Constitution, slavery was still legal. As Chief Executive, sworn to preserve the Union, Lincoln could not alienate them. Little wonder, then, that he moved so cautiously on the slavery issue, holding as long as he could to the principles he had enunciated during his campaign for the presidency.

However, before the war was many months old, the slavery question arose in an unexpected way. General John C. Fremont, ardent abolitionist and Republican presidential candidate in 1856, was in command of the Union Army's Western Department. Unable to suppress recurrent prosouthern guerrilla activity, he issued a proclamation invoking martial law. Acting on his own authority he proclaimed that the property of all persons who continued to bear arms against the federal government was to be confiscated and their slaves freed. As soon as Lincoln learned of the proclamation, he wrote his western commander asking him to modify it to reflect Congress' recent order providing for the confiscation of all property used in rebellion against the Union only after a judicial proceeding.

When Fremont refused, Lincoln himself revoked the proclamation. This drew a storm of protest from the abolitionists, and in a letter to the newly elected Illinois Senator, Lincoln outlined his position. "No doubt the thing was popular in some quarters, and would have been more so if it had been a general declaration of emancipation," he noted, but he pointed out that a company of Kentucky volunteers, upon hearing of the order, had thrown down their arms and disbanded, while the legislature of that state had refused to vote any further assistance to the war effort. "I think to lose Kentucky," Lincoln said, "is nearly the same as to lose the whole game. Kentucky gone, we can not hold Missouri, nor, as I think, Maryland. . . . We would as well consent to separation at once, including the surrender of this capitol."[42] For similar reasons, the President continued to refuse the eagerly proffered services of free Negroes in the Union armies. At the moment he was unwilling to do anything that might lose him the support of the border states.

Yet he could not ignore entirely the demands of the abolitionists who were growing increasingly dissatisfied. The more vigorous enforcement of the prohibition on the slave trade did not placate them, since the government was continuing to enforce the fugitive slave laws just as vigorously. When Lincoln was compelled to remove Fremont from his command, they renewed their pressures. Another consideration was that many influential persons in England favored the southern cause; only strenuous efforts of the antislavery cohorts, aided by the war news, prevented the British government from recognizing the Confederate States. But liberal opinion in England would eventually turn against the North if steps were not taken to bring an end to slavery. Under these pressures Lincoln sent a special message to Congress in March, 1862, finally recommending a move in that direction.

The proposal was really quite modest. He suggested that Congress provide financial aid to any state that adopted a program of its own for the gradual, compensated emancipation of the slaves within its jurisdiction, thus avoiding the direct involvement of the federal government. If the border states could be persuaded to support such a program, they might forever be weaned from their sister states in the South, since slavery was the only common bond between them. And if the states which had seceded were thus put on notice that they would receive no support from the border states, they would be quick to lay down their arms and cease their rebellion.

Behind the scenes, Lincoln actively pressed for support of this program. He wrote to prominent Democrats already on record as opposed to the scheme and asked them to reconsider their position. Only $1 million, or less than what it cost to pursue the war for half a day, he pointed out, would buy all of Delaware's slaves at $400 a head. Next, he called in congressmen from the border states for a long, friendly talk at the White House. Fervently he tried to persuade them how important the measure was to the Union cause. A month later Congress approved the resolution the President had requested. Since it merely declared the will of both Houses without providing any funds for carrying out the proposal, Democrats and Republicans alike joined in supporting it. But the ultimate fate of the scheme was presaged by the fact that not a single senator or representative from the border states had cast an affirmative vote for the resolution.

Still, Lincoln continued to press his scheme. He called the representatives of the border states to the White House. Asserting that the war would end much sooner if they would vote for a resolution endorsing gradual emancipation, Lincoln told the assembled lawmakers: "Let the states which are in rebellion see . . . that . . . they cannot, much longer maintain the contest. . . . I do not speak of emancipation *at once,* but of a *decision* at once to emancipate *gradually.* Room in South America for colonization, can be obtained cheaply, and in abundance; and when numbers shall be large enough to be company and encouragement for one another, the freed people will not be so reluctant to go."[43] But Lincoln was no more successful in this latest attempt to win over the support of the border states for his emancipation scheme than he had been in the past. When the legislators left the White House, twenty-two of their number promptly published a statement criticizing his position; only eight supported the President.

Meanwhile, however, Lincoln had moved ahead on other fronts, prodded by a far more radical Congress. For years southern objections had prevented the United States from recognizing either of the two Negro republics, Haiti or Liberia. Now, in the spring of 1862, with the southern representatives no longer present, both Houses by large majorities approved an exchange of diplomatic representatives, despite the fears voiced by one Ohio representative. "How fine it will look," he said, "to welcome here at the White House an African, full-blooded, all gilded and belaced, dressed in court style, with wig and sword and tights and shoe-buckles, and ribbons and spangles, and many other adornments which African vanity will suggest." But Lincoln himself had no objection to a Negro being appointed. "You can tell the President of Haiti," he said, "that I shan't tear my shirt if he does send a nigger here!"[44] Within a year, the first Negro diplomat in history had been accredited by the American government.

At the same session Congress redeemed a Republican campaign pledge and abolished slavery in the territories; it forbade military commanders from returning runaway slaves to their rebel masters, and it enacted a bill providing for the gradual, compensated emancipation of all slaves in the District of Columbia. When he signed the bill, Lincoln stated that he had "ever desired to see the national capital freed from the institution in some satisfactory way."[45]

But Lincoln was afraid to move too rapidly. When General David Hunter, commanding Union forces in South Carolina, Georgia, and Florida, issued a proclamation freeing all the slaves within his jurisdiction, the President countermanded it, as previously he had revoked General Fremont's order. When the time came for such a proclamation from "a necessity indispensable to the maintenance of the government,"[46] Lincoln said, he would issue it, not a commander in the field. Meanwhile, he warned the citizens of the border states to proceed as rapidly as possible with a program of gradual, compensated emancipation before it was too late.

From the earliest days of his political life, Lincoln had believed that colonization offered the only constructive solution to the nation's Negro problem, and he had long supported the efforts of the American Colonization Society. Now, in appropriating $1 million to pay slaveholders in the nation's capital to free their bondsmen, Congress, to Lincoln's delight, voted an additional $100,000 "to be expended under the direction of the President of the United States, to aid in the colonization and settlement of such free persons of African descent now residing in said District . . . as may desire to emigrate to the Republic of Hayti or Liberia, or such other country beyond the limits of the United States as the President may determine."[47] This was followed two months later by an actual appropriation of $500,000. Lincoln turned enthusiastically to the task of executing this legislative mandate.

His most immediate problem was to find a suitable site for the proposed colony. Liberia appeared unsatisfactory on many grounds, including both distance and the cost of transportation. Moreover, previous attempts to develop a haven for American Negroes there had not been particularly successful. Far more promising was a site in Chiriqui Province, Panama, where a group of American investors claimed they had found rich coal deposits and said they would welcome Negro colonists. Now, Lincoln turned at once to the next task—winning the support of the Negroes who would have to emigrate.

He called a group of them to the White House—the first time a delegation of Negroes had ever met with the President. "You and we are different races," he began. "We have between us a broader difference than exists between almost any two races. Whether it is right or wrong, I need not discuss; but this physical difference is a great disadvantage to us both. . . . Your race suffer very greatly, many of them, by living among us, while ours suffer from your presence. In a word, we suffer on each side. . . . But for your race among us there could not be war, although many men engaged on either side do not care for you one way or the other. . . . It is better for us both, therefore, to be separated. . . . There is an unwillingness on the part of our people, harsh as it may be, for you free colored people to remain with us."[48]

Despite the great respect and deep love that the Negroes felt toward Lincoln himself, his blunt talk, widely reported in their own press, failed to dispel the traditional Negro antipathy toward colonization. The Chiriqui plan, however, was soon abandoned for other reasons. The opposition of the neighboring Central American republics was too great. Lincoln next approached the various European powers, to see if they would agree to resettling American Negroes within the borders of their already existing colonies in South America. The response was only lukewarm. Still undaunted, Lincoln turned to Haiti. There one promoter said he was prepared to resettle 5,000 Negroes immediately, offering them homes, employment, schools, and hospitals. Lincoln was so eager to get on with the project that he signed a contract without adequately investigating, and a few hundred Negroes actually set out for Haiti in April, 1863. But most of them returned disillusioned within the year. Only the caution of Secretary of State William Seward prevented the government's becoming more deeply involved in this scheme.

Lincoln's quest for a suitable colonization site was made more urgent by a decision he had reached in the summer of 1862. The time had come, he had decided, to proclaim the freedom of all slaves whose masters were still in open rebellion against the federal government. If his Administration were to retain the support of the abolitionists in this country and of the liberals in Great Britain, he knew he must do at least that. Moreover, public opinion was coming more and more to favor such a step. The northern armies were floundering in the field, the enlistment quotas were going unfilled. The Union cause required new life, new meaning for the continuing bloodshed. Lincoln announced his decision to his Cabinet in July, but Seward advised waiting for a Union victory before issuing the proclamation. Otherwise, at the end of a long series of northern defeats, it might seem an admission of weakness. Lincoln agreed.

Meanwhile, the abolitionists continued to castigate Lincoln for not taking a more vigorous stand against slavery. Nearly every day Charles Sumner and Henry Wilson, the radical Senators from Massachusetts, and Thaddeus Stevens, the radical Representative from Pennsylvania, were at the White House to urge on the President a firmer policy. Church groups supplemented these visits with memorials of their own. Horace Greeley, in an editorial in his New York *Tribune* entitled, "the Prayer of Twenty Millions," bitterly attacked Lincoln for not acting more forcefully. Slavery, he insisted, was the inciting cause and sustaining base of treason. No intelligent champion of the North could believe it possible to put down the rebellion, while at the same time upholding its cause.

In reply, Lincoln was unequivocal. "My paramount object in this struggle," he wrote Greeley, "*is* to save the Union, and is *not* either to save or to destroy slavery. If I could save the Union without freeing *any* slave I would do it, and if I could save it by freeing *all* the slaves I would do it; and if I could save it by freeing some and leaving others alone I would also do that. What I do about slavery, and the colored race, I do because I believe it helps to save the Union; and what I forbear, I forbear because I do *not* believe it would help to save the Union."[49]

Then came news of the battle at Antietam Creek, which, with only slight exaggeration, could be considered a northern victory. Six days later, on September 22, Lincoln announced that if the rebellion were not ended by January 1, 1863, he would proclaim the freedom of all slaves in those areas where federal authority was still being resisted. Confronted by the war's exigencies, he retreated somewhat from his previously held principle that gradual emancipation and compensation were essential.

He did, however, make one last determined effort to give substance to this principle. In his annual message to Congress, in December, 1862, he proposed three constitutional amendments, which would enable Congress to provide financial assistance to any state that agreed to abolish slavery by 1900, to compensate those slaveholders whose bondsmen had been freed by the fortunes of war, and to appropriate money for the colonization of freed Negroes in an area outside the United States. Lincoln defended the delay of emancipation in this plan by stating that it would save the Negroes "from the vagrant destitution which must largely attend immediate emancipation. . . ." In the meantime, they would remain with their old masters, who would give them wages at least until new laborers were procured. He supported compensation because "the liberation of slaves is the destruction of property" and he questioned whether the South had been more responsible than the North for the continuation of slavery. He advocated colonization as a means of allaying the fears of many that the "freed people will swarm forth and cover the whole land." He ended by declaring, "The dogmas of the quiet past, are inadequate to the stormy present. . . . Fellow-citizens, *we* cannot escape history. . . . In *giving* freedom to the slave we *assure* freedom to the *free.* . . ."[50]

Meanwhile, the exigencies of war were forcing Lincoln to retreat on still another issue. From the beginning of the conflict he had consistently and steadfastly refused to accept Negroes in the Union armies on the grounds that this "would turn 50,000 bayonets from the loyal Border States against us." Many in the North opposed the use of Negro soldiers on other grounds; they feared that they would lack fighting qualities, that putting guns in their hands would simply incite slave insurrections, that making them into soldiers would bring about a subtle though significant change in their social status. But as the northern casualties mounted and it became increasingly difficult to find white replacements, public attitudes began to change. "We beg leave to say," the New Hampshire Governor and Executive Council wrote Lincoln, "that our reading, intelligent, patriotic young men are inquiring into the propriety of wasting their strength and energy in daily and nightly watching of rebel states and other property, or . . . digging trenches, piling fortifications and the like, while

strong and willing hands await only to be invited . . . that
they may show their appreciation of the glorious boon to
freedom."[51] A Negro weekly continued to ask what many
white citizens must have been thinking, "How long will white
Americans submit to be drafted solely because their colored
fellow-countrymen are rejected?"[52]

On January 1, 1863, the deadline set by Lincoln for an
end to all open rebellion passed. On that day he issued his
Emancipation Proclamation. "I do order and declare that all
persons held as slaves within said designated states, and parts
of states, are, and henceforward shall be free; . . . And upon
this act, sincerely believed to be an act of justice, warranted
by the Constitution, upon military necessity, I invoke the
considerate judgment of mankind, and the gracious favor of
Almighty God. . . ."[53] Appended to the Proclamation was an
announcement that the President was thereby authorizing the
enlistment of freed Negroes in the Union Army and Navy.

Events had finally overtaken Lincoln. Though opposed to
slavery himself, he had held off from actively interfering with
that institution as long as he possibly could. He had restrained
his military commanders, his civilian advisors, and his abolitionist followers. He had entreated the border states to accept
compensated emancipation. But time had run out. In 1863
the position of the North was sufficiently precarious that Lincoln, as Commander-in-Chief, could no longer deny the North
a moral cause to sustain its war effort. Nor could he deny any
longer the advantage of Negro manpower. Writing a year
later, Lincoln revealed the considerations that had shaped his
action: "I am naturally anti-slavery . . . yet I have never understood that the Presidency conferred on me an unrestricted
right to act officially upon this judgment and feeling. . . .
When, early in the war, Gen. Fremont attempted military
emancipation, I forbade it, because I did not then think it an
indispensable necessity. When a little later, . . . the Secretary
of War suggested the arming of the blacks, I objected, because
I did not yet think it an indispensable necessity . . . in March,
and May, and July 1862 I made earnest, and successive appeals to the border states to favor compensated emancipation.

... They declined the proposition; and I was, in my best judgment, driven to the alternative of either surrendering the Union, and with it, the Constitution, or of laying strong hand upon the colored element ... I ... confess plainly that events have controlled me."[54]

NOTES

1. Sandburg, Carl, *Abraham Lincoln,* Harcourt, Brace, New York, 1954, p. 267.

2. *Documents of American History,* Henry Steele Commager, ed., F. S. Crofts, New York, Vol. I, p. 278.

3. *Abraham Lincoln, Selected Speeches, Messages, and Letters,* T. Harry Williams, ed., Rinehart, New York, 1957, p. 5.

4. Hofstadter, Richard, *The American Political Tradition and the Men Who Made It,* Vintage Books, New York, 1961, p. 109.

5. Commager, *op. cit.,* Vol. I, p. 325.

6. *Abraham Lincoln, Selected Speeches, Messages, and Letters, op. cit.,* p. 36.

7. *Ibid.,* pp. 37–8.

8. *Ibid.,* p. 39.

9. *Ibid.,* pp. 39–40.

10. Nevins, Allan, *Ordeal of the Union,* Scribner's, New York, 1947, pp. 107–8.

11. *Idem.*

12. Thomas, Benjamin P., *Abraham Lincoln,* Knopf, New York, 1960, p. 143.

13. *Abraham Lincoln, Selected Speeches, Messages, and Letters, op. cit.,* p. 44.

14. *Ibid.,* p. 45.

15. *Ibid.,* pp. 47–8.

16. *Ibid.,* p. 49.

17. *Ibid.,* p. 55.

18. *Ibid.,* pp. 50–2.

19. *Ibid.,* p. 60.

20. *Ibid.,* pp. 64–5.

21. *The Collected Works of Abraham Lincoln,* Roy P. Basler, ed., Rutgers University Press, New Brunswick, N.J., 1953, Vol. III, p. 43.

22. *Idem.*

23. *Ibid.,* pp. 97–9.

24. *Ibid.,* p. 231.

25. *Ibid.,* p. 233.

26. *Abraham Lincoln, Selected Speeches, Messages, and Letters, op. cit.,* pp. 109–11.

27. *Ibid.,* p. 76.

28. *Ibid.,* p. 107.

29. Hofstadter, *op. cit.,* p. 116.

30. *The Collected Works of Abraham Lincoln, op. cit.,* p. 112.

31. *Abraham Lincoln, Selected Speeches, Messages, and Letters, op. cit.,* p. 97.

32. *The Collected Works of Abraham Lincoln, op. cit.,* p. 301.

33. *Abraham Lincoln, Selected Speeches, Messages, and Letters, op. cit.,* p. 113.

34. *Ibid.,* pp. 129–30.

35. Hayes, Melvin L. *Mr. Lincoln Runs for President,* Citadel, New York, 1960, pp. 59–60.

36. *Abraham Lincoln, Selected Speeches, Messages, and Letters, op. cit.,* p. 133.

37. *Ibid.,* p. 135.

38. *Ibid.,* pp. 138–9.

39. Carman, Harry J., and Syrett, Harold C., *A History of the American People,* Knopf, New York, 1955, Vol. I, p. 601.

40. *Abraham Lincoln, Selected Speeches, Messages, and Letters, op. cit.,* p. 162.

41. Catton, Bruce, *Glory Road,* Doubleday, Garden City, New York, 1955, p. 246.

42. *Abraham Lincoln, Selected Speeches, Messages, and Letters, op. cit.,* p. 167.

43. *Ibid.,* pp. 185–6.

44. Quarles, Benjamin, *Lincoln and the Negro,* Oxford, New York, 1962, pp. 99–100.

45. *Ibid.,* p. 104.

46. *Abraham Lincoln, Selected Speeches, Messages, and Letters, op. cit.,* p. 182.

47. Quarles, *op. cit.,* p. 109.

48. *Complete works of Abraham Lincoln,* John C. Nicolay and John Hay, eds., Century, New York, 1894, pp. 222–3.

49. *Abraham Lincoln, Selected Speeches, Messages, and Letters, op. cit.,* pp. 190–1.

50. *Ibid.,* pp. 202ff.

51. Quarles, *op. cit.,* p. 154.

52. *Idem.*

53. *Abraham Lincoln, Selected Speeches, Messages, and Letters, op cit.,* p. 213.

54. *Ibid.,* pp. 261–3.

6 Victory Without Commitment

In the spring of 1865 the South lay devastated. The Civil War had ended, but its ugly scars remained. "The fields were trampled down," wrote a young Georgia girl. ". . . The dwellings that were standing all showed signs of pillage, and on every plantation we saw the charred remains of the gin-house." In Virginia matters were much the same. "Hanover Junction," reported Whitelaw Reid, editor of the New York *Tribune*, "presented little but standing chimneys and the debris of destroyed buildings."[1] Through these scenes of havoc and destruction passed the remnants of a once proud army, not in orderly columns but singly or in pairs, clad in tattered gray and begging scraps of food from a populace that already had too little to eat; 250,000 of their comrades had been killed, many more had been wounded.

"It was not merely the ruin of war in a physical sense," Paul Buck has noted. "The utter prostration of the South was only in part a story of devastation, burnt cities, bankrupt financial institutions, torn-up railways, depleted farms, and a disrupted labor force. More disastrous was the impoverishment of spirit that came with defeat. . . ."[2] Nevertheless, the returned men tired of war, wanted most to go to work "to repair their ruined fortunes."[3]

What plan did the North have for dealing with the South? On what basis were the rebellious states to be brought back into the Union? The North had achieved its primary aim, to preserve the nation. Moreover, in the final months of the war the North had reached a broad consensus that victory meant the final and irrevocable destruction of slavery. On that one point alone had agreement been reached. But what was to become of the Negroes once they secured their freedom? While publicists and statesmen were slow even to recognize the problem, small groups of dedicated individuals, many of them Army chaplains, worked to educate and train the multitude of Negroes rapidly being liberated from slavery. With only meager means, they accomplished a great deal. As the war drew to a close, they were joined by others from the North. Initially their efforts were directed toward basic education, but soon they included elementary education in hygiene, agriculture, the use of money, and other facets of everyday life which the freedman would soon need to know. But these were only temporary expedients; a long-range plan was needed.

The group that should have had such a plan ready had none. For over thirty years the abolitionists had devoted their energies to bringing an end to slavery, but they had deliberately given little thought to what would happen once the Negro actually gained his freedom. "Do not allow yourself to be drawn away from the main object," the American Anti-Slavery Society had warned its agents. "Let the *principle* be decided on, of immediate abolition, and the plans will easily present themselves."[4] With single-minded devotion, the abolitionists had pursued this strategy.

Thus when the Thirteenth Amendement abolishing involuntary servitude was approved, they considered their work to be at an end. "The American Anti-Slavery Society under the lead of Mr. Garrison, . . . [was] disbanded," the ex-slave, Frederick Douglass, later recalled; "its newspapers were discontinued, its agents were withdrawn from the field, and all systematic efforts by abolitionists were abandoned." Douglass and Wendell Phillips, the great abolitionist leader, felt there was still work to be done, that the society "had not fulfilled its mission, which was, not merely to emancipate, but to elevate the enslaved class." Emancipation had left the Negro with "neither money, property, nor friends—nothing but the dusty road under his feet. . . . He was in a word literally

turned loose, naked, hungry, and destitute, to the open sky."
When Douglass and Phillips suggested that as a measure of
minimum protection, the Negro ought to be guaranteed the
right to vote, Garrison would hear nothing of it and said it
was too much to ask at that time. Thus, "against Mr. Garrison's leadership, and the surprise and joy occasioned by
emancipation, it was impossible to keep the association
alive. . . ."[5]

The crusade against slavery had been primarily a religious
movement. The abolitionists regarded that institution not
merely as a social evil, but, even more importantly, as an absolute sin against God's divine order. Theodore Weld, one of
the earliest of the abolitionist leaders, said that the sin was
"the inflictions of slavery on the *mind*—its prostration of conscience . . . its destruction of personality—its death stab into
the soul of the slave."[6]

The majority of abolitionists thought of freedom as an
abstract ideal, not necessarily associated with human beings.
They could demand an end to slavery while disdaining the
slave himself. As long as the Negro was actually free, they
could no longer distinguish between him and the many other
races at the bottom of the social spectrum. When emancipation finally came, the majority of abolitionists retired into
obscurity, while the more dedicated of their leaders turned
their energies to other causes.

The Congress, the political body most immediately concerned, also had no systematic plan for dealing with the formerly rebellious states or the newly freed slaves. In fact, during
the crucial first eight months following the southern defeat, the
Congress was not even in session. During the 1864 session,
however, a bill concerning each of these issues had been
passed. The first of these, the Wade-Davis bill, had laid down
terms on which the secessionist states were to be readmitted
to the Union. It was passed by both houses while the war was
still in progress, but Lincoln refused to sign the measure into
law, claiming he did not want to be "inflexibly committed to
any single plan of restoration."[7]

The second measure, which actually became law, attempted to deal with the Negro problem specifically. Enacted in March, 1865, only a little more than a month before Lincoln was assassinated, it established a Freedmen's Bureau charged with the "supervision and management of all abandoned lands and the control of all subjects relating to refugees and freedmen from rebel states."[8] Under its provisions, former slaves and loyal southerners who had lost their property could rent up to forty acres from the public domain for a period of three years, with the right to purchase the property at the end of that time. To meet the need for more immediate assistance, the bill authorized the Secretary of War to issue provisions, food, and clothing to the refugees and freedmen in the meantime.

While it seemed to offer former slaves the prospect of acquiring land, the bill actually ignored the realities of their position. The Negroes were the most impoverished of any group in the South. How were they to pay the required rent, much less accumulate sufficient savings in three years to purchase their forty acres? Moreover, the best of the public lands in the South had long since been appropriated by others. How were the Negroes to find among those portions of the public domain still available a sufficient amount of cultivable land so that they could support themselves and their families? Only in the West were such fertile tracts still to be found, but the Civil War was being fought to preserve the West for free white labor. What congressman would support the measures necessary to transport large numbers of former slaves beyond the Missouri? Here, then, was only a stopgap measure, as revealed by the fact that the Bureau was to remain in force only "during the present war of rebellion and for one year thereafter."[9] It was quite far indeed from being a comprehensive plan for rehabilitating a war-devastated region and guaranteeing the freedom of four million former slaves.

While Congress as a whole had not thought out the problem, one member of that legislative body had. Thaddeus Stevens, the brooding Republican Representative from Pennsylvania, had long been an active foe of slavery. As early as 1836, as state legislator, he had opposed the spread of the

South's "peculiar institution" into the territories, as well as any prohibition on the activities of the antislavery forces.

As a sworn enemy of the South and its distinctive way of life, Stevens was elected to Congress in 1848 by his Quaker constituents on an antislavery, Whig platform. In the debates that soon followed on the territorial question he stated, "I cannot listen to the recital [of Southern control of the nation's destiny] without feeling the burning blush on my countenance, that the North with her overwhelming millions of free men, has for half a century been tame and servile enough to submit to this arrogant rule."[10]

A decade later Stevens became the strident voice of radical Republicanism. On several occasions his bitter speeches, roundly denouncing the South and its institutions, nearly touched off a general melee on the House floor. When, after Lincoln's election in 1860, the southern states threatened to secede from the Union, Stevens cautioned against compromise. "It is time," he declared, "to decide whether this nation exists by the sufferance of individual States or whether it required a constitutional majority to absolve them from their allegiance. . . . If . . . it should be decided that we are *one people* and the government possesses sufficient power to coerce obedience, the public mind will be quieted, plotters of disunion will be regarded as traitors, and we shall long remain a happy and united people."[11]

It was in a speech to his Lancaster, Pennsylvania, constituents on September 6, 1865, that Stevens outlined his plan for dealing with the defeated South. "Heretofore," he explained, "Southern society has had more the features of aristocracy than democracy. . . . It is impossible that any practical equality of rights can exist where a few thousand men monopolize the whole landed property. . . . How can republican institutions," Stevens asked, "free schools, free churches, free social intercourse exist in a mingled community of nabobs and serfs, of owners of twenty-thousand-acre manors, with lordly palaces, and the occupants of narrow huts inhabited by low white trash?"[12]

In September, 1865, Stevens proposed that the victorious

North expropriate the holdings of the South's largest landowners as a war indemnity. Each recently freed Negro adult
male would then receive an outright gift of forty acres; the
remaining millions of acres would be distributed among the
poorer white farmers at a reasonable price. The wealth and
power of the South's former ruling oligarchy would thus be
destroyed, and a new class of small, free farmers would be
created. Most important, the social and economic structure of
southern society would be recast in the northern image. "If
the South is ever to be made a safe republic," Stevens declared, "let her land be cultivated by the toil of its owners, or
the free labor of intelligent citizens. This must be done, even
though it drive the nobility into exile. If they go, all the
better. It is easier and more beneficial to exile seventy thousand proud, bloated and defiant rebels than to expatriate four
million laborers, native to the soil and loyal to the Government."[13]

If this plan were carried out under the Constitution,
Stevens pointed out, the rebellious states would have to be
treated as conquered provinces. "In reconstruction," he said,
"no reform can be effected in the Southern States if [as some
claim] they have never left the Union." For then they would
still have the right to vote on the measures designed to bring
about reform, and they would certainly vote to defeat those
measures. "But reformation *must* be effected; the foundation
of their institutions, political, municipal and social, *must* be
broken up and *relaid* or all our blood and treasure have been
spent in vain. This can be done only by treating and holding
them as a conquered people."[14]

The reaction to Stevens' plan, even in the Republican
press, was generally unfavorable. "We protest against any warfare against Southern property . . . ," Greeley's New York
Tribune declared, "because the wealthier class of Southerners, being more enlightened than the ignorant and vulgar, are
less inimical to the blacks."[15] But what the *Tribune* overlooked was the fact that Stevens' plan was designed to eliminate some of the economic roots of lower class white hostility
to the Negro. One of the few to appreciate Stevens' plan was

the American correspondent of the Paris *Le Temps*. "A question is never settled," he wrote, "until it is settled right. The real misfortune of the Negro race is in owning no land of its own. There cannot be real emancipation for men who do not possess at least a small portion of soil."[16] The name of the correspondent was Georges Clemenceau.

Undaunted by the negative reaction in the Republican press, Stevens tried to give substance to at least a portion of his plan when Congress finally reconvened in the winter of 1865–1866. Both then and when he tried the next year, Congress overwhelmingly defeated the confiscation bills.

Almost alone among the leaders in the North Stevens understood the institutional changes that would have to be made in the South if the freedom granted the Negro were to be anything more than simply a change in form. If the former slave was unable to own his farm, he would not long be able to retain his political and civil freedom. But in pressing the Negro's case, Stevens was looking beyond the welfare of only that minority. He knew that without reforms the South could never contain truly democratic institutions, that its poorer white citizens would never be able to advance beyond a degraded status, and that the northern way of life itself would be endangered if an unreconstructed South rejoined the Union. But he was asking for a complete social revolution, and this was further than most people in the North were prepared to go. Moreover, as Lincoln had earlier pointed out, if Congress might today compel southern landowners to give up their property, what would prevent it from doing the same tomorrow to the far more wealthy northern businessmen, manufacturers, and financiers? It was this haunting thought which produced so cool a reception to Stevens' plan in the North, regardless of its other merits.

Lincoln himself had long advocated an alternative plan. Instead of confiscating the property of the large landowners, he preferred to compensate them for the loss of their slaves. In part, this reflected his belief that the North shared equally in the blame for the evil of slavery. "We of the North as well as you of the South," he had said, "shall pay fairly for our complicity in that wrong. . . ."[17] But he also believed that "a gradual and not sudden emancipation [would be] better for all."[18] This had been the manner in which slavery had been eliminated in the British West Indies, peacefully and with a minimum of social friction, and this was the way he hoped to see it eliminated in the United States. Thus, as late as February, 1865, with the Emancipation Proclamation over a year old and the South almost ready to admit defeat, Lincoln startled his Cabinet by once again proposing gradual compensated emancipation. Only the vehement opposition of his closest advisors prevented the President from actually requesting $400 million from Congress to pay southerners for the loss of their slaves.

As for the Negroes themselves, Lincoln still did not believe that they could ever live at peace with their white neighbors. Despite the repeated evidence of the impracticality of such a plan, he hoped that some way might still be found to transport the newly freed Negroes to some other land. Shortly before the end of the war, he said to General Benjamin F. Butler, "I am troubled about the negroes. We are soon to have peace. We have got some one hundred and odd thousand negroes who have been trained to arms. When peace shall come I fear lest these colored men shall organize themselves . . . into guerrilla parties, and we shall have down there a warfare between the whites and the negroes." The President asked General Butler whether he could transport large numbers of Negroes to Liberia or South America. The answer was disappointing. Butler soon reported that "negro children will be born faster than your whole naval and merchant vessels, if substantially all of them were devoted to that use, can carry them from the country."[19]

In a different way, Lincoln showed the same awareness of underlying and economic factors as had Stevens. Lincoln's proposal of colonization recognized that land and slaves had been the basis of antebellum southern wealth. To confiscate even one without disturbing the other would disrupt the economic equilibrium of the region. Lincoln therefore wanted to stretch the abolition of slavery over a long period of time;

the painful readjustments could be made that much easier. In addition, the compensation which was to be paid could be used to make the same type of investments that men of wealth in the North were making. Thus, instead of leaving the South impoverished, abolition would lead to a new prosperity, a new kind of property. And the Negro, if he chose to remain in the South, would share in the prosperity. Lincoln proposed to transform the South. However, just as the northerners were unwilling to strip the southern ruling class of their property, as Stevens proposed, so they were unwilling, as Lincoln proposed, to enhance the defeated rebels' wealth and power by converting their former slave property into new capital.

Although Lincoln never completely rejected this plan for gradual compensated emancipation and simultaneous Negro colonization, he did attempt to formulate acceptable alternatives. His first essay in that direction had been the Proclamation of Amnesty and Reconstruction, issued in December, 1863. This provided that when one-tenth of the number of voters in a rebel state in 1860 swore allegiance to the federal government, it would be taken back into the Union and all property except slaves restored to its citizens. All slaves were to be guaranteed their freedom and provision made for their education. The response in Congress to this "one-tenth" proposal was mostly unfavorable, and the Wade-Davis bill, with its "one-half" provision and other stipulations, was its counterproposal. But, as we have seen, Lincoln refused to accept this plan. In his last public address, he said of his own suggestion that "he distinctly protested that the executive claimed no right to say when, or whether members should be admitted to seats in Congress." Besides, he added, "as bad promises are better broken than kept, I shall treat this as a bad promise, and break it, whenever I shall be convinced that keeping it is adverse to the public interest."[20]

He went on to urge acceptance of Louisiana's reconstruction plan, even though the number of voters supporting the new regime was less than desirable and the right to vote was not conferred on the Negroes. But under the circumstances, he felt, it seemed better to approve the plan than to dis-

approve it: 12,000 Louisianians previously in rebellion
against the federal government had sworn allegiance to the
Union, "held elections, organized a state government, adopted
a free-state constitution, giving the benefit of public schools
equally to black and white, and empowering the legislature to
confer the elective franchise upon the colored man." They
even agreed to supply a badly needed vote in favor of the
Thirteenth Amendment abolishing slavery. "Now, if we reject, and spurn them," Lincoln said, "we do our utmost to
disorganize and disperse them. We in effect say to the white
men 'You are worthless, or worse—we will neither help, nor
be helped by you.' To the blacks we say 'This cup of liberty
which these, your old masters, hold to your lips, we will dash
from you, and leave you to the chances of gathering the
spilled and scattered contents in some vague and undefined
when, where, and how.'"[21]

Meanwhile, Lincoln refused to join the growing debate as
to whether the rebellious states were actually within the
Union or not. "I have *purposely* forborne any public expression upon it," he said. "As appears to me that question has
not been, nor yet is, a practically material one, and that any
discussion of it, while it thus remains practically immaterial,
could have no effect other than the mischievous one of dividing our friends." The question was, he concluded, "good for
nothing at all—a merely pernicious abstraction."[22] The important goal at the moment was to establish loyal governments in the rebellious states so that their citizens could lay
down their arms. Whatever concessions could be wrung from
these regimes regarding the status of the Negro—and abolition of slavery was the absolute minimum—would be to the
good. Later, when the rebellion was finally ended, Congress
could take up the task of actual Reconstruction. Just as that
moment arrived, however, Lincoln was assassinated.

The man who succeeded Lincoln, Andrew Johnson, could
not delay in formulating a definite plan of Reconstruction.
The rebel armies had surrendered, loyal state governments
had to be organized. But while Lincoln had headed a nation
still at war, Johnson found himself in control of eleven ex-

hausted, badly defeated states; where Lincoln had been flexible and sensitive to congressional criticism, Johnson was to become hard and unyielding.

A tailor by trade, Johnson came from eastern Tennessee, where Jacksonian democracy was, and still is, the orthodox political creed. He had rapidly ascended the political ladder, rising from state legislator to governor and United States Senator, by continually bucking the regular party organization and appealing directly to the people by opposing the "interests." Aware of his humble origins, he bore a special animus toward class privilege of all sorts. Once, after being snubbed by a leading citizen in his home town of Greeneville, he warned bitterly, "Some day I will show the stuck-up aristocrats who is running the country. A cheap purse-proud set they are, not half as good as the man who earns his bread by the sweat of his brow."[23] Even as governor, he continued to make an occasional suit. Nevertheless, Johnson yearned to be accepted by those he considered his social betters. Not even his growing wealth and rising social position were sufficient to remove this need.

Johnson tended to see only the abstract principles involved in any problem. Certain principles, such as states' rights, loyalty to the Union, and strict constitutionalism, had sustained and carried him so far since his youth. These principles had led him to remain loyal to the federal government when Tennessee seceded from the Union, to agree to Lincoln's request that he take over as the state's wartime military governor, and to rule the conquered western portions of the state with a firm and unyielding hand. These principles had resulted in his being chosen as Lincoln's running mate in 1864, and these were the principles which he brought with him to the presidency.

The eight months that intervened between the day he took the oath of office and the next session of Congress provided Johnson with ample time in which to put a Reconstruction plan into effect. The provisional governments which had already been set up in Tennessee, Arkansas, and Louisiana he let stand. In the remaining eight southern states he appointed temporary governors, charged with calling a constitutional convention to draft a new republican government. The President let it be known that the new constitutions would have to contain at least three provisions: repeal of the articles of secession, abolition of slavery, and repudiation of the Confederate debt.

The first two requirements met little opposition. As Governor William Sharkey of Mississippi said, "The negroes are now free—free by the fortunes of war—free by proclamation —free by common consent . . . , and it is too late to raise questions as to the means by which they became so."[24] The third requirement, however, threatening even greater financial ruin to the South, met stiffer resistance. When the North Carolina convention showed signs of refusing to accept this provision, Johnson said quite firmly, "Every dollar of the debt created to aid the rebellion against the United States should be repudiated finally and forever. The great mass of the people should not be taxed to pay a debt to aid in carrying on a rebellion which they in fact, if left to themselves, were opposed to."[25] North Carolina finally voted to approve the debt-repudiation provision, but South Carolina continued to balk.

The President laid down one more stipulation. Each state would have to ratify the Thirteenth Amendment. Since this involved little more than what they had already agreed to in their own constitutional conventions, nearly every one of the former rebel states did so. Only Mississippi, still defiant, refused. But this was as far as Johnson was prepared to go in defining the Negro's new status. The President had suggested to those engaged in constitution-making that they give at least a portion of their former slaves the right to vote. "If you could extend the elective franchise to all persons of color who can read the Constitution of the United States in English and write their names," he telegraphed Governor Sharkey of Mississippi, "and to all persons of color who own real estate valued at not less than two hundred and fifty dollars . . . you would completely disarm the adversary and set an example the other States will follow." This, he said, would establish in Mississippi the same Negro suffrage as prevailed in the states in the North. "I hope and trust your convention will do this, and as a consequence the radicals, who are wild upon the negro franchise, will be completely foiled in their attempts to keep the Southern States from renewing their relations to the Union. . . ."[26] But when the various state conventions refused to take his advice, Johnson did not press the matter further.

There was one other important aspect of Johnson's Reconstruction plan. Since all those who had taken up arms against the federal government were guilty of treason, President Johnson issued a proclamation of general amnesty. This carried full and complete pardon for all those who had taken part in the late rebellion except for several important groups. At the height of the war, Lincoln had issued a similar proclamation, promising a pardon to any of the rebels who agreed to lay down their arms and swear allegiance to the Union. He too had excepted certain persons, primarily the leaders in the Confederate government. Lincoln's proclamation had been a war measure, designed to bring about an end to hostilities. Johnson's was a peace measure, designed to bring about Reconstruction. Moreover, whereas Lincoln had excepted only seven classes, Johnson now excepted fourteen, including all those who owned more than $20,000 in property.

These 160,000 former rebels could be prosecuted for treason, could be denied all civil and property rights, could be barred from voting or holding office. Johnson had said, immediately on taking office, that "treason must be made infamous and traitors must be impoverished."[27] But even those excepted by proclamation could win a pardon by appealing directly to the President, renouncing their former misdeeds and attesting to their present remorse. Thus, throughout the summer of 1865 petitions poured into the President's office, while the wives of high Confederate officers still in prison traveled to Washington to make their pleas in person. However, in these early months relatively few pardons were granted.

By December all the state conventions except that of Texas had met and adopted new constitutions. Most of the pro-

visional governors had been relieved of office, and the new
governments had taken over control.

To Johnson loyalty was a simple matter. Certain of the
southern states had attempted to secede from the Union, but
the great majority of their citizens could not be held responsible for this. "Many humble men, the peasantry and yeomanry
of the South," he said, "who have been decoyed, or perhaps
driven into rebellion, may look forward with reasonable hope
for an amnesty . . . it was the wealthy men of the South who
dragooned the people into Secession."[28] These were his ancient foes, the southern aristocrats, and since they had violated
their oaths of loyalty to the Constitution, they would have to
pay the penalty. And only by publicly recanting, by admitting
their recent guilt and promising to sin no more, could they
remove the stigma of disloyalty. Reconstruction for Johnson,
then, was an individual, personal problem. It had to take
place in the hearts of the men who had led the South into rebellion.

As far as the rebellious states themselves were concerned,
Johnson felt that there was no problem. Disputing Stevens'
contention that they were now conquered provinces, he insisted that the southern states had never really left the Union
and that, purged of their disloyal governments, they were fit to
reoccupy their accustomed places in the legislative halls of the
nation. "General," the President had told one of the North's
military leaders in May, "there's no such thing as reconstruction. These states have not gone out of the Union. Therefore
reconstruction is unnecessary."[29] And when the editor of the
Boston *Advertiser,* in reporting an interview with the President, used the word "reconstruction," Johnson reminded him
that he had actually said, "restoration." It was restoration not
Reconstruction that the President desired. Moreover, as Johnson was treated to reassuring deference by a continual stream
of prominent southern visitors, some respectfully seeking a
pardon for friends or relatives, others commending him for
his generous, understanding treatment of their defeated region, he came to feel that even the southern ruling classes
were less and less in need of reconstruction.

The recently freed Negroes, he felt, could take care of themselves. First, the South still needed their labor and consequently would not deal with them harshly. If Negroes needed protection, they could look to the recently re-established civil authorities. Actually like many men with his social origins, Johnson had little sympathy for the Negro. He had told an audience many years before, "This is a white man's government."[30]

Although the President was satisfied with the progress of reconstruction, many were not. One of these was Charles Sumner, the radical Senator from Massachusetts and stalwart friend of the Negro. His initial reaction to Johnson as President had been favorable. Writing about him, Sumner said, "I had a long conversation with him mainly on the rebel states and how they shall be tranquilized. Of course my theme is justice to the colored race. He accepted this idea completely and indeed went so far as to say 'that there is no difference between us.'"[31] For Sumner the test of the President's intentions was his stand on Negro suffrage. Shortly Sumner learned that there *was* a difference between them.

Sumner was almost alone among the principal leaders of the North in his insistence on Negro suffrage at that time. Even Thaddeus Stevens looked askance at the proposal to extend the ballot to the ex-slaves. Many who favored it as a natural right, such as the Reverend Henry Ward Beecher, the famed abolitionist preacher, thought it would "be attained at too high a price if it involved the right of the Federal government to meddle in State affairs."[32] William Cullen Bryant, writing in the New York *Post,* opposed Negro suffrage on similar grounds. As far as this issue was concerned, Johnson still enjoyed the confidence of the North.

But there were other disquieting notes. With the President's blessing, Carl Schurz, the well-known German-born journalist and Republican leader, had undertaken a tour of the South that summer to learn first hand about conditions. He discovered a deep antagonism between the races, as the former slaves and former masters tried with difficulty to adjust to their new social relationship. "In many districts," Schurz reported, "the colored people were in a panic of fright and the whites in an almost insane irritation against them."[33] Many of the former slaveholders believed that the Negroes would not work except under compulsion. This indeed seemed true, for many former bondsmen exercised their new freedom by walking off the plantations. Vagrancy was soon widespread. The white population was prepared to prevent such large-scale departures, through violence if necessary. In some states, Schurz said, "the planters were making extraordinary efforts to hold their former slaves together on their plantations, so that when the hoped-for restoration of slavery came, they might have less difficulty in identifying and reclaiming . . . [them]." As a result, "the cases of murder or mutilation of straggling freedmen increased in number."[34]

Schurz' account of conditions in the South proved quite embarrassing to the President. When Schurz finally returned to Washington to make a personal report, Johnson at first refused to see him but finally granted him a perfunctory interview. Stung by the President's refusal to take seriously the conditions he had discovered, Schurz prepared a written report, which soon fell into the hands of a congressional group.

While most southerners were prepared to accept the edict of the battlefield, Schurz found that this acceptance was only grudging. "The Union was still hateful to a large majority of the white population of the South," he reported; "and as to the abolition of slavery, emancipation, though 'accepted' in name, was still denounced by a large majority of the former master class as . . . 'unconstitutional' [which] was still desiring, hoping, and striving to reduce the free negro laborer as much as possible to the condition of a slave."[35] This was done, Schurz said, through the enforcement of specially enacted Black Codes. "Various parish or county governments, organized under the authority of the provisional governors, anticipating the restoration of slavery or so much of it as might be found practicable, adopted ordinances or regulations putting the negroes under the strictest police control, stripping them almost completely of the right of free movement enjoyed by everyone else, and of the right to dispose of their persons and property. . . ."[36]

Attempts by northern missionaries to establish special schools for the Negroes were fiercely resisted. A Freedmen's Bureau official told Schurz, "The whites esteem the blacks their property by natural right, and, however much they may admit that the relations of masters and slaves have been destroyed by the war and by the President's emancipation proclamation, they still have an ingrained feeling that the blacks at large belong to the whites at large."[37]

"Here was the great opportunity of the Federal Government," Schurz said. "Had it . . . [made] the South clearly understand that the 'States lately in rebellion' would certainly not be restored to full self-government until the introduction of free labor should have been . . . successfully accomplished and the rights of the freedmen reasonably secured, the Southern whites would, instead of striving to reverse the new order of things, have . . . [given it their support,] thus avoiding the worst troubles.[38] But with treason liquidated and the wealth of the planter class destroyed, Johnson and the South were no longer really estranged.

To offset the unfavorable impression Schurz was creating, President Johnson ordered General Ulysses S. Grant to make a brief reconnaissance of southern conditions. His report, delivered soon after the Congress reconvened, differed markedly from that of Schurz. "I am satisfied," General Grant said, "that the mass of thinking men of the south accept the present situation of affairs in good faith." He had, however, sensed the deepseated hostility of the whites toward the Negroes. "It cannot be expected," Grant added, "that the opinions held by men at the south for years can be changed in a day, and therefore the freedmen require, for a few years, not only laws to protect them, but the fostering care of those who will give them good counsel, and on whom they can rely."[39] The General had talked to the South's leaders; Schurz had talked with their followers. Both reports, in their own way, were accurate.

Meanwhile, disturbing news continued to come from the South. Having received no instructions to the contrary from the President, the leaders of that region had proceeded with their own plans for regulating the behavior of their former slaves. In Mississippi, for example, if a freedman quit his job before the expiration of his contract, under the labor laws he forfeited the wages he had earned. In addition, he could be arrested and forcibly returned to his former employer. Persons who encouraged him to quit were subject to a fine and imprisonment. Under the vagrancy laws, Negroes over eighteen who had no lawful employment could be fined and, if unable to pay, could then be hired out to anyone who would pay the fine for them. Finally, under the penal laws, freedmen were forbidden to carry arms of any sort. If convicted of such an offense, they could again be hired out to anyone who would pay their fine. These various Black Codes were widely condemned throughout the North. "The men of the North will convert the state of Mississippi into a frog-pond," the Chicago *Tribune* declared, "before they will allow any such laws to disgrace one foot of soil in which the bones of our soldiers sleep and over which the flag of freedom waves." Such laws, the New York *Tribune* added, show that the South will not "stop short of the extermination of the black race."[40]

The Black Codes helped to alert many in the North to what was happening in the South, but they were truly shocked when among those elected to the first postwar Congress from that region were the vice president, four generals, three colonels, and six members of the Confederate Congress. At the state level ex-rebel military and civilian leaders were in even greater evidence. Though many still remained unpardoned by the President, their constituents had defiantly elected them to office. Mississippi still refused to ratify the Thirteenth Amendment, and in both Georgia and South Carolina prominent citizens questioned the right of the federal government even to legislate in these areas. By the end of 1865, although President Johnson was convinced that the former secessionist states were ready to be restored to the Union, many in the North had begun to doubt it.

Nevertheless, the President seemed to have lost very little

of his earlier popularity in the North. "I think I may assure you," the Reverend Beecher wrote Johnson, "that the religious men of the North and West, are rapidly growing into a confidence in your patriotism, and wisdom, second only to that which they felt for Mr. Lincoln—a confidence which I am sure will increase. . . ."[41] In part, Johnson's continued support was a reflection of the fact that he still had not made his position entirely clear. "Those who have counted upon the President's treachery to the principles upon which he was elected," *Harper's Weekly* declared, "have reckoned without their host. . . . There is nothing in the acts or words of the President to justify the insinuation that he wishes to intrust the political power of the late rebel States exclusively to the class to which for his whole life he has been bitterly opposed."[42] The continued support for Johnson was also a reflection of the fact that the North had not clearly made up its own mind as to what it wanted from the South. It did not like the Black Codes, and it did not like the election of former Confederate officers, but it was agreed on little else.

Still, there was a growing uneasiness over the President's position. "I am getting very tired of this state of not knowing exactly where we are," wrote the editor of *Harper's Weekly* privately. "It must soon end for Johnson must express himself in his Message."[43] There was uneasiness, too, over the President's lack of firmness in protesting the treatment of Negroes in the South and in sanctioning the formation of the state governments controlled by ex-rebels. Meanwhile, praise was lavished on Johnson by the notoriously prosouthern Democratic press. ". . . the President's course in regard to the reconstruction of the Southern States," the Lancaster *Intelligencer* said gloatingly, ". . . is much more in accordance with Democratic doctrine than with the fanatical creed and the crude political theories of the radical abolitionists."[44]

In December Congress finally convened, and the President sent his annual message. He reviewed the actions he had taken, but he left unanswered more questions than he settled. On the one hand, he seemed to imply that no further steps toward Reconstruction were necessary. "The adoption of the

amendment," the President said, "reunites us beyond all
power of disruption. . . . It would remain for the States, whose
powers have been so long in abeyance, to resume their places
in the two branches of the national Legislature, and thereby
complete the work of restoration." On the other hand, Johnson seemed to admit that Congress had the right to approve
the new governments that had been organized in the South.
"Here it is for you, fellow-citizens of the Senate, and for you,
fellow-citizens of the House of Representatives, to judge, each
of you for yourselves, of the election, returns, and qualifications of your own members."[45]

The reaction in Congress and throughout the North was
generally favorable, though the response seemed to spring
more from a desire to avoid criticism of the President than
from any genuine enthusiasm for what he had said. The Republicans, especially in light of their own lack of unity, had
no wish to pick a quarrel with their leader in the White
House. Nevertheless, the Congress had already taken several
precautionary steps. On its first day it established a fifteen-
member Joint Committee on Reconstruction, a move that was
warmly supported by most moderate Republicans, including
those closest to the Administration. The Congress had also
prevented the seating of any of the newly elected southern
representatives. In the House, when the Clerk was challenged
for not calling the names of the new members from the
former rebellious states, he was upheld by a large majority,
again including many Republican supporters of the Administration. For they recognized that once the southern members
were seated, all control over Reconstruction would pass out
of the hands of Congress.

Throughout the next several weeks an air of indecision
hung over Washington. Then, in February the bill to extend
the life of the Freedmen's Bureau was passed. In thus voting
Congress broadened the Bureau's responsibilities to include
protection of the Negro against the various Black Codes.
Every Republican Senator voted in favor of the bill, and it
passed the House with almost unanimous Republican support. Since the party leaders in Congress had been in almost

constant touch with the White House while the bill was under consideration, it was generally assumed that the President
would not hesitate to sign the extension. But, to the amaze-
ment of his own supporters, he vetoed it.

In an accompanying message, Johnson stated that he considered the bill unconstitutional, since it would lead to an
expansion of the military power in peacetime and to an in-
vasion of civil judicial functions. He balked at supporting the
indigent. He questioned whether the freedmen were really as
vulnerable "as may at first be imagined," and he looked forward to their establishing themselves "through their own
merits and exertions." He warned against disturbing unnecessarily "the commerce and credit of the country." But his most
trenchant objection was that the Bill referred to certain of the
States "as though they had not been 'fully restored in all their
constitutional relations to the United States.' "[46] In the President's view, the members of Congress from the southern states
had a right to be seated and vote on all matters affecting their
future.

Not a word from the President about the Black Codes.
Not a sign of recognition that the bill had been supported by
almost the entire Republican membership in Congress. Most
disturbing of all, the President seemed to indicate that he
would thenceforth veto every piece of legislation touching the
South unless the representatives from that region were seated.
Here was a barely disguised challenge to the authority of
Congress to legislate on the subject of Reconstruction.

The President won a temporary victory when his veto was
subsequently upheld, but it was not long before the struggle
between him and the Congress resumed, this time with victory for the latter. On March 13 Congress passed the bill carrying the title "An Act to protect all persons in the United
States in their Civil Rights, and furnish the Means of their
Vindication." It made citizens of all persons born in the
United States and pledged the power of the federal government to safeguard their civil rights. This was Congress' second
effort to protect the freedmen from the Black Codes and from
the recrudescence of white power in the South. Many well-

informed persons, in and out of Congress, assumed that Johnson would sign the bill and thereby outflank his opponents. But once again they were mistaken, for on March 27 Johnson announced his veto of the Civil Rights measure.

Once again he explained his reasons. The bill as passed by both Houses of Congress, he said, would exceed the powers granted that branch of government under the Constitution. "In all our history," the President declared, "in all our experience as a people living under Federal and State law, no such system as that contemplated by the details of this bill has ever before been proposed or adopted."[47] To the objections he had raised against the Freedmen's Bureau bill, Johnson now added several others. He did not think it "sound" policy to make citizens of the Negroes while eleven of the states most vitally affected were still barred from taking their seats in Congress. He questioned whether granting citizenship to those who had just emerged from slavery into freedom, who were "unfamiliar with our institutions and our laws," would not, in effect, discriminate against worthy foreigners. The bill seemed to aim at "a perfect equality of the white and colored races," whereas it has "frequently been thought expedient to discriminate between the two." Its enactment would make it impossible for any state ever to "exercise any power of discrimination between the different races," even in regard to voting and holding office. "In fact," Johnson said, "the distinction of race and color is by the bill made to operate in favor of the colored and against the white race." If the bill were approved, he maintained, the federal system would be further undermined and the centralization of government authority dangerously increased. Finally, the bill could only "resuscitate the spirit of rebellion. . . ."[48]

The President's views on Reconstruction—or as he preferred to regard it, restoration—were now clearly revealed. As far as he was concerned, the southern states were already reconstructed. Congress should therefore seat their elected representatives and complete the process. The President was opposed to all efforts to have the federal government provide protection for the freedmen. This would involve an undue drain on the national treasury, increase federal powers at the expense of states' rights and prevent the Negro from learning self-reliance. Of the Black Codes he had no overt or even implied criticism. In fact, he wanted the southern states left free to discriminate against their colored citizens as they saw fit.

On almost any one of these issues Johnson could count on considerable support, not only among the members of the party which had elected him to office, but throughout the North. But no Republican could support him on a policy that, in its totality, was essentially a southern policy. For once the elected representatives of the recently rebellious South were seated in Congress, they would join with their Democratic allies in the North and take over control of the federal government. This had happened before the Civil War; now the South would have the advantage of even more votes. Previously, its Negro slaves had been counted at only three-fifths of their number for purposes of determining representation in the national legislature; now, as freedmen, they would be counted in full. Southern representation in Congress would be vastly increased—eighteen additional members, it was estimated—and with it the southern voice in national affairs. The Republican Party would become a minority party, and the measures it had finally succeeded in getting through Congress while the southerners were absent—measures, such as the tariff, internal improvements, and a sounder banking system, that were so important to the North's continued industrialization and prosperity—would be endangered. The North would have fought a costly war only to see the fruits of victory snatched away.

These practical considerations were reinforced by humanitarian ones. Although the North had not gone to war to free the Negro, in the course of that bloody struggle it had incurred certain moral obligations, to those who had fallen in battle as well as to the Negroes themselves. It could not now allow the South to re-enslave the Negro in all but name—for that was the obvious intent of the various Black Codes. As more and more Republican members of Congress came to understand the logical consequences of the Johnson policy, they went over to the opposition.

The Republican leaders in Congress had tried to prevent an open break with the President. "Soon after Congress met," Senator Lyman Trumbull of Illinois said, "it became apparent that there was a difference of opinion between the President and some members of Congress in regard to the condition of the rebellious States, and the rights to be secured to freedmen." In the following months he and the other Republican leaders in Congress had met frequently with the President to try to iron out that difference. When Johnson was reported reluctant to sign the Freedmen's Bureau bill, "he was informed of the condition of the civil rights bill then pending in the House, and a hope expressed that if he had objections to any of its provisions, he would make them known to his friends, that they might be remedied, if not destructive to the measure; that there was believed to be no disposition on the part of Congress, and certainly none on my part, to have bills presented to him which he could not approve. He never indicated to me," Trumbull concluded bitterly, "nor, so far as I know, to any of its friends, the least objection to any of the provisions of the bill till after its passage."[49]

The Republican congressional leaders had thought they were negotiating with the President the provisions of a badly needed piece of legislation. But to President Johnson the leaders were simply another special interest group. Politely he had listened to their arguments, but when it came time to act, he proceeded on the basis of his own principles. On the grounds of strict constitutionalism and states' rights, he vetoed the bill which would do violence to these beliefs.

With this latest veto, the break between the President and Congress was complete. No room for further compromise existed. The mood, particularly in Congress, became ugly. "Every unregenerate rebel lately in arms against the government," Senator Oliver Morton of Indiana, hitherto the most conservative of Republicans, told his constituents, "calls himself a Democrat. Every bounty jumper, every deserter, every sneak who ran away from the draft calls himself a Democrat.

. . . The Democratic party may be described as a common sewer and loathsome receptacle, into which is emptied every element of treason North and South, every element of inhumanity and barbarism which has dishonored the age."[50] With passions running at such heat, the tone of Congress became increasingly that of its radical members, such as Charles Sumner and Thaddeus Stevens, while the level of its acts sank to those of petty ward politicians. But the directing hand in both instances belonged to the same moderate Republicans who had tried so hard only a short time before to reach an understanding with the President. They girded for the upcoming struggle by first unseating the recently elected Democratic Senator from New Jersey on most questionable grounds; then, with the necessary votes in their pocket, they had both Houses override the President's veto. Later, they had the Congress pass another Freedmen's Bureau bill, and when the President once more vetoed it, they easily secured enough votes to enact the measure anyway.

After their final break with Johnson in the spring of 1866, the Republicans faced two major problems. The first and most immediate task was to fashion an alternative Reconstruction policy that would not turn control of the national government over to the southern Democrats, but there was a closely related problem: to win acceptance for that alternative policy in the upcoming fall congressional elections. A major obstacle in both cases was the all-too evident lack of unity within the Republican Party itself over the issues of Negro suffrage, the basis of future southern representation in Congress, disenfranchisement of former Confederate officers and others. Here Johnson, now completely estranged from the party which had made him President, made it easier for the Republicans. Opposition to his policies became the standard around which the party rallied. "Diversity of opinion is rapidly disappearing," an Ohio Republican wrote. "It is not now so much a difference . . . as to whether we will or will not support Johnson but as to how we shall deprive his evident defection of its power of mischief . . . I cannot but regard his vetoes as an escape from all his promises of protection to the freedmen on the hypocritical pretence of constitutional objections. His last message hands the Freedman over helplessly to the tender mercies of state legislation and his exasperated master."[51]

Even while their leaders had been trying to reach some understanding with the President, the Republicans in Congress had been working on an alternative Reconstruction plan. In order to prevent the South from rejoining the Union with an even larger representation in Congress than before, there were only a limited number of alternatives. One was to continue refusing to seat the southern Representatives; to treat the former rebellious states as Stevens had proposed, as conquered provinces. However, while this might be a temporary expedient, useful for accomplishing certain reforms, it certainly could not be a permanent solution.

Another option was to refuse to count the Negro altogether for purposes of representation. Instead of counting as three-fifths of a man, he would count as no man at all. Then the southern Representatives could return to Washington, but in much fewer numbers than before the war. However, since this would disenfranchise the Negro permanently, many in the North would oppose it.

The only practical alternative, the Republican congressional leaders gradually came to realize, was to grant the Negro the right to vote. This, it was hoped, would provide a broad base for the Republican Party in the South. However, this plan, too, had disadvantages. Many northerners were opposed to Negro suffrage. Only the previous fall, three states —Connecticut, Wisconsin, and Minnesota—had specifically rejected amendments to their state constitutions designed to give Negroes the right to vote. In fact, only six northern states gave their colored citizens this privilege. In the Congress itself the proponents of Negro suffrage were in the minority; Senator Charles Sumner of Massachusetts was the only prominent member of this group. Even Thaddeus Stevens, as already mentioned, was opposed to granting the ex-slaves the right to vote until they were better equipped to take advantage of it. "The infernal laws of slavery," he said, "have prevented them from acquiring an education, understanding the commonest laws of contract, or of managing the ordinary business of life."[52]

In any case, even if the ex-slaves in the South were given the right to vote, the Republicans in the North believed that the southern whites would prevent the Negroes from casting their ballots. To avoid this, several suggestions were made. Stevens had already proposed that the number of representatives in Congress be based, not on a state's total population but on the number of its qualified voters. Thus, if the southern states prevented their Negro citizens from voting, their representation in Congress would be proportionately reduced. Although Stevens still believed his confiscation program to be the best plan for dealing with the South, he now recognized the improbability of its ever being enacted.

Stevens' suggestion, however, was unacceptable to New England, for the voting eligibility requirements of those states were so stringent that they would be penalized as fully as the South. Senator William Fessenden of Maine suggested instead that the states simply be prohibited from denying the suffrage to their citizens "on account of race, creed or color."[53] Finally the Republican leaders in Congress reached a compromise. Discrimination in voting would be broadly prohibited, and those states that persisted in denying suffrage to their Negro citizens would have their representation in Congress proportionately reduced. Just as the Negro slaves had been liberated as the outgrowth of a war fought between white factions for control of the West, it was proposed that they be given the right to vote to enable the victorious faction to remain in power.

The northerners looked to other safeguards to prevent the return to national power of the prewar southern oligarchy. While the great majority of that class had been excepted from the provisions of Johnson's general amnesty proclamation, and they were thus ineligible to vote or hold office, the President's subsequent actions had largely nullified that policy. As the number of requests for pardons piled up, Johnson found it impossible to consider each individually, and he began re-

laxing his standards. He hired an extra clerk, an ex-Confederate colonel, to handle the mounting load; he allowed the provisional governors to recommend those to be pardoned; he
relied on informal "pardon brokers," men and women with
special access to his office; and he began granting pardons to
ex-Confederate officers simply because they had been elected
to office. Thus, many of the leaders of the prewar southern
aristocracy received pardons.

The Republicans in Congress were afraid that if the southern leaders were returned to their former positions of power,
their first act would be to have the federal government assume the Confederate war debt or perhaps even repudiate the
federal war debt. Either move would be a severe blow to the
North's interests. To preclude these possibilities the Republicans agreed to place a positive prohibition on them, and to
make the safeguard even stronger by including this prohibition as part of the new Fourteenth Amendment to the Constitution. This Amendment also provided penalties in the
form of reduced representation in the Congress on any state
that denied suffrage to male citizens over twenty-one years of
age and further specified the conditions under which officials
who had sworn to uphold the Constitution and had engaged
in rebellion could again hold office. It also included the major
parts of the Civil Rights Act, so recently enacted over the
President's veto. This, then, as embodied in the Fourteenth
Amendment, was Congress' initial Reconstruction program,
which was then submitted to the states for ratification.

The Republican legislators then returned to their next
task, to win an endorsement for their alternative Reconstruction policy at the polls over the bitter opposition of President
Johnson and the northern Democrats. Again the President
made it easier for them. In an extensive campaign tour, Johnson presented an increasingly bizarre figure out of touch with
reality. He equated his current struggle over Reconstruction
policy with his earlier struggle to keep Tennessee in the
Union. ". . . having fought traitors in the South," he declared,
"I am prepared to fight traitors in the North." He spoke repeatedly of a flag with thirty-six, not twenty-five stars; of leav-

ing the Constitution in the people's hands. He compared himself with Jesus Christ, insisting that he was being persecuted
only because he wished to pardon those who had repented.
"Hang eight million people!" he exclaimed. "Who ever heard
of such a thing? Yet because I refuse to do this, I am called a
traitor!" When heckled he tried to answer, usually with disastrous results.[54]

For most northerners the implications of Johnson's Reconstruction policy had already been driven home with dramatic fury by a bloody race riot in New Orleans. The provisional governor, finding his Unionist regime endangered by
the resurgence of southern Democrats, called a constitutional
convention to take the right of suffrage away from the ex-
Confederates and give it to the Negroes. The Democrats, already in control of the New Orleans city government and
determined to prevent the convention from taking place,
armed the police and turned them loose on the convention
delegates. In the ensuing melee, forty persons were killed and
160 wounded, all but one of them Negroes or white Unionists.
General Phil Sheridan, after investigating the riot, accused
the New Orleans mayor and police of attacking the convention delegates "with fire-arms, clubs, and knives, in a manner
so unnecessary and atrocious as to compel me to say that it
was murder."[55] But the President, in a speech delivered at St.
Louis, excoriated the radicals, both North and South, charg-
ing them with contributing to the tensions that had provoked
the riot.

By the time he returned to Washington, the President had
lost his last remaining shred of dignity and his last remaining
support among northern Unionists. "Mr. Johnson's haste to
take the wrong side at the atrocious massacre of New Orleans," the Reverend Beecher now declared, "was shocking."[56]
The November elections, already foreshadowed by the earlier
results in Maine, were a complete defeat for the President and
a smashing victory for the congressional Republicans. Nevertheless, President Johnson continued his battle with Congress.
With his encouragement, every southern state refused to
ratify the Fourteenth Amendment, with the exception of

Johnson's home state of Tennessee. When the Tennessee legislature finally approved the Amendment, Johnson's successor as governor cabled the Senate, "We have fought the battle and won it. . . . Give my respects to the dead dog of the White House."[57] Tennessee's Representatives to Congress were promptly seated, but the Republican leaders in Congress immediately said that this unique case could by no means set a precedent, that Tennessee had, in fact, demonstrated its loyalty to the Union in other ways.

Nevertheless, the southern states, with Johnson's encouragement, had rejected Congress' minimum terms. When he could have intervened to make those terms less onerous, he had remained aloof. When the terms had been set, he announced his opposition to them. His own lack of firmness in dealing with the South had encouraged the leaders of that region to defy northern opinion ever more boldly. And when the Congress had indicated its dismay, he had intimated to the South that the northern representatives did not truly reflect the views of their constituents. Thus he reinforced the south's tendency to underestimate the depth of anti-South feeling in the North. By now, of course, Johnson himself failed to understand the region of which fate had made him the leader. The balance of power had shifted unmistakably away from the President to the Congress, and the South would have to pay the price for listening to such pleasing but ill-founded advice.

Despite the recent election results, the new Congress, which reconvened in December, 1866, was not in a radical mood. It again rejected, for example, Stevens' last attempt to win approval for his confiscation scheme. But as the weeks went by and southern intransigence, encouraged by President Johnson, became more apparent, the Congress leaned to the extreme. There were continuing reports of southern atrocities against both Negroes and white Unionists. Two incidents in particular aroused northern indignation. One involved six South Carolinians, accused of killing three Union soldiers on guard duty, and the other a prominent Virginia doctor who had admitted shooting and killing a Negro of acknowledged good character for passing his carriage on a narrow road and "thus insulting" his wife and daughter who were inside. In both cases the accused were freed by civilian courts after being found guilty by military tribunals. According to the southern judges in each instance, the military tribunals lacked jurisdiction under existing law. Under these circumstances, the great majority in Congress became convinced that some form of federal military rule was absolutely essential for the proper reconstruction of the South.

Consequently in March, 1867, Congress passed a series of Reconstruction Acts. These set up five military districts, each commanded by a brigadier general with broad civil powers and together covering all the former rebellious states except Tennessee. This military rule was to continue until specially summoned conventions "elected by the male citizens . . . of whatever race, color or previous condition,"[58] had framed new state constitutions, specifically guaranteeing the Negroes the right to vote. When this was done and the Fourteenth Amendment was ratified, Congress would then seat the Southern representatives and remove the military governments. To prevent the President from frustrating these objectives, the Congress took two further actions: it prohibited him from removing any federal officeholder without prior Senate approval, and it sought to prevent him from relieving from command General Grant, the man to whom the various military governors were to report and who in turn was to be directly responsible to Congress.

President Johnson, however, was as unyielding as ever. Vetoing each of the Reconstruction Acts in turn, he condemned them as unconstitutional, as forcing a military despotism on nine million persons, and as seeking to change the structure and character of the state governments. His most bitter denunciation was reserved for the unconcealed purpose of the measures, which was to foist on the southern states unlimited Negro suffrage. "The negroes," he said, "have not asked for the privilege of voting; the vast majority of them have no idea what it means. . . ." Decrying "the policy or impolicy of Africanizing the southern part of our territory," he declared, "if universal suffrage for blacks as well as whites is a *sine qua non,* the work of reconstruction may as well begin in Ohio as in Virginia, in Pennsylvania as in North Carolina."[59]

It was true that both Ohio and Pennsylvania still denied the Negro the ballot; Ohio, in fact, would shortly vote against Negro suffrage. But Johnson failed to perceive that the depth of anti-Negro feeling in the North was quite different from that in the South, that consistency was not a political necessity nor even a political virtue. The issue before the country was not the northern Negro; it was the southern Negro. Specifically, it was how to protect the southern Negro and, with him, Republican rule throughout the nation.

The various Black Codes, the testimony before the Joint Committee on Reconstruction, the New Orleans riot, and other reports of southern recalcitrance had steadily added new supporters to the cause of Negro suffrage. At first only a few, such as Charles Sumner, favored so drastic a measure because they believed that the Negro was as entitled to cast his ballot as the white man. Their ranks soon were joined, however, by those who saw Negro suffrage as the only means by which four million one-time slaves and untold thousands of white Unionists could be protected against the vengeance certain to arise once the former slaveholders and ex-Confederate officers regained political power. The North could and did retain a deprecating attitude toward the Negro. But it could not acquiesce, so soon after the end of a bloody war, to the virtual re-enslavement of the Negro. Nor could it ignore the southern white Unionists.

But the great majority of those who now insisted on the Negro's right to vote were those who recognized that what was actually at stake was the political hegemony of the nation. Too much blood and treasure—the blood and treasure of too many white men—had been spilled to emancipate the North from southern political domination. What the North had won on the field of battle it had no intention of now losing through the ballot box. Thus, while Johnson was worried about the possible "Africanization" of the South, Republicans in the North were concerned about their ability to stay at the helm of the national government. They had no intention of relinquishing control, surely not to a band of unreconstructed rebels. And if giving the Negro the vote was the only way they could hold on to power, they were for it, regardless of what they had said before. As Stevens said, "It prevents the States from going into the hands of rebels, [and] giving them the President and the Congress for the next forty years."[60] Or as even Sumner admitted, "The colored vote was a necessity. . . ."[61]

Once this had been recognized, the North was prepared to do whatever was necessary to make Negro suffrage a reality, and this included placing the entire South under military rule, an extension of federal authority it would normally never have condoned. Johnson's vetoes were therefore easily overridden, and his appeal for equal treatment of Ohio and Virginia ignored. And when the President, ignoring Congress' specific prohibition, continued to remove those federal officers who displayed too great a zeal in enforcing the Reconstruction statutes, the Republicans were prepared even to remove him from office. Meanwhile, military Reconstruction proceeded under Congress' watchful eye.

NOTES

1. Carter, Hodding, *The Angry Scar, The Story of Reconstruction*, Doubleday, Garden City, N.Y., 1959, p. 32.

2. Buck, Paul H., *The Road to Reunion 1865–1900*, Little, Brown, Boston, 1938, p. 31.

3. *Ibid.*, p. 37.

4. Barnes, Gilbert Hobbs, *The Antislavery Impulse, 1830–1844*, Peter Smith, Gloucester, Mass., 1957, p. 248.

5. Douglass, Frederick, *Life and Times of Frederick Douglass*, Collier Books, New York, 1962, pp. 376–8.

6. Barnes, *op. cit.*, p. 79.

7. *Documents of American History*, Henry Steele Commager, ed., F. S. Crofts, New York, 1947, Vol. I, p. 439.

8. Commager, *op. cit.*, Vol. II, p. 1.

9. *Idem.*

10. Korngold, Ralph, *Thaddeus Stevens, A Being Darkly Wise and Rudely Great*, Harcourt, Brace, New York, 1955, p. 86.

11. *Ibid.*, p. 118.

12. *Ibid.*, p. 283.

13. *Idem.*

14. *Ibid.*, p. 282.

15. *Ibid.*, p. 283.

16. *Ibid.*, p. 284.

17. *Abraham Lincoln, Selected Speeches, Messages, And Letters,*

T. Harry Williams, ed., Rinehart, New York, 1957, p. 263.

18. *Ibid.*, p. 178.

19. Korngold, *op. cit.*, p. 152.

20. *Abraham Lincoln, Selected Speeches, Messages, and Letters, op. cit.*, p. 287.

21. *Ibid.*, pp. 288-9.

22. *Ibid.*, pp. 287-8.

23. McKitrick, Eric L., *Andrew Johnson and Reconstruction,* University of Chicago Press, Chicago, 1960, p. 87.

24. McCarthy, Charles H., *Lincoln's Plan of Reconstruction,* McClure, Phillips, New York, 1901, p. 460.

25. *Ibid.*, p. 455.

26. *Ibid.*, p. 461.

27. McKitrick, *op. cit.*, p. 91.

28. *Ibid.*, p. 140.

29. *Ibid.*, p. 91.

30. Winston, Robert W., *Andrew Johnson, Plebeian and Aristocrat,* Henry Holt, New York, 1928, p. 252.

31. *Memoir and Letters of Charles Sumner,* Edward L., Pierce, Sampson Low, Marston, London, 1893, p. 242.

32. McKitrick, *op. cit.*, p. 171.

33. *The Reminiscences of Carl Schurz,* Frederick Bancroft and William A. Dunning, McClure, New York, 1908, Vol. III, 1863-69, Chapter VI.

34. *Ibid.*, p. 188.

35. *Ibid.*, p. 184.

36. *Ibid.*, p. 188.

37. *Ibid.*, p. 189.

38. *Ibid.*, p. 201.

39. Commager, *op. cit.*, Vol. II, pp. 10-11.

40. Carman, Harry J., and Syrett, Harold C., *A History of the American People,* Knopf, New York, 1956, Vol. II, p. 22.

41. McKitrick, *op. cit.*, p. 171.

42. *Ibid.*, p. 180.

43. *Ibid.*, p. 181.

44. *Ibid.*, p. 182.

45. *Ibid.*, pp. 255-6.

46. Commager, *op. cit.*, Vol. II, pp. 12ff.

47. McKitrick, *op. cit.*, p. 315.

48. Commager, *op. cit.*, Vol. II, pp. 15ff.

49. McKitrick, *op. cit.*, pp. 316-7.

50. *Ibid.*, pp. 318-9.

51. *Ibid.*, pp. 315-6.

52. Korngold, *op. cit.*, p. 306.

53. McKitrick, *op. cit.*, p. 335.

54. *Ibid.*, p. 432.

55. *Ibid.*, p. 426.

56. *Ibid.*, p. 427 footnote.

57. *Ibid.*, p. 361.

58. Commager, *op. cit.*, Vol. II, p. 30.

59. *Ibid.*, p. 41.

60. Korngold, *op. cit.*, p. 374.

61. *Memoir and Letters of Charles Sumner, op. cit.*, p. 319.

7 In Search of a Permanent Majority

THE REPUBLICANS HAD OPTED for a Reconstruction program based on Negro suffrage. The question was whether they could make it work.

If Negro suffrage should prove inadequate for establishing a Republican stronghold in the South, the Democrats would fall heir to most of that region's votes in the Congress and in the Electoral College. And, since Negroes now were counted fully, the number of southern votes would be vastly augmented. If the southern representatives who returned to the halls of Congress were members of the Democratic Party, they would then join with their colleagues in the North to wrest control of the national government from the Republicans. In this event much recent legislation aimed at speeding the economic development of the East and West might be jeopardized. This legislation included the protective tariff, railroad land grants, and the national banking system, policies considered essential to the country's continued growth and prosperity. Public policy and party advantage were therefore closely intertwined.

The Republicans were therefore prepared to take any steps necessary to make their Reconstruction program succeed. Thus the situation in which they found themselves after they had stripped President Johnson of his last remaining power was rife with irony. The North had undertaken the recent war to preserve the Union and to uphold the Constitution; now it was to find itself forced to delay the re-establish-

ment of the first and to trod lightly over the latter. Just prior
to the war, many Republicans had condemned President
James Buchanan for exerting political pressure on the Supreme Court in the Dred Scott Case; now many Republicans
were themselves to put pressure on the nation's highest tri-
bunal. They were, moreover, to demand of the South what in
their own northern states they were unwilling to concede: the
civil, political, and social equality of the Negro.

Many of the steps that the Republicans took, once they
launched their program, went against the nation's historical,
legal, and moral grain. Many in the party were disturbed by
these highhanded actions, but they kept their criticisms to
themselves, at least initially, for they were unable to come forward with a more satisfactory plan. Unique conditions, they
told themselves, required unique solutions. The logic of
events had forced the Republicans to build their Reconstruction program around the principle of Negro suffrage. Once
committed to that policy, they had to try to make it work as
well as possible.

For the next quarter-century—in fact, until the election
of President William McKinley in 1896—the Republican
Party found its own fate intricately linked with the success of
that policy. From time to time, it would abandon that policy,
hoping to form a more effective alliance with the old southern
leadership instead; but eventually, when such an alternative
policy proved a failure, as it inevitably did, the Republicans
were forced to turn once more and place their hopes on the
Negro. This search by the Republicans for some means by
which they could bring the Civil War to a final conclusion
without endangering their control of the national government
was the major theme of American politics from the passage
of the Reconstruction Acts until the end of the century.

The basis for a Republican Party in the South was to be
the recently freed Negroes, now secured in their right to vote,
but the hopes of the Party went beyond this one group alone.
In the several decades prior to the Civil War, the southern
Democrats' chief opposition had come from the Whigs, the
political heirs of the old Federalist tradition. Like their

counterparts in the North, the southern Whigs drew their support primarily from the affluent members of the community who were likely to be interested in internal improvements such as railroad promotion.

The southern Whigs had tried to prevent the disruption of the Union, and in the months following Lincoln's election they had continued to oppose any move toward secession in their own home states. But when open conflict came and they were forced to choose between loyalty to their country and loyalty to their state, many of them, like Robert E. Lee, decided to choose their state. Many soon achieved prominence in the new Confederate government, just as earlier many had achieved prominence in the Democratic Party. With the war over, however, they were eager to reach some sort of understanding with the Republican Party in the North. In this they were joined by those Whigs who had not renounced their loyalty to the federal government and had become leading southern Unionists, aiding the northern war effort whenever circumstances permitted.

Except for one issue, the Southern Whigs had every reason to support the Republican Party; many one-time northern Whigs were, in fact, now prominent in its councils. On questions affecting internal improvements, railroad land grants, and a favorable environment for private property, the southern Whigs and northern Republicans were as one. Only on the issue of the Negro's future status were they still divided, and on this issue the southern Whigs now seemed ready to make certain concessions. Most of them had already accepted the fact that slavery could not be restored; now they were coming to realize that some form of suffrage would have to be extended to the Negro. As James L. Alcorn, the Mississippi Whig leader, had already warned, unless the South won over the friendship of the Negro, its path would lie "through a way red with blood and damp with tears." Although he earlier opposed secession, Alcorn had been a general in the Confederate armies. He told his fellow Mississippians, "I propose to vote with [the Negro]; to discuss political affairs with him; to sit, if need be, in political counsel with him . . . to pluck our common liberty and our common prosperity out of the jaws of inevitable ruin."[1] One of the richest of the Mississippi Delta planters, Alcorn realized that even if the Negroes did obtain the right to vote, he and the other large landholders would still be able to control them. In many of the other southern states Whigs were coming around to a similar view.

There was one other group on whom the Republicans could count, a group which, along with the one-time southern Whigs, would supply the leadership for the Negro masses. These were men born in the North who, through various ways, had found their way South. Some had served in the Union armies, had liked the land over which they fought, and had decided to settle there after the war. Others had resigned military commissions to take posts in the Freedmen's Bureau. Some had even come before the war, lured by the South's need for professional men. After the war others were attracted by the manifold opportunities. Because the straitened circumstances of so many southerners, some of the richest cotton-growing lands in the world could be purchased on extremely favorable terms. Valuable coal and iron lands could also be obtained at rock-bottom prices. There were also political opportunities. Loyal unionists were in great demand to staff the numerous federal offices throughout the South, and who could better fill them than transplanted Yankees? Whatever reason brought large numbers of northerners to the South, they seemed sure to align themselves with the Republican Party, regardless of their previous political affiliation, for the fulfillment of their own ambitions depended to a large extent on Republican power in the South.

With the support of these three groups Republican regimes were in fact soon established throughout the South. This was done primarily through the several military commanders appointed under the Reconstruction Acts, who proceeded to draw up lists of eligible voters, excluding all those who had ever served under the Confederate government. The standards that were to be applied were never spelled out, and so each registrar became something of a law unto himself. Since the military governments were considered extralegal, no appeal was possible. In this way, approximately 150,000 southerners were struck from the voting rolls. When it was found that the disenfranchised included many of the old southern Whigs, there was considerable embarrassment in the North, and Congress was forced to enact the first of several successive amnesty laws.

Once the electorate had been purged in this way, state conventions were called and delegates elected to draft new constitutions, this time guaranteeing Negroes the right to vote. The revised organic laws contained many democratic features copied from the constitutions of various northern states. These included provisions for the establishment of free public schools and the abolition of imprisonment for debt, both features that subsequent regimes would retain.

When the work of drafting these new constitutions was completed, the next task was to secure their ratification at the polls. Here the secondary instrument for implementing Republican policy in the South came to the fore. The Union League of America had been organized in Philadelphia early during the war to counteract prosouthern feeling in the North, and later its agents, infiltrating the South, consolidated local resistance to Confederate authority. When the war was over, the League had turned its attention more directly to the Negroes. As early as May, 1865, Chief Justice Salmon P. Chase, after a tour of the South at President Johnson's behest, had reported that "everywhere throughout the country colored citizens are organizing Union Leagues." Within two years every southern state had its local chapters; South Carolina alone had eighty-eight. The League's white organizers, aided by employees of the Freedmen's Bureau, first initiated prospective Negro members into the secrets and rituals of the group and then, in the words of one organizer, began "their quiet instruction . . . into their rights and duties."[2]

The Union League's membership in the South was primarily Negro, but it included many whites, particularly in the larger southern cities where the Union League club was the rallying point for local Republicans, The leadership, especially at the higher levels, however, was primarily white. The head of the Union League in Alabama, for example, was John Keffer, a white Pennsylvanian who reported directly to the wealthy Philadelphia capitalists who paid his expenses. What had thus been fashioned was a highly effective political machine, controlled by northern Republican interests and capable of mobilizing large numbers of Negro voters. Though new to the South, it was similar to the machine that had long been used in the North to organize the immigrant vote. It was this political machine which was expected to provide the margins necessary to secure ratification of the new state constitutions. Since the 1868 presidential elections were fast approaching, the Republicans were in some hurry.

In seven of the ten southern states still remaining outside the Union, the Republicans were able to bring about a speedy ratification, though not without difficulty. In Alabama, for instance, the new state constitution was initially defeated because, although the majority of the votes cast were in favor of it, so many white voters stayed away from the polls in protest that it failed to win the approval of 50 per cent of the electorate as required under the Reconstruction statutes. Congress promptly remedied this situation, however, by repealing the 50 per cent requirement. Mississippi, meanwhile, rejected the constitution outright, while in Virginia and Texas the Republican leaders were so unsure of their control that they preferred not to risk an election. The seven states that did approve their new constitutions and the Fourteenth Amendment were quickly readmitted to the Union, and their newly elected representatives were seated.

The new governments that came to power in these seven states seemed to confirm the soundness of the Republicans' Reconstruction policies. All seven owed their loyalty to the national Party, one-time southern Whigs and transplanted northerners sharing the power in varying proportions. In South Carolina, for example, one of the two United States Senators was a graduate of the state college, class of 1843, a local planter and, after the war, a businessman in Columbia. The speaker of the state House, also a native South Carolinian, was the son of a former state Chief Justice. As secretary to the secessionist governor in 1861, he had gained notoriety by raising the Confederate flag over Fort Sumter after its federal garrison had capitulated. The other United States Senator and the newly elected governor were both transplanted northerners. The former had come to Charleston before the war to head the state normal school, while the latter had been a general in the Union armies, later serving as head of the Freedmen's Bureau in South Carolina. In some of the states, such as Georgia and North Carolina, old-line Whigs seemed to have the greater voice; in others, such as Louisiana and Florida, transplanted northerners seemed to be the dominant factor. But, whatever the case, the two groups worked together to assure Republican control.

Though it was mainly their votes which had put the Republicans in power, the Negroes played only a minor role in all but a few of the southern states. In South Carolina their influence was probably greatest: From the very beginning they formed a majority in the lower House, but later, even when a Negro lieutenant governor presided over the state Senate, effective control rested in the hands of whites. This was also true in Louisiana, even though Negroes held such high elective posts as lieutenant governor and state treasurer. Forty-two Negroes also sat in the Louisiana legislature, but they were far too few to command a majority. In the other newly admitted states, the Negroes had even less influence. Their representation in the various legislatures was much smaller, and they controlled hardly any important offices. Still, the dominant white groups were careful to make concessions to the Negroes, for it was recognized that their votes were essential for sustaining the Republican regimes in power.

While northern Republicans had every reason to be cheered by the gains they were making in the South, it was mainly the presidency in which they were interested. Here, too, their Reconstruction policies seemed to be a success. With General Ulysses S. Grant as their candidate in 1868 the Republicans captured 214 out of the 294 electoral votes cast. The Democratic candidate, Horatio Seymour, had attacked his

opponents for subjecting the South to "military despotism
and negro supremacy,"[3] but the Republicans still won handily
and at the same time managed to retain control of both
Houses of Congress. The electoral votes of several newly admitted southern states added significantly to Grant's winning
margin. Four years later, when Grant ran for re-election, the
Republicans did even better, garnering 286 out of the 352
electoral votes cast, despite the fact that a large number of dis-
affected Republicans had joined forces with the Democrats.
Two years earlier Virginia and Mississippi had finally been
readmitted to the Union with Republican state governments,
and the electoral votes of those two states had added to Grant's
margin.

But even at the height of the Republican Party's power, a
closer look at the election returns would have revealed certain
ominous signs. Grant's popular margin in 1868, despite the
fact that he had run as a widely acclaimed wartime military
commander, was only 300,000 votes. Four years later his
margin had increased to 750,000 votes, but he had lost the
electoral votes of several southern states: Texas, also readmitted in 1870, Georgia, Kentucky, Maryland, and Missouri.
The unusually prosperous times had resulted in Grant's receiving the North's entire electoral vote, but prosperous times
would not last forever. When they finally did come to an end,
the Democrats could be expected to pick up strength in the
North. Then the Republican Party's strength in the South
would become even more important.

But several events were eroding the Republican position
in the South. Already the Republicans had not been able to
muster the same strength in Georgia as in some of the other
southern states, and soon after Georgia was admitted to the
Union, the legislature voted to expel its Negro members.
Congress retaliated by refusing to seat one of the Georgia
Senators. When the legislature continued to defy Congress,
federal troops were ordered back into the state to complete
the unfinished task of Reconstruction. Twenty-two Democrats
found sitting in the legislature, despite the fact that they had
been disenfranchised under the Fourteenth Amendment, were

themselves expelled and their places taken by loyal Republicans, including the three Negroes previously unseated. By this means Republican rule in Georgia was firmly re-established.

But the Democrats had not been alone in voting to expel the Negro representatives. They had been joined by the moderate Republicans, previously the old Whig element. To them the sight of Negroes in the legislative halls had been too disturbing. The moderates had also broken with the more radical members of their party over the choice for United States Senator. With the help of the Democrats they had been able to elect a candidate of their own. The Democrats, by supporting the moderate Republicans, hoped to split the Republican coalition; and as time went on and the economic issues became subordinate, they were increasingly successful. They were helped by President Grant and his followers in Congress, who consistently favored the transplanted northerners in matters of patronage at the expense of the one-time Whigs. Once the question became, Is Georgia to be dominated by Negroes and northerners? the Republican Party was on the wane. For then the former Whigs had no choice but to desert the Republican Party, stripping it of even the outward appearance of local support.

Similar developments were taking place throughout the South. In Mississippi, for example, the Whigs from the start had been the dominant element within the Republican Party. They had elected Alcorn as governor and had then embarked upon a program of rebuilding the levees, providing state aid to railroads, reducing the tax on land, and hiring out state prisoners to assure adequate protection to the Negro. Alcorn's antipathy to northerners was well known, and they felt they did not receive a fair share of the state's offices. Moreover, while the Whigs seemed willing enough to promise political equality to the Negro, they did not make more than a token effort in that direction. Therefore when Alcorn resigned as governor in 1873 to take a seat in the United States Senate, the transplanted northerners and the Negroes joined forces to nominate their own candidate on the Republican ticket.

He was Adelbert Ames, a native of Maine, an ardent supporter of equal rights for Negroes, and the son-in-law of Benjamin Butler, a leading radical Republican in Congress. Stung by the refusal of the Republican convention to name his candidate for the position, Alcorn decided to run for governor himself on an independent ticket. This time the Democrats backed the more radical faction in their effort to split the Republican party. With their support, as well as the active backing of President Grant, Ames was easily elected governor, and the Whigs began drifting slowly back into the Democratic fold.

It was not only through political maneuver that the Republican coalition was whittled down. Great social and economic pressure was also brought to bear. Anyone who called himself a Republican was ostracized by the great majority of southern whites. Those who had only recently come to the South were derisively called "carpetbaggers," supposedly to point out how little they had brought with them. Those who were natives were even more disdainfully called "scalawags." But for carpetbaggers or scalawags the treatment was the same. A young native of New Jersey, moving to South Carolina to take up duties as assistant to a state senator who was himself a transplanted northerner, found that he and his young bride were almost universally regarded as social pariahs. He wrote, "South Carolinians from low-lying plantations . . . made us realize that we were undesirables. In the [hotel] dining room we were demonstrably shunned, without any advances on our part to provoke it; and on one occasion, as my wife went up a stairway she met two South Carolina ladies coming down. They drew close to the wall lest gown touch gown across the wide space from wall to banister."[4] Like many others who had come South hoping to make their home there, he was finally forced to leave the region forever.

The pressure was relentless. In Canton, Mississippi, the *Mail* published the names of those white citizens who were henceforth to be avoided by "every true woman." In other cities the methods were more informal but no less effective. There was only one escape other than to leave the South. A prominent native southerner told a Negro leader that he was leaving the Republican Party for the sake of his family. "No white man can live in the South in the future and act with any other than the Democratic party," he said, "unless he is willing and prepared to live a life of social isolation and remain in political oblivion."[5] Those who refused to make the apostasy were denounced as "obnoxious radicals." But even the vilest carpetbagger could become a respected citizen and later hold high public office if he switched his party allegiance. In the face of such pressure, many southern Republicans succumbed.

Other kinds of pressure, especially those applied to Negroes, were more violent. Throughout the South the whites organized themselves into bands of night riders, known variously as the Knights of the White Camellia, the White Brotherhood, the Council of Safety, and the '76 Association, but most commonly as the Ku Klux Klan. Swooping down under cover of darkness, they attempted through intimidation to prevent Negroes from exercising their newly won voting rights. Often they went further. In South Carolina a group of about forty whites gathered one night in 1871 and proceeded to the home of a local Negro leader. According to the attorney who later prosecuted the case, they "broke in his door, took him out, fastened a rope about his neck, took him to the woods near by, and hung him till he was dead." That same night, "they visited divers other houses of colored people, threatened them, took them out, robbed them of their arms, and informed them that, if they should vote again, they would be killed. . . ."[6] Whipping recalcitrant Negroes was quite common, and even whites were not immune.

Union League organizers and former Freedmen's Bureau officials in particular were favorite targets of the Klan. As one southern editor declared in 1868, "If to every tree in our forest-like streets were attached a rope; and to the ends of each rope a Northern or Southern Radical, gathered from the Loyal League assembled in our courthouse, then might we once more live in peace and harmony."[7] Those who performed the actual deeds of violence for the Klan were gen-

erally young men of low origins with little or no education.
But directing them, in the higher reaches of the secret organization, were many of the leading citizens of the South,
ex-Confederate officers and prominent members of the Democratic Party. They were determined to break the grip of the
Republican Party in the South, and in their eyes violence was
justified by the need to protect southern culture against the
alien horde.

Since the Klan had widespread support among the South's
whites, Republican state officials found it extremely difficult
to suppress its activities. Here federal troops were of little
help. Greatly reduced in number since the Civil War and
confined for the most part to regular army posts, they were
inadequate to counteract the growing terror. Therefore the
Republican state governments throughout the South, as soon
as they came to power, appealed to Congress to repeal the
law forbidding the former Confederate states to organize their
own militias. When Congress assented, Republican-controlled
militia forces were frantically formed in many of the southern
states. Negroes were openly invited to join, but this merely
sharpened the racial conflict and militia members themselves
soon became the targets of Klan violence.

The state militias were able to police the major cities and,
during election periods, some of the rural areas, but were
unable to protect the Negroes in outlying regions against the
Klan. Republican leaders in the South appealed to President
Grant who sent Congress a special message requesting specific
legislation to deal with the situation. Its concern aroused,
Congress voted to strengthen federal control over elections,
giving federal courts the power to appoint election supervisors
and making interference with them a federal offense.

Congress followed this with the enactment of an even more
stringent law, known as the Ku Klux Act. This gave the
President the right to suspend the writ of *habeas corpus* and
declare martial law whenever a southern state proved unable
or unwilling to protect its colored citizens. The measure was
opposed even by certain Republicans, but it was reluctantly
passed. It was, in a sense, the next logical step in the Re-

publicans' continuing efforts to force the South to accept
Negro suffrage, efforts that had already included enactment
of the Fifteenth Amendment and several Reconstruction Acts.

In certain rural counties in South Carolina, the President
actually suspended the writ of *habeas corpus* and declared
martial law. Many persons were arrested, and some Klan
members were even convicted when they were brought to the
larger cities and tried before juries composed of Negroes and
white Republicans. But the leaders were not convicted, and
when arrests were also made in North Carolina and Mississippi, juries would not convict even the rank and file. The
members of the Klan who were arrested refused to reveal
who their leaders were, and others in the white community
were no more helpful. Thus, this attempt to use the army to
implement Republican policy in the South failed to break
the back of the Ku Klux Klan or even to halt the drive by the
Democrats to regain political power. It merely delayed temporarily the counter-restoration.

The Democratic leaders were engaged in the deadly serious game of testing the North's resolve. They were determined
to rid the South of Republican and radical influence, but
they knew that they had to proceed cautiously. Rash southern
acts had already resulted in massive federal intervention.
Nevertheless the Republican base of support in the South was
slowly but surely being eroded. More and more transplanted
northerners and one-time Whigs were finding it expedient
either to switch over to the Democratic Party or leave the
South entirely; more and more the Negroes were becoming
too intimidated to vote. The Republican regimes were becoming increasingly isolated.

The nature of these regimes did not enhance their political popularity. Many were quite frankly dedicated to narrow
class interests. Throughout the South taxes had been greatly
increased in order to erect public works, encourage railroad
construction, and pay off the mounting state debts. It made
no difference that the money often went to maintain the state
credit, to provide urgently needed improved means of transportation, and to establish for the first time schools and other

public institutions, all of which were essential to the South's further industrial growth. Many small landowners knew only that their taxes had been increased at a time when they were having personal financial trouble and for this reason alone opposed the various Republican regimes.

Another factor making for opposition was that the state governments had become greatly centralized, with local authority undermined. Many of the governors had been given extraordinary powers, including the right to order out the militia and appoint most local officials. The legislatures could for only slight cause declare any office vacant and fill it as they wished. Most significant, boards appointed by the governor could go over the ballots and determine which should be counted. These provisions, greatly concentrating political power in the hands of the state governments, had been specifically written into the constitutions in order to buttress Republican rule. But they were provisions easily abused, and many native southerners considered them an undue restriction of their political liberties.

In addition, many of the state governments seemed blatantly corrupt. Public offices were frequently sold to the highest bidder, and it became almost impossible to transact even minor public business without paying off some political figure. To compensate for this extra expense, many contractors had no hesitancy in padding their bills. The cost of government thus reached previously unheard of heights as a favored few received extremely profitable contracts. Florida, for example, paid more for printing in 1869 than it had for its entire government nine years earlier. Construction contracts were awarded and railroad franchises granted with a similar show of favoritism and lack of regard for the public interest. Often, however, it was the minor forms of graft which rankled most. South Carolina's legislators, sitting in a state house which had cost $200,000 to refurbish when it should only have cost $18,000, voted to reimburse the Speaker of the House for $1,000 lost in a horse race. One governor, while drunk, was persuaded by a burlesque performer to sign a new issue of railroad bonds. In Louisiana the senators and representatives, as well as the clerk, sergeant-at-arms, doorkeeper, and page, received an average of $113.50 a day for "traveling and other expenses" while the legislature was in session.

This state of affairs, however, did not mean that only the Republican state governments in the South were corrupt. The Republican administrations in the North or the Democratic regimes that succeeded them in the South also left much to be desired. These were the Grant years, when corruption was rife even at the national seat of power.

The Republicans in the South were caught in a dilemma. As their base of popular support narrowed, they were forced more and more to rely on those who had some special narrow interest to advance, and in the process they would inevitably alienate others.

Moreover, their hopes of retaining power in the South depended to a large extent on the support of that region's colored citizens. To assure that support, it was necessary to make at least a token gesture toward Negro equality. But this would alienate large numbers of the party's southern white supporters, whether one-time Whigs or recently arrived northerners. For no white man could long survive in the South without positively affirming his belief in the doctrine of white supremacy. The few who tried were either killed or driven from the South. The others simply ignored whatever qualms they might have had and went along with their neighbors. On political and economic issues white men might divide, but on race questions, not. As time went on, southern whites found it more and more difficult to remain within the Republican Party. And as they began to drift away from the party, Republicans were forced to rely more and more on their Negro supporters.

Thus it was the question of race that finally came to distinguish the two parties. Once the issue was drawn in so sharp a manner, the Republican Party in the South was finished. The whites could not and would not support it. The Negroes alone were insufficient to sustain it. In 1869 the Republicans were finally driven from power in Tennessee, and a year later they were unseated in Georgia, North

Carolina, and Virginia. It seemed only a matter of time before the other Republican regimes in the South, now sustained
mainly by federal power, would also be overthrown.

Meanwhile, many persons in the North were growing
disillusioned with the Republicans' Reconstruction policies
and their attendant consequences. There were dissidents even
within the Republican Party. They were disturbed particularly by the corruption of the Grant Administration and by
its strong-arm policy toward the South. The two were closely
linked. Carl Schurz had had first-hand acquaintance with the
way in which Republican politicians manipulated Negro
votes in Missouri. As early as 1870 Horace Greeley had written
in the columns of his New York *Tribune* that it was time to
"have done with Reconstruction." The country, he added, "is
. . . sick of it. So long as any State is held in abeyance, it will
be plausibly urged that the Republicans are afraid to trust
the people. Let us give every State to herself."[8]

Many of the leading magazines were also becoming dis-
affected with the Republicans' southern policies. Most vocal
was the *Nation,* founded by E. L. Godkin during the war
as an antislavery organ. Soon after Grant had been elected
and the Fifteenth Amendment specifically guaranteeing
Negroes the right to vote had been ratified, it called for an
end to all further efforts in the freedmen's behalf, pointing
out that "there is no political machinery to protect ignorance
and inexperience completely against skill, vigor, and un-
scrupulousness, and the Southern whites boast the possession
of all three."[9] Then, at the height of the Ku Klux Klan's
activities, it took the position that the wisest procedure was
"to leave every Southern state to its own people."[10] If the
Negroes were treated badly in the South, the *Nation* argued,
in the vein of its laissez-faire beliefs, they would soon quit
that region and the southern states that needed their labor
would thus pay a penalty. The *Nation* was not opposed to
the attempts of the federal government to deal with the Klan.
But it felt it was unwise to pass laws without providing the
men and funds to enforce them. Godkin did hint, however,
that he would not have liked to see the federal government

provide those men and funds. "Even though a man fights for his country, as the Negro did," the *Nation* said, "the nation owes him nothing. Far more important is the Constitution and its limitations on central authority."[11]

Like the editor of the *Nation,* many northerners who at one time had strongly supported the efforts to protect the southern Negro now began to defect. Without deep prejudice themselves, they were for the most part public-spirited citizens who wanted only what they thought best for the country. But when they saw where radical Reconstruction was leading the nation, they balked. They balked at keeping the memories of the recent conflict alive, at the federal government's exercising such detailed control over the states, at the high cost of maintaining federal troops in the South, and at making the Negro a permanent ward of the government. Above all else, they balked at the corruption that was part and parcel of radical Reconstruction.

Other northerners had more practical reasons for opposing the Republicans' Reconstruction policies. The merchants and manufacturers with commercial interests in the South complained that the continuing political turmoil was bad for business. The "western expansionists" considered it a mistake to devote so much energy to the South and to the Negro; in their eyes, the country's destiny lay between the Mississippi and the Pacific, and it was there that the nation ought to focus its attention. Others in the North were completely without sympathy for the Negro. Soon after the Civil War, the American correspondent for the London *Spectator* had described their attitude. He wrote that loathing for the negro "pervades all classes here. . . ." He said that people feared that "if political privileges are given to the negro, political position and social intercourse must inevitably follow. The negro at the ballot box means the negro in Congress, in all public places, in the parlor, at the table, in the marriage bed."[12] Since that had been written, anti-Negro feeling in the North had grown even stronger.

These various divergent forces, sharing only a common antipathy for the Republicans' Reconstruction policies, joined together in 1872 to support Greeley as their presidential candidate. From the Republican ranks, besides Greeley himself, came Schurz, Chief Justice Salmon P. Chase, Senator Lyman Trumbull of Illinois, former United States Ambassador to Great Britain, Charles Francis Adams, and others. Forming their own Liberal Republican Party, they drafted a platform that demanded "immediate and absolute removal of all disabilities imposed on account of the Rebellion." The platform proclaimed the belief that "local self-government, with impartial suffrage, will guard the rights of all citizens more securely than any centralized power."[13] Democrats, whose only hope of victory lay in uniting behind Greeley, also nominated him as their presidential candidate. But with times so prosperous, few persons in the North were willing to risk a change in administration. Grant won.

In 1873, however, the worst depression the country had ever known set in. With the arrival of bad times came increased hostility toward the Republicans' Reconstruction policies as well as the other aspects of the Grant Administration. As one northerner described the attitude of the people in his part of the country during the bitter year of 1874, "hard times and heavy taxes make them wish the 'nigger,' 'everlasting nigger,' were in ———— or Africa. It is amazing the change that has taken place in the last two years of public sentiment."[14] The elections that year bore witness to the shift in mood. In what amounted to a virtually Democratic sweep, the Republicans lost eighty-five seats in the House as well as control of that branch for the first time since the Civil War. Their losses in the Senate were not as great, but only because of the indirect method by which Senators were still chosen. Even if the Republicans still had the will to make their Reconstruction policies work, they no longer had the votes.

As his second term neared its end, President Grant became increasingly reluctant to bring federal power to bear to prevent the southern Democrats from returning to power. When in 1875 Governor Ames of Mississippi requested that federal troops be sent to Mississippi to bolster his faltering regime, the President turned the request aside with the comment, "The whole public are tired of the annual autumnal outbursts in the South."[15] With the support of the national government denied, the Republican regime in Mississippi soon collapsed. That same year the Democrats took over in Texas; they had already gained power the year before in Alabama and Arkansas. This left only Florida, South Carolina, and Louisiana still under Republican rule, and it seemed only a question of time before they, too, would slip into the Democratic column. It was now quite clear that whoever succeeded Grant as head of the Republican Party would have to devise a new policy for dealing with the South.

As their presidential candidate in 1876, the Republicans chose Ohio governor Rutherford B. Hayes, a long-time supporter of his party's Reconstruction policies. As early as 1866, while still a Representative, he had warned the South not to be deceived by Andrew Johnson, telling its leaders that the congressional plan of Reconstruction offered "the best terms you will ever get—and they should be promptly accepted."[16] Campaigning for nomination as governor in 1867, he had fully endorsed radical Reconstruction, and a year later, when his party nominated Grant for president, he warmly supported the Republican candidate as one who "has begun the work of reconstruction in a masterly way and with marked success." Even as late as 1871 he said that "the Administration is right on the South and the Democracy wrong."[17] Soon after, however, Hayes became alienated by Grant's policies and began to consider himself a Liberal Republican. Like Greeley, he began to favor a milder policy toward the South, and to question the wisdom of radical Reconstruction, although as far as the public knew, he still supported the Republicans' policies.

As soon as Hayes was nominated as presidential candidate, he came under increasing pressure to declare his intention of pursuing a milder policy toward the South. A leading journalist in the North advised him to promise not to interfere with the affairs of that region "except when the clearest and extremist necessity demanded it," while Schurz urged him to declare that "the Constitutional rights of self-government must be respected." But Hayes was unwilling to go that far. He said that the phrase, "local self-government [seemed] to smack of the bowie knife and revolver." It "has nullified the Fifteenth Amendment in several states, and is in a fair way to nullify the Fourteenth and Thirteenth." He was willing to promise the South "honest and capable local government," free of federal interference, but only on condition that the whites respect the Negroes' political and civil rights. Hayes made these terms known to the South when he publicly announced his acceptance of the Republican nomination.[18]

Despite this hint of a milder policy toward the South, the Republicans ran on the same "bloody shirt" platform in 1876 as before. Ever since the Civil War they had found that the surest appeal to the voters of the North was to charge their Democratic opponents with being the party of treason and then to cite the latest reports of violence in the South as evidence that the Democrats were still trying to undo the results of the great conflict. During the campaign Hayes himself made few public statements, but he gave the strategy his private support. This stategy, however, seemed to have lost its effectiveness. Samuel J. Tilden, the Democratic candidate, received 4,300,590 votes; Hayes only 4,036,298. The Republican nominee believed he had lost the election. "I don't care for myself," he said the day after the election, "and the party, yes, and the country, too, can stand it, but I do care for the poor colored men of the South. . . . The result will be that the Southern people will practically treat the constitutional amendments as nullities, and then the colored man's fate will be worse than when he was in slavery . . ."[19]

But Hayes had been ready to concede defeat too soon. Although Tilden had captured a majority of the popular vote and even led in the Electoral College, the results in the three southern states, still under Republican rule, were still in doubt. In all three states the Republicans controlled the returning boards which had to certify the election results, and in all three states they certified their own party's slate. When the Democrats challenged their decisions, it was up to Congress to decide the matter. The Constitution simply declared:

"The President of the Senate shall, in the presence of the Senate and House of Representatives, open all the certificates and the votes shall then be counted." It did not specify, however, whether the Senate or the House would actually do the counting, a crucial matter since the first was controlled by Republicans and the second by Democrats. Throughout the winter months the controversy raged.

As the history books reveal, the crisis was finally overcome when the southern Democrats agreed to support Hayes, as part of a larger compromise. Hayes promised, in return, to withdraw the Federal troops from the South, thus permitting the Democrats to oust the remaining carpetbagger regimes.

As C. Vann Woodward has made clear in his important study *Reunion and Reaction,* this bargain was actually part of a much larger compromise, involving the same southern Whigs on whom the Republicans had once placed their hopes of reconstructing the South. Though they had once again risen to positions of power as Democrats, they felt uncomfortable within a party dedicated mainly to the interests of the northern working classes and the southern yeoman farmers. A former southern Unionist wrote of them: "I find that I was right in calculating upon these old union Whigs who pursued the same course that I did during the war, but went over to the Democracy upon the questions involved in the reconstruction or because of occurrences since. I have known for the last three years that they were dissatisfied with their party affiliations and were held to them only because they could see no satisfactory place to go to."[20]

These southerners were increasingly at odds with the party over a number of specific issues. Though it was they who supplied the bulk of the Democratic vote, it was the northerners who dictated Party policies. This was particularly true in the case of internal improvements. Since the Civil War more federal funds had been spent on internal improvements in New York state alone than in the entire South. Now that the Democrats were in power, the South wanted its fair share and came forward with a detailed program of public works, designed to rescue the South from its economic depression.

But when the southerners sought congressional approval for these projects, they found that the northern members of their Party were opposed. The Democrats had campaigned on a platform of "Retrenchment and Reform," and the northerners who controlled the party through their congressional seniority were determined to carry out that pledge. What little support the South received in its quest for federal funds to finance internal improvements came from the Republicans.

The same had happened to another measure urgently desired by the southern Whigs, repeal of the Southern Homestead Act. This law, enacted in 1866, had set aside over 47 million acres of public lands for occupancy by small homesteaders, including freedmen. In the ten years the law was in effect more homesteading took place in the South, proportionate to the land available, than in any other area of the nation. The southern Whigs much preferred to see the public lands thrown open to speculators and large holders, such as themselves. Again it was the northern Democrats who blocked their way and the Republicans who finally provided the votes necessary to bring about the law's repeal in 1876.

Thus the stage was set for a rapprochement between the dissatisfied southern Democrats and the Republicans who were casting about for some means of retaining their control over the national government. Hayes and his advisors wished to have the support of the southern Democrats in order to insure a Republican administration in Washington, four years later if not sooner. The ex-Whigs sought assurances that a Republican President would abandon Grant's policy of favoring radical northerners in the South at the expense of native whites. They also hoped to gain Republican support for an extensive program of public works throughout their region. If he wished to develop allies in the South, Hayes was told, "avoid the carpetbaggers . . . and address yourself to the material and Industrial interests of the South."[21] Hayes indicated his willingness: "Assure any of our Southern friends that I am impressed with the necessity of a complete change of man and policy. . . . This, more fully interpreted means, not only the entire right of self-government, but also a large and liberal policy in respect to matters of internal improvements."[22] Hayes laid down only one condition: if control of their states were turned over to them, the conservative Democrats would have to promise not to mistreat the Negroes.

Aware that his party's Reconstruction policies were no longer capable of assuring continued Republican rule in Washington, Hayes now sought to shift the basis of its support in the South. The transplanted northerners were to be jettisoned and the Negroes abandoned to the promised mercy of the old planter class. In this way, it was hoped, the southern Whigs might once and for all be wedded to the Republican Party, and the mistake President Grant had made in supporting the "carpetbagger" Adelbert Ames over the "scalawag" James Alcorn as Republican leader in Mississippi finally be rectified. "It is very thoroughly understood here by Southern men," the New York *Herald's* Washington correspondent reported reliably on February 15, 1877, "that Mr. Hayes means, if he should become President, to cut adrift from the carpet-baggers and make an alliance with respectable party leaders of Whig antecedents in the South."[23]

After several years, when the odium that clung to the Republican Party in the South had disappeared, these one-time Whigs would be able to announce formally their new party allegiance. Then the Republican Party would become a truly national organization. In fashioning his new policy toward the South, Hayes was thinking even more of the future than the present.

Many Republicans were skeptical of this change in Party direction. They saw little to be gained from giving up the only source of Party strength south of the Mason-Dixon line in exchange for a vague promise of Whig support in the future. And many of them had qualms about abandoning the Party faithful in the South. In a public letter, James Blaine expressed his "profoundest sympathies" for the ousted Republican leaders in South Carolina and Louisiana, while

Benjamin Wade, the one-time Ohio Senator who had seconded Hayes' nomination at the 1876 Republican convention, lamented the plight of the Negro. "I feel that to have emancipated these people and that to leave them unprotected would be a crime as infamous as to have reduced them to slavery when they were free," he said. "And for Hayes to do this to the men who had at the hazard of their lives given him the votes without which he could never have had the power to do this terrible injustice! No doubt he meditates the destruction of the party that elected him."[24] But, despite this opposition within his own ranks, Hayes proceeded with his plan to transform the basis of the Republican Party in the South.

Soon after being sworn into office, Hayes took the first step toward implementing his part of the recent bargain by naming as his Postmaster General David Key of Tennessee, the first southerner to hold a Cabinet appointment since the Civil War. This was not a small gesture, since Key would control one of the most important sources of federal patronage. There then followed the withdrawal of federal troops from South Carolina and Louisiana, the last two states where army bayonets were still being used to implement Reconstruction policy. Finally, in his inaugural address, Hayes mentioned that federal funds might be provided for public works in the South. After taking these initial steps, Hayes made a tour of the South accompanied by his Postmaster General, in an effort to rally southern Democrats behind his Administration.

On this trip he also sought to convince the Negroes that his policies would, in the long run, best serve their interests. In Atlanta Hayes told a Negro audience that their "rights and interests would be safer if this great mass of intelligent white men were let alone by the general Government." The audience, according to newspaper accounts, responded with "immense enthusiasm and cheering for several minutes."[25] At Nashville Hayes stated his belief that "the majority of people of the South—the white people of the South—have no desire to invade the rights of the colored people."[26] He pointed to the example of Wade Hampton, newly installed as Governor of South Carolina following the withdrawal of federal troops.

Hampton was acting—as Hayes hoped all southern leaders would—with consideration, understanding, and tolerance for the Negro. He promised the colored citizens of his state equal justice, better schools, protection from white racists, and appointment to minor offices.

Meanwhile, James Garfield, Hayes' chief lieutenant in the House, was expressing the hope that the day was not too far distant when "the constitutional rights of the negro shall be as safe in the hands of one party as it is in the other; and that thus in the south as in the north men may seek their party associates on the great commercial and industrial questions rather than on questions of race and color."[27]

To accomplish this political sleight of hand, however, proved more difficult. Northern Republicans continued to criticize the abandonment of the carpetbagger regimes in the South, while many southerners complained that Hayes was not moving quickly enough to fulfill his promises to them. The President found himself more and more caught in the middle, unable to satisfy either group. In the fall of 1877, the first break between the northern Republicans and the southern Democrats followed the latter's failure to support Garfield for Speaker of the House. But the true test of Hayes' southern policy came in 1878. The southern conservatives had pledged to respect the Negroes' right to vote, but the congressional elections of that year revealed that they could not be trusted. Negroes were kept from the polls by every sort of pressure and coercion, including murder. Ballot boxes were stuffed in some localities, and in others Negro voters were forced to support the Democratic ticket. Of the 294 counties in the so-called black belt—those areas of the South where Negroes outnumbered the whites—only sixty-two went Republican, a decline of more than 50 per cent in two years. Counties that had gone Republican in 1876 now failed to record a single Republican vote. As a result, the Democrats for the first time since the Civil War won control of the Senate. They also increased their majority in the House. Surveying these election results, Hayes said unhappily, "I am reluctantly forced to admit that the experiment was a failure."[28]

There were several reasons for that failure. The continuing hard times had cost the Republicans many votes and had at the same time made the North unwilling to vote the South the federal funds it desired to finance internal improvements. Moreover, since the South had already accomplished its primary objective, the removal of the last remaining federal troops, it was less eager to bargain with the Republicans. Finally, the South's leaders had never believed that Hayes would insist on their protecting Negro voting rights, and in any case they were unwilling to jeopardize their own political control. The one-time Whigs, like the President, found themselves in a position in which it was difficult to maneuver. The realities of political life required that as Democrats they had to support their party's candidates, on whose success their own political fortunes depended. Moreover, they could not risk leaving the Democratic Party in the South. The race issue was still paramount, and anyone not calling himself a Democrat was suspect in the eyes of most southerners. Thus the one-time Whigs at most could lend assistance to the Republican Party only during presidential elections, and even then only covertly. These ambivalences do not make permanent, enduring political alliances.

The Republicans now understood this. Outraged by the recent election, they reverted to their previous policy toward the South. They accused that region's leaders of continuing disloyalty to the nation, of seeking to undo the results of the Civil War. They demanded that southern representation in Congress be reduced, that the election laws be enforced more vigorously. Even Hayes joined in the clamor. He called on Republicans to defeat any candidate "unless he will undertake to carry out in good faith the pledges made in all our platforms in regard to the rights of colored citizens; unless he will support laws providing the means required to punish crimes against them; and unless he will oppose the admission of any man to either house of Congress whose seat has been obtained by the violation of the Fifteenth Amendment. The right of suffrage," he said, "is the right of self-protection. Its free exercise is the vital air of republican institutions."[29] He asked for this, even though it meant his own political doom. For the Republicans, it was a return to the "bloody shirt."

On the basis of such an appeal, the Republicans nominated James Garfield for President in 1880, since Hayes had declared at the beginning of his Administration that he would not be a candidate for re-election. During his campaign Garfield had strongly exploited the sectional theme. "We shall stand by [the Negroes]," he had declared, "until the sun of liberty . . . shall shine with equal rays upon every man, white or black, throughout the Union."[30] But, like his predecessor, Garfield realized that such an appeal could not long continue to give the Republicans victory. He himself was elected with a majority of only 10,000 votes out of the nine million cast, less than 0.01 per cent of the total. Since Hayes' policy of reconciliation had proved a failure, Garfield was faced with the necessity of finding yet another alternative. Like his predecessor, he understood that time was required for resolving the southern problem in order that the salubrious effects of education and business expansion could make themselves felt. But before he could fully develop such a policy, an assassin's bullet struck him down.

His successor, Chester Arthur, also realized the necessity of formulating a new Republican policy for the South. Like Hayes, he recognized the need to abandon the fully discredited Republican organizations throughout that region, now composed mainly of federal officeholders and their Negro allies. But, whereas Hayes had sought to form an alliance with the one-time Whigs, Arthur sought to join forces with their bitter enemies, the Independent Democrats. Primarily economic radicals, the Independents had broken with the more conservative members of their party over such issues as the unlimited coinage of silver, national banks, Greenbacks, and the readjustment of state debts. They were certainly strange bedfellows for the head of the Republican Party, but as Arthur explained to a prominent Georgia Negro, "I have made up my mind that a permanently defeated Republican party is of little value in any State, North or South, and that if any respectable body of men wages war on the Bourbon Democracy, with reasonable prospects of success, it should be sustained."[31]

If such an alliance were to succeed, the Republican Party would have to turn its back on its colored followers in the South, for the Independents were for the most part unsympathetic toward the Negro. Though the Independents were concerned primarily with economic matters, the classes from which they drew their major support were sensitive on racial matters. Lacking the social position of the conservative Democrats, they were far more concerned with keeping the Negroes in their place. And, though their leaders might promise the Negroes fair treatment under the law, they themselves would not have tolerated any attempt to treat the Negroes as political equals. To win their support, it was necessary to soft pedal the racial question. This Arthur was fully prepared to do, despite his previous record as an avid waver of the "bloody flag."

In fact, he was the first President since the Civil War to ignore the issue in his formal messages. Throughout his Administration he consistently avoided speaking out in favor of civil rights for the southern Negro, despite several incidents which aroused widespread resentment in the North. Arthur was criticized as he attempted to pursue this new policy, but he was able to silence most of his detractors at least temporarily. Frederick Douglass, by now a party wheel horse wholly dependent on presidential patronage, defended Arthur's southern policy as a "decent movement looking to the abolition of the color line in American politics."[32]

The test of this new approach came in the 1883 election, fought primarily over local offices throughout the South. Again an election proved a sad revelation to a Republican President. The Democrats, employing the same extralegal methods as before, easily defeated the Independents, supported by the Republicans. In some areas of the South the Democrats' opponents were too intimidated even to attempt to vote. A riot in Danville, Virginia, resulted in the death of four Negroes, while in Hazelhurst, Mississippi, the white chairman of the county Republican Committee, defying a warning to stay away from the polls, was murdered. The Bourbons, however, did not rely solely on violence. Pointing out the support the Independents were receiving from the Republicans, they conjured up all the alleged evils of Black Reconstruction. In the face of such a specter, economic questions became secondary, and southern whites lined up almost as one behind the regular Democratic Party. Arthur's attempt to overcome the Republican Party's reputation as "nigger lovers" had not been successful. The stigma that remained had even rubbed off on those whom the Republicans supported. Again a Republican President, faced with the obvious failure of his policy to establish a new basis for the party in the South, reacted by resurrecting the "bloody shirt." An investigation of the "Alleged Election Outrages in Virginia and Mississippi" was ordered, and the results were reported with gusto throughout the North.

In 1884 the Republicans nominated as candidate for president James Blaine, a bitter political foe of Arthur. He had decided on still a different way of dealing with the South. Like Arthur, he was determined to ignore the existing Party organization, but, instead of favoring the economic radicals, he hoped to win the support of the South's emerging business groups by emphasizing the tariff and currency questions. He stated in his acceptance letter that the South needed "capital and occupation, not controversy." By voting the Democratic ticket, he said, southern businessmen were using "their Electoral votes to destroy their own future."[33] During the campaign in West Virginia Blaine made the new Republican policy even more explicit. Businessmen throughout the South, he said, are "all interested in a protective tariff, and the question is, which do they prefer, to gratify prejudice or to promote general prosperity!" West Virginia can "lead the way," he declared; "she can break this seemingly impregnable barrier of the Solid South . . . solid on what? Solid on prejudice, solid on a tradition, solid upon doctrines that separate the different portions of the Union." Blaine urged his listeners "to join in a union not merely in form, but a union in fact, and to take part in the solution of the industrial and financial problems of the time."[34]

The citizens of West Virginia voted in October, before most of the rest of the nation, and when his appeal failed to carry even that most industrialized of all southern states, Blaine became alarmed. During the last few weeks of his campaign, in a futile effort to turn the tide, he unfurled the Bloody Flag. Nevertheless, he lost to Grover Cleveland by a very narrow margin.

Benjamin Harrison, the Republican candidate four years later, became convinced that an appeal to the South on the same broad economic issues, while again downgrading the importance of the race issue, would this time be successful. In his letter accepting the nomination, Harrison, once an ardent supporter of Negro rights, declared that the "colored people do not ask special legislation in their interest." They desire only "the common rights of American citizenship."[35]

This time the Republicans seemed to have found the winning formula. Harrison was elected, and for the first time since 1872 the Republicans captured both houses of Congress. Most important, Harrison had made serious inroads into the Democratic Party's southern strength. Although he did not carry a single southern state, he came close in several, losing in Virginia by only 1,539 votes out of 304,093 cast and in West Virginia by only a slightly larger margin. In fact, Harrison received more southern votes than any other Republican candidate since the end of Reconstruction. It appeared that if the Republicans could continue to make the tariff issue paramount they might finally become a national party in practice as well as in name. As the President-elect declared, "the best manner in which to break the solid South will be to interest democrats and republicans in an economic way. This, should the republican party remain in power for eight or twelve years, will cause a split in the South on economical questions, probably the only way in which a split could occur."[36]

In his inaugural address, Harrison requested that the old race issue be buried. "Shall the prejudices and paralysis of slavery continue to hang upon the skirts of progress?" he

asked. Recommending an alliance between southern protec-
tionists and the Negro, the President said he was opposed to
"a special Executive policy for any section of the country."[37]
In the succeeding months, despite the continuing opposition
of a minority within his Party, Harrison set about the task of
implementing this new policy. He appointed Negroes only to
minor positions, and then only if they did not involve having
contact with or exercising authority over whites. He also
threw his support behind the new white Republican organizations being organized throughout the South to hold the pro-
tectionists together.

For Harrison, as for his predecessors, the real test of his
policy was the next local elections, scheduled to take place in
1889. Judging that their strength was greatest in Virginia and
Louisiana, the Republicans chose to contest a governorship in
the former state and a congressional seat in the latter. Men
and money were poured into the contests. Yet despite these
strenuous efforts, both Republican candidates were defeated
by wide margins. The Party's leaders had apparently mis-
calculated. Wade Hampton, Democratic Senator from South
Carolina, pointed out their mistake. The Republicans, he
said, were "trying to win by introducing the Economic question in the South. But as long as the matter of local self-
government demands our attention our people cannot divide
on this issue. Whether a man is a Protectionist or a Tariff
Reformer, the safety or welfare of his home is paramount.
. . ."[38] Hampton himself had advised his fellow Democrats to
emphasize the racial issue in the campaign.

As on previous occasions when their efforts to crack the
solid South failed, the Republicans now began to adopt a
more militant course. Many in the party had consistently opposed the abandonment of the Southern Negroes in the hope
of attracting native white support. This reflected in part their
concern for the Negro himself and in part their skepticism
that such a policy would work. These "Stalwarts," as they
were known, insisted that the colored people of the South, if
adequately protected in their right to vote, offered the surest
hope of establishing a Republican base in that region. Now

they were joined in their demand for Negro voter protection
by some of the younger Republicans in Congress—in particular, by Henry Cabot Lodge, Representative from Massachusetts. One of the first members of that body to hold a doctoral
degree, he had strong convictions not only about the Negro
but about the sanctity of the ballot. "We must have fair elections," he said, "if we are going to carry on our system of
government successfully, but we must have something more.
We must have an absolutely popular belief that the elections
are fair. . . ."[39] Certainly no one hearing the reports on the
recent southern elections could believe that this obtained in
a large part of the country. Congress, Lodge felt, should act
with regard to the situation. With the southern votes always
in the Democratic column, the Republican Party would face
a major hurdle in becoming a truly national political force.
When Congress reconvened in December, 1889, Lodge saw to
it that he was named chairman of the Select Committee on the
Election of the President, Vice-President, and Representatives
in Congress.

Many of the Republican leaders, including those who had
worked so hard only a few months before to crack the solid
South on the tariff issue, were now beginning to agree with
Lodge. The President had signaled the change in party mood
by calling for greater federal protection of the Negroes' voting
and civil rights. Republican leaders in Congress soon followed, especially when testimony before the Lodge committee
revealed the extent of voting irregularities throughout the
South. "No fair man can sit in Committee," one congressman
wrote, ". . . and hear testimony and arguments in seventeen
contested cases without becoming thoroughly *convinced* of
the absolute lawlessness in elections in a large portion of the
South." Said an influential Senator, "That some law must be
passed is now apparent."[40] The result, as reported by the
Lodge committee, was a bill that called for the appointment
of federal supervisors in every congressional district, armed
with the power to inspect registration lists and otherwise see
that the elections were honestly conducted. In the larger cities
they were even to go from house to house, informing registered

voters of the time, place, and mechanics for casting their ballots. The supervisors were to report to a three-man board of canvassers, appointed by the federal circuit courts, and the boards of canvassers in turn were to certify all election results to Congress. This measure was carefully thought out, designed to end once and for all the biennial autumnal controversies over alleged election frauds, but Democrats promptly labeled it a Force Bill.

The fight, in and out of Congress, was bitter. In the House opponents argued that the measure, if enacted, would unnecessarily exacerbate sectional feelings just as the scars of the recent war showed signs of healing. They also charged that it would lead to an undue centralization of governmental authority. Outside the legislative halls, the South threatened an economic boycott of the North if the bill were enacted, while northern merchants, even without being threatened, saw no reason to stir up such a controversy. Many in the North, moreover, saw no point in pressing the South to grant the Negro equal voting rights when he still seemed ill equipped to exercise that privilege. Yet, despite this opposition, the bill passed the House on July 2, 1890, by a vote of 155 to 149. With Speaker Read exercising firm party discipline, only two Republicans voted against the measure. At the same time, not a single Democrat voted for it.

In the Senate, however, the measure bogged down. It was toward the end of the session, with the calendar crowded, that a group of eastern Republicans insisted that the McKinley bill raising tariff rates be given priority. To their surprise, they received support from a group of western Republicans, normally opposed to higher tariffs. The westerners had earlier received the support of southern Democrats for an eagerly sought piece of silver legislation, and in return they now agreed to help the southerners postpone action on the Lodge bill. The Republicans were not opposed to providing additional voting safeguards, but they were far more concerned about other legislation. And so the Lodge bill was put over until the next session.

In the interim the congressional elections went against the

Republicans. Though they retained control of the Senate, their majority was reduced from fourteen to eight, which made enactment of the Lodge bill even more difficult. When the western Republicans continued to support the southern Democrats, the measure was doomed. A new congressional alliance had been forged, linking South and West, and it augured ill for the Negro. The southern Democrats realized that time was on their side, that the longer they delayed congressional action on a federal elections bill, the less likely it was to be enacted. Republican sentiment in favor of such a measure had already begun to recede. Then came the presidential election of 1892, in which Grover Cleveland, again the Democratic candidate, chose to make the Force Bill and the McKinley tariff the major issues. Harrison tried to neutralize the first of these by proposing that an impartial commission be appointed to study the question of election laws, but to no avail. The Democrats kept intoning, "No Force Bill! No Negro Domination in the South!" The federal elections bill was dead. Meanwhile, the southern Democrats were working in their own way to solve the problem of voting irregularities by disenfranchising the Negro.

The re-election of Cleveland marked the end of an epoch, a third of a century during which the Republicans had searched unsuccessfully for some formula by which they might become a truly national party, dominant throughout the country. Though they had won five of the seven presidential elections since 1868, their margin in all but one had been uncomfortably small. A closer look at the election returns, moreover, revealed that the Republicans were, in fact, a minority party during most of this period. They had failed to make even a small crack in the "Solid South" once federal troops had been removed from that region. Though they had sought to form various political alliances, in each instance the legacy of slavery, the Civil War, and Reconstruction had undermined their efforts. They had now run out of alternative policies, except to allow time to run its course.

The re-election of Cleveland also marked the end of the previously close ties between the Negroes and the Republican

Party. As the memory of the Civil War receded into the background and the nation grew increasingly less tolerant of its colored citizens, the Republicans discovered that the Negro had been transformed from a political asset into a political liability. Their Party's espousal of Negro suffrage had long cost it the support of most southerners; now it was beginning to cost it the support of many northerners as well. Since it had little to lose and much to gain, the Republican Party was prepared to turn its back once and for all on the Negro. This change in party mood had long been heralded; its most recent manifestation had been the Republicans' reluctance during the 1892 campaign to support forthrightly a federal elections bill. Now the change in Party mood was confirmed by Harrison's appointment, during his last month in office, of an ex-Confederate officer to the Supreme Court. Only a few lone Republican voices protested. The Negro was to learn that he could no longer count on the continued protection of the Party of Lincoln.

NOTES

1. Wharton, Vernon Lane, *The Negro in Mississippi, 1865–1890*, University of North Carolina Press, Chapel Hill, 1947, pp. 140–3.

2. Franklin, John Hope, *Reconstruction after the Civil War*, University of Chicago Press, 1961, p. 124.

3. *National Party Platforms, 1840–1960*, compiled by Kirk H. Porter and Donald Bruce Johnson, University of Illinois Press, Urbana, 1961, p. 38.

4. Shenton, James P., ed., *The Reconstruction, A Documentary of the South After the War: 1865–1877*, Capricorn Books, New York, 1963, p. 195.

5. Wharton, *op. cit.*, p. 183.

6. Shenton, *op. cit.*, p. 154.

7. Franklin, *op. cit.*, p. 158.

8. De Santis, Vincent P., *Republicans Face the Southern Question, The New Departure Years 1877–1897*, Johns Hopkins Press, Baltimore, 1959, p. 35.

9. *Nation*, New York, February 25, 1869, p. 144.

10. *Nation*, New York, March 23, 1871, p. 192.

11. *Idem.*

12. *Nation*, New York, September 28, 1865.

13. *National Party Platforms, 1840–1960, op. cit.*, p. 44.

14. De Santis, *op. cit.*, p. 40.

15. Franklin, *op.cit.*, p. 150.

16. De Santis, *op. cit.*, p. 67.

17. *Ibid.*, p. 68.

18. *Ibid.*, p. 54.

19. Hirshson, Stanley P., *Farewell to the Bloody Shirt*, Indiana University Press, Bloomington, 1962, p. 24.

20. Woodward, C. Vann, *Reunion and Reaction, The Compromise of 1877 and the End of*

Reconstruction, Little, Brown, Boston, 1951, p. 44.

21. De Santis, *op. cit.,* p. 57.
22. *Ibid.,* p. 71.
23. Woodward, *op. cit.,* p. 208.
24. Hirshson, *op. cit.,* p. 24.
25. Woodward, *op. cit.,* p. 229.
26. Hirshson, *op. cit.,* p. 39.
27. *Ibid.,* p. 25.
28. *Ibid.,* p. 49.
29. *Ibid.,* p. 58.
30. *Ibid.,* p. 81.
31. *Ibid.,* p. 107.
32. *Ibid.,* p. 116.
33. *Ibid.,* p. 124.
34. *Ibid.,* pp. 124–5.
35. *Ibid.,* p. 164.
36. *Ibid.,* p. 171.
37. *Ibid.,* pp. 177–8.
38. *Ibid.,* p. 186.
39. *Ibid.,* p. 203.
40. *Ibid.,* pp. 203–4.

8 The Reconstructed South

On April 24, 1877, federal troops were ordered to withdraw from their positions surrounding the Louisiana State House in New Orleans and return to their barracks. For nearly six months the state, as well as the rest of the nation, had been in turmoil over whether the Republicans or Democrats had won the November elections. In Louisiana both parties claimed victory, and each had installed its own gubernatorial candidate in office in a different part of the capital. Once Rutherford B. Hayes was inaugurated as President, he had taken steps, in line with the deal he had made with the southern Democrats, to remove the Republicans from office in Louisiana. Now, with the actual withdrawal of federal troops, the final step had been taken, marking the end of Republican rule in Louisiana. By coincidence, it occurred exactly fifteen years after federal troops had first occupied New Orleans.

To celebrate the happy occasion church bells were rung throughout the state and cannons were fired. The rest of the South shared the feeling of relief, for Louisiana was the last southern state to be redeemed from radical Republican rule; the Democrats had taken over in South Carolina only two weeks before. The North, it seemed, had finally abandoned its efforts to reconstruct the South in its own image. The South hoped henceforth to be master of its own fate.

However, although the South had achieved political self-rule within a federal system, it had not yet gained economic independence. Northern merchants and businessmen still controlled the greater part of its commerce. Moreover, its economy rested on the export of an agricultural staple the price of which was subject to fluctuations in the world market. At the same time, the South was faced with a surplus of agricultural labor. Many of the region's leaders recognized that industrialization offered the only hope of overcoming these weaknesses in the economy, but the South lacked many of the preconditions for industrialization, such as railroads and schools. It also lacked an entrepreneurial tradition; in fact, its culture scorned the ethic of the countinghouse and factory. If the South were to industrialize, it had to obtain outside capital, but its well-known hostility toward foreigners and Yankees dissuaded many men of wealth from investing their funds there. Thus, political independence brought with it many problems.

In addition, the South was burdened with the legacy of 200 years of Negro slavery. Now that its "peculiar institution" had been destroyed, the South had somehow to forge a new relationship between the races. The North had attempted to provide a solution to this problem, but the overwhelming mass of southerners had rejected it. Now the South had to find a different solution and at the same time attempt to cope with its serious economic disabilities. The two problems were not wholly separate. For as time went by and the North proved itself increasingly loath to interfere in southern affairs, southern leaders found that it was possible to achieve, if not a definitive solution to the South's economic problems, a *modus vivendi* with its colored citizens, largely at their expense. The next quarter-century of southern history was to witness the working out of that *modus vivendi*.

History is an irreversible process, and many of the institutions introduced into the South by northerners were not easily rooted out. They had already become an intricate part of southern society and, although they were modified, they were there to stay. This was true of both the public schools and tenant farming.

Before the Civil War it had been a crime to teach a slave to read or write in the South. But formal education had been denied not only to all Negroes but to most whites as well. Hardly a single southern state had a public school system of which it could boast, and the few schools that did exist required at least some payment of tuition. As a result, only a handful of even the white school-age population had attended regular classes in the antebellum South. During the war itself an initial effort was made to overcome this deficiency, at least as far as the Negro was concerned. Northern philanthropic groups, acting on their own, organized schools in those areas of the South that were brought under federal control. Chaplains and regular army officers joined in their efforts; at least 1,000 northern men and women, it was estimated, were serving as teachers to the newly freed Negroes at the end of the war.

These efforts did not stop with the armistice. In fact, ever larger numbers of dedicated northerners, many of them former abolitionists, now journeyed southward to teach school. By 1869 there were 9,500 of them throughout the former Confederacy. Southern leaders began urging southerners to assume the task of educating the freedmen themselves, in order to guard against the baleful influence of the "Yankees." As the editor of a Mississippi newspaper noted, "A Southern teacher would instill into the young, Southern ideas of the relative social positions, rights and duties of the races."[1] But local whites who would teach in the Negro schools were almost impossible to find.

By 1870, when it finally ceased operations, the Freedmen's Bureau had expended $5 million on Negro education. At that time, the Bureau estimated, 250,000 former slaves were attending classes throughout the South. Yet these efforts were only a small part of what was needed to raise the great mass of freedmen from their former state of almost total illiteracy. The native whites, as soon as they had regained control of their state governments after the armistice, had finally recognized the need to provide free public education, but in almost all cases the local systems that were set up completely excluded Negroes.

This situation soon changed, however, when the North imposed radical Reconstruction on the South. In every state

new constitutions were written, establishing for the first time
a system of statewide schools and guaranteeing Negroes as well
as whites free public education. By 1870 the new statewide
school systems were in operation throughout the South. Because of fears that mixed classes would lead to "race mongrelization," classes were integrated in only two states—South
Carolina and Louisiana. It was also in these two states and in
Mississippi that Negroes had their greatest success in electing
members of their race to office. But even in those states with
separate school systems, Negroes for the first time began to
receive a significant portion of the funds allocated to public
education. They did not always receive a proportionate share,
but they seldom received much less than their share. Moreover, under the radical Republican regimes the total amount
of funds made available for education was vastly increased.
Mississippi, in the first year that it operated a state-supported
school system, spent more money on education than on all
other government services. While many native whites might
rebel at the cost, by the end of Reconstruction free public
education had become an institution that all southerners were
prepared to accept at least in principle.

Even more fundamental to the Reconstruction of the
South was the system of tenant farming which had developed,
with northern encouragement, as a substitute for the old slave
plantations. The large landowners, of course, would have much
preferred the system of quasi-slavery envisioned by the various
Black Codes, just as they would have much preferred the system of white education only. For the Black Codes would have
enabled them to continue working their soil as they always
had, albeit without the stronger social control and greater
moral stigma of legalized slavery. The North, however, had
made clearly known its unwillingness to sanction any such
system for again bringing together land-capital and labor in
the South.

The northerners who were sent South by the Freedmen's
Bureau to aid the newly freed slaves found a situation which,
in the first year after the war, was becoming increasingly cha-
otic. Many Negroes, for a very large number of reasons,

had left their former plantations and were congregated in the various southern cities. Unable to find employment there, they had become dependent on the Freedmen's Bureau for subsistence. Others, after being paid off from the previous year's crop, had rushed to those same cities to spend what for most of them was the first money they had ever earned in their lives. Stirred by rumors that they would soon receive forty acres and a mule of their own, they were reluctant to enter into new labor contracts for the coming year. The planters were loud in their protests that something be done about the situation.

The Freedmen's Bureau now found thrust upon it the task of reordering the entire socioeconomic relationship between land-capital and labor throughout the South. Somehow it had to reconcile many conflicting interests: those of the recently freed Negroes in obtaining fair working conditions; those of the nearly destitute southern planters in a stable, low-wage working force; and those of the northern merchants in a return to "normal," prewar business conditions. The Bureau's response to the various demands made upon it in the winter of 1865–1866 was pragmatic and opportunistic.

It had been suggested that the Freedmen's Bureau set a minimum wage to compensate the Negroes for their unequal bargaining power in dealing with their former masters. But General Howard, the head of the Bureau, had refused on the grounds that economic conditions varied too greatly throughout the South to set a single standard. Instead, he left it up to his regional assistants to decide what wages would be fair given the local situation. As a guide, he suggested that the Negroes now receive the same rate at which their masters had been able to hire them out while they were still slaves. Occasionally Bureau officials actually took advantage of their power to annul a contract on the grounds that it offered the Negroes insufficient compensation, but in general they allowed a wage scale that was little above subsistence. In light of the depressed economic conditions Bureau officials encountered throughout the South, this was hardly surprising.

Bureau officials, recognizing the limitations of the southern

situation, soon offered the planters an alternative to a wage
system. If they chose, they could enter instead into a crop-sharing agreement with their former slaves. In return for working
the planter's lands, the Negroes were to receive up to one-half
the proceeds from the cotton eventually sold, giving them a
proprietary interest in the cotton they were growing. With
this incentive the freedmen no longer required the same close
supervision that had been necessary under slavery. Moreover,
since the Negroes shared in whatever return the cotton later
brought in the open market, they were forced to assume part
of the risk arising from falling prices. For these and other
reasons, the planters preferred the crop-sharing arrangement
over the wage system. Despite some misgivings, the Freedmen's Bureau gradually acquiesced in the shift in the form of
the contract.

The sharecropping arrangement, as it developed under
the aegis of the Freedmen's Bureau, led to one other institutional change: the planters began leasing the land to their former slaves. While it then appeared that the large southern
estates had been broken up, in reality they remained as extensive as ever, even if their ownership shifted to northern migrants or new men of power from the South. The fact that the
leases were renewable each year assured the owners of the same
effective control they had enjoyed when they had worked the
land themselves. The legal form of tenancy was simply
another way of controlling the Negro laborer.

If the planters had gained any unfair advantage, Bureau
officials hoped to offset it somewhat through the provisions
they insisted be written into the various labor contracts.
Many of these provisions simply recognized practices long
common in the South. At the end of the year, the Negroes had
certain safeguards. Throughout the South, protective provisions were incorporated into the contracts the Freedmen's
Bureau drafted, such as the fact that they could file a crop
lien against any employer who failed to pay the wages and
other forms of compensation due them under the contract.

On the other hand, planters could withhold up to half
the Negroes' wages until the end of the cotton season. Negroes

who quit before that time without just cause forfeited the entire sum. This tied the Negro to a particular employer for the entire year, assuring him of a stable labor force while his cotton crop was still in the field.

By 1870, just as the Freedmen's Bureau was preparing to cease operations, the sharecropper system had already become deeply entrenched in the South. By its means cotton production had reached three-fifths of its prewar level, and the other southern staples were recovering nearly as fast. Yet even while the Bureau had been at the height of its power, it had had difficulty supervising the various labor and land contracts. Nevertheless, it had been able to offer the Negroes some protection. Its mere presence had had a deterring effect. But when the Bureau was abolished, the planters were free to exploit the sharecropping system without interference, for the end of the Freedmen's Bureau coincided with the fall of the radical Republican regimes throughout most of the South. With the state and local courts now in the hands of the planter class and their allies, the rural merchants, the Negroes were without hope of legal redress in the case of any contract dispute. Completely at the landlord's mercy, they were forced to labor throughout the year for little more than subsistence. In any given area large landowners discussed and agreed among themselves about the terms they would offer their Negro tenants. At the same time they pledged not to sell the Negroes land or lease them a plot of ground if they had previously quit on one of their number. This close cooperation among the large landowners destroyed not only what little economic independence the Negroes had but also whatever political freedom they had recently come to enjoy. Elections were conducted in the open, where any landlord could see how his tenants voted; those who voted against his wishes found themselves without a contract for the coming year. In this way, the planters did not usually have to resort to violence to control the Negro vote in their districts.

This system of farm tenancy was made even more oppressive by the system of agricultural credit that developed alongside it. To supply the Negro fieldhands and sharecroppers

with groceries, clothing, seed, fertilizer, and various implements between the time a crop was planted and the time it
was picked or harvested, a new class of merchants began
settling in the southern countryside. At first they simply advanced the supplies to the large planters, who in turn
advanced them to their Negro laborers. A native southerner,
describing the emerging labor system of his region, commented in 1875, "The planter usually, and I may say nine
times out of ten, does not get a dime. The merchant has got
him in debt, and [appropriates for himself] the proceeds; and
if there is any [left] over—if the negroes are entitled to any—
they get it."[2]

Later, as the farm tenancy system became more common,
the merchants began advancing the supplies directly to the
Negroes. In fact, many planters themselves—those who were
able to accumulate the necessary capital—began operating
their own stores. Then the full burden of the credit system
fell on the ex-slaves.

As one southern Governor remarked, "The Negro skins
the land and the landlord skins the Negro."[3] When the cot-
ton-picking season was over, the sharecroppers found that they
had to turn over practically their entire crop, first to the
owner of the land and second to the storekeeper who supplied
them with credit. Often they were the same. Not very adept
at commercial transactions and not very likely to win a
friendly hearing in court, the Negroes were seldom able to
secure fair treatment when it came time to settle accounts. In
one of the many stories that soon began to make the rounds in
the South, a Negro sharecropper was shown his ledger entries
and told that the debits from the supplies advanced to him
during the year exactly balanced the credits from his share of
the cotton crop.

"Then I don't owe you nothin', Capt'n?" the Negro asked.
"No, you don't owe me a cent."
"An' you don't owe me nothin'?"
"You saw the books."
"Then what's I gonna do with them two bales I ain't done
hauled in yet?"

"Tut, tut! Just look at that! Here's two pages stuck to-gether. I'll have to add this whole account up again."[4]

The Negroes, once they had contracted an initial debt, were usually required to buy all their supplies from the same store, as a rule the one located on the plantation itself, and it was then a simple matter for the proprietor to charge what-ever he wished. Whites as well as Negroes were caught up in the system. "The poor, ignorant, colored and white man, rent-ing small farms and relying on the merchants for advances to make his crop," a contemporary southern observer noted, "were . . . compelled to pay the exorbitant interest, fre-quently of fifty per cent and not unusually of seventy or ninety per cent. A coat which cost the merchant one dollar, was fre-quently sold for two; a pound of meat that cost six cents was sold for twelve; a hat which cost fifty cents was sold for $1.50. . . ." And the legal whip held over the sharecroppers' heads was the crop lien. "I have seen colored men," that same southerner reported, "who . . . after paying such debts to the merchants as were incurred in making said crop, [did] not have enough money to buy a suit of clothing for anyone of the family. I have also seen the taking of all of the crop by the merchant, and also, the horse or mule and other chattels which were given as collateral security for the debt. . . ."[5]

Besides the economic bind in which he found himself, the Negro was subject to various social controls. One was the con-vict lease system. Under slavery, the masters themselves had administered punishment for all but the most serious crimes. However, now that slavery had been abolished, it was neces-sary to devise a substitute that would deter petty crime but would not overtax the penal system. As a solution, the south-ern states began leasing their convicted prisoners to private individuals and corporations. On the one hand, this turned what otherwise would have been a financial burden into an important source of state revenue. On the other hand, it led to dreadful conditions.

In most states there were no laws limiting the hours or types of work that could be demanded of the convicts, and if a prisoner died, the contractor was seldom held responsible.

Convicts were put to work, chained and in gangs, in the
water-filled mines of Alabama and Arkansas and in the tur-
pentine camps of Florida and North Carolina; their "prisons"
were either huge rolling wagons or hastily built windowless
stockades. These accommodations were, the Alabama prison
inspectors reported in 1882, "as filthy, as a rule, as dirt could
make them, and both prisons and prisoners were infested with
vermin." The inspectors found that the "convicts were ex-
cessively and sometimes cruelly punished; that they were
poorly clothed and fed; that the sick were neglected, inso-
much as no hospitals had been provided. . . ."[6] Not surprisingly, the death rate among leased convicts sometimes reached
as high as 25 per cent a year.

Though whites were often the victims of this system, it
was primarily the Negroes who suffered. They comprised the
great bulk of leased convicts, for under southern justice, they
were particularly vulnerable. In Mississippi, for example, the
theft of any property worth $10 or more could result in a
prison sentence of up to five years, and a Negro was likely to
receive the maximum penalty. In fact, one of the customary
ways of dealing with a particularly troublesome or rebellious
Negro was to see that he wound up on a chain gang.

In extreme cases, direct physical violence was employed.
Sometimes it was legalized "murder," such as when a Negro
was sentenced to death by an all-white jury on the basis of
insufficient evidence. How frequently this occurred no one
will ever know. Some figures are available, however, on the
number of extralegal killings. Between 1882, when Tuskegee
Institute first began keeping a record, and 1901 an average of
about 150 lynchings a year took place in the South—one
lynching every few days, since a single lynching occasionally
took more than one life. While many of the victims were undoubtedly Negroes who had violated the South's rigid sexual
taboos, many others were Negroes who had simply rebelled
against the racial *status quo*. The greater the threat a Negro
posed to white control, the more likely it was that he would
be killed, to set an example to others if nothing else. Again
no one will ever know for sure, but it is probably not inaccu-

rate to say that between 1877 and 1890 an entire generation of Negro leaders was deliberately decimated. Those who were not killed outright were tarred and feathered or beaten, driven out of the South or forced into submission. During these years the South turned to terror as a means of social control.

Although the sharecropping system—like the public schools, a legacy of radical Reconstruction—was later modified, it remained essentially the same as when the Freedmen's Bureau first helped to shape it. Yet few persons in the North could have foreseen that the sharecropping system would become, even after the overthrow of Republican rule, the South's dominant socioeconomic institution, just as the slave plantation had been before it. Few could have foreseen, either, that it would become such a vehicle of oppression once the protective cover of the Freedmen's Bureau was removed. For both of these developments were due in great part to the serious economic straits in which the South found itself after 1873.

After the end of the Civil War the South had made slow but steady progress toward full recovery. By 1873 it was approaching prewar levels of production in most of its agricultural staples. Then came the most severe depression this country had ever experienced. Though the effects were felt far more in the North, the South, which had not shared to the same extent in the previous prosperity, found itself set back even further. What happened to cotton prices foreshadowed what happened to the southern economy as a whole. From a high of eighteen cents a pound shortly after the war, cotton prices fell to half that figure in 1878. Meanwhile, production fell off. That same year the total value of the southern cotton crop, which had been $293 million only eight years before, plummeted to $193 million. The South's other great staples, such as tobacco and sugar, had not recovered as quickly from the war, but now they, too, suffered a fall in price. Even more serious for future growth, the depression virtually dried up northern investment in the South.

Then, in the 1880's, although the rest of the country recovered and made new economic gains, the south remained in the same depressed condition. Cotton prices, instead of rising again, held to their same low levels, and even declined somewhat. The problem now was not so much insufficient demand as oversupply. Newer lands, especially in Texas, were being brought into production at a time when the textile industry's rate of growth had begun to slacken and other sources of supply were also being opened up.

The South's sugar growers suffered even more severely from world competition as well as from the continual fluctuation in price and output. Tobacco production was somewhat more stable, but these growers were caught in the grip of powerful buyers, who often acted in concert to keep prices low.

Throughout the 1880's, then, southern agriculture experienced hard times. In Mississippi local leaders reported an exodus from the plantations "so strong and wide as to threaten whole sections of our country with desolation" while in Alabama a planter noted sadly that "want and gaunt, haggard despair have prevailed everywhere in the Black Belt." In Louisiana a farmer told of "old fields abandoned in every direction," and in Virginia a prominent citizen of that state said that "since the Red man left us tobacco-seed the farming interest has not been so depressed."[7] Adding to the plight of southern agriculture was the nation's return to specie payment, which had the effect of making money scarcer, forcing up interest rates, and adding to the South's real debt burden. The country's fiscal policies also redounded to the South's disadvantage. A protective tariff was the source of most government revenue, and this had the effect of raising the price of practically every manufactured item the South had to purchase, while it was forced to rely for income on the sale of agricultural products on an unprotected world market. Since the South still had no control over its fiscal, monetary, and tariff policies, it remained in what was basically colonial vassalage to the North.

The 1890's brought a new depression in the North and an even further decline in southern agriculture. Cotton prices hit rock bottom in 1894 at 4.6 cents a pound, less than it cost to grow the cotton. Total production had increased nearly threefold since 1873, but the value of the entire cotton crop in 1894 was $2 million less than it had been in that previous depression year. A similar decline occurred in the value of the South's other staples. These economic setbacks were compounded by certain natural calamities. "Flood, drought, and plague competed with debt, mortgage and bankruptcy as causes of suffering," notes C. Vann Woodward. "Crevasses in the levees of the lower Mississippi in 1891, 1892, and 1893 resulted in floods that made thousands homeless and reduced many to the point of starvation. The floods drowned stock, destroyed property valued at several millions, and rendered much of the overflowed land unproductive for years. Drought followed flood. Lack of water cut Louisiana rice production from 182,000,000 pounds in 1893 to 76,000,000 pounds in 1895. Drought in 1896 caused an almost total loss of crops in the hill country of Louisiana, Mississippi, Arkansas and Texas. . . . In 1892 a new and terrifying enemy began an invasion from Mexico that in future years was to overrun the cotton kingdom—the boll weevil."[8]

From the end of radical Republican rule in the South on into the twentieth century, continuing hard times exaggerated the worst features of the farm tenancy system. And the hard times were made even worse by the growth in the South's population during this same period. In 1870 not quite five million Negroes lived in the South. Within twenty years the number had grown to 6.7 million; by 1910 it had reached 8.7 million. The growth in the South's white population was even more startling. From a base of 8.6 million in 1870, the number of whites soared to 13 million in 1890 and 20.5 million in 1910, a 238 per cent increase over the entire period. This, despite the substantial outmigration of whites. Though the growth of North and West was almost as rapid, it was accomplished largely through foreign immigration, a phenomenon which the South's conditions and attitudes discouraged. The South's population increase was mainly from native stock. Little wonder, then, that some said the South's most important product was babies.

Thus, the South, in addition to its other serious economic problems, was faced with the task of finding employment for an exploding population. One solution, of course, was industrialization, which provided employment for so many immigrants in the North. This was a solution the South attempted. As soon as the debris from the 1873 depression had been cleared away, northern capitalists again began looking for investment opportunities in the former Confederacy. This time they were welcomed with open arms.

The result in too many cases was limited to the exploitation of the South's great mineral and forest resources. When these had been extracted, northern capital withdrew, leaving the region with only the memory of former employment. But, gradually, local industries of a more permanent nature began to emerge in various parts of the South, taking advantage of some special endowment. In Alabama and Tennessee a steel industry was founded on the iron and coal deposits surrounding Birmingham and Chattanooga. In South Carolina and Georgia cotton mills grew up on the basis of cheap labor, cheap cotton, and water power. In North Carolina and Virginia tobacco processing and manufacturing were founded on the ready availability of the raw product. In Mississippi cottonseed-oil mills and in Louisiana sugar refineries were developed. Added to this was the growth throughout the South of an improved transportation network. Between 1870 and 1880 only 2,650 miles of railroad were built, making a total of 13,259 miles. But in the next decade another 14,396 miles were added, which more than doubled the region's total mileage. The South's harbor facilities were also expanded, especially in the Gulf region. After $8 million in federal funds were spent to widen the Mississippi River below New Orleans and $7.5 million to dredge Galveston harbor, these two cities became the leading ports in the nation, second only to New York.

As a result of these burgeoning industries, nonagricultural employment in the South increased substantially between

1870 and 1890, though few Negroes derived any benefit. By tacit agreement, the jobs in these new industries were reserved almost exclusively for whites. In fact, in many parts of the South community leaders worked assiduously to bring a new mill or plant to their town mainly to provide employment for the redundant white population in the surrounding countryside. The town merchants who joined in these efforts were perhaps thinking of the prosperity that the new industry would bring, but the nearby large landowners were more interested in the over-all social problem. They were, they said, simply trying to help the "poor whites." Theirs, however, was a much larger interest, for they recognized that the existing economic order might eventually collapse if something were not done about the lack of employment opportunities for the great mass of southern whites. As things then stood, there was no room for them in agriculture, except on the same degraded level as the Negro sharecroppers. The "poor whites," finding their position gradually worsening, might one day be led to make common cause with the Negroes against the large landowners. But by promoting an industrial society limited to whites only, the old planter class hoped to give the lesser members of their race a new place in southern society, retaining their former allegiance against the blacks and siphoning off the worst of the social discontent. Thus as late as 1891 only 7,500 Negroes were employed in all of southern industry.

Not only the new jobs but many of the old as well were now reserved exclusively for the whites. Before the Civil War most of the South's artisans had been Negroes, who, as slaves, had been rented out by their masters on a daily basis. In fact, Negroes had performed most of the skilled labor in the antebellum South. Now, however, under the pressure of an expanding white population this began to change. White workers began taking over jobs previously performed only by Negroes, pre-empting all but the least desirable positions, just as they were in the South's newer industries. In 1870 the New Orleans city directory listed 3,460 Negroes as carpenters, cigar makers, painters, clerks, shoemakers, coopers, tailors, bankers, blacksmiths, and foundry hands; by 1904, only one-tenth that number were employed in those trades, despite a 50 per cent increase in the city's Negro population. "It is possible now," one southerner wrote in the latter year, "to live in New Orleans as free from any dependence on the services of Negroes as one could be in New York or Boston."[9]

The Negroes' role in the emerging industrial order, then, was to fill the jobs no white men would take—that and to keep the great mass of white workers in line. For if any white worker had a mind to protest against his wages or working conditions, there were literally thousands of Negroes eager to take his place at lower wages and under worse working conditions. In fact, to make the threat explicit, the Tennessee Coal and Iron Company in Birmingham, after labor difficulties in the 1890's, began giving jobs to Negroes "as motormen, blacksmiths, masons, machine runners, linesmen, rockmen, machinists, pipe men, etc., which were formerly considered white men's jobs."[10]

With most industrial occupations closed to them, the South's Negroes had little choice but to continue to live on the land. This was just what the large landowners wanted, for it assured them of an adequate and cheap supply of labor. Meanwhile, they saw to it that the Negroes' only other avenue of escape was cut off. Northern migration was positively discouraged, and labor recruiters from other parts of the country were made unwelcome. Several southern states, in fact, passed laws against "enticement." An incident after the Mississippi River overflowed its banks in 1890 clearly revealed the landowners' attitude. When the federal government offered army rations to help feed the Negro tenants displaced by the flood waters, the Governor of Mississippi, under pressure from the large planters, turned down the offer. A Mississippi editor admitted that the governor's actions might "seem pretty rough on the darkies,"[11] but he pointed out that the army rations would lessen the Negroes' dependence on the planters. The control of labor, he added, must not be endangered.

Thus the Negroes' place in the southern economy was fixed. Just as in the past, they were henceforth to till the soil. However, even though most of the new industrial employment was reserved exclusively for whites, it proved insufficient to provide enough jobs for the exploding white population. To their dismay and resentment, many whites found that they had no choice but to become tenant farmers themselves. By 1900 white sharecroppers were beginning even to outnumber Negro sharecroppers in the South. Despite the best efforts of southern leaders, the unsatisfactory labor situation had only grown worse.

The exploding population and the decline in agricultural prices posed a problem for the South in yet another area. This was in education, where the first of these two factors—the growth in population—led to an increase in the demands made upon the various school systems while the second—the agricultural depression—meant a drying up of the funds available to support them. When the southern Democrats finally regained control of their state governments in the early and middle 1870's, one of their first acts was to reduce public expenditures. The cutback affected white and Negro schools alike, for under the various state constitutions appropriations for education were made on a per capita basis. Moreover, there seemed no way to change this. The Negroes were still a potent enough political force to prevent repeal of these constitutional provisions. Besides, it was feared that the Supreme Court would frown on any attempt to discriminate between the races. It was, in fact, this need to treat the white and colored schools equally that made conservative Democrats from these regions of the South where Negroes were in the majority so vehemently opposed to increased school appropriations. Though the Negroes paid hardly any taxes, they received the overwhelming share of the funds spent on public education. "Here in the Black Belt," the Montgomery *Advertiser* said, "where the country white people pay the taxes and the negroes go to school, there is considerable sentiment to the effect that taxation for public schools is a burden to the white people, not a benefit."[12]

The large landowners had other reasons for wishing to see the amount of state aid to education reduced. Convinced of the Negroes' inherent inferiority, they felt that any money spent on Negro schools was wasted. Besides, they asked, what did a man need to know to work in the fields? The attitude was probably best expressed by the Rev. Robert Dabney, a prominent Virginia clergyman and the biographer of Stonewall Jackson. "If our civilization is to continue," he argued, "there must be at the bottom of the social fabric a class who must work and not read. Now grant that the free public school does all that its wildest boasts can claim; that it elevates the negroes out of this grade. Then the only result will be that white people must descend into it and occupy it." Dr. Dabney asked what would happen if the Negro were actually trained to become a social equal, as some suggested. "Then will he not demand it? Of course he will. If those negro schools are to fail they should be abolished without further waste. If they are to succeed they only prepare the way for that abhorred fate, *amalgamation.*"[13]

These arguments carried little weight with the whites from those parts of the South where the Negroes were much fewer in number. "Now, don't give us any of the old chestnuts—'Educate a negro and you spoil a good field-hand'—'a man ought to educate his own children'— . . . ," a newspaperman from the hill country of Alabama declared. "We have heard all this, over and over, and yet we believe in our heart of hearts that it is right to enlighten every human being into whom God breathed the breath of life . . ." If educating Negro children was the only way they could obtain state assistance in educating their own children, these whites were fully prepared to do just that. "Were we to refuse education to the Negro and cut off the white children, too?"[14] one northern Alabama state legislator asked.

The conservatives' answer, however, was affirmative, and it was they who controlled the Democratic Party. As George Cable, the renegade Southern journalist, explained, "The friends of ample free schools in the South cannot elect legislative majorities that will vote for them. . . . [t]he white Southerner will not league with the Negro on a Negroes' plank; and he cannot in his own exclusively white party command a majority willing to vote a sufficient school tax."[15] Thus, by 1887 Alabama was contributing only about 72 cents a year per child toward the education of its youthful citizens. Other southern states were no more inclined to be generous.

But as the pressure of population mounted, the demand for increased state aid grew, especially among the whites outside the Black Belt regions. As Alabama's superintendent of education, Solomon Palmer, said in his report for 1890, "Alabama must—by some means—largely increase her school fund if she keeps pace with other states, and meets the growing demand of her school population." It was Palmer who suggested how, at least in Alabama, the long bedeviling dilemma might be overcome; how, on the one hand, the constitutional requirement that school funds be apportioned on a per capita basis might be satisfied while, on the other hand, the conservatives' objection that this gave back to the Negroes far more than they contributed in taxes were met. What Palmer proposed was that state aid be distributed to local authorities on a per capita basis, ignoring racial distinctions, and that the local authorities then be allowed to divide the funds between the two races on the basis of "who will probably attend each school."[16]

Palmer's proposals won ready approval from the state legislature, and through a similar ploy Mississippi found that it could do the same. In 1886 its average monthly salary for white teachers was $31.37, compared to $27.40 for Negro teachers; by 1895 it was $33.04, compared to $21.53. The effectiveness of such devices was still limited by what many southerners thought were the constitutional prohibitions against such outright discrimination, and these fears were not to be proved false for yet another decade. Meanwhile, the South had found another partial solution for one of its pressing problems—again at the expense of the Negro.

It was not only the question of public education that divided the upcountry farmers and the bottomland planters. They bitterly fought one another on virtually every public issue that touched on their respective economic interests. The upcountry farmers tended toward self-sufficiency, tilling their

small plots of ground with no other labor than that of their
immediate families. The rocky, barren soil barely provided
them with a living, but they remained fiercely independent,
supplementing their meager income by hunting and fishing.
The bottomland planters, on the other hand, produced for
the world market, cultivating extensive tracts of land with the
help of Negro labor. Rich and powerful, they readily identified with their fellow capitalists in the North, eager to join
with them in developing the South's industrial potential.

The mutual dislike of upcountry farmers and bottomland
planters, however, transcended their economic differences.
The hill people were, in the words of one bottomland aristocrat, "probably the most unprepossessing [breed] on the
broad face of the ill-populated earth." He added, "I can for-
give them as the Lord God forgives, but admire them, trust
them, love them—never. Intellectually and spiritually they
are inferior to the Negro, whom they hate." The bottomland
planters, in turn were referred to by the upcountry farmers
as "those elegant, smooth mannered, oily tongued bondhold-
ers . . . and members of financial boards," those *"thieves, ty-
rants and cowardly murderers* who are crushing out the life
and liberty."[17] of the South. This deep antagonism had existed before the Civil War when the two were roughly divided
into the Democratic and Whig Parties; now, even though
radical Reconstruction had been overthrown and they were
thrown together in the same political party, the antagonism
ran as deep as ever.

The issues over which they fought were many and diverse.
In addition to education, they disagreed as to whether the
federal government should discontinue printing Greenbacks,
whether corporate interests should be favored, whether the
convict lease system should be retained, whether a ceiling
should be placed on interest rates, whether crop liens should
be abolished, and many other questions. One of the most important issues dividing the two factions within the Democratic
Party during the early 1880's was the question of the various
state debts, contracted during and immediately following
Reconstruction primarily to finance the construction of new

railroads and extend old ones. By 1874 these debts had grown to approximately $275 million throughout the South, an increase of over $100 million since the beginning of Reconstruction. With the onset of a major depression the year before, the burden of this debt had become truly oppressive, and the upcountry farmers demanded that the amount be scaled down. Talk of repudiation, even partial repudiation, thoroughly alarmed the Whig-industrialist wing of the Democratic Party, many of whom were bottomland planters. It would, they argued, destroy public faith in the various states' credit and discourage northern investment in the South. "This contest," a conservative Democratic newspaper in Nashville declared, "is a struggle between ill-disguised communism and conservatism. The appeals of the repudiation party are all directed to . . . arousing that feeling against all accumulations."[18]

In many states the old Whig-planter class completely dominated the Democratic Party, leaving the radicals with no choice but to bolt, at least on the local level. In 1874 independent candidates first began making their appearance in Georgia. Three years later, with "no general principle in common except the spirit of revolt against the dictates of the solid Democracy,"[19] they had become a familiar part of the Georgia political landscape. Independent candidates also rose to challenge the conservative Democrats in South Carolina, Arkansas, and Tennessee.

With regard to national issues, there was at first no reason for the insurgents to leave the Democratic Party. On perhaps the most important of these, the Greenback question, the Party platform joined with the radicals in calling for monetary reform. But in 1878 the "hard money" faction began taking over control of the Democratic Party machinery, and two years later they succeeded in having an "honest money" plank incorporated into the national platform. No longer comfortable even within the national Democratic Party, many of the southern radicals now went over to the Greenback-Labor Party, which gave the insurgents for the first time a badly needed common ideology.

In Virginia and Tennessee, where the question of the state debt was paramount, the insurgents ran as "Readjusters" or "Low-Tax Democrats," as the latter to avoid any possible confusion with the Republicans. They were most successful in Virginia, where they captured control of the state legislature in 1879 and the governorship in 1881. When the Readjusters finally forced through a measure reducing Virginia's state debt of $31 million by nearly a third, they set the stage for other reforms. Taxes on landed property were reduced, and those on corporations and railroads increased. The mechanics' lien law was tightened, labor unions were given the right to organize, Granger legislation was enacted, the whipping post was abolished, and the laws against dueling were enforced for the first time in years. Most important, the system of public education was rescued from near collapse. Only two years before the state had faced the prospect of having to close nearly half its schools; now the appropriations for education were increased by 50 per cent, teachers' salaries that were in arrears were paid, and new schools were opened.

The radicals' success in Virginia, however, was unusual. In the other southern states they captured only a scattering of elective offices. The conservatives, deeply entrenched in power, stooped to any tactic to hold on to the reins of government, and the radicals found it extremely difficult to make inroads against them. Their only hope, the radicals decided in many cases, was to join forces with the local Republicans, a policy which President Arthur encouraged. It was an unholy alliance, for the Republican Party stood for all that the radicals opposed, and many of the radical leaders had long been pilloried in the Republican press as unreconstructed rebels and bloody murderers. But a local Alabama Republican leader explained the rationale for such an alliance. "Why, then, did I and the mass of Republicans here support the Greenback-Labor candidate?" he asked. "Let us frankly tell you. There are questions of more vital importance in Southern politics than banking and currency. . . . They are issues such as fair elections, an honest count, free thought, free speech, free government itself. . . . The Republicans felt bound . . . to stand by the Greenbackers upon this issue. We had a common grievance, and we made a common cause against it."[20]

Nevertheless, the alliance left the radicals open to Democratic charges that they were working to bring about the return of Republican and Negro rule in the South. Lucius Lamar, Mississippi's conservative Democratic Senator, denounced the leaders of the Greenback-Labor Party as "selfish and unscrupulous men who have publicly made a shameless partnership with the Negroes of Mississippi," while in Virginia a newspaper editor characterized the political struggle in the following manner. "It is black against white; ignorance against intelligence; vice against virtue; barbarian against civilization." These were cynical tactics: conservative Democrats openly supported Negro Republicans, knowing that the more closely the Republican Party was identified with the Negro, the more easily it would be alienated from the great mass of southern whites. Thus it was Lamar himself who provided Blanche Bruce and the other Negro Republicans in his state with most of their federal patronage. "Bruce and Lamar," complained the leader of the white Republicans in Mississippi, "humbug the different [Republican] administrations and keep up negro rule in the Rep. party in order that fear of negro rule in the State may keep white men in the Dem. party."[21]

In addition, the conservative Democrats were able to hold on to their power primarily because of the large number of Negro votes they controlled. It was the "black belt" areas, where Negroes greatly outnumbered whites, that consistently gave the old Whig elements of the Democratic Party the large electoral majorities they needed in order to overcome the up-country, anti-Bourbon vote. The planters did not control these votes simply through intimidation and violence. As they had promised President Hayes, the old Whigs were prepared to provide the Negroes with a certain minimum protection. They were even willing to look after the Negroes' vital interests, as long as these did not threaten their own political and economic control. The old plantation paternalism had simply been transplanted to a new social setting. As South Carolina's

Wade Hampton told a group of Negro voters, "The best friends of the colored men are the old slaveholders."[22] Thus the conservatives consistently refused to go along with the demands that the Negroes' civil liberties be curtailed, and they were even willing to reward their colored followers with occasional minor offices. But, if need be, the planters were fully capable of using all the political and economic power at their command to make sure that their Negro fieldhands voted solidly for the conservative candidates. As sharecroppers and tenant farmers, the Negroes were in a poor position to resist.

No matter how cynical the conservative Democrats' tactics were, they worked. Once allied with the Republicans, the radicals found they could not escape the stigma of "betraying the South." Democratic politicians in the South knew as well as any Republican precinct captain in the North how to exploit sectional conflict and once they raised the specter of radical Reconstruction, the great bulk of southern whites forgot their economic differences and rushed to join the conservative Democrats' banner. "In general," says Vernon Wharton, writing of Mississippi, "the policy of the Democratic party in the state and in the counties was to brand any effort toward independent political action as a return to Republicanism in disguise and as a threat to white supremacy."[23] With the lines thus drawn, the radicals hardly stood a chance.

But in case the race issue proved insufficient, the Democrats were fully prepared to use even more drastic methods. "Ballot boxes were stuffed," Wharton reports, "fraudulent returns were made, and thousands of opposition votes were thrown out on technicalities. . . . With mock solemnity, newspapers reported that boxes containing anti-Democratic majorities had been eaten by mules or horses."[24] In this way, the threat to conservative Democratic rule was overcome throughout the South. Even in Virginia the Readjusters were finally driven from office, after a race riot in Danville brought the whites out to the polls in 1883 in greater numbers than ever before. At one mass meeting held just before the election, an ex-Confederate general and one-time Whig declared that "the negroes must know that they are to behave themselves and keep in their proper places."[25] Once Virginia's conservative Democrats were safely ensconced in power, they took steps to make sure they would not soon be turned out again. As one of their leaders later recalled, the election laws were amended "so that the officers of election, if so inclined, could stuff the ballot boxes and cause them to make any returns that were desired."[26]

The voices of protest had been silenced throughout the South—but only temporarily. Before the decade was over, the same causes of disaffection, the feeling that the agricultural interests of the nation were being sacrificed to the rampant industrialism, had spawned a new protest movement, the Populists. Their source of support lay in most of the same upcountry and pine hill areas that ten years earlier had supported the Greenback and Readjuster movements, but to the old list of grievances many new ones had been added. As debtors, the Populists still wished to see the amount of currency in circulation expanded, but, in addition, they called for the abolition of the national banking structure and the establishment of a commodity credit system. They demanded that the government take back from the large land companies the extensive lumber and mineral-bearing tracts it had previously sold them at scandalously low prices, and they demanded that the government also take over the nation's railroad and telegraph lines.

The movement was essentially an agricultural protest against the Bourbons in the South as well as a revolt against northern economic domination. A Texas editor complained that "corporate greed and monopoly have concentrated the wealth into the hands of a few hundred men, who are as essentially the masters of the people as were the feudal barons of the middle ages the masters of the peasants." Meanwhile, a Virginia Populist charged that the conservative leaders of his state were working to "hand us over bound hand and foot to foreign dividend hunters." He added, "But it is said: 'It will never do to drive capital away from the state. You must attract it by offering it inducements'—said inducements being liberty to fleece the people. . . . Our reply to all this loathsome mammon-worship is that you are bartering away Virginia's birth-right for a miserable mess of pottage."[27]

Faced with this new challenge to their political rule, con-servative Southern Democratics resorted to the same cynical tactics as before. On the one hand, they skillfully sought to exploit the race issue. The Populists had attempted to deal with this problem in a somewhat different manner than the earlier radicals. From the Party's very beginning, instead of closing the door to Negro membership, it had invited colored delegates to join its highest councils. The issue was first fought out at the Texas convention of the new Party. "I am in favor of giving the colored man full representation," said the con-vention president in granting a Negro delegate's request that he be seated. "He is a citizen just as much as we are, and the party that acts on that fact will gain the colored vote of the South."[28] His ruling was upheld by the convention and later in most of the other southern states.

However, the Populists were not prepared to make any concessions on the question of social equality. "This is a white man's country," a Virginia Populist declared, "and will always be controlled by the whites." Nevertheless, they hoped to appeal to the Negroes on the basis of common economic interests. "Let it once appear plainly," predicted Tom Wat-son, Georgia's Populist leader, "that it is to the interest of a colored man to vote with the white man, and he will do it. . . . The accident of color can make no difference in the interest of farmers, croppers, and laborers," he told the two races. "You are kept apart that you may be separately fleeced of your earnings." A white Texan put it another way. "They are in the ditch just like we are."[29] In addition to their stressing common economic grievances, the Populists denounced lynch laws and the convict lease system, both of which affected pri-marily the Negro.

Although the Populists protested that they had no inten-tion of granting the Negroes social equality, it made no differ-ence to the conservative Democrats, who still accused them of seeking to undermine white supremacy. The Populists also tried to avoid the mistake of the Greenbackers and Readjusters and refused in most cases to join forces with the Republicans. But, when the Republicans decided to make an election issue of the so-called Force bill, Henry Cabot Lodge's proposal to establish federal voting registrars, the Populists lost important votes. Though they themselves had come out strongly against the measure, the fact that the issue was raised at all tended to divide the South once more along racial lines. "But for the Force Bill," said the Richmond *Dispatch*, "the South might possibly have listened to the appeals of some of the new parties." In the columns of that same newspaper a Virginia Democrat added that the bill's effect "will be to draw the color line more intensely and to weld the South more solidly together."[30]

But it was mainly through outright election fraud that the conservative Democrats succeeded in holding off the Populist onslaught in the presidential election year of 1892. In Virginia the Populists claimed they were cheated out of victory in four of the state's congressional districts. "The Democrats," they charged, "have deliberately thrown out the returns of their own judges in precinct after precinct until the majorities are fixed to suit themselves." The Georgia election was, in the words of the Populists, a "solemn farce," the ballots counted in Augusta, for example, being twice the number of legally registered voters. "It is needless to attempt to disguise the facts of the Alabama election," a Democratic Party organ admitted quite candidly: "The truth is that [Reuben F.] Kolb [the Populist gubernatorial candidate] carried the state, but was swindled out of his victory by the [entrenched Democratic] faction, which had control of the election machinery and used it with unblushing trickery and corruption." What made Kolb's defeat so bitter for the Populists was the fact that the Negro votes had once again supplied the margin of defeat. Kolb had captured a majority of white votes cast, but the state's twelve black counties had gone for his Democratic opponent by a margin of 26,000 votes, more than twice what he needed to win. "Undoubtedly the defeat of the popular will by the ballot-box stuffers," a prominent Alabama politician and editor wrote one of his friends, "would justify revolution after the manner of our fathers. There was the same condition of affairs in the state during the reconstruction period—the same crimes against the ballot box."[31]

But, as C. Vann Woodward has pointed out, the Democrats could no longer justify the use of such tactics on the same grounds as before. A Virginia Populist editor remarked, "It is no excuse to say that these iniquities are practiced to 'preserve white civilization.' In the first place it was white men who were robbed of their votes, and white men who were defrauded out of office." This continual resort to election skulduggery, as well as the conservative Democrats' almost abject dependence on the Negro vote, undermined their support even among their own followers. The two were closely connected, for the election laws were most openly flouted precisely in those areas where the Negro vote was greatest. When in 1896 the Democrats again defeated the Populists in Louisiana, despite the fact that they had carried only one-fifth of the counties with white majorities, the New Orleans *Times-Democrat* sarcastically commented that white supremacy had once more been "saved by negro votes."[32]

This time, however, unlike the early 1880's, the radicals' defeat at the polls failed to discourage them. Convinced that only the conservative control of the Negro vote had prevented them from winning a resounding victory, the Populists resolved to take steps to counter the cause of their defeat. On the one hand, they had lost many white votes because of their alliance with the Negro; on the other hand, they had seen the colored vote cynically manipulated to defeat them. If the conservatives could exploit the race issue to attract lower-class white support, the Populists could do the same, only with greater enthusiasm. They themselves came from that stratum, and they knew how best to express its traditional enmity toward the Negro. And what better way was there to express that centuries-old antagonism than to disenfranchise the Negro? This would not only win the support of most southern whites; it would also make it impossible for the Democrats ever again to manipulate the Negro vote in order to perpetuate themselves in power.

Mississippi had already shown the way. In 1890 it had approved a new state constitution denying the right to vote to any person unable to read or explain its provisions. Wharton explains, "There was a general understanding that the interpretation of the constitution offered by an illiterate white man would be acceptable to the [voting] registrars; that of a Negro would not."[33] Through this device the great majority of Negroes in Mississippi were disfranchised, leaving only 8,615 eligible Negro voters, compared to 68,127 eligible white voters. And in 1892 the Supreme Court handed down a decision which upheld the constitutionality of the literacy requirement. Henceforth the immediate thrust of southern radicalism was to disfranchise the Negro.

Such an objective received the support of even most conservative Democrats. They had no intention of being left behind on the race issue. Even more important, many of them had grown tired of the perennial election frauds. "It is true that we win these elections," said the conservative New Orleans *Times-Democrat*, "but at a heavy cost, and by the use of methods repugnant to our idea of political honesty and which must, in time, demoralize the people of Louisiana." A Virginia Democrat agreed. "Cheating at elections," he warned, "is demoralizing our whole people." But perhaps most important of all, the conservative Democrats hoped that by disfranchising the Negro they would disfranchise the poor whites as well, and thus undermine the basis of Populist support. It was "not the negro vote which works the harm," a Virginia conservative said, but "the depraved and incompetent men of our own race."[34]

Beginning with South Carolina in 1895 and ending with Oklahoma in 1910, nearly every state in the South held a constitutional convention in order to change its voting requirements, and the others changed them through legislative act. The question in all these conventions was not whether disfranchisement would take place, but how and of whom. The radicals sought to disenfranchise only Negroes, but the conservatives sought also to remove poor whites from the rolls. The difficulty, from the radicals' point of view, was that the requirements had to be general enough to pass constitutional scrutiny yet stringent enough to be effective, and the more stringent they were, the more whites they barred from voting. The only way to solve this was to provide some loophole through which whites could be registered but Negroes not. Thus, almost every state adopted some variant of the Mississippi "understanding" clause whereby a prospective voter, even if illiterate, could cast his ballot if he demonstrated to the registrars that he was capable of "understanding" the state constitution. Afraid that even this loophole, liberally interpreted, would disfranchise too many white voters, the Louisiana constitutional convention adopted what came to be known as the "grandfather" clause, whereby anyone who had voted prior to January 1, 1867, was automatically entitled to vote in future elections, together with his sons and grandsons. In other states where the radicals were dominant, the same clause or a variant was adopted.

But one requirement for which there was no loophole was adopted by every southern state—the poll tax, which had to be paid before a man could vote. In some states any unpaid tax from previous years also had to be paid. As a result, in every state large numbers of whites were disfranchised. To this extent, the conservatives had their way.

In the long run, however, it was the radicals who gained. Though the Spanish-American War soon put all talk of reform temporarily aside, as the nation again turned its attention to domestic problems, the Populists' successors found that they no longer had to worry that fraud and intimidation in the Black Belt would cancel out their electoral majorities in the white counties. The Negro voter, as a significant factor, had been virtually eliminated. In Louisiana, for example, 164,088 whites and 130,344 Negroes had been qualified to vote before the constitutional convention of 1898; after the new voting requirements went into effect, 125,437 whites and only 5,320 Negroes were able to register. The situation was much the same in the other southern states. The Negro had been disfranchised, it was said, "to prevent the Democratic election officials from stealing their votes." To at least one delegate attending the Virginia constitutional convention, this seemed to "punish the man who has been injured."[35] However, this was neither the first nor the last time that southern whites found at least a partial solution to a pressing problem at the expense of the Negro.

Though the elimination of the Negro from politics may have helped to make later elections in the South more honest, it left the Negro himself in a helpless position. Deprived of the right to vote, he no longer had any means of protecting himself against the forces of race hatred. At the same time, Negro disfranchisement seemed to have upset the delicate social balance that had previously held these forces in check. At the various constitutional conventions called to disfranchise the Negro, it was only the old patricians—such men as Wade Hampton of South Carolina—who spoke out in behalf of their former slaves. Thomas Jones, a former governor of his state and a patrician like Hampton, told the Alabama convention the story of Robert E. Lee's reply to the question of why he took so great an interest in a certain lowly soldier— "Because he is under me." Said Jones, "The Negro race is under us. He is in our power. We are his custodians . . . we should extend to him, as far as possible, all the civil rights that will fit him to be a decent and self respecting, law-abiding and intelligent citizen. . . . If we do not lift them up, they will drag us down."[36] But in the new political environment created by Negro disfranchisement, men of his type, extremely conservative yet solicitous of the Negro's welfare, were unable to survive.

The political leadership of the South now fell to a new group, men able to unite the South behind a program of racism and reform. In the process, the Populist movement was absorbed by the new, more liberal Democratic Party. As a leading southern educator wrote, "disfranchisement of the negroes has been concomitant with the growth of political and social solidarity among the whites."[37] With the dominant race no longer divided into bitterly opposed political parties, it was possible to disenfranchise the Negro more effectively than ever before through the "white primary." Since the Democrats now usually were unchallenged in the general elections, except for token Republican opposition, it was the primaries, restricted by law to whites only, that determined the South's political fortunes.

Thus in the Progressive era that followed, the nation was treated to the spectacle of racism and reform marching hand in hand throughout the South. The same legislatures which voted to tax the corporations, regulate the railroads, adopt the initiative and referendum, prohibit alcoholic beverages, and allow labor to organize also voted to discriminate against the Negro in every aspect of his life. It was not until 1887 that the first "Jim Crow" statute was enacted in the South. That year the Florida legislature passed a law requiring separation of the races on all trains, and in the next few years, several of the other southern states enacted similar legislation. The conservatives who were in control of those states had hoped— futilely, as it developed—that this concession to popular prejudice would win the support of the poor whites and stem the mounting Populist tide. However, it was not until the turn of the century, under the various Progressive regimes, that the great bulk of "Jim Crow" legislation was enacted. Local ordinances supplemented the various state laws. Separation of the races was required in the schools, at work, in the hospitals, at public amusements—in fact, in every area of everyday life. One Progressive journal even demanded that the farm lands in North Carolina be segregated, while the New Orleans town fathers went so far as to require separate white and Negro prostitutes in different parts of the city.

But the various "Jim Crow" laws were only part of the story. As C. Vann Woodward has pointed out, the Negro became the outlet for all the South's pent up aggression. "Economic, political, and social frustrations had pyramided to a climax of social tensions. No real relief was in sight from the long cyclical depression of the 'nineties, an acute period of suffering that had only intensified the distress of the much longer agricultural depression. Hopes for reform . . . had likewise met with cruel disappointments and frustration. There had to be a scapegoat."[38] Many southerners did not care that the Negro, as the Populists had pointed out much earlier, was more a victim than a cause. Frustrated beyond endurance and uncertain whether conditions would ever improve, they frequently exploded by assaulting, and on occasion even murdering, Negroes who offended them—often by merely existing. The efforts by politicians to outdo one another in depicting the Negro's baseness and inhumanity simply egged the mobs on. It is little wonder that the years from 1890 to 1915 have been called the nadir of Negro history. In some ways the former Africans were even worse off than they had been under slavery.

NOTES

1. Wharton, Vernon Lane, *The Negro in Mississippi, 1865–1890,* University of North Carolina Press, Chapel Hill, 1947, p. 244.

2. Bond, Horace Mann, *Negro Education in Alabama, A Study in Cotton and Steel,* Associated Publishers, Washington, D.C., 1939, pp. 120–1.

3. Shannon, Fred A., *The Farmer's Last Frontier, Agriculture, 1860–1897,* Farrar and Rinehart, New York, 1945, p. 77.

4. *Ibid.,* p. 93

5. Bond, *op. cit.,* p. 121.

6. Woodward, C. Vann, *Origins of the New South, 1877–1913,* Louisiana State University Press, Baton Rouge, 1951, pp. 213–4.

7. *Ibid.,* p. 177.

8. *Ibid.,* p. 270.

9. *Ibid.,* p. 361.

10. Bond, *op. cit.,* p. 232.

11. Wharton, *op. cit.,* p. 96.

12. Bond, *op. cit.,* p. 152.

13. Dabney, Charles William, *Universal Education in the South,* University of North Carolina Press, Chapel Hill, 1936, Vol. I, p. 158.

14. Bond, *op. cit.,* pp. 152–3.

15. Cable, George W., *The Negro Question, A Selection of Writings on Civil Rights in the South,* Doubleday, Garden City, N.Y., 1958, p. 209.

16. Bond, *op. cit.,* pp. 155–6.

17. Woodward, *op. cit.,* p. 76.

18. *Ibid.,* p. 92.

19. *Ibid.,* p. 77.

20. *Ibid.,* p. 81.

21. *Ibid.,* pp. 103–4.

22. *Ibid.,* p. 79.

23. Wharton, *op. cit.,* p. 204.

24. *Idem.*

25. Pearson, Charles Chilton, *The Readjuster Movement in Virginia,* Yale University Press, New Haven, Conn., 1917, p. 164.

26. Woodward, *op. cit.,* p. 105.

27. *Ibid.,* p. 251.

28. *Ibid.,* p. 256.

29. *Ibid.,* pp. 257–8.

30. *Ibid.,* p. 255.

31. *Ibid.,* pp. 261–2.

32. Woodward, C. Vann, *The Strange Career of Jim Crow,* Oxford University Press, New York, 1955, p. 62.

33. Wharton, *op. cit.,* p. 215.

34. Woodward, *Origins of the New South, 1877–1913, op. cit.,* pp. 326–30.

35. *Ibid.,* p. 327.

36. *Ibid.,* p. 339.

37. Woodward, *The Strange Career of Jim Crow, op. cit.,* p. 76.

38. *Ibid.,* p. 64.

9 The Mind of the North

THE CHANGE that gradually took place in the mood of the North after 1876 is in some ways the most important part of the Reconstruction story. The North continued to dominate the nation, politically, economically, and culturally, throughout the final quarter of the nineteenth century. In whatever direction it moved, the nation was sure to follow. By the same token, in whatever direction it refused to follow, the nation could not long continue.

The change in northern mood did not spring from internal sources alone. No sooner had Robert E. Lee surrendered than the defeated South began impressing upon the victorious North its view that the Negroes could not be made to work except by coercion, that the former slaves were inherently incapable of governing themselves, and that only the white southerners really understood and knew how to deal with them. Even after efforts at radical Reconstruction were overthrown, the spokesmen for the South continued to hammer at these points. They sought to convince the North that the Negro problem was best left to the South to handle. At first, the North would hear none of this, but later, as its own efforts to deal with the problem of the Negroes met only with frustration, it began to listen to the South's argument more sympathetically. As the memories of war began to recede and the people of the North came to have more and more contact with the South, they found more in common with the white southerner than with the Negro.

After their earlier unhappy experiences, Southerners hesitated to again invite northern retaliation. The South's treatment of the Negro was influenced at least in part by what it considered to be the mood of the North, and slowly that mood began to change. Northern magazine articles, politicians' statements and Supreme Court decisions clearly revealed the new temper, and cautiously, the leaders of the South began testing it. They found that the North was prepared to accept their view that the Negro was primarily a southern problem, one to be dealt with by southerners. This meant that they were free to work out their own solution, one evolved in the best interests of the white population, without fear of outside interference.

It is not possible to understand why the Negro, by the turn of the century, had sunk to so low a position without understanding what lay behind this change in northern mood. When the North in 1877 relinquished its control of the South, it realized that it was placing the Negro in great jeopardy. Senator Bejamin Wade of Ohio echoed the feelings of many when he said that the Administration had attempted to "put these colored people under the iron heel of their most bitter enemies, and reduce them to a condition unfortunately worse than before they were made free."[1] Yet the North seemed to have no alternative. To a large extent, the southerners had already regained control themselves. Then too, the Depression of 1873 had greatly undermined the strength of the Republican Party and its program of radical Reconstruction. Without control, how could the North protect the Negro? For the next quarter-century the North was to try to find some way of reconciling the realities of political life that made a return to radical Reconstruction impossible with the moral obligation it had inherited from the Civil War to act as the freedmen's guardian.

Since it was limited to proffering only indirect assistance, the North turned to education as the most important instrument which it could bring to bear in the Negro's behalf. In his inaugural address, a speech that heralded the North's new "hands-off" policy toward the South, President Rutherford B. Hayes himself suggested that the federal government help the South to educate its Negro citizens. During his four years in

office, Hayes returned to this theme time and again. "To
perpetuate the Union and to abolish slavery were the work
of the war," he declared toward the end of his term. "To
educate the uneducated is the appropriate work of peace."[2]

As early as 1870 Representative George Hoar of Massachusetts had introduced a bill which sought "to compel by
national authority the establishment of a thorough and efficient
system of public instruction throughout the whole country."[3]
When the Hoar proposal was denounced as too drastic, a
Mississippi Republican, Legrand W. Perce, introduced a
milder measure, which narrowly passed the House but failed
to advance any further.

Toward the end of the Hayes' Administration a new effort
to revive federal aid to education received the support of most
southern Democrats and easily passed the Senate, but it was
then buried in the House, never even emerging from committee, the first of many such bills to suffer the same fate.
Undaunted, the Republicans the next year endorsed the
principle of federal aid to education in their party platform.
"The work of popular education," they declared, "is one left
to the care of the several States, but it is the duty of the National Government to aid that work to the extent of its constitutional power. The intelligence of the Nation is but the
aggregate of the intelligence in the several States, and the
destiny of the Nation must be guided, not by the genius of
any one State, but by the aggregate genius of all." The platform
reiterated the party's earlier belief that the Constitution
should be amended "to forbid the appropriation of public
funds to the support of sectarian schools."[4]

The Republican standard bearer James A. Garfield had
been much impressed by a recent book, *A Fool's Errand,* by
Albion W. Tourgee, a northerner who had gone South after
the Civil War, with a clarion call for education. "The
Nation nourished and protected slavery," Tourgee wrote.
"The fruitage of slavery has been the ignorant freedman, the
ignorant poor-white man, the arrogance of the late master. . . .
Now, let the Nation undo the evil. . . . Let it educate those
whom it made ignorant. It is not a matter of favor to the

black, but of safety to the Nation. . . ." Responding to critics who asked how this could be done "without infringement of the rights of the States," Tourgee's hero said, "when the Nation has smarted enough for its folly, it will find a way to undo the evil, whether the State-Rights Moloch stand in the way or not."[5]

Garfield decided on a two-pronged program, education and civil service reform. His answer to the southern white minority's control of the Negro majority was to make the members of the majority "as trained and intelligent as the minority itself." The race problem would be solved only when Negroes exhibited "the native hungering and thirsting for knowledge that the Creator has planted in every child to the last possible degree of their ability, so that the hands of the people shall reach out and grasp in the darkness the hand of the Government extended to help, and by the union of effort the two will bring what mere legislation alone cannot immediately bring."[6]

Mortally wounded by an assassin's bullet six months after his inauguration, Garfield never had a chance to implement this program. His successor, Chester Arthur, had little sympathy for the needs of education or for the plight of the Negro. The outlook for federal aid grew even worse after 1884 when Grover Cleveland was elected as the first Democratic President since James Buchanan. While the Negroes' fears that his election would presage a return to slavery soon proved false, Cleveland was a fiscal conservative, a states' righter opposed to expanding the scope of federal power. Though bills to aid education passed the Senate in 1886 and in 1888 by large margins, they inevitably bogged down in the House, where the Democrats were in the majority and the President was more able to exert his influence.

In the fall of 1888, however, the outlook for federal aid to education brightened considerably when Benjamin Harrison was elected President and the Republicans captured control of both houses of Congress for the first time since Grant's second Administration. Though the Republican platform four years earlier had included only a passing reference to federal aid for education, the plank on which Harrison had run was unequivocal. "In a Republic like ours," it declared, "where the citizen is the sovereign and the official the servant, where no power is exercised except by the will of the people, it is important that the sovereign—the people—should possess intelligence. The free school is the promoter of that intelligence which is to preserve us a free Nation; therefore, the State or Nation, or both combined, should support free institutions of learning sufficient to afford every child growing up in the land the opportunity of a good common school education."[7]

When, in his first message to Congress, Harrison strongly supported a program of direct federal aid for education, the outlook seemed even brighter.

Once again, as he had done five times previously, Senator Henry W. Blair of New Hampshire introduced legislation providing federal aid to education. The bill, as amended, would have committed the federal government to a ten-year program of grants to the states, beginning with $7 million the first year, increasing to $15 million the third year, and then gradually declining to $5 million the last year. The basis for distributing these funds among the states was to be the number of illiterates over ten years old. Again, since about three-fourths of all illiterates were in the South, and about 70 per cent of them were colored, the bill would have primarily benefited the South and particularly the Negro. Each state, in order to qualify for these funds, was required to establish "a system of free common schools for all of its children of school age, without distinction of race or color, either in the raising or distributing of school revenues. . . ."[8] However, at the South's insistence, segregated schools were to be permitted.

Once again the measure passed the upper chamber, though this time by the smallest margin ever, only ten votes. A majority of Democrats supported the measure, but the defection of many others presaged the bill's ultimate defeat. This stiffening of Democratic opposition was due in large part to the fear that if the measure were enacted, it would redound mainly to the Republicans' political advantage; that if the

Treasury surplus were thereby drained, it would lead to demands that the tariff be increased. In the North Democrats were under pressure from their Catholic constituents, who viewed the measure as a threat to their own parochial school system. In the South Democrats were swayed by fears that the measure would lead to renewed federal interference in the South's tangled race relations. "The chief factor [in defeating the Blair bill]," a prominent northern educator later said, "was Southern political bourbonism."[9] A southern colleague agreed, pointing out that many persons from his region were afraid that improved education would make the Negroes more difficult to control.

But it was in the House that the Blair bill was actually buried. The story of the behind-the-scenes maneuvering has been lost to history, but it is probably safe to say that the measure had such a low priority among Republicans that they preferred not to force the issue. Since the bill would mainly benefit the South, Republicans could hardly be expected to work up much enthusiasm for it, especially since so many southern Democrats were now opposed to it. Perhaps the best clue to the northern attitude was the reaction of the press. In the West most newspapers either ignored the Blair bill entirely or mildly disapproved of it. "The principle that where the National money goes," warned the Salt Lake City *Daily Tribune,* the paper with the largest circulation in the Rocky Mountain region, "there goes also the National authority and supervision is a correct one. . . . [I]ndeed, we do not see how it can be safely ignored." The *Tribune* hoped to see the bill amended so that the funds would be distributed on a different basis, one more likely to benefit the West, but "if the change should kill [the measure] altogether," it added, "there would be no occasion for wet eyes."[10]

Only in New England was there any enthusiastic support for the measure. All three Boston papers endorsed the Blair bill, the *Traveller* accusing opponents of being "short-sighted" in attacking the measure on economic grounds. "True economy," it declared, "demands the building of the school house and the establishment of the school, since on these the safety and perpetuity of our institutions depend." The *Journal* agreed, responding to criticisms of the way in which the federal funds were to be distributed. Calling illiteracy a "disease," it declared, "If there is any better or more natural course than to apportion the remedy in ratio to the extent of the disease, we do not know what it is."[11]

In New York City none of the major newspapers supported the Blair bill, not even the avowedly Republican *Tribune.* Most vociferous in its opposition was the *New York Evening Post,* edited by E. L. Godkin and quoted extensively throughout the country. Convinced that passage of the Blair bill would lead to complete federal control over education, an editor of the *Post* inveighed against the "present tendency to paternalism in government" and warned that "recourse to Washington for school money would inevitably harm the schools in the States by weakening the spirit of self-reliance."[12] Besides, it argued, with the South's growing prosperity, the time had passed when it needed special assistance. True or not, these and similar arguments had their effect on the members of Congress. Two years later, when the Blair bill was revived once more, it failed even to clear the Senate. The North had finally given up the idea of aiding the Negro through a broad program of federal grants to education.

As early as 1871, the *Nation* had suggested outmigration as the most effective cure for southern mistreatment of the Negro. "Our business," the widely respected weekly declared, "is now to leave every Southern state to its own people, first because this is the only practical course, and secondly because it is the only wise one. Those victimized can leave the state, and so in the long run the state will suffer for its defects. This may be a slow remedy but it is a sure one."[13] In a small way Negroes had been leaving the South ever since the end of the Civil War. A few had gone North, a few had settled on western homesteads, and some had even moved to other parts of the South. There had been considerable movement but, as yet, no significant regional distribution of the Negro population. In fact, it was not until 1878 that outmigration from the South began to assume large-scale proportions. In that year thousands of Negroes from the lower Mississippi delta began heading for the Great Plains.

They were driven westward by a series of disastrous events that had brought death and ruination to many Negro farm families. A yellow fever epidemic had followed on the heels of a drought that destroyed a large part of the 1878 cotton crop. To these natural calamities were added falling prices and mounting debt. Finally, the Negroes were beginning to feel the full effects of the North's withdrawal from Southern affairs. A congressional committee later summed up the testimony of many of these migrants: "The land owners, planters, and the old master-class generally, deal unfairly with them, having had their labor for nothing when they were slaves. These men, now they are free, endeavor by various devices to get it for next to nothing; work as hard, faithfully and constantly as they may, live as plainly and as sparingly as they may, they are no better off at the end of the year than at the beginning. They say that they are the dupes and victims of cunning and fraud in signing contracts which they cannot read and cannot fully understand; that they are compelled to trade at stores owned in whole or in part by their employers, and that they are paid with orders and not with money. They say that they have to pay double the value of nearly everything they buy; . . . that land owners are in league to prevent land-owning by Negroes; that when they work the land on shares they barely make a living; that outside the towns and cities no provision is made for education, and, ground down as they are, they cannot employ teachers to instruct their children; that they are not only the victims of fraud and cunning, but of violence and intimidation; that from their very poverty the temples of justice are not open to them; that the jury box is virtually closed; that the murder of a black man by a white man is followed by no conviction or punishment."[14]

Early in 1879 the westward flow of blacks quickened. Once again the rumor spread that the federal government was about to provide every Negro with forty acres and a mule. By spring the flow had become a torrent, some 40,000 Negroes pulling up stakes from Mississippi, Louisiana, Alabama, and

Georgia and heading west. Sympathetic observers soon referred to it as the "Exodus." "Hopeless, penniless and in rags," one historian has written, "these poor people were thronging the wharves of St. Louis, crowding the steamers on the Mississippi River, hailing the passing steamers and imploring them for a passage to the land of freedom, where the rights of citizens are respected and honest toil rewarded by compensation."[15]

In vain did Frederick Douglass try to dissuade the members of his race from leaving the South, their natural home, where, he said, they had "a monopoly of the labor market." In the South, Douglass pointed out, the Negro had much greater political power because of his larger numbers. "The business of this nation," he said, "is to protect its citizens *where they are,* not to transport them where they will not need protection."[16] Besides, "there was something sinister in this so-called exodus, for" . . . the agents of railroad companies ". . . were to receive one dollar per head upon all such passengers."[17] His efforts to halt the "stampede," however, were to no avail. Other Negro leaders continued to urge their followers westward, and in Nashville a colored convention asked Congress to appropriate $500,000 to enable southern Negroes to resettle in "those states and territories where they can enjoy all rights which are guaranteed by the laws of the Constitution of the United States."[18]

At first the migrants were greeted with open arms. Local Republicans, eager to distinguish their own behavior from that of the Democrats in the South, made a special effort to assist the newcomers. In Kansas, where over 25,000 Negroes eventually sought to settle, one group was met by the Governor himself, who welcomed them to "the state made immortal by Old John Brown."[19] It was not long, however, before this initial hospitality gave way to hostility. The first wave of Negro migrants was easily absorbed by the local labor market, but as more and more of them continued to arrive in Kansas, the supply soon exceeded the demand. Unfortunately, few Negroes had any idea of how to operate the various types of agricultural machinery already prevalent on Kansas farms, and not many of them had the money to buy farms of their own. As a result, they began to gather in the cities, unable to find work. Many had come to Kansas unprepared for the cold weather they encountered. Clad only in light cottons, sometimes even without shoes, they easily succumbed to sickness and death. All of this put a great strain on local charity, with the consequence that many communities began discouraging the migrant from settling in their midst.

To help alleviate the Negroes' plight, the Kansas Freedmen's Relief Association was formed, with headquarters in Topeka and branches in various other cities. It succeeded in raising $25,000 in cash and $100,000 in food and clothing; one-sixth of the former and one-fourth of the latter came from Great Britain. With this money a colony was established in Wabaunsee County, fifty miles west of Topeka, where land was sold to the Negroes for $2.65 an acre, only one-tenth of which was required as a cash down payment. Elsewhere throughout the country a National Emigration Aid Society was organized, with Senator Windom of Minnesota, a proponent of federal support for Negro migration, and many other leading Republicans as sponsors. Perhaps most active of all in the Negroes' behalf was General Thomas Conway of New Jersey, a former Freedmen's Bureau official. Besides soliciting funds, he persuaded many wealthy northerners either to donate land outright or to permit Negro migrants to settle on their estates. Meanwhile, in Congress, Speaker John Garfield sponsored a resolution authorizing the Secretary of War to supply the colored migrants in Kansas with army rations.

On May 28, 1879, President Hayes noted in his diary that the migration of Negroes out of the South was continuing, and he was certain that this would lead to "altogether favorable" results. "The tendency," he wrote, "will be to force the better class of Southern people to suppress the violence of the ruffian class, and to protect colored people in their rights."[20] Others in the North, however, were less happy about the exodus. Business interests, in particular, were concerned lest the southern economy be disrupted. "Can the South or the North be benefited," the New York *Commercial Bulletin* asked, "by encouraging the migration of that labor upon which our chief commercial crop is dependent? Can we afford to undermine the prosperity, nay the very existence of Southern trade by diverting from that section the population on which its industry is dependent?"[21] And when conventions of southern planters appealed to the North to help stem the outflow, the New York *Journal of Commerce* replied, "We can assure the Southerners, once and for all, that, excepting a few incurable fanatics who have little money or influence, the people of the North feel no desire to break up the present Southern labor system, and will contribute a hundred dollars to transport the refugees back to their homes from Kansas, to every dollar given by any rabid hater of the South toward depriving the capitalists of the only labor available to them."[22] In St. Louis, twenty-five merchants gave an even more positive reply to the southern appeal. They petitioned the city's steamship companies to raise their rates so high that no Negro could afford to book passage up river.

Southerners were not above using more direct methods to bring a halt to the outmigration. Senator John J. Ingalls of Kansas charged on the Senate floor that at least twenty Negroes were murdered for attempting to flee their homes in the South. In May, at the height of the exodus, a group of Mississippians threatened to sink any boat carrying Negroes up the Mississippi River. This so frightened the shipowners that they refused to take on any more Negro passengers, leaving 1,500 of them stranded along the Mississippi's banks. Incensed by this act, Conway wrote to President Hayes, demanding federal protection for the Negro migrants. "Every river landing is blockaded by white enemies of the colored exodus," he explained, "some of whom are mounted and armed, as if we were at war, their object being to force the negroes back to the places they left." Deputy sheriffs, he added, armed with writs of attachment for debts allegedly owed southern planters, were arresting the colored migrants and returning them to the counties from whence they came, "much as they used to do under the old fugitive slave law."[23] Hayes promised that federal authorities would see to it that any vessel transporting

Negro migrants was allowed to pass up river unmolested. Physical "resistance to lawful business carried on upon a National highway such as the Mississippi would be rebellion," the President declared, "and there would be no doubt that the Government would afford its protection."[24] When Hayes' views were made known, southerners abandoned their efforts to close the Mississippi River to Negro migrants. Yet this was as far as the President was willing to go.

While Conway was mainly concerned about the welfare of the Negroes, other Republicans were more interested in the political implications. Senator John Sherman of Ohio, for example, while supporting the Party's efforts to help the Negro relocate in the North, felt that if the migrants "could be directed into Indiana it could still be better. The trouble is that it is rather late now for political results next year, but it would be useful for the future."[25] Meanwhile, in North Carolina, the Negroes themselves had formed an emigration society. Two of their leaders were brought to Indiana and assured that members of their race would find agricultural employment there. Within a few months the first group of fifty Negroes had left North Carolina for the Hoosier State.

Enraged by what he felt was an underhanded political maneuver to shift his state into the Republican column, Senator Voorhees demanded a congressional investigation. Indiana, he declared, "will accept everybody who comes there, black, or white, or red . . . ; but we do no more want this population colonized upon us in large squads, battalions, regiments and corps than the people of California want the Chinese landed upon them. . . . What we object to is not black people coming to Indiana legitimately and orderly in the natural way of emigration, but . . . to its being pointed out and designated as a field for emigrant aid societies to operate upon. If that be going on in Indiana . . . for political purposes . . . , the sooner it is known the better. . . . "[26]

The fact was that Indiana had no room for any large number of Negro migrants. "We have no public waste-lands for people to take up cheaply," Senator Voorhees said. "If there are agents going South saying to the negroes down there that they can get so much per day for cultivating land and various things of that kind in Indiana, the sooner these unfortunate people are undeceived the better for them."[27]

The investigation that Senator Voorhees demanded was finally agreed to, and in the hearings that ensued both the Republican leaders' role in the relocation movement and the very real grievances that prompted the Negroes to leave the South were disclosed. Meanwhile, however, the exodus had come to a halt even more suddenly than it had begun. From Kansas and the other western states reports began filtering back to the South that conditions in the promised New Canaan were not as inviting as they had been advertised. The climate was colder than most Negroes were accustomed to, the only lands available were generally barren, and jobs were difficult to come by. Senator Voorhees was right: there was no place for the Negroes in Indiana or any other northern state. In fact, at least a third of the migrants returned home to the South.

Meanwhile, many people in the North had come to believe that the Negro problem would eventually solve itself. On the basis of a few isolated statistics and some dubious reasoning they had come to the conclusion that the Negro in America was gradually dying out. The ex-slave had been able to survive so far, it was felt, only because first his white master and later the Freedmen's Bureau had looked after him. Now, left to his own devices and inherently incapable of taking care of himself, he was about to become extinct. This belief was reinforced by occasional reports that Negro communities in the South were declining. However, the 1880 census returns, which revealed an increase, not a decrease, in the Negro population, soon put an end to such speculation. "One of the most disheartening ethnological speculations concerning us," Frederick Douglass wrote, "has been that we shall die out—that, like the Indian, we shall perish in the blaze of Caucasian civilization. The census sets to rest that heresy concerning us."[28]

Now the fear arose that the Negro population was growing too rapidly, that this would make a solution of the nation's race problem that much more difficult. Even southerners began to share this fear. In 1889 Senator M. C. Butler of South Carolina introduced a bill "to provide for the migration of persons of color from the Southern States,"[29] in the belief that a lessened concentration would aid race relations. Other proposals of a similar nature followed. One southern Senator wanted the United States to annex Cuba and set up a Negro republic there. Another urged the setting aside of territory in the United States. A third favored the emigration of the "better class" of colored people to Africa. Still another suggested a protectorate over Haiti. It was the same solution to the Negro problem that Americans had proposed ever since the formation of the American Colonization Society in 1816. And for much the same reason none of these latter-day proposals received serious consideration. The North was unwilling to provide the sums necessary to relocate the very large number of southern Negroes, even if this were practical, and the South was unwilling to lose the principal source of its labor supply. Outmigration was foreclosed as a possibility to all but a few Negroes for at least another thirty-five years.

The federal government's failure to help the Negro either to become better educated or to resettle in some other region meant that the great majority of former slaves had no choice bu to remain in the South as agricultural laborers. Only one possible means of escape still remained—to break into the industrial job market. Whether this would happen depended to a large extent on local attitudes, but in one important way the North could still make its influence felt, for the emerging trade union movement was led mainly by white men in the North.

Samuel Gompers, the founder of the American Federation of Labor, was initially sympathetic towards organizing the Negro worker. "If the colored man is not permitted to organize," he said, "if he is not given the opportunity to protect and defend his interests, if a chance is not given him by which he could uplift his condition, the inevitable result must follow, that he will sink down lower and lower in his economic scale and in his conception of his rights as a worker and finally find himself . . . absolutely dependent (worse than chattel slavery) in the hands of unfair and unscrupulous employers."[30] At Gompers' insistence the Federation in 1890 declared that it "looks with disfavor upon trade unions having provisions which exclude from membership persons on account of race or color."[31] Three years later it reaffirmed this position, declaring that "the working people must unite and organize, irrespective of creed, color, sex, nationality, or politics."[32]

The test of Gompers' policy came when the National Association of Machinists applied for an A.F. of L. charter in 1890. Drawing its membership mainly from the South, it was one of only two national unions which specifically excluded Negroes. Gompers told its leaders that they would have to strike the "white only" clause from the union's constitution before it could be admitted to the A.F. of L. When they refused, Gompers chartered a rival organization, the International Machinists' Union of America, composed of several northern locals and placing no restriction of Negro membership. Similarly, when the International Brotherhood of Blacksmiths, another "lily-white" union applied for an A.F. of L. charter, it, too, was turned down until it eliminated the objectionable clause from its constitution. As Gompers explained to the latter's officers, "If, as you say, there are no Negro blacksmiths, then there is no need to specifically exclude them. If, on the other hand, there are blacksmiths who are colored men, the inevitable is presented to you, that either you must make friends of them or if you will not they will prove enemies to you and play into the hands of employers who may always be willing to take advantage of you. If the question were not a humanitarian one, then enlightened self-interest should prompt us all to declare our desire to organize our fellow workers instead of discriminating against [them.]"[33]

Gompers well understood that any racial cleavage among the laboring classes would be exploited by employers, but he soon found that he was caught on the horns of a dilemma. White workers, particularly in the South, would not join any union organization that accepted Negroes on an equal basis.

Aside from the question of white supremacy, they complained that the Negroes frequently pulled the local wage level down. Officials of the Brotherhood of Locomotive Firemen, for example, complained to Gompers that colored firemen were working for 25 to 50 per cent less than their white counterparts, and that the white members feared if the Negroes were admitted to the Brotherhood, their own wages would fall. Gompers tried to argue that this was all the more reason to accept the Negroes as members. "This question of race and color," he wrote, "is more of a bugaboo urged among some workingmen to frighten them from performing their duties. It is simply preposterous. During the agitation for the abolition of slavery . . . unthinking people of the time could not understand that one could desire [such a step] without falling absolutely in love with the slaves. This mistake seems to be repeated in our day only in another way. . . ."[34] But such arguments were to no avail.

Gompers came to realize that the growth of the Federation was being retarded by racial conflict. In an effort to resolve this dilemma he made the first of several retreats on the race question when he informed the machinists' union that it need only remove the "white only" clause from its constitution but that it would still be free to accept for membership only those whom it desired. This the machinists' union finally agreed to do, placing the ban on Negro members in its secret ritual instead. The A.F. of L. then accepted it for affiliation, knowing full well that it continued to discriminate against Negroes. As Gompers told the Brotherhood of Locomotive Firemen when he sought to bring them into the Federation on the same basis: "Does the A.F. of L. compel its affiliated organizations to accept colored workmen? I answer no! Decidedly not. No more than it compels organizations to accept Americans, Frenchmen, Englishmen, Irishmen, or even Hottentots. . . . The International Association of Machinists formerly had the 'color line' provision in its constitution. It eliminated the objectionable declaration and became affiliated with the A.F. of L. . . . Yet I venture to say . . . that they are more than pleased with their affiliation, that their autonomy and independence is as fully recognized today as any time in the existence of the organization."[35] The locomotive firemen at least were not hypocrites. Their president informed Gompers that the firemen "do not care to belong to an organization that is not honest enough to make public its qualifications of membership."[36]

As another way out of the dilemma in which the labor movement found itself, Gompers began sanctioning the formation of separate white and Negro locals. "Inasmuch . . . as many white workmen will not belong to the same local organization with black men," Gompers explained to those who protested this change in policy, "and will not meet with them as members of the same local union, it might be more advantageous to go to work gradually to accomplish the desired end. In other words, have the Union of white men organize, and have the Union of colored men organize also, both unions to work in unison and harmony to accomplish the desired end." Then, giving expression to his feelings of frustration, he added, "It is useless to be simply trying to ram our heads through stone walls; recognizing conditions which exist is the best way we can secure the organization of all in a way which must ultimately bring about a unity of feeling and action among all toilers."[37]

But Gompers found that he was forced to retreat even further. When it became impossible to form councils in the South with both white and Negro members, he finally agreed to the establishment of separate councils for the two races, just as he had already agreed to the establishment of separate locals. As a result, southern Negroes found themselves abandoned by organized labor.

In 1897 Booker T. Washington, Frederick Douglass' successor as the leader of his race, accused the trade union movement of holding back the Negro's advancement. The A.F. of L., at its annual convention that year, promptly denounced the accusation as untrue. It then reaffirmed its traditional stand against excluding Negroes from union membership. Among those enthusiastically supporting the resolution was the president of the still "lily-white" machinists' union.

Though the A.F. of L. had discovered the value of resolutions as a substitute for action, organized labor had still not escaped from its dilemma. No one understood this better than Gompers himself. Taking the floor in support of the antidiscrimination resolution, he declared, "If we do not give the colored men the opportunity to organize, the capitalist will set him up as a barrier to our progress. . . . It is not a question as to the color of a man's skin, but the power that lies in organization."[38]

Yet the inescapable fact was that organized labor had turned its back on the Negro. In 1902 W. E. B. Du Bois reported that forty-three national unions had not a single colored member. And of the more than a million working men who belong to the A.F. of L., only 40,000 were Negroes. Abandoned as they were by the trade unions, Negroes were easily recruited as strike breakers, and even when they were not actually so employed, they served to keep local wages and working conditions below what they otherwise would have been.

Forgetting what he had previously said about the need for unity among the working classes and what would be the probable consequence of excluding Negroes from the labor movement, Gompers now denounced colored workmen for being "cheap workers" and for demanding "special privileges." They had so conducted themselves, he told the United States Industrial Commission in 1899, "as to be a continuous convenient whip placed in the hands of the employers to cow the white men and to compel them to accept abject conditions of labor."[39] Meanwhile the A.F. of L. published an article by a white Georgia organizer who argued that the Negro was incapable of being unionized because he did not possess "those peculiarities of temperament such as patriotism, sympathy, etc., which are peculiar to most of the Caucasian race, and which alone make an organization of the character and complicity of the modern labor movement possible. . . ." The Negro, he added, was not only distrustful of other colored workers, prejudiced against whites, and characterized by "abandoned and reckless disposition"; he was also willing to work for next to nothing and remain "the happiest and most contented individual imaginable."[40] Since he represented such a menace to the white worker, the only solution was to ship him to Liberia or Cuba. In 1905, in tune with the nation's growing racist temper, Gompers himself warned that "Caucasians are not going to let their standard of living be destroyed by negroes, Chinamen, Japs or any others."[41]

The A.F. of L. president was not the first northerner to turn on the Negro in despair. Most northerners had already preceded him. Frustrated in their efforts to incorporate the colored man into the broader spectrum of American life, they had come to rationalize this failure by pointing to the Negroes' own alleged inherent limitations. Most northerners preferred to believe not that the Negro was too intimidated to exercise his right to vote, but that he was incapable of self-government. If he was too deprived to acquire even an elementary education, they preferred to believe that he was incapable of mental discipline. If he was too exploited to rise above his station as an agricultural laborer, they preferred to believe that he was improvident and lazy. And if he was unhappy in the North, they preferred to believe that he could thrive only in a warm climate. The Negro had become a burden that most northerners no longer wished to bear. And so they sought to transfer that burden to the Negro himself. Shortly after Henry Cabot Lodge's Force Bill went down to defeat in 1891, Senator George Hoar of Massachusetts, a long-time champion of the negro wrote that the colored people should "cultivate the virtues of integrity, industry and frugality. . . [T]he negro question is to be settled in this country by the personal worth of the Negro. When he attains that, all other things will be added unto him!"[42]

To give credence to this process of rationalization, the North began developing its own stereotype of the Negro. One literary historian has pointed out the seven aspects of this stereotype, as revealed in northern fiction and drama: The Contented Slave, The Wretched Freedman, The Comic Negro, The Brute Negro, The Tragic Mulatto, the Local Color Negro, and the Exotic Primitive. "All of these stereotypes," he says, "are marked either by exaggeration or omission; they all agree in stressing the Negro's divergence from an Anglo-Saxon norm to the flattery of the latter."[43] They also contained just enough truth to make them plausible. But, most important, they described the Negro as many people in the North wanted to believe he existed. Joel Chandler Harris, for example, has old Uncle Remus declare, "Hit's [education is] de ruinashun er dis country. . . . Put a spellin'-book in a nigger's han's, en right den en dar' you loozes a plow-hand. . . . What's a nigger gwineter 'larn outen books? I kin take a bar'l stave an' fling mo' sense inter a nigger in one minnit dan all de schoolhouses betwixt dis en de State er Midgigin. . . . Wid one bar'l stave I kin fa'rly lif' de vail er ignunce."[44]

Harris and most of the others who wrote about the Negro—men such as Mark Twain and Thomas Nelson Page—were southerners. The magazines which published their stories, however, were controlled by northerners. This was no mere coincidence. *Scribner's,* followed by *Lippincott's, Harper's Monthly* and the *Atlantic Magazine,* had deliberately sought out southern writers and opened its pages to them. Editors looked to the elimination of the old themes of sectional conflict from our literature, replacing them with "a sane and earnest Americanism."[45] Tacitly discouraging "any expression of the old hostility" from their contributors, the editors of *Scribner's,* later the *Century Magazine,* sought to "increase the sentiment of union throughout our diverse sisterhood of States."[46] Southern authors were given a free hand to write about their region, even to emphasize its distinctiveness, just as long as they did not do so in the same old truculent, provincial spirit as before the war. "Let's see to it, North and South," said *Scribner's,* "that the Centennial [celebration] . . . reconciles all the old differences . . . [and makes for] fraternal good will among all sections and all states."[47]

Nothing symbolized the theme better than the popular tale of the northern cavalry officer falling in love with the rebellious southern belle, a tale first suggested by southern writers but repeated over and over again by northern imitators. The story was given a new twist when the daughter of Julia Ward Howe, author of "The Battle Hymn of the Republic," wrote a book telling of a New England school girl's romance with a southern youth. One result of all this was to foster the myth of the Old South, the antebellum society of white-columned mansions, gracious ladies, and Negroes singing in the fields. This sentimental portrait had a warmth and softness that contrasted sharply with the vulgarity and harshness of postwar northern society, and it was for this reason that it found such a ready acceptance among northern readers. But another result, perhaps unintentional but real nevertheless, was to provide the North with its unflattering stereotype of the Negro.

Scholars as well as writers supplied the rationale for this shift in sentiment. Sociologists such as William Graham Sumner of Yale helped to popularize in this country the ideas of social Darwinism, a doctrine that argued against man's inherent equality. In Sumner's words, "Nothing is more certain than that inequality is a law of life. . . . No two persons were ever born equal. . . . Thus if you asked Thomas Jefferson when he was writing the first paragraph of the Declaration of Independence, whether in 'all men' he meant to include negroes, he would have said that he was not talking about negroes."[48] Meanwhile, historians such as John Burgess of Columbia helped to rewrite history in such a way as to emphasize the superiority of the Anglo-Saxon race.

The North had come increasingly to "understand" the problem the South faced because of its Negro population, and with understanding had come sympathy. Paul Buck has compiled a list of attitudes that, he says, had become common among northerners by the turn of the century: "1. The mass of Negroes are unfit for the suffrage; 2. The only hope of good government in the South rests upon the assured political supremacy of the white race; 3. The Negroes are the American peasantry; 4. One race or the other must rule, and the true interests of both races require that the control should be in the hands of the whites; 5. If there be a race problem, time and education can alone supply its solution; 6. Northerners when confronted with the race problem at home show the same prejudices southerners do—In fact, the attitude of the Anglo-Saxons toward the Negro the world over is essentially the same; 7. The Negro is better off in southern hands; 8. The history of the Negro in Africa and America 'leads to the belief that he will remain inferior in race stamina and race achievement.' "[49]

Among the prominent northerners identified with one or more of these views were E. L. Godkin, Carl Schurz, Charles Eliot Norton, Senator Hoar, A. W. Tourgee, Charles Francis Adams, T. W. Higginson, and Albert B. Hart. "Few Northerners," concludes Buck, "could be found at the close of the century who did not subscribe to the greater part of this credo. A tremendous reversal of opinion had materialized. The unchanging elements of the race problem had become apparent to most observers and the old impatient yearning for an immediate and thorough solution had passed away."[50] Besides, many northerners felt that the nation had more important matters to concern itself with. "Who or what is he," asked the *Nation* after warning against the federal government's becoming involved in educating the Negro or in protecting his voting rights, "that we should put the interests of 55 million whites of the continent in peril for his sake?"[51]

The readjustment that took place in the northern mood is nowhere more clearly reflected than in the decisions of the Supreme Court. Slowly and systematically, from 1873 onward, it withdrew from the Negro the protection afforded him by the Thirteenth, Fourteenth, and Fifteenth Amendments, as well as subsequent civil rights legislation. These decisions could hardly be said to represent the influence of southerners on the Court, as had been charged in the controversy surrounding the earlier Dred Scott decision. William Woods of Georgia, appointed to the Supreme Court in 1880, was the first southerner so named since 1852; while Lucius Q. Lamar of Mississippi, appointed in 1888, was the first Democrat since 1862. With the exception of John Marshall Harlan of Kentucky, appointed in 1881, they were still the only two southerners sitting on the Court in 1896 when it handed down its famous decision in *Plessy v Ferguson*. Harlan, however, had fought in the Union Army during the Civil War.

These decisions did not represent a conservative Court, irresponsive to the public will, simply interpreting the law as it saw fit. Ever since the beginning of the Civil War the

Supreme Court had attempted to avoid lagging behind the changing values of the country. Congress had actually withdrawn from it appellate jurisdiction over the Reconstruction Acts and even, for a short time, had reduced the number of the Court's members in order to prevent President Johnson from making any appointments. Faced with the threat of still further curbs on its powers, the Supreme Court had scrupulously avoided offending public opinion as reflected by Congress. Lamented ex-President James Buchanan, "What is to become of the Supreme Court of the United States—the conservative branch of the Government? . . . I cannot help thinking we have fallen on evil times."[52] Consequently, when the Supreme Court took a moderate position with respect to civil rights, it did so only after carefully testing the current drift of the North's mood.

The first sign of the Supreme Court's changed attitude came with its decision in the Slaughterhouse cases of 1873. Though these primarily involved the power of the states to regulate economic activity, the court's majority, in rendering its opinion, severely restricted the scope of the Fourteenth Amendment. It held that that Amendment was never intended "to transfer the security and protection of all . . . civil rights . . . from the States to the federal government"; nor was it intended "to bring within the power of Congress the entire domain of civil rights hitherto belonging exclusively to the States."[53] Two years later the Court went even further when it held that the Fourteenth Amendment did not necessarily confer the right to vote on all citizens of the United States. "It is true that the United States guarantees to every State a republican form of government," the Court said, but it went on to point out that "No particular government is designated as republican."[54] Each state was therefore free to limit the right to vote as it saw fit, subject only to the restrictions of the Fifteenth Amendment.

These decisions, though greatly narrowing the scope of the Fourteenth Amendment, did not touch on the Negro question directly. A year later, however, in 1876, the Supreme Court handed down two rulings which specifically curtailed the federal government's power to protect the Negro's political rights.

Then, in *U.S. v Cruikshank,* which involved an attempt to prevent Negroes from voting in Louisiana, the defendants were charged specifically with conspiring to violate the Negroes' right to peacefully assemble, petition for redress of grievances, bear arms, and vote. The Court ruled that all of these rights except the right to vote had existed before the Constitution was adopted and were therefore not encompassed by the 1870 Civil Rights Act. As for the right to vote, the Court's decision in *U.S. v Reese* was reaffirmed. "We may suspect," the majority opinion said, "that race was the cause of the hostility, but it is not so averred."[55] The defendants had also been charged with conspiring to falsely imprison and murder Negroes who sought to vote. The Court, however, denied that this was a violation of the Fourteenth Amendment's due process clause. That clause, it held, merely protected citizens against the violation of their rights by the states, not by other private citizens. Only the states themselves could prohibit such acts.

"The practical effect of these decisions," says Charles Warren in his authoritative history of the Supreme Court, "was to leave the Federal statutes almost wholly ineffective to protect the negro, in view of the construction of the Amendments adopted by the Court, the lack of adequate legislation in the Southern States, and the extremely limited number of rights which the Court deemed inherent in a citizen of the United States, *as such,* under the Constitution."[56] The southern states were thus assured, in effect, that they could continue to control the Negro vote through threats and physical violence without fear of federal interference. These decisions also presaged the later Court rulings upholding various state laws intended to disfranchise the Negro directly, first through the literacy test and later through the "grandfather" clause and the white primary.

And yet the decisions met with little criticism in the North. The *Independent,* for example, hailed the decision with the comment that "Southern questions, so far as they are purely State questions, must be left to the States themselves.

. . . The General Government cannot authoritatively deal with them, without producing more evils than it will remedy." *The New York Times* remarked that the "United States have neither the power nor the obligation to do police duty in the States. . . ."[57] Even the more partisan Republican papers, such as the Chicago *Tribune,* while recognizing that the decisions made the task of protecting Negro voting rights in the South more difficult, felt that the only remedy was new legislation that met the Supreme Court's constitutional objections. But Congress showed no inclination to enact such legislation.

Having dealt a severe blow to the Negroes' political rights in the 1870's, the Supreme Court proceeded to do the same to their civil rights in the 1880's. Under the Civil Rights Act of 1875 it was a misdemeanor, punishable by a $500 fine, to discriminate against any citizen of the United States using various public facilities. In enacting this law, Congress had declared in a preamble that "we recognize the equality of all men before the law, and hold it is the duty of government in all its dealings with people to mete out equal and exact justice to all. . . ."[58] The philosophy as well as the practical effect of this law was challenged in what came to be known as the Civil Rights Cases, decided by the Supreme Court in October, 1883. Seven separate incidents of discrimination were involved, ranging from denial of a theatre seat to denial of hotel accommodations. Only two of the cases, however, had originated in the South.

In light of its earlier decisions, it came as no surprise when the Supreme Court refused to uphold the constitutionality of the 1875 Civil Rights Act under the Fourteenth Amendment. However, some persons had hoped that it would be upheld under the Thirteenth Amendment. Justice Joseph Bradley, speaking for the majority, conceded that Congress, under that Amendment, did have the power to enact legislation "for the obliteration and prevention of slavery with all of its badges and incidents." He then asked if the denial of access to public accommodations subjected a person "to any form of servitude or tend to fasten upon him any badge of slavery. If it does not, then power to pass the law is not found in the Thirteenth Amendment. . . ." Weighing the conflicting arguments, Justice Bradley finally came to the conclusion that "mere discriminations on account of race or color were not regarded as badges of slavery. . . ." He therefore held that the denial of access to public accommodations "has nothing to do with slavery or involuntary servitude, and that if it is a violation of any right of the party, his redress is to be sought under the laws of the State." As a further point, he noted that "when a man has emerged from slavery . . . there must be some stage . . . when he takes the rank of a mere citizen, and ceases to be the special favorite of the laws. . . ."[59]

Justice Harlan was the lone dissenter. The majority, he felt, had reached its decision on too narrow and artificial grounds. He said that he could not "resist the conclusion that the substance and spirit of the recent Amendments of the Constitution have been sacrificed by a subtle and ingenious verbal criticism."[60] In a more prophetic vein, he added that he expected that the country would enter upon an era of constitutional law, when the nation would no longer protect slavery and the slaveholder.

But once again the leading organs of public opinion in the North found favor with the Court's decision. "The decision settles the point forever," said the *Nation,* "that the Fourteenth Amendment merely adds new limitations upon State action . . . and does not change in any way the fundamental structure of the Government." The *Independent* agreed. "In this way, and in no other way," it said, "can our duplicate system of government be harmoniously and successfully worked." Though "several leading colored men have expressed great indignation and disappointment, the Court is clearly right. The question as to the class of rights involved belongs exclusively to the States. There is the proper place to look for a remedy against any abuse. . . ." *The New York Times,* meanwhile, declared that "The Court has been serving a useful purpose in thus undoing the work of Congress. . . . The fact is, that, so long as we have State governments, within their field of action we cannot by National authority prevent the consequences of misgovernment."[61]

In 1896, in its sweeping decision concerning *Plessy v. Ferguson,* the Supreme Court for the first time dealt with the question of whether a state could use its police power to enforce racial discrimination. The case involved a Louisiana statute requiring separation of the races on all railroad cars. The lower federal courts, in four separate cases, had already upheld similar state laws, as had the newly established Interstate Commerce Commission on three other occasions. The Supreme Court itself had handed down contradictory rulings in this area. In one case it had struck down, as being an undue restriction on interstate commerce, an earlier Louisiana law forbidding segregated seating on trains. Then in a later decision it had upheld, on the narrow grounds that it was *not* an undue restriction on interstate commerce, a Mississippi law *requiring* segregated seating on trains. But *Plessy v Ferguson* was the first time the Supreme Court ruled directly on the question of whether a state could use its police power to enforce racial discrimination.

The Court, speaking through Justice Henry B. Brown of Michigan, framed the constitutional question in this way: Was the state requirement enforcing segregation on public carriers a reasonable extension of its police powers? The answer, in the Court's opinion, was yes. In such matters, Justice Brown said, "there must necessarily be a large discretion on the part of the legislature. . . .[I]t is at liberty to act with reference to established usages, customs, and traditions of the people. . . ." Justice Brown agreed that "the object of the [Fourteenth] Amendment was undoubtedly to enforce the absolute equality of the two races before the law," but he argued that "in the nature of things it could not have been intended to abolish distinctions based on color, or to enforce social, as distinguished from political equality, or a commingling of the two races upon terms unsatisfactory to either." As if to cinch the matter, he remarked, "We cannot say that . . . the separation of the two races in public conveyances is . . . more obnoxious to the Fourteenth Amendment than the acts of Congress requiring separate schools for colored children in the District of Columbia, the constitutionality of which does not seem to have been questioned. . . ." He then added, "If one race be inferior to the other socially, the Constitution of the United States cannot put them upon the same plane."[62]

Again Justice Harlan delivered a scathing denunciation of the majority's reasoning. "In respect of civil rights, common to all citizens," he said, "the Constitution of the United States does not . . . permit any public authority to know the race of those entitled to be protected. . . . Our Constitution is color-blind, and neither knows nor tolerates classes among citizens. In respect of civil rights, all citizens are equal before the law. . . . The arbitrary separation of citizens, on the basis of race, while they are on a public highway is a badge of servitude wholly inconsistent with the civil freedom and the equality before the law established by the Constitution. It cannot be justified upon any legal grounds. . . ."[63] Harlan, however, was unable to persuade any of his colleagues to join him in his dissent. They, like the country at large, wanted surcease from the continual agitation over the Negro problem. The Northern press, for example, generally let the decision pass with little or no comment. As Professor Logan points out, *The New York Times* misspelled Plessy's name and put its brief notice of the decision on page three under railroad news. Thus the Supreme Court gave its official sanction to the doctrine of "separate but equal" public facilities, a decision that was not to be overturned until 1954. Henceforth the Negro could by law be made a second-class citizen.

The Supreme Court had stood by giving tacit approval while the Negro was stripped first of his political rights, and then of his social rights. But there were limits beyond which it would not go. In *Strauder v West Virginia*, for example, a case decided in 1880, the Court held unconstitutional a state statute limiting jury duty to white persons. That same year, in *Ex Parte Virginia*, it went even further when it upheld the right of the federal government to hold in custody a county court judge charged with excluding Negroes from jury duty. A minority of the Court, however, did argue that the exercise of such power by the federal government would reduce the states to "a humiliating and degrading dependence upon the Central Government; engender constant irritations and destroy that domestic tranquillity which it was one of the objects of the Constitution to ensure. . . ."[64] Similarly, in *Ex Parte Yarbrough*, handed down in 1884, the Supreme Court upheld the right of Congress to protect the Negro's right to vote, as such, on the grounds that "it is . . . essential to the successful working of this government that the great organisms of its executive and legislative branches should be the free choice of the people."[65] Yet even the basic rights to vote and to serve on juries were stripped of any real meaning when the Supreme Court, in later decisions, refused to declare illegal the various subterfuges the South invented to abrogate them.

The Supreme Court's handling of the Negro problem was merely one more step in the final reconciliation of the North and South. Charles Warren reflected the feelings of many northerners when in assessing its decisions in this area thirty years later he declared that they "were most fortunate." As he explained, "They largely eliminated from National politics the negro question which had so long embittered Congressional debates; they relegated the burden and duty of protecting the negro to the States, to whom they properly belonged; and they served to restore confidence in the National Court in the Southern States."[66] This reconciliation was accomplished, not by the South's softening its own attitude towards colored people, but rather by the North's adopting the southern view. Whatever doubt may have existed about this change in nothern mood was soon dispelled once the United States embarked upon its imperialistic adventure against Spain in 1898. Almost overnight this country found itself the ruler of nearly eight million colored people, stretching from the Philippines to Puerto Rico, "a varied assortment of inferior races," according to the *Nation,* "which, of course, could not be allowed to vote."[67]

This new imperialistic temper had its roots primarily in the North. Those who were most conspicuous in giving it expression—men such as Theodore Roosevelt, Senator Albert Beveridge, and Josiah Strong—were all native to that region, and some—such as Henry Cabot Lodge and William Chandler —had even been identified at one time with the Negro cause. What had happened during these years was that the nation's drive toward westward expansion, temporarily brought to a halt by the Pacific waters, had now sought an outlet across the oceans. To many in the North it seemed that the United States desperately needed a new frontier. In the minds of some, this was necessary for economic reasons. "American factories," declared Senator Beveridge of Indiana in 1898, "are making more than the American people can use; American soil is producing more than they can consume. Fate has written our policy for us; the trade of the world must and shall be ours. . . . And we will get it as our mother England has told us how."[68] In the minds of others this was necessary for religious and cultural reasons. Josiah Strong, a minister for the home missionary society, wrote in his widely read *Our Country* of the American people's historic mission to spread the great values of civil liberty and "spiritual Christianity" throughout the world. For men such as Theodore Roosevelt, it was simply a matter of redeeming the nation's manhood.

There were other wellsprings as well. There was, first of all, the example of the other European nations carving up that portion of the world where claims had already been staked out. "The great nations," wrote Senator Henry Cabot Lodge in *The Forum* of 1896, "are rapidly absorbing for their future expansion and their present defense all the waste places of the earth. . . ." The United States, he warned, must not "fall out of the line of march."[69] There was also the hope, expressed by at least one Texas congressman, that a more venturesome foreign policy would stifle the rising social discontent at home. To the Secretary of State he wrote: "Why . . . just think of how angry the Anarchistic, socialistic and populist boil appears on our political surface, and who knows how deep its roots extend or ramify? One cannon shot across the bow of a British boat in defense of this principle [the Monroe Doctrine] will knock more pus out of it than would suffice to inoculate and corrupt our people for the next two centuries."[70]

Through this new imperialistic temper ran a strong sense of national pride. "We're a gr-reat people," Finley Peter Dunne has his Irish saloonkeeper, Mr. Dooley, say. "We ar-re that. An' th' best iv it is, we know we ar're."[71] With it went the belief that the United States could never do any wrong. Simply because his country had embarked upon it, Roosevelt was able to declare that the Spanish-American War was "the most absolutely righteous foreign war"[72] of the nineteenth century. But through this new imperialistic temper also ran a strong feeling of racial superiority. "God has not been preparing the English-speaking and Teutonic peoples for a thousand years for nothing but vain and idle self-contemplation and self-admiration," declared Senator Beveridge. "No! He has made us master organizers of the world to establish system where chaos reigns. He has given us the spirit of progress to overwhelm the forces of reaction throughout the earth. He has made us adept in government that we may administer government among savage and senile peoples. Were it not for such a force as this the world would relapse into barbarism and night. And of all our race He has marked the American people as His chosen nation to finally lead in the regeneration of the world."[73]

No matter how peculiar to the North this imperialistic temper may have been, southerners quickly recognized its affinity to their own way of thinking. When Senator Hoar of Massachusetts delivered a speech on the Senate floor, arguing that the United States should retain possession of the Philippines, Senator John J. McLaurin of South Carolina thanked him "for his . . . announcement of the divine right of the Caucasian to govern the inferior races," a position which "most amply vindicated the South." McLaurin's senior colleague, Ben Tillman, echoed the same theme. "No Republican leader, not even Governor Roosevelt," he said, "will now dare to wave the bloody shirt and preach a crusade against the South's treatment of the negro. The North has a bloody shirt of its own. Many thousands of them have been made into shrouds for murdered Filipinos, done to death because they were fighting for liberty." Even northerners recognized the affinity. "If the stronger and cleverer race," wrote the editor of the *Atlantic Monthly,* "is free to impose its will upon 'new-caught, sullen peoples' on the other side of the globe, why not in South Carolina and Mississippi?"[74]

With this recognition came an even greater tolerance for the southern position. "Northern men . . . ," reported *The New York Times,* "no longer denounce the suppression of the Negro vote [in the South] as it used to be denounced in the reconstruction days. The necessity of it under the supreme law of self-preservation is candidly recognized." That same year, the leader of Negro disfranchisement forces in Alabama exulted that "we have now the sympathy of thoughtful men in the North to an extent that never before existed."[75] The Spanish-American War, which brought large numbers of northerners and southerners to the colors for the first time since a similar imperialistic venture against Mexico half a century earlier, witnessed the final reconciliation of the two sections in more ways than one. The new note of unity was struck by President McKinley in his second inaugural address. "We are reunited," he said. "Sectionalism has disappeared. Division on public questions can no longer be traced by the war maps of 1861."[76] The North and South had finally buried their differences, but, in the process, the Negro had lost an important ally.

NOTES

1. Hirshson, Stanley P., *Farewell to the Bloody Shirt, Northern Republicans and the Southern Negro, 1877–1893*, Indiana University Press, Bloomington, 1962, p. 34.

2. *Ibid.*, p. 87.

3. Lee, Gordon C., *The Struggle for Federal Aid, First Phase, A History of the Attempts to Obtain Federal Aid for the Common Schools, 1870–1890*, Teachers College, Columbia University, New York, 1949, p. 42.

4. *National Party Platforms, 1840–1960*, compiled by Kirk H. Porter and Donald Bruce Johnson, University of Illinois Press, Urbana, 1961, p. 61.

5. Tourgee, Albion W., *A Fool's Errand*, Harvard University Press, Cambridge, 1961, pp. 387–9.

6. Hirshson, *op. cit.*, p. 92.

7. *National Party Platforms, op. cit.*, p. 81.

8. Lee, *op. cit.*, p. 91.

9. *Ibid.*, p. 159.

10. *Ibid.*, p. 130.

11. *Ibid.*, p. 131.

12. Hirshson, *op. cit.*, p. 195.

13. *Nation*, March 23, 1871, p. 192.

14. Logan, Rayford W., *The Negro in American Life and Thought, The Nadir, 1877–1901*, Dial Press, New York, 1954, pp. 125–6.

15. *Ibid.*, p. 134.

16. *Life and Times of Frederick Douglass, The Complete Autobiography*, Collier Books, New York, 1892, p. 435.

17. *Ibid.*, p. 428.

18. Van Deusen, John G., "The Exodus of 1879," *Journal of Negro History*, XXI, 1936, p. 121.

19. Logan, *op. cit.*, p. 133.

20. Hirshson, *op. cit.*, p. 67.

21. *Ibid.*, p. 70.

22. *Ibid.*, p. 71.

23. *Ibid.*, p. 69.

24. *Idem.*

25. *Ibid.*, p. 76.

26. *Congressional Record*, 46th Congress, 2nd Session, p. 156.

27. *Idem.*

28. *Life and Times of Frederick Douglass, op. cit.*, p. 506.

29. Logan, *op. cit.*, p. 135.

30. Mandel, Bernard, "Samuel Gompers and the American Negro Worker, 1886–1914," *Journal of Negro History*, 1955, p. 41.

31. Spero, Sterling D., and Harris, Abram L., *The Black Worker—The Negro and the Labor Movement*, Columbia University Press, New York, 1931, p. 87.

32. Mandel, *op. cit.*, p. 34.

33. *Ibid.*, p. 38.

34. *Ibid.*, p. 40.

35. *Ibid.*, p. 39.

36. *Ibid.*, p. 40.

37. *Ibid.*, p. 43.

38. *Ibid.*, p. 45.

39. *Ibid.*, pp. 48–9.

40. *Ibid.*, p. 47.

41. *Ibid.*, p. 46.

42. Hirshson, *op. cit.*, p. 249.

43. Logan, *op. cit.*, p. 162.

44. *Ibid.*, pp. 162–3.

45. Buck, Paul H., *The Road to Reunion, 1865–1900*, Little, Brown, Boston, 1938, p. 221.

46. *Ibid.*, p. 222.

47. *Ibid.*, p. 134.

48. Logan, *op. cit.*, p. 168.

49. Buck, *op. cit.*, p. 296.

50. *Ibid.*, p. 297.

51. *Nation*, January 23, 1890.

52. Warren, Charles, *The Supreme Court in United States History*, Little, Brown, Boston, 1926, Vol. II, p. 464.

53. *Documents of American History*, Henry Steele Commager, ed., F. S. Crofts, New York, 1947, Vol. II, p. 71.

54. *Ibid.*, p. 85.

55. *Ibid.*, p. 604.

56. *Idem.*

57. *Ibid.*, pp. 605–7.

58. Logan, *op. cit.*, p. 107.

59. Commager, *op. cit.*, Vol. II, p. 87–8.

60. Warren, *op. cit.*, p. 613.

61. *Ibid.*, pp. 613–14.

62. Logan, Rayford W., *The Negro in the United States*, Van Nostrand, Princeton, N.J., 1957, p. 131–3; Konvitz, Milton R., *A Century of Civil Rights*, Columbia University Press, New York, 1961, p. 128.

63. Logan, *The Negro in the United States, op. cit.*, pp. 134–5.

64. Warren, *op. cit.*, p. 610.

65. Commager, *op. cit.*, Vol. II, p. 90.

66. Warren, *op. cit.*, p. 608.

67. Woodward, C. Vann, *The Strange Career of Jim Crow*, Oxford University Press, New York, 1955, p. 54.

68. Curti, Merle, *The Growth of American Thought*, Harper, New York, 1943, p. 668.

69. *Ibid.*, p. 667.

70. *Ibid.*, pp. 668–9.

71. Beale, Howard K., *Theodore Roosevelt and the Rise of America to World Power*, Johns Hopkins Press, Baltimore, 1956, p. 23.

72. *Ibid.*, p. 26.

73. Curti, *op. cit.*, p. 675.

74. Woodward, *op. cit.*, pp. 54–6.

75. *Idem.*

76. *Inaugural Addresses of the Presidents of the United States from George Washington 1789 to John F. Kennedy 1961*, U.S. Government Printing Office, Washington, D.C., 1961, p. 179.

10 The War for Democracy

ON APRIL 2, 1917, both Houses of Congress assembled for an extraordinary early morning session to hear the President of the United States speak. Most Representatives were already in their seats when, at 8.32 A.M., the Senators began filing into the House side of the Capitol en masse, nearly all of them holding American flags in their hands. The Justices of the Supreme Court and members of the diplomatic corps had already preceded them. A minute later, the Speaker of the House announced, "The President of the United States."

Woodrow Wilson, author of "The New Freedom," walked directly to the rostrum. As he proceeded to recite a list of German "crimes" against the United States, the members of Congress listened intently, without interrupting. Then, when the President declared that "We will not choose the path of submission—," his words were suddenly drowned out by a burst of applause, led by the Chief Justice himself. No one in the chamber doubted any longer that the United States was about to declare war on Imperial Germany. From then on, the President was interrupted frequently by applause. Finally, about three-fourths of the way through his thirty-six-minute address, he paused, then said firmly, "The world must be made safe for democracy." At first, only one man, Senator John S. Williams of Mississippi, caught the full significance of that sentence. "Alone," according to *The New York Times,* "he began to applaud, and he did it gravely, emphatically—and in a moment the fact that this was the key word of our war against Germany dawned on the others, and one after another, followed his lead until the whole host broke forth in a great uproar of applause.''[1]

The editors of the radical Negro journal, the *Messenger*, later read the President's words, but instead of clapping they mocked. Why should Negroes, they asked, who enjoyed none of the rights of which the President spoke, flock to the colors and perhaps die for a country that denied them both justice and freedom?

Although the vast majority of Negroes agreed with this statement of injustice, they followed the recommendation set forth by W. B. Du Bois in an editorial written for the *Crisis*, entitled "Close Ranks." "Let us, while the war lasts," he said, "forget our special grievances and close our ranks shoulder to shoulder with our own white citizens. . . ."[2]

One reason that the majority of Negroes supported the war effort was their deepseated, if unspoken, conviction that their progress was indissolubly linked to the progress of the nation. Despite ill treatment, despite their subjection to exploitation, depredation, and injustice, they were nevertheless considerably better off than they had been under slavery. Those who looked backward had no difficulty in perceiving where they had made gains. In the antebellum South, it had been a crime to teach a Negro to read or write; as a result, at the outbreak of the Civil War the entire Negro population, with but minor exceptions, was illiterate. The decennial figures after the Civil War show a rapid decline in the proportion of the Negro population that was illiterate. By 1880 the illiteracy rate for Negroes had been reduced to about 57 per cent; by 1900, to 44 per cent, and by 1910, to 30 per cent. This was truly astonishing progress.

Also substantial was the progress in the area of higher education. During the three post-Civil War decades, about 2,000 Negroes—many of them the children of slaves—graduated from colleges in the South, and another 4,000 from northern colleges. These were, of course, the intellectual elite. Du Bois found that just over half of the group became teachers or academic administrators, including presidents of institutions, heads of normal schools, and principals of city schools; 17 per cent were clergymen, and the same proportion were professionals, primarily physicians; over 6 per cent were merchants, farmers, or artisans; and 4 per cent were in the civil service.

The Census of 1910 showed even more clearly the progress the Negro had been able to make during the half-century after the Civil War. Since five out of six Negroes were still living in the South, the Census data provided an indication of the status of the southern Negro as well as of the Negro's place in the nation. About 200,000 owned farms, and 800,000 were tenant-operators with a stake in the profits of their enterprise. Another 800,000 were farm laborers. There were 65,000 professionals, primarily teachers and ministers. About 40,000 were owners or managers of small businesses, most of which catered exclusively to Negroes. Another 40,000 were clerks or sales workers, again employed primarily in Negro establishments. There were 115,000 skilled workers and about 260,000 semiskilled workers, most of whom had found a niche in southern industry.

But if these gains were impressive, equally impressive was the magnitude of the gap that continued to mark the educational and economic achievements of the two races. In 1910 650 per 1,000 Negro children aged 10 to 14 were enrolled in school, compared with 835 white children. But these enrollment figures do not reflect the fact that most Negroes attended schools that were less adequately equipped, where the teaching staff was less competent and where instruction was provided for a shorter period of time. Thus, the discrepancy in education between the races remained large.

While many Negroes had succeeded in moving a rung or two up the occupational ladder, many others remained at the bottom. In 1910 2.4 out of the approximately 4.7 million Negro men and women in the labor force were earning their livelihood, such as it was, as farm laborers or other types of laborers or service workers. And many owned farms that produced little or held jobs that carried more impressive titles than salaries.

It was against the backdrop of the continuing wide gap

between the races that Booker T. Washington appeared. He stated again and again that the key to the Negro's progress lay in the acquisition of knowledge and skills; that only in that way could he secure a place in the economy of the South. He could afford to wait for his full political and civil rights. In his famous Atlanta address, he said: "The wisest among my race understand that the agitation of questions of social equality is the extremist folly, and that progress in the enjoyment of all privileges that will come to us must be the result of sincere and constant struggle, rather than of artificial forcing. No man that has anything to contribute to the markets of the world is long in any degree ostracized."[3]

Washington succeeded in establishing himself as the leader of the American Negro community from the time of his Atlanta address in 1895 until his death twenty years later, but he had only a few years of uncontested power. In 1903 W. E. Burghardt Du Bois, Massachusetts-born and the first Negro scholar trained at Harvard, was teaching at Atlanta. He set about to challenge Washington's autocratic hold on the Negro community, and particularly the positions which he advocated. Washington, according to Du Bois, was foolhardy in asking the Negro to give up, "at least for the present, three things—First, political power; Second, insistence on civil rights; Third, higher education of Negro youth."[4] Du Bois argued that Washington would fail in his efforts to make artisans, businessmen, and property owners of Negroes because they could never defend their economic rights without political rights. Washington's insistence on thrift and self-respect was self-defeating, said Du Bois, because submission to civic inferiority would "sap the mankind of any race in the long run." He said that efforts to establish common schools and industrial training for Negroes would fail for lack of Negro college-trained teachers. Du Bois considered it a grievous error when Washington agreed to permit the nation to shift "the burden of the Negro problem to the Negro's shoulders,"[5] since Du Bois realized that the Negro needed a great deal of help. "Negroes must insist continually, in season and out of season, that voting is necessary to modern mankind, that color discrimination is barbarism, and that black boys need education as well as white boys."[6]

In May, 1905, Du Bois issued a call for "aggressive action on the part of men who believe in Negro freedom and growth." Twenty-nine Negroes responded. Meeting in Niagara Falls, Canada, in July, they demanded "free speech, a free unsubsidized press, mankind suffrage, and an end to distinctions based on color and race."[7] The next year they met in Harper's Ferry, and the year after in Boston. This movement was met by deep hostility from Negro and white alike. The Negro press, controlled by Washington, sought to destroy Du Bois, and there was only derision from those white papers who took note of these Negro malcontents. The Niagara Movement was the first organized Negro protest movement in the twentieth century that set its sights upon the achievement of first class citizenship for the Negro. While it did not survive as an independent organization, it provided Negro leadership for the years ahead.

As noted earlier, after the defeat of the federal election and education bills at the beginning of the 1890's, the last of the northern white liberals who had been concerned about the nation's unmet responsibilities toward the freedman had withdrawn from the struggle. They had made repeated efforts on his behalf, but for many years they had been unable to persuade their fellow citizens, and they had turned their attention to other issues.

But recent developments in both the South and North had pinched anew their consciences. In the fall of 1906 there had been an ugly race riot in Atlanta. Four Negroes were killed, many more were injured, and there had been much looting and burning of Negro homes. For several days the city was paralyzed, all transportation stopped, and factories closed. When the rioting subsided, many Negroes sold their property and left Atlanta.

Rioting and murder of innocent Negroes were not restricted to the South. Pennsylvania, New York, Ohio, and Indiana had each witnessed repeated outbreaks of racial violence. But it was a brutal riot in Springfield, Illinois in

1908 that finally touched the nation's conscience. Here, in the city where Lincoln had lived, his memory failed to restrain the white mob. The riot was touched off by a strumpet's charge that she had been raped by a Negro. "For three days, the arson, the mayhem, and the murder" reigned. Sixty people were killed or injured. The howling mob shouted, "Lincoln may have freed you, but we'll show you where you belong!"[8] In seeking the cause of the riot, William English Walling, an able journalist, reported that the townsfolk reportedly told him, "Why, the niggers came to think they were as good as we are!"[9] Walling was appalled, not only by the fact that 6,000 peaceful and innocent Negroes were driven in fear of their lives from the town in which they had lived for half a century, but also by the fact that the leaders of the white community, including churchmen, sought to put the blame for the riot on the general inferiority and unfitness of the Negro for free institutions.

Walling warned that unless the Negro were treated on a plane of "absolute political and social equality . . . [the South] will soon have transferred the race war to the North. . . . Yet who realizes the seriousness of the situation, and what large and powerful body of citizens is ready to come to their [Negroes'] aid?"[10]

The shame of Springfield, following the bloody riots in Atlanta, finally led a group of New York liberals to call a conference in 1909 "for the discussion of present evils, the voicing of protests, and the renewal of the struggle for civil and political liberty."[11] The call was written by Oswald Garrison Villard, grandson of the great abolitionist, and several Negro leaders were invited to participate. This conference led to the establishment of the National Association for the Advancement of Colored People, a biracial organization dedicated to achieving equality for the Negro in American society. From the start the organization advocated complete political and social equality for the Negro. It placed major reliance on a Legal Redress Committee and on its monthly journal, the *Crisis,* to advance its cause. Du Bois became director of publicity and research.

Thus, during the first decade of the twentieth century the Negro was totally disenfranchised throughout the South. Racial segregation, in all its ugliness, was firmly entrenched, supported by law in the South and by custom in the North, and race riots and lynchings provided the means by which white citizens gave vent to their frustrations. It was inevitable that the Negro's loss of political power through disfranchisement would be reflected not only in the actions of local and state officials, but even in the attitudes and programs of the men elected to national office.

During Theodore Roosevelt's first Administration some white conservatives feared that the former "Rough Rider" might try to undo the policy of William McKinley, who had sought to eliminate the race issue from national politics. And for a time it seemed that Roosevelt was less interested in wooing the white South than in doing justice to the Negro. He had been in office only a few weeks when he invited Booker T. Washington to the White House. This shocked the South, since it appeared to herald a return to the former Republican policy of wooing the Negroes. Then, two years later, Roosevelt refused to withdraw the appointment of a leading Negro to the position of Collector of the Port of Charleston, South Carolina, despite strong southern protests. When he also refused to dismiss arbitrarily a Negro postmistress in Mississippi, many Negroes saw Roosevelt emerging as a second Lincoln.

In 1904 the Republican platform included a plank to impose the penalties provided in the Fourteenth Amendment upon states that interfered with the constitutional rights of citizens to vote. The Democrats warned that "the race question has brought countless woes to this country. The calm wisdom of the American people should see that it brings no more. To revive the dead and hateful race and sectional animosities . . . means confusion, distraction of business, and the reopening of wounds now happily healed. North, South, East and West have but recently stood together in the line of battle from the walls of Pekin to the hills of Santiago, and as sharers of a common glory and a common destiny, we should share fraternally the common burdens."[12]

But it was soon clear that these were campaign statements, not policy positions. Shortly after his election Roosevelt demonstrated that he was not really as friendly toward the Negro as some had believed. Though he had earlier denounced lynchings, he now failed to recommend legislation to put an end to these extralegal practices. His underlying attitude toward the Negro was perhaps best revealed in his attitudes about Negro education. While preparing a speech on the subject, he indicated that he would favor industrial and agricultural training for Negroes but nothing beyond that. When his advisor suggested that Negroes needed teachers, he agreed that there must be normal schools. But when he was asked where the teachers were to be trained, the President replied, "Ah, I see. Once you start in education you cannot stop."[13]

A further clue to his attitude is found in his handling of the Brownsville riot. In August, 1906, several companies of the Negro Twenty-fifth Regiment stationed in Brownsville, Texas, became involved in a racial riot with the townsfolk, as a result of which one man was killed and several others were injured. Roosevelt acted summarily and dismissed the entire battalion without honor, thus disqualifying them from further governmental service, military or civilian. Senator "Pitchfork" Ben Tillman, leader of the southern racists, called it "executive lynching."[14] Senator Foraker of Ohio insisted that the men should have been given a fair trial and after years of effort succeeded in securing congressional approval for reinstating those who were otherwise eligible to serve. By the end of his term, the Negroes were glad to see Roosevelt go.

Before the election of 1908, Taft did what no Republican candidate had done before. He toured the South in search of votes. And, though he failed to carry a single southern state, he continued to follow the policy of reconciliation expressed in his inaugural address, which alone among the inaugural addresses in this century dealt at length with the "negro race, its progress and its present condition." Before presenting this appraisal Taft indicated his satisfaction with the "good feeling between the South and the other sections of the country." Taft stated that "the Thirteenth and Four-teenth Amendments have been generally enforced and have secured the objects for which they are intended." While this was not so for the Fifteenth Amendment, he expressed the hope that if the South wished to protect itself against domina-tion by "an ignorant, irresponsible element," it would do so by excluding both unqualified whites and unqualified Negroes from voting. Reviewing the nation's efforts to give the Negro the vote in order to protect his own interests, Taft concluded that "the movement had proved to be a failure."

The President was encouraged by the interest shown by the leaders of the white community in industrial education for Negroes. He considered the progress that the Negro had made in the last fifty years to be "marvelous" and looked for-ward to further gains in the next twenty-five years. He stated that "The Negroes are now Americans" and that they "must base their hope on the results of their own industry, self-restraint, thrift, and business success, as well as upon the aid and comfort and sympathy which they may receive from their white neighbors in the South."[15]

Shortly after taking office Taft returned to the South, where he delivered a series of addresses stressing his belief that the southern white man was the Negroes' best friend. Although he had stated in his inaugural that he had not the "slightest race prejudice or feeling,"[16] he told Negro students in a North Carolina college that in his opinion the best solution to the race question was emigration and concluded that "Your race is adapted to be a race of farmers, first, last and for all times."[17]

The election of 1912 highlighted the plight of the Negro. Northern Negroes who were permitted to vote could select the regular Republican ticket, which was a vote for Taft, the man who in the preceding four years had demonstrated his inability to cope with their problems. They could cast their ballot for the dissident Bull Moose ticket, which was a vote for Roosevelt, the man who had thrown his support to the "lily-white" delegates in the Bull Moose convention. Or they could cross over and support the Democratic ticket, which was a vote for Woodrow Wilson, a native of Virginia who had practiced law briefly in Atlanta before relocating in the North.

Badly treated as they had been by the Republicans, both regular and Bull Moose, the majority of Negroes were not inclined to defect to the Democrats. But Oswald Garrison Villard saw the opportunity of securing considerable numbers of votes for Wilson if the Democratic candidate would give some assurance of sympathy and understanding toward the Negro. This Wilson was willing to do. He said that he wished to see "justice done to the colored people in every matter; and not mere grudging justice, but justice executed with liberality and cordial feeling." He also promised that if he became president, the Negroes could count upon him "for absolute fair dealing, for everything by which I could assist in advancing interests of their race in the United States."[18] Wilson received many more Negro votes than any previous candidate of the Democratic Party, even though these votes were not crucial to his victory.

With Wilson's election, the Democrats gained control of both houses of Congress, enjoying a comfortable margin in the Senate and an overwhelming majority in the House. This was the first time since the Civil War that the Democrats dominated the federal government. Wilson had been elected as the spokesman of "The New Freedom," but it was not long before the Negroes learned that they were not to be its beneficiaries. In fact, they were to find their already severely circumscribed rights further constricted.

In the legislative arena a flood of extremist proposals were submitted, all of which aimed at the further segregation of Negroes. These included a bill to prohibit Negroes from being commissioned in the Army or Navy and a bill requiring separate accommodations for white and Negro civil servants. The ways of the South were to become the ways of the nation, if some Democrats were to have their way. Most of these bills—and, according to Professor Franklin, there were more than twenty of them—never came to a vote. But they reflected the temper of the times, as did various actions taken in the executive department to replace Negroes with whites and to segregate the two races. Booker T. Washington said of this period that he had never seen the colored people so "discouraged and embittered."[19]

Early in 1913 Villard submitted to Wilson a proposal for a National Race Commission that would make a nonpartisan scientific study of the status of the Negro, with particular reference to his economic condition. Although initially intrigued by the proposal, the President eventually turned it down for fear of offending the South. He said that he was "absolutely blocked by the sentiment of Senators, not alone Senators from the South by any means, but Senators from various parts of the country." Wilson wrote to Villard that he "thought segregation to be in the interest of the colored people as exempting them from friction and criticism in the departments."[20] He later told Villard that he would never name a colored man to office in the South "because that would be a social blunder of the worst kind."[21] Du Bois, who had supported Wilson, summarized the situation in the NAACP's 1913 report. "Everywhere," he wrote, "we have witnessed efforts to officialize caste."[22]

The years preceding the outbreak of World War I had been marked by a recrudescence of reformism and progressivism. Much in the American scene came in for caustic comment and critical reappraisal, particularly the dominance of the monied interests and their control over the nation's destiny. The muckraking journalists threw a powerful searchlight on the corruption and degredation that was rampant in politics, industry, and other important sections of national life. But for the most part they had little to say about the country's treatment of Negroes, possibly because they still represented a small minority in the North, the area that attracted most of their attention.

In 1908 Eugene V. Debs, the Socialist candidate for president, had polled over 400,000 votes, and in 1912, slightly over

900,000. The Socialists had developed a long list of major criticisms about America, but their Party platform even in 1912 had made no mention of the Negro's plight.

These years had also seen the Progressive movement make important political inroads by advocating the use of governmental power to prevent the serious human waste resulting from unbridled competition in the market place. The platform of the Progressive Party, whose standard bearer in 1912 was Theodore Roosevelt, had contained these ringing words, "The supreme duty of the Nation is the conservation of human resources through an enlightened measure of social and industrial justice."[23] Again, while the platform contained a separate section on "The Immigrant," it remained silent on the Negro.

The Democratic standard bearer, Woodrow Wilson, had campaigned on the philosophy of "The New Freedom," and around this he had built his first inaugural. Wilson, too, was deeply concerned about the human cost of industrialization. He looked forward to a government that would serve all people, not only the favored few. He talked of "equality of opportunity, the first essential of justice in the body politic"[24] but never, not even by indirection, did he take cognizance of the Negro and of the extent to which government had failed him.

America was on the move again; there was a promise of a better life for all—at least for all white Americans. The situation of the Negro was much more equivocal. While he was no longer a slave, no longer illiterate, and no longer without any property, he was still on the fringe of American society. The years since the beginning of the twentieth century had seen him retrogress with respect to his political and civil rights. He was beyond the pale of democracy.

And then the unexpected happened. Europe was plunged into war, and before long the United States became directly involved. World War I and its aftermath brought about major changes in the position of the Negro that no one could possibly have foreseen. For many decades the Negro had looked to the nation for aid and succor; now the nation looked to the Negro.

There had been a slow, steady increase in the number of Negroes in the Northeast and the North Central states in the two decades preceding the outbreak of the war. In 1910, however, approximately nine out of the total of ten million Negroes were still living in the South, and of these about seven million were on southern farms. This skewed geographic distribution was largely responsible for the way in which national policy toward the Negro had evolved. The North long ago had turned the problem of the southern Negro back to the southern white population to work out as it saw fit. And the number of Negroes in the North was not sufficiently large to create more than periodic concern or conflict.

For many years the North had been preoccupied with the absorption of its European immigrant population. This steady stream of "seething masses" had provided a seemingly unlimited supply of cheap, unskilled labor. The outbreak of war in Europe first dramatically cut and then virtually eliminated this inflow. Meanwhile, the spur which the war had given to the American economy made the demand for labor even greater than ever. It was to fill this gap that the Negro began moving North.

During the century's second decade more than 300,000 Negroes born in the South migrated to the Middle Atlantic and North Central States to stay. Many more went North but for various reasons drifted back South. Jobs were the magnet. Negroes found opportunities in established industries—such as iron, steel, coal, meat packing, railroads, and many others—that had long relied on immigrants to fill the dirty or dangerous jobs at the bottom of the employment ladder. They were also employed in many of the industries specifically connected with the war—such as munitions plants, shipyards, and automobile and truck plants—which had not had time to build up an exclusively white labor force. In the burgeoning war economy, a considerable number of opportunities in the service sector were also opened to Negroes.

The flow of Negroes to the North was partly spontaneous,

but it was also stimulated by recruiters who went South for the specific purpose of enticing Negroes to leave their farms, holding out the promise of better jobs and a less hostile environment in the North. Since the Negro provided the core of the southern agricultural labor supply, the plantation owners did not let them go easily. Some southern communities passed ordinances requiring recruiters to pay fees of $1,000 or more. The conventional response of the southern leadership, however, was to resort to intimidation of both the Negro and the recruiter. Warned that they would be beaten, or even killed, if they were caught leaving the community, many Negroes thought twice about the advantages of migrating North. War had also stimulated the economy of the South, and even Negroes had an opportunity to share in some of the gains. Cotton prices advanced from about 11 cents in 1915 to 29 cents by the end of the war and in the following year shot up to 35 cents.

However, not all southerners benefited from this advance. Much of the South had been ravaged between 1915 and 1917 by the boll weevil, which decimated large cotton-growing sections of Louisiana, Mississippi, Alabama, Georgia, and Florida. And much of what the weevil did not destroy was lost as a result of devastating floods. Many farmers, both white and Negro, were wiped out during these years.

Since the number of productive cotton plantations was thus reduced, the opposition of many southerners to the Negroes' seeking employment elsewhere, either in the North or in the expanding urban communities in the South, was moderated. Between 1910 and 1920 the number of Negroes in the rural South declined from about 6.5 million to 6.1 million, and the number of Negroes in urban communities in the South increased by about the same amount, from over 1.5 to almost 1.9 million.

The impact of the war and the postwar boom on the occupational situation of the Negro is reflected in a number of statistics. Negro males employed as farm laborers declined from 944,000 in 1910 to 828,000 in 1920. By the same token there was a considerable increase, approximately 300,000, in

the number of Negro males employed as semiskilled workers
or as service workers or laborers in the nonfarm sector. The
numbers employed as skilled workers or foremen also increased from 114,000 to 149,000. Thus the war and postwar
boom made it possible for many Negroes to move up at least
one rung.

The active involvement of the United States in the war
after 1917 also altered the status of the Negro and his relationship to the white majority. During the hostilities about
3.7 million men served on active duty, with slightly more than
half of the total serving overseas. When the country entered
the war, it was assumed that enlistments would provide sufficient manpower to meet the greatly expanded needs of the
Army and Navy, but before long it became necessary to resort
to a system of compulsory military service. During the short
period that the services relied on voluntary enlistments, many
Negroes applied but few were accepted. As in each earlier war
in which the nation had been engaged, the initial posture was
to exclude the Negro. However, once the draft was instituted,
Negroes were registered, and many were accepted. Over 350,-
000 served on active duty. In fact, the proportion of Negro
registrants who were eventually drafted exceeded the proportion of white men. This reflected in part the disinclination
of southern draft boards to defer Negro registrants. Of the
many millions of selectees who were examined for service,
only 43,000 were rejected for mental or educational deficiency. Thus the much lower educational qualifications
of many Negroes did not prevent their being drafted.

Negro soldiers pressed for an opportunity to serve as
officers and, after much agitation, the War Department finally
established a separate camp for this purpose. Before the war's
end, some Negroes even received commissions at nonsegregated camps. The Secretary of War, Newton D. Baker,
recognizing the many possible sources of conflict that would
result from the induction of large numbers of Negro soldiers,
appointed Emmett J. Scott, Booker T. Washington's secretary,
as Special Assistant in matters affecting the "interests of ten

million Negroes of the United States and the part they are to play in connection with the present war."[25]

The sources of conflict went far beyond the issue of officer training for Negroes. The South looked askance at providing military training for Negroes. Moreover, the training of northern Negroes in segregated southern locations inevitably led to trouble. From the Negroes themselves there were repeated complaints that they were indiscriminately assigned to labor battalions. There were further complaints that the white officers assigned to them were blatantly prejudiced. Training camps were troubled by constant friction between military police and Negro soldiers, and overt conflict on occasion between Negro troops and the surrounding civilian population. After a riot at Houston, Texas, in which Negro troops killed 17 white people, 13 Negro soldiers were summarily tried and hanged and forty-one were imprisoned for life.

Many Negro troops served overseas, primarily as members of labor battalions. Some, however, were used in combat, and several regiments distinguished themselves for bravery, winning acclaim of both French and American generals. Nevertheless, racial conflicts followed the troops overseas. Many American white soldiers were incensed when French girls went out with Negroes. They even warned the French military and civilian population not to fraternize with Negro troops, though without success. For the first time in 300 years large numbers of American Negroes were exposed to a population that was not overly concerned with the question of color. For the first time they enjoyed the same freedom as was vouchsafed white men. Some Negro intellectuals were so shaken by the contrast in the conditions at home and those they experienced in France that when the war ended they found it impossible to return to the United States.

The war also made it necessary to enlist the support of the Negroes on the home front. They were asked to buy Liberty Bonds, to cooperate in food conservation drives, and to join in fund-raising campaigns for the Red Cross, the "Y," and similar organizations. As Will Alexander put it: "For the first time in the history of the South, Negroes were asked to join in a common community effort." Alexander reported that when he went through the deep South on a Liberty Loan campaign he was repeatedly asked by the local chairman to say something "about the colored boys in the Army. . . . We'll have whites and Negroes together in the courthouse. . . . The Negroes have got a lot of money. . . ."[26] Under the pressure of war the American Federation of Labor found itself forced to reconsider its long-standing policy of condoning *de facto* racial discrimination in its constituent unions. It even sat down to discuss the problem with a group of Negro leaders.

The war was over within nineteen months, but it brought in its wake new disturbances in race relations. Large numbers of Negroes left southern farms for the urban centers of the South or the North never to return. Many Negroes who had been living in southern cities at the war's outbreak moved North. The large number who had served in the Armed Forces had gained new knowledge and skills through travel and new experiences and, above all, by gaining access to new jobs and higher incomes.

The war led to other improvements. For the first time in the nation's history, government agencies began consulting with Negro leaders. Sometimes consultation was initiated by the government itself. On other occasions Negro leaders requested an opportunity to place before key officials their special problems. And because of the war, their requests were granted. The large-scale migration to several northern cities—particularly New York, Philadelphia, and Chicago—during and after the war helped to create Negro communities large enough to provide the basis for economic expansion, political advances, and cultural contributions. Above all, these large urban communities increased the Negro's sense of security. Even before the United States entered the war, Oscar DePriest, a Negro, was elected Alderman by the community already settled on the South Side of Chicago. Two years later, Negroes in New York City were able to send one of their members, Edward A. Johnson, to the State Assembly. The substantial increases in population in these principal northern cities, together with improved job opportunities, provided a broadened base both for the growth of a Negro professional and business group and for strengthened cultural and protest movements.

Hundreds of thousands of young Negroes brought home with them memories of the greater freedom they had enjoyed during their military service in Europe. The contrast between their experiences overseas and life at home was sharp—so sharp, in fact, that many were profoundly shaken. The Rev. Francis J. Grimké declared that Negro troops in France had sniffed that country's "free, invigorating liberty-loving air" and that when they returned home: "There has got to be a change. . . . They know now what it is to be a man, and to be treated as a man. And that spirit will remain with them. It cannot be quenched. It will rather be sure to communicate itself to others."[27] While the soldiers were waiting to be transported back to the United States and demobilized, reports reached Washington that many Negro servicemen were out of control. Having tasted freedom, they would cause serious difficulties, it was feared, when they returned to their home communities. The War Department asked Dr. Robert R. Moton, Booker T. Washington's successor at Tuskegee Institute, to review the situation of Negro troops and to counsel them about the adjustments which they would have to make on their return. In France he warned the soldiers that they could not expect to enjoy the same freedom at home that they were experiencing at the hands of the grateful French. The soldiers deeply resented Dr. Moton's advice. Du Bois, writing in the *Crisis* in May, 1919, caught the mood: "We return from fighting. We return fighting. Make way for Democracy! We have saved it in France and by the Great Jehovah, we will save it in the U.S.A., or know the reason why."[28]

The war and immediate postwar years saw a new Negro, a man who had pride in his heritage and himself and who, through poetry, prose, music, the dance and the theater, was able to create works of beauty out of his travail and sufferings as well as out of the lighter and more humorous facets of his life. These years witnessed the literary movement that came to be known as the "Harlem Renaissance."

The Negro community, and particularly its ever broadening leadership group, came to appreciate that for the first time it could help to shape its own destiny. A new mixture of impatience, determination, and aggressiveness was coursing through the veins of those who for so long had been beaten and intimidated into silence and submission.

This new mood and outlook was undoubtedly aided and abetted by friendly whites who also had been affected by participating in a war to save democracy. Some of America's leading writers—such as Eugene O'Neill, Carl Van Vechten, and H. L. Mencken—made constructive use of Negro materials in their own writings and otherwise encouraged Negroes to press their claims to equality. There were flirtations between white liberals and radicals on the one hand and the "New Negro" on the other, but they did not blossom into any lasting union.

However, the number of friendly whites, sincere and insincere, was miniscule in comparison to the millions whose contact with Negroes during the war years left them in a critical and even hostile mood. Many white soldiers from the North and West were thrown together with Negroes for the first time in their lives. Since most Negroes came from seriously deprived environments the whites were startled and disturbed by what they saw. Thus, their military experience failed to soften the view of many whites toward the Negro. Among the reasons for this was that during their training they were exposed to southern mores as well as the segregationist views of their southern barracks mates.

Many factors led to an exacerbation of race relations on the home front, particularly after the troops came home. At that time, although business in general remained at a satisfactory level, many war industries were cut back or liquidated. Moreover, the already severe pressure on housing—the result of interrupted construction and an increasing population—was greatly intensified. Meanwhile, the country was undergoing a very rapid increase in prices, which pinched many groups on fixed incomes. All of these factors combined to create a combustible situation.

Unfortunately, the war for democarcy had not brought about any basic changes in the long-prevailing negative attitudes of the white community, both in the North and in the South, toward the Negro. If anything, prejudice, discrimination, and ostracism increased.

The Ku Klux Klan, revived shortly before the war, saw its membership grow rapidly in the next few years. By the war's end it had achieved considerable strength in the Middle West as well as in the South. The revival of the Klan cast a shadow of what was to come.

There were repeated incidents in the months following the return of the troops from abroad. The lynching of Negro soldiers in uniform was frequent, and in the summer of 1919 blood ran in the streets. This was "The Red Summer," when many whites were determined to force the Negroes back into subservience. They did not balk at violence or even murder to impress Negroes with the fact that they were and must remain second-class citizens. Violence increased as more and more Negroes for the first time decided to protect themselves at any cost. As Claude McKay later wrote, they were determined not to die "like hogs . . . but fighting back."[29]

Many were killed, both black and white, in the twenty-five race riots that erupted that summer in every part of the country, East and West, North and South. The worst riot was in Chicago, where for thirteen days the city was without law and order, even though the militia was called out on the fourth day of rioting. When the fighting ceased, the casualty rolls showed that thirty-eight had been killed—fifteen whites and twenty-three Negroes—and 550 injured, twice as many Negroes as whites.

Adding to the Negroes' plight was the fact that the federal government itself was fanning the fires of racial animosity and hatred as a backwash of its fears about the forward march of Bolshevism. Attorney General A. Mitchell Palmer was convinced that Negroes were being attracted to the Communist Party by its promise to carve out a separate black state. Representative James F. Byrnes had earlier made the same charge. Negro leadership, he said, "appeals for the establishment in this country of a Soviet government," and he went on to explain that "the incendiary utterances of would-be Negro leaders . . . are responsible for racial antagonism in the United States."[30]

The Justice Department, after much deliberation, concluded that some Negro leaders were indeed actively included in a Bolshevik conspiracy. In support of this view, the Department cited the following facts: "First, an ill-governed reaction towards race rioting. Second, the threat of retaliatory measures in connection with lynching. Third, more openly expressed demands for social equality. . . . Fourth, the identification of the Negro with such radical organizations as the I.W.W. and an outspoken advocacy of the Bolshevik doctrine."[31]

But the response of the Negro masses to the Ku Klux Klan, to persecution by the federal government, and to the violence and hatred of the whites was not Bolshevism but an escape into racial chauvinism. Marcus Garvey, a man of many skills if no steady occupation, came to Harlem from Jamaica to lead the Negroes back to Africa, where they would be their own masters. In this country Garvey collected large sums, hoping to establish a steamship line. He founded a Church and a Court of Ethiopia and conferred many titles on his more important followers. Before he was sent to jail for using the mails to defraud, he had succeeded in convincing a great many Negroes that they could never expect justice from the white man. They had no option, he argued, but to throw their lot in with the "Pure Black Race." His grandiose plans and projects came to naught, but his efforts to make Negroes look realistically at the white man seared deep.

In support of his "Back-to-Africa" movement Garvey had pointed to the fact that the Senate in 1921 had refused to approve the Dyer antilynching bill previously passed by the House. Southern opposition to the bill had been tacitly aided and abetted by disinterested Republicans from the North and

West, although their own party platform had urged "Congress to consider the most effective means to end lynching in this country which continues to be a terrible blot on our American civilization."[32]

Lynchings, race riots, and accusations of Bolshevism were mean rewards for Negroes who had helped the nation in the factory and on the battlefield to win a costly victory over a dangerous and determined foe. Now they faced another attack. Leaders of the white community stated that the mental testing that had been part of the military call-up had provided unequivocal evidence of the inherent inferiority of the Negro, an inferiority that justified his being relegated to an inferior position in American society.

The Army had made use of two simple tests, known as Alpha and Beta, to assess the ability of men to meet the demands of military service. As the results became known, it was clear that the average of the scores made by Negroes was far below the average of those made by the white population. Here indeed was "scientific" proof of the widely held belief that the Negro was genetically inferior to the white man. Even when the results were analyzed by region, the poor showing of the Negro was incontestable. The southern Negro scored much lower than the southern white; the northern Negro much lower than the northern white.

It was not until several years later that a few academicians, reviewing the materials with care, perceived that the conclusion of the inherent inferiority of the Negro could be challenged by the very same data that had been used to make the point. They called attention to the fact that the median scores of Negroes in eight northern states were exactly the same as the median scores for whites in eight southern states. The test scores, they said, apparently reflected environmental opportunity, not genetic endowment. But before correction was made and publicized and before it was buttressed by additional studies showing that Negroes in the North, when permitted to attend better schools for longer periods of time, had scored significantly higher than Negroes in the South, a wide segment of the American public was convinced that their racial deprecation of the Negro had a sound scientific basis.

The desire of the country to inter its war experience and to return to good and tried ways was clearly demonstrated in the stinging defeat handed President Wilson when he sought Senate approval for the treaty establishing a League of Nations. This mood carried into the 1920 election, when Warren G. Harding was elected on the promise of a "return to normalcy." The nation wanted to get back to peace and prosperity as quickly as possible.

There was no reason for the small minority interested in the improvement of race relations to be encouraged by the substitution of Harding for Wilson, weak as Wilson had been in this sphere. Shortly after Harding's election, Dr. Moton, President of Tuskegee Institute, and a group of white southerners called on him to discuss racial issues in the South. Harding had not been briefed, and he mistook the group for politicians seeking favors. During the course of a short and embarrassing interview it became clear that the President had never heard of Tuskegee, had no idea who Dr. Moton was, and, for that matter, did not recognize the name of Booker T. Washington.

And yet, shortly thereafter, he made a major address at Birmingham, Alabama, in which he laid down the nation's new stance toward the Negro. A return to the *status quo ante,* Harding declared, was impossible as well as undesirable. The war and the restrictions on immigration had transformed the race problem from a regional to a national—in fact, an international—issue in light of America's dedication to the enhancement of democracy. The President argued that with immigration vastly reduced, the North and West would bid for Negro labor and the South would be able to retain the manpower it needed to work its farms only if it dealt justly with the Negro. "Politically and economically there need be no occasion for great and permanent differentiation," he said, but then, reflecting the North's latest view of the problem, he called for "absolute divergence in things social and racial."

The President desired that qualified Negroes be permitted to vote, and that unqualified white men be denied the right to vote. He insisted "upon equal educational opportunity for both . . . ," although he knew that this did not mean that both would be "equally educated within a generation, or two generations, or ten generations." He stated that the nation had an interest in seeing that the "South shall not be encouraged to make its colored population a vast reservoir of ignorance, to be drained away by the process of migration into all other sections." Having stressed that there must be no "racial amalgamation," the President made a fervent plea for "partnership" of the races. He stated that he looked forward to the break-up of two traditions: the solidly Democratic white South and the solidly Republican black race.[33]

In commenting on the President's appeal for political equality for the Negro while denying him social equality, *The New York Times* pointed out that his political equality has its place "beside, or near, his social equality . . . and the labor unions . . . have taken effective means to restrict his economic equality to about the same extent as the other two." The *Times* foresaw the antagonism of the South that Senator Pat Harrison of Mississippi expressed: "I am against any such theory because I know it is impractical, unjust, and destructive of the best ideals of America. Place the Negro upon political and economic equality with the white man or woman and the friction between the races will be aggravated."[34]

Echoes of much of what Harding said could be traced back to Hayes and Garfield, and even to Grant and Lincoln. But he presented a new emphasis. He recognized that World War I had transformed the racial problem from a regional into a national one. He sensed that the control of immigration would affect the demand for Negro labor outside the South. Most important, he voiced a desire for the greater participation of the Negro in the American economy and society within the limits of continued social differentiation. The South would have none of this, and the North was unwilling to press the matter. And so as the memory of the war for democracy receded, the Negro was once again forgotten.

NOTES

1. *The New York Times*, April 3, 1917.

2. Redding, Saunders, *The Lonesome Road, The Story of the Negro's Part in America*, Doubleday, Garden City, N.Y., 1958, p. 219.

3. Washington, Booker T., *Up From Slavery, an Autobiography*, Bantam Books, New York, 1959, pp. 157–8.

4. Du Bois, W. E. Burghardt, *The Souls of Black Folk, Essays and Sketches*, Fawcett, Greenwich, 1961, p. 48.

5. *Ibid.*, p. 53.

6. *Ibid.*, p. 51.

7. Redding, *op. cit.*, p. 197.

8. *Ibid.*, p. 199.

9. Swados, Harvey, *Years of Conscience, The Muckrakers*, World, Cleveland, 1962, p. 197.

10. Redding, *op. cit.*, p. 199.

11. *Idem.*

12. *National Party Platforms, 1840–1960*, compiled by Kirk H. Porter and Donald Bruce Johnson, University of Illinois Press, Urbana, 1961, p. 134.

13. Dykeman, Wilma, and Stokely, James, *Seeds of Southern Change, The Life of Will Alexander*, University of Chicago Press, Chicago, 1962, p. 60.

14. Franklin, John Hope, *From Slavery to Freedom, A History of American Negroes*, Knopf, New York, 1961, p. 434.

15. *Inaugural Addresses of the Presidents of the United States from George Washington 1789 to John F. Kennedy 1961*, U.S. Government Printing Office, Washington, D.C., 1961, pp. 194–6.

16. *Idem.*

17. Logan, Rayford W., *The Negro in the United States, A Brief History*, Van Nostrand, Princeton, N.J., 1957, p. 66.

18. Franklin, *op. cit.*, p. 445.

19. Villard, Oswald Garrison, *Fighting Years, Memoirs of a Liberal Editor*, Harcourt, Brace, New York, 1939, p. 237.

20. *Ibid.*, p. 238.

21. *Ibid.*, p. 239.

22. National Association for the Advancement of Colored People, *Annual Report*, 1913, p. 8.

23. *National Party Platforms, 1840–1960, op. cit.*, p. 177.

24. *Documents of American History*, Henry Steele Commager, ed., F. S. Crofts, New York, 1947, Vol. II, p. 264.

25. Franklin, *op. cit.*, p. 449.

26. Dykeman and Stokely, *op. cit.*, p. 50.

27. Thorpe, Earl E., *The Mind of the Negro: An Intellectual History of Afro-Americans*, Ortlieb Press, Baton Rouge, 1961, p. 212.

28. *Idem.*

29. Redding, *op. cit.*, p. 234.

30. *Ibid.*, p. 233.

31. *Idem.*

32. *National Party Platforms, 1840–1960, op. cit.*, p. 236.

33. *The New York Times*, October 27, 1921.

34. *The New York Times*, October 29, 1921.

11 The New Federalism

As established by the founding fathers, the government of the United States was one of limited powers. The separate states, jealous of their sovereignty, had been reluctant to relinquish any of their prerogatives, and in order to obtain ratification of the Constitution, it had been necessary to agree to an amendment reserving to the states all powers not specifically delegated to the federal government. Even so, some persons feared that a new engine of tyranny had been created, one that would dwarf the old colonial administration, and they sought to curb the new government's powers even further. It was the Federalists, led by Alexander Hamilton, who opposed any such move. Only a strong national government, they argued, could protect against foreign aggression, assure unhampered trade between the various states and maintain the sanctity of the public credit.

Although the Federalists were eventually successful in establishing a strong central government, the preponderance of power still remained with the individual states. The majority of Americans preferred it that way. They genuinely believed that their own political liberty was best served by a government with limited powers. And they were willing to make an exception only during a major armed conflict, such as the Civil War and the First World War. But even then, once the hostilities were ended, the power of the federal government was curtailed again just as quickly as was practicable. When Harding waged his campaign of 1920 on the platform of a "return to normalcy," he advocated among other things the speedy withdrawal of the federal government from the many new spheres into which the exigencies of the recent war had forced it to enter. His overwhelming victory indicated that the vast majority of Americans desired a return to the basic pattern, where the fulcrum of power remained with the states.

The New Era that began with Harding gained momentum under Coolidge and reached its zenith under Hoover. These were the years when more decisions were made on Wall Street than on Pennsylvania Avenue. They were prosperous years for many but by no means all Americans. They were also years when Negroes like many laboring men, lost some of the gains that they had made during World War I.

In 1928 Herbert Hoover finally accomplished what every Republican presidential candidate since Rutherford B. Hayes had dreamed of: he broke the solid South. Shattering traditional political patterns, Hoover carried seven states below the Mason-Dixon line—Virginia, West Virginia, North Carolina, Kentucky, Tennessee, Florida, and Texas. His success was due, in great part, to the fact that his Democratic opponent was a Roman Catholic and had run on an antiprohibition platform. But it was also due to the fact that he had courted southern white votes at the expense of the Negro. At the Republican national convention, for example, Hoover's forces had ignored the Negro Republican leaders from several southern states, voting to seat instead the "lily-white" factions opposing them. During the campaign itself, many important Negro leaders in the South refused to campaign for him and several northern Negro newspapers even supported his Democratic opponent, although the Democratic Vice-presidential candidate was from Arkansas and the Party platform promised to respect states' rights and local self-determination.

Even after the election Hoover continued to ignore the Negro. He hoped, he said, to build up a Republican Party in the South "such as could commend itself to the citizens of those states."[1] The new Administration was careful, therefore, to do nothing to offend its southern supporters. On the social side there was the First Lady's embarrassingly long delay in inviting to tea at the White House, as protocol required, Mrs. Oscar DePriest, wife of the first Negro Representative elected since the early 1900s; the Vice President's refusal to shake hands with the Negro members of a delegation that had called on him; and the inferior accommodations on separate ships assigned to the Negro Gold Star Mothers invited by the government to visit their sons' graves in Europe. On the political side there was the President's silence in the face of continued lynchings throughout the South; his unwillingness to appoint Negroes to the offices they traditionally had held under Republican Presidents, and his nomination to the Supreme Court of John J. Parker, on record as having said that the "participation of the Negro in politics is a source of evil and danger . . ."[2]

The Hoover Administration had reflected, as closely as any administration ever had, the belief that that government was best which governed least. However, Hoover's inability to stem the deepening depression laid the basis for a recrudescence of the federal power. This new federalism was a response initially to the domestic crises of a depression and then to the foreign crises of fascism and, subsequently, communism. These three challenges to American democracy required vast changes in the nature and structure of our basic institutions.

When Franklin Roosevelt took office in March, 1933, the nation's economy and the society itself were dangerously close to dissolution. "Values have shrunk to fantastic levels," the new President declared in his inaugural address, "taxes have risen; our ability to pay has fallen; government of all kinds is faced by a serious curtailment of income; the means of exchange are frozen in the currents of trade, the withered leaves of enterprise lie on every side; farmers find no markets for their produce; the savings of many years in thousands of families are gone. More important, a host of unemployed citizens face the grim problem of existence, and an equally great number toil with little return. Only a foolish optimist can deny the dark realities of the moment."[3]

Roosevelt was realistic about the state of the nation. But

neither in the Democratic platform of 1932 nor in his inaugural address did he mention the Negro. The platform had stressed the continuous responsibility of government for human welfare, and "equal rights to all."[4] Toward the end of his address Roosevelt stated that he aimed "at the assurance of a rounded and permanent national life."[5] But nowhere was there a promise on which the Negro could build new hope. And yet a flicker of hope was tendered, and time proved it to be justified. During the campaign Roosevelt had declared that "These unhappy times call for the building of plans that rest upon the forgotten—the forgotten man at the bottom of the economic pyramid." When asked by a Negro journalist, "Is the Negro included in the plan you have to end the plight of the mass of the people?" Roosevelt replied, "Absolutely and impartially."[6]

The Negro had heard such promises before. He preferred to wait and see. But he did know one thing: it would be difficult for Roosevelt to do less than had his predecessor in the White House.

The outstanding characteristics of the New Deal were its venturesomeness and energy. In his inaugural address Roosevelt had declared that "I am prepared under my constitutional duty to recommend the measures that a stricken nation in the midst of a stricken world may require."[7] In the first three years of his Administration he tried a variety of approaches in an effort to revive the depressed economy and to shore up its foundations. Although they were directed at stimulating the economy at large, the various policies which came to comprise "The New Federalism" could not fail to affect the Negro.

Uppermost among the problems with which the new Administration had to deal was the decline in jobs and income over the preceding three years. About 13 million persons were unemployed, or approximately one out of every four persons in the labor force. Meanwhile, the gross national income had declined from about $104 billion in 1929 to $56 billion in 1933.

The new Administration threw the full weight of its very

considerable prestige behind the newly established National Industrial Recovery Administration. Each industry was encouraged to draw up codes of fair competition which were to bring an end to destructive price competition, reduce the hours of work, raise wage rates, and, through other regulations, bring about a better balance among capacity, output, and demand. Many southern employers insisted that they could not afford to pay the same wages as their northern competitors, and most codes provided for regional differentials. A much more difficult question was the stance that should be adopted with respect to racial differentials.

Wage differentials based on race were widespread throughout the South and, to a lesser extent, in other regions. In the face of the large-scale unemployment of white workers, the elimination of these differentials would probably, as many employers warned, lead to the replacement of Negroes by white workers. Despite the much higher incidence of unemployment among Negroes, most colored leaders opposed incorporating racial differentials in the codes for fear that they would thereby become permanent. As wage rates advanced, many employers did in fact replace Negroes with whites. Since many of them had lost their jobs as a result of the NRA, Negroes were not unhappy when in 1935 the Supreme Court declared the Act unconstitutional. This much is certain: the principal industrial recovery action initiated by the New Deal had a deleterious rather than a constructive influence on the employment of Negroes. Many were employed in sectors of the economy outside the reach of the Act or where effective codes came into existence only shortly before the end of the experiment. But many Negroes who were attached to major industries subject to its jurisdiction fared badly.

Many more Negroes earned their livelihood in agriculture than in manufacturing, however, and the several New Deal agricultural and rural rehabilitation efforts had the greatest direct impact on the economic welfare of approximately 40 per cent of all Negro males and 30 per cent of all Negro females attached to the agricultural work force. The primary vehicle of the New Deal's efforts to help farmers was the Agricultural

Adjustment Act, which provided for the payments of cash benefits to those who agreed to limit their output by plowing under their crops or by slaughtering their livestock. In 1930, approximately 180,000 Negro farm owners and managers were in the South. This group was in the best position to benefit from the federal government's cash payments. The 300,000 tenants and the almost 400,000 sharecroppers were in a much more equivocal position. While government payments were supposed to go to tenants, there were repeated complaints during the early years of the program that the landlords simply pocketed them.

Partly because of the Agricultural Adjustment Act and partly because of developments parallel in time—such as the exhaustion of the soil, mechanization, the boll weevil, and the loss of important overseas markets—there was a striking reduction in the number of Negro tenants and sharecroppers during the 1930's, especially the second half. They declined from about 700,000 in 1930 to 500,000 in 1940. The New Deal's agricultural program helped Negro farm owners and later farm tenants, but to the extent that it made it profitable for white landlords to reduce the number of Negro tenants and farm laborers it also had an adverse effect on Negro farmers.

Washington's efforts to help the farm population of the South went far beyond payments for crop and livestock control, however. As the federal government developed various banking and credit institutions, farmers who had previously had only limited access to agricultural credit or had been forced to pay exorbitant interest rates had a new source of funds. Toward the latter part of the 1930's the Farm Security Administration, the successor agency to the Resettlement Administration, began a large-scale economic rehabilitation program for farm families who previously had never been able to acquire title to the land they worked. Through a system of rentals and loans, the Administration made it possible for considerable numbers of previously landless Negro farmers to become owners. Powerful southern politicians became concerned when they realized that Washington bureaucrats were not only advocating crop diversification and other innovations but were also ignoring the color line. The status quo was being disturbed.

The New Deal was active on a great many related fronts, all of which contributed to improving the condition of southern Negro farmers. Soil-conservation programs were increased, and there was a marked expansion in farm and home demonstration work. The federal government also took a hand in furthering cooperative activities among farmers. Meanwhile, adult educational efforts taught farmers more effective agricultural methods. These also included instruction in a wide range of basic subjects, including health, reading, and the housekeeping arts. Next to road building, rural electrification probably contributed the most to transforming the rural South, and it was during the New Deal years that the program received its greatest encouragement. The Tennessee Valley Authority, in particular, represented a major regional rehabilitation effort.

It was Myrdal's considered opinion, after a careful assessment of the evidence, that "Negroes have received a substantial share in the F.S.A. benefits—almost as much, as a matter of fact, as would correspond to their population ratio in Southern farm areas."[8] He pointed out, however, that there was evidence, statistical and other, which pointed to discriminatory treatment in phases of the program administered locally.

There was no single impact of the new agricultural policies on southern Negroes. Many benefited substantially; others benefited some; still others were injured. Some were even forced off the land on which they and their parents and grandparents before them had lived. Since state and local officials were responsible for implementing most of the new federal programs, few Negroes in the South received equitable treatment. Nevertheless, many of them—like, of course, many more white farmers—were helped indirectly by the federal government's efforts to assist agriculture and to energize the South. An Alabama tenant farmer helped by the FSA told of his experience: "We was laying flat down . . . without food or clothes and this Administration . . . excepted(!) my petition and now we are standing with iron props on four sides of us."[9]

During the 1930's there was a steady outflow of Negroes from southern farms into southern cities and a resumption of the migration North. Between 1930 and 1940 the total Negro population increased from 12 to 13 million, and by the end of the decade this increase was distributed roughly equally between the South and the North, all of it in urban centers. In the cities of both regions the Negro population had increased by 20 per cent.

This inflow into the cities continued throughout the decade, in spite of the fact that most Negroes were unable to find employment. With millions of white workers unemployed or working only short hours, the Negro's position in the job market became even more vulnerable than before. Only the relief programs instituted by the federal government prevented the total demoralization of both the Negro and the white communities. The range of governmental relief programs was considerable, from the Public Works Administration, where men were paid prevailing wages, to the distribution of surplus commodities to destitute families. The fact that in the middle 1930's roughly one-half of the Negro families in the urban North were on the relief rolls led Myrdal to conclude that "large-scale public relief [was] . . . the one bright spot in the recent economic history of the Negro."[10] In 1939 the Works Progress Administration provided the basic earnings for one million Negro families, or roughly one out of every seven in the nation.

Meanwhile, the National Youth Administration provided modest but still significant wages for Negro youths who participated in its study-work programs that enabled them to continue in school and at the same time earn some income. Often these students were the only wage earners in their families. At the same time, approximately 200,000 young Negroes participated in the Civilian Conservation Corps between 1933 and 1942 and thereby earned a modest wage while they raised their educational, health, and social level. Initially, the officials of the CCC tried to exclude the Negro, and in the early years of the program they were grossly underrepresented; but Negro pressure combined with the efforts of friendly white liberals within the government, eventually achieved an enrollment of Negroes which accounted for roughly 10 per cent of the total.

The passage of the Social Security Act in 1935 initiated the development of a series of programs designed to provide an income for unemployed groups handicapped by old age or major physical handicaps, as well as for families unable to provide adequately for their dependent children. While Negroes did not qualify for aid as readily as whites under some of these programs, and local white administrators, particularly in the South, discriminated against them in varying degrees, the fact that these federally administered programs became firmly fixed in the social and economic structure of the country gave the Negro population a new source of succor. For the first time since the establishment of the Freedmen's Bureau, Negroes in want could look to the federal government for help. They were no longer completely at the mercy of the local white leadership whose dispensation of charity, particularly in the South, had for so long been guided by an over-all strategy of discrimination aimed at keeping the Negro vulnerable and subservient.

The elaborate relief and rehabilitation structure erected by the federal government during the 1930's went even further in undermining white control over local Negroes. Prior to the establishment of these programs, Negro men and women, as well as boys and girls, had to accept the prevailing wages and working conditions or remain unemployed. They had no alternative. But the work relief and public assistance programs resulted in minimum standards being set more by professional estimates of need than by reliance on local practice. Many Negroes found that their standard of living on relief was higher than it had been earlier, even when they had been fully employed. Thus, the New Deal helped to break the economic exploitation of southern Negroes.

Other New Deal programs as well affected the Negro's welfare. With federal funds supplying the stimulus, new schools, hospitals, roads, bridges, airports, recreational sites, and other community facilities were constructed throughout the South. Although the white population was the principal beneficiary of these efforts, a considerable part nevertheless spilled over into areas from which Negroes could profit. Of the $91 million in federal funds spent on new schools in the South, about $7 million went for Negro schools—a relatively small amount but substantial when considered against the previously low level of capital expenditures.

The New Deal also saw increased governmental efforts in the field of housing. The Home Owners Loan Corporation and the Federal Home Loan Banks tried to save the homes of those who could not otherwise meet their mortgage payments. The Federal Housing Administration became a major factor in the new home construction market by backing up private building with government guarantees. Although a few Negroes did receive housing loans, the total impact of the FHA on the members of that race was negligible, since both its overt and covert policies were aimed at protecting current market values, which reinforced the existing segregated pattern in residential housing.

But Negroes did receive some direct housing help. The U.S. Housing Administration, in particular, was responsible for subsidizing home construction for low-income groups. By the time the United States entered World War II, it had helped to construct about 120,000 dwelling units, of which 40,000 were for Negro occupancy. Thus, approximately 3 per cent of the urban Negro population was able to live in subsidized housing. This low-cost housing program, continued and expanded after the war, did have drawbacks, however, the most serious being the manner in which it intensified in many cities, both North and South, the effective segregation of the Negro population.

Another dimension of the New Deal was the passage of the National Labor Relations Act in 1935 and the Fair Labor Standards Act of 1938. The first greatly facilitated the growth of industrial unionism, and the second put a floor under wages and a ceiling on hours of work. Although the shortage of jobs tended to make most trade unions more exclusionist than ever, the large-scale organizing efforts in steel, automobiles, textiles, and other sectors of the economy laid the basis for gains in Negro employment once the demand for labor strengthened. And although the Wage and Hour Act did not cover the two largest segments of Negro laborers—farm workers and domestic workers—a significant number of Negro workers nevertheless benefited from the establishment of federal standards.

The programs fashioned by the Roosevelt Administration were in large measure directed to helping the lower third of the population—those who were poorly housed, poorly clothed, and poorly fed—and the Negro was more than proportionately represented among these groups. While many Negroes did not benefit from some of the New Deal measures, and while a considerable number were actually injured by others, on balance the major recovery and reform measures proved a boon to them. In seeking to stimulate the economy and alleviate the effects of depression, the federal government during the 1930s did more to assist the Negro than any government, federal, state or local, had done in the entire prior history of the nation. The government had not suddenly become deeply concerned about the Negro, but it was determined to play an active role in directing the economy and in improving the status of vulnerable groups in the society—and the Negro was in the direct path of these efforts.

There was, moreover, a definite shift in sentiment among those at the top of the federal government. The President was friendly yet cautious, but the First Lady was unstinting in her devotion to the cause of the Negro. Meanwhile, Harold Ickes and Frances Perkins lined up in support of the Negro against other members of the Cabinet, such as Henry A. Wallace, who believed that "The New Deal is undertaking to do too much for Negroes."[11] The Roosevelt Administration did appoint Negroes to office in sufficiently large numbers and sufficiently important positions that they were able to exercise considerable influence on the formulation and implementation of policies. The "Black Cabineteers," as they were called, represented a major advance in the Negro's struggle for his political rights.

Ickes had written in his diary, "While I have always been interested in seeing that the Negro has a square deal, I have never dissipated my strength against the particular stone wall of segregation. I believe that wall will crumble when the Negro has brought himself to a high educational and economic status."[12] During the days of the New Deal an increasing number of Americans became interested in seeing that the Negro got a square deal.

The outbreak of war in Europe in 1939 found the domestic crisis at home eased but by no means solved. Business was better, and employment had increased from the low levels prevailing in 1933; yet the economy was still operating at a level far below its potential. The position of the Negro continued to be unfavorable. The economic debacle of the 1930's had prevented him from adding to the gains that he had been able to make during World War I and the postwar years in the private sector of the economy. However, the New Deal provided him with access to government services that had previously been denied him.

World War II metamorphosed the American economy in a way that the New Deal in all its six years had been unable to. In 1939 the gross national income stood at $91 billion, of which $5 billion represented the federal government's purchase of goods and services. By 1944 the national income had risen to $211 billion, and the federal government's share was $89 billion. While part of this increase represented an advance in prices, most of it reflected gains in real output. During these five years there was, of course, a very rapid expansion of employment in the nonagricultural sector of the economy. The number of workers in that sector jumped from about 30.5 million in 1939 to almost 42 million in 1944, an increase of 37 per cent. While a large part of the new labor supply was furnished by white men who had been unemployed, white adolescents who left school, and white girls and women who had not previously worked, the employment expansion was so explosive that employers were forced to accept

Negro men and women in jobs where color bars had previously prevailed. The opportunities for Negroes in the civilian labor market during the war were further increased by the need to replace the large number of young men who had been called to active military duty. At the war's peak there were over 12 million men in the armed services.

The substantially enlarged numbers of Negroes in the major cities of the East and Middle West as a result of the continuing migration northward that had been under way meant that they were able to exert leverage on the federal government as it attempted to mobilize the nation's resources in the fight against Fascism. The assault by the President's press secretary on a Negro policeman in New York City on the eve of the 1940 election was neutralized only through the appointment of Negroes to high office in the War Department and the Selective Service System. Some months later, in June, 1941, Negroes had organized a march on Washington under the leadership of A. Philip Randolph to protest their continued exclusion from many defense jobs. The Negro leadership agreed to cancel the march only after President Roosevelt promised to establish a Fair Employment Practices Committee. The Executive Order establishing the Committee provided that "there shall be no discrimination in the employment of workers in defense industries or Government because of race, creed, color, or national origin . . ."[13] While it would not be easy to weigh the specific contributions of FEPC to broadening opportunities for Negroes during the war years, southern conservatives were sufficiently impressed with its work to thwart after the war's end the establishment of a permanent federal agency concerned with fair employment.

As World War II drew to a close, government officials and others concerned with the future of the economy were afraid that peace would bring a major depression. The memory of the large-scale unemployment characteristic of the whole of the 1930's could not be wiped out in less than four years. The overwhelming vote in favor of the Employment Act of 1946 testified to two facts: the nation's continuing fear of unemployment and its conviction that the federal government ought to pursue policies aimed to prevent such a recurrence. But, despite fears to the contrary, the postwar labor market remained strong—at least until the Korean conflict—and Negroes were able to add to their wartime gains.

A comparison of their occupational distribution and income level for 1940 and 1950 indicates the substantial progress Negroes had made. Between 1940 and 1950 the number of Negro males in the nonfarm sector increased from 1.8 million to 2.8 million; during this same period the number in the farm sector declined from about 1.3 million to 900,000. This shift out of farming into manufacturing and the service sectors of the economy had a significant improvement factor built into it. And the detailed figures show further gains. For instance, the number of Negro males in the white-collar occupations almost doubled, rising from 175,000 to 325,000. The number of skilled workers and foremen more than doubled, from 135,000 to 300,000. Most of the increased employment was, however, represented by Negroes who obtained semiskilled, service and laboring jobs.

Negro women also made significant employment gains. They, too, were able to shift out of agriculture into the industrial and service sectors of the economy. They, too, were able to secure more jobs in the white collar occupations, from about 100,000 in 1940, to about 250,000 in 1950.

The 1940's witnessed many dynamic changes in the labor market, and the Negro was able to profit from almost all of them. The shift out of agriculture into industry and trade was perhaps the basis for his greatest gain. He could usually double and frequently triple his money income through this shift alone. Although Negroes continued to be heavily concentrated at the bottom of the urban job ladder, the wages paid to unskilled and semiskilled workers increased relatively more rapidly during the decade of the 1940's than the wages of the more highly skilled. Negroes benefited substantially from this differential rate of increase. Moreover, during this decade fringe benefits proliferated, and an increasing proportion of all Negroes were employed under contracts that in-

cluded these new benefits. The continued tightness of the
labor market, moreover, made it possible for many workers,
including Negroes, to earn a considerable amount of overtime
pay. Since many had been able to join unions early in the
war, they were able to bid for better jobs as they became
available, and many succeeded in advancing at least one or
two rungs up the skill ladder. Their union membership and
their accruing seniority meanwhile offered them greater protection against layoffs.

These many developments resulted in marked increases in
the money and real income earned by Negroes. The increasing numbers now residing in urban centers, especially in the
North and West, had access to markedly improved public
services, such as schools, hospitals, libraries, and recreational
facilities. Of course the white population also improved its
position, but the evidence is clear that Negroes not only
made very substantial absolute gains but also narrowed the
gap between their situation and that of the white majority.
These substantial gains were the direct result of the United
States' involvement in World War II and the prosperity that
followed in its wake. However great the costs of World War
II in terms of life and treasure, the Negro population as a
whole was markedly better off five years after its termination
than it had been at its outbreak.

One source of the Negroes' improved situation was their
experience in the Armed Services. During the course of
World War II almost 1 million Negroes served on active duty.
On VE Day there were more than 500,000 Negro troops overseas and less than 200,000 in the United States. Most Negroes
profited from their military service in various ways. Several
hundred thousand were taught to read and write, and most
were introduced to health services far beyond any they had
previously known. Many had an opportunity to acquire skills
that proved helpful to them when they returned to civilian
life. The hundreds of thousands of Negro servicemen honor-
ably discharged were entitled to veterans' benefits, which enabled them to go back to school, take special training, secure
loans to purchase a home and enjoy other types of assistance

that could speed their civilian adjustment. Even more important, they spent several years in an organized military society which, though basically segregated, brought them into close contact with whites. Since most Negroes had been born and brought up in the South, they had never lived in communities where legal segregation did not prevail. Many spent some part of their military career in the North or West, and many served overseas.

The Armed Services provided a crucible for the active exposure and interaction of Negroes from different parts of the United States who had undergone different life experiences. Educated Negroes from the North were incensed when they encountered for the first time the full blast of southern segregation; and their outrage left its mark on many southern Negroes who had taken their world for granted, not because they liked it, but because they had known no other.

The fact that the United States was engaged in mortal combat with an enemy whose ideology was anchored in racism made it easier for the Negro leadership in the United States to press, even while the war was still in progress, for reforms aimed at reducing segregation and discrimination in the Armed Services. While the President and his senior advisors were disinclined to enter upon any social reforms that might slow the war effort or reduce the nation's military efficiency, the Negro leadership did secure some concessions on the ground that they would lead to an improved utilization of manpower and would strengthen the total war effort. When the United States entered the war, military leaders widely believed that the Negro was not a good fighting man and that he could be useful only in labor battalions. Only under pressure from the White House and the Secretaries of War and Navy were they willing to modify this position, and then only within narrow limits. They agreed to induct Negroes in proportion to their ratio to the population as a whole. All branches of the service eventually became open to them, and they were permitted to attend desegregated officer candidate schools. Late in the war they even served in combat units on a partially integrated basis. In addition, the Army reduced or eliminated discrimination against Negroes in the use of recreational and transportation facilities. Although there had been many "breakthroughs" during the course of the war, at the end of hostilities segregation in the Army and Navy was still largely intact. During the immediate postwar years there was some further relaxation of conventional practices but no radical innovations.

In December, 1946, President Truman established a Committee on Civil Rights under the chairmanship of Charles E. Wilson. Its report, entitled *To Secure These Rights,* concluded that "We need to guarantee the same rights to every person regardless of who he is, where he lives, or what his racial, religious or national origins are." The Committee specifically recommended that "The Armed forces should expand efforts, already under way, to develop genuinely democratic attitudes in officers and enlisted men."[14] But this would require, first, programs to eliminate the many segregated practices that were still in force. In 1948 Truman was ready to take another step. In July he issued an executive order proclaiming a national policy for the Armed Forces of "equality of treatment and opportunity for all persons in the armed services without regard to race, color, creed, religion, or national origin."[15] The order created a Committee on Equality of Treatment and Opportunity in the Armed Services, thus providing a goad to the Department of Defense to take action to achieve stated objectives. Thereafter progress was made, but it was slow.

Although the White House and the Negro leadership, with the help of friendly whites, never ceased their pressure on the Department of Defense to intensify its actions to eliminate segregation, the process would have taken much longer had it not been for the manpower exigencies created by the Korean conflict. The Army and the Air Force had to expand the number of their combat-ready troops in a short time. Since neither department had adequate cadres to meet this urgent requirement and at the same time staff the duplicated facilities that a segregated service required, training centers were the first to be desegregated. When the Army began to sustain serious losses in action, it became hard pressed to find adequate replacements. Consequently, with General Ridgway's concurrence, it dropped racial designations on troops shipped overseas as replacements. As a result, combat units were soon on their way to being desegregated. With training centers at home and combat units in Korea desegregated, it was relatively easy to complete the process in Europe and other overseas commands. Once again manpower stringencies had proved more telling than social mores. As in the civilian economy, so in the armed services, the barriers to the use of Negro manpower fell when the white community had no satisfactory alternative.

By 1954 the armed forces had complied with Truman's order, which was reaffirmed by Eisenhower. Thereafter, from the moment he was sworn in as a member of one of the services until he received his discharge papers and was mustered out, the Negro serviceman lived in an integrated world. He shared barracks with white servicemen. He ate in the same mess, at the same table. He attended the same church and used the same recreational centers. He was assigned to the same unit. He was hospitalized in the same ward. Never before in the history of this nation had Negroes lived in a fully integrated environment. For the first time large numbers of Negroes and white had the personal and direct experience of living with each other on a basis of equality.

Still another dimension of federal power came to be employed on the Negro's behalf under the stimulus of "The New Federalism." In the closing decades of the nineteenth century the Supreme Court, reflecting the mood of the North, had greatly circumscribed the power of the federal government to intervene directly to protect the Negro's rights. At about the time that the New Deal was launched, the Court became increasingly sensitive to the violation of these rights. The Court's new stance was first revealed in its review of the famous Scottsboro case. Nine young Negroes early in the 1930's were charged with having raped two young white women and were found guilty and sentenced to death. On appeal, the United States Supreme Court found in *Norris* v

State of Alabama in .1935 that the "continuous and total exclusion [of Negroes] from juries because there were none possessing the requisite qualification cannot be sustained . . ."[16] The systematic exclusion of Negroes from juries was henceforth *prima facie* evidence of denial of equal protection guaranteed by the Fourteenth Amendment. Since legal intimidation had long been used by the South as an instrument of racial control, the Supreme Court took an important step in the Scottsboro case to protect the southern Negro from this type of judicial abuse. The Supreme Court had never completely forsaken the Negro in cases involving the violation of his rights in the courtroom, but after 1935 it became increasingly sensitive to all forms of coercion applied against Negro defendants, particularly in capital cases. The Court would no longer stand aside and permit technicalities to hide discrimination.

Three years later, in the case of *Missouri ex rel Gaines v. Canada,* the Supreme Court took a momentous step toward reinterpreting *Plessy v Ferguson,* which had been the law of the land for more than four decades. Examining for the first time the question of whether separate accommodations were in fact equal, the Court concluded that if a state wanted to maintain a system of public education that provided separate facilities for white and Negro students, it would have to provide substantially equal opportunities for Negroes within the state. Young Gaines had sought to study law and the state of Missouri had offered to pay his tuition in an out-of-state school. But Chief Justice Hughes in his opinion recognized that this offer of the state was not "equal," since clear advantages attach to studying in the state where one intends to practice. The Court's opinion left the Missouri no option but to admit Gaines to the University. The fact that Gaines dropped from sight and never enjoyed his victory in court did not diminish the impact of the Court's judgment.

Shortly after the end of World War II additional cases involving the admission of Negroes to law schools or the graduate faculties of state universities in the South came before the Supreme Court. In each instance it went to the substance of the issue of equality and, when it found that the opportunities offered Negroes were not truly equal, decided against the defendants.

The South read the handwriting on the wall. Since segregation in elementary and secondary schools was in jeopardy under a rule of law that looked to the substance of equality, it set about energetically to improve the facilities and teaching staffs of Negro schools.

The extent of the South's effort is suggested by the increase in expenditures for instruction per pupil in average daily attendance between 1940 and 1953, the year before the Court handed down its decision in the Brown case. During 1939–1940 Mississippi spent for each white child an average of five times as much as it spent for each Negro child. In Louisiana the gap was more than three to one, in Alabama and Georgia a little less than three to one, and in the other Southern states the ratio was only slightly better. After 1939–1940 the South increased its expenditures for the education of white children about threefold, but it made an even greater effort with respect to Negro children. On the eve of the Brown decision the gap in annual expenditures in Florida, North Carolina, and Alabama was less than 10 per cent, and in Arkansas and Louisiana the gap in favor of the whites was almost one-third. Only Mississippi lagged far behind, its expenditures for white children still being more than double those for the education of Negro children. But even Mississippi had made a real effort in the preceding period: while it doubled its expenditures for white children, it had increased its expenditures for Negro children more than fivefold.

However, the South soon discovered that increasing the pay of teachers, making more and better books available, and increasing other expenditures for current operations was not enough to stay the Supreme Court's hand. It would also have to narrow the gap between the quality of facilities available to white and Negro children. In 1947–1948 the average value of property, buildings and equipment available to white children in every southern state was at least more than twice the value of similar property available to Negro pupils. In several of the states—Alabama, Mississippi, South Carolina, Florida, and Louisiana—the differential in favor of white pupils was three or four to one. Although almost all of the southern states made desperate efforts in the years immediately preceding the Brown decision to build new schools for Negroes, they had started too late and the gap was too large. The several cases involving Negro complaints of unequal schools were certain to reach the Supreme Court before the South could demonstrate that it had in fact lived up to the doctrine of "separate but equal." But even if they had, in fact, been equal, it is doubtful whether the Supreme Court would have sanctioned the continuance of segregated schools. In *Brown et al v Board of Education of Topeka et al*, the Court declared: "We conclude that in the field of public education the doctrine of 'separate but equal' has no place. Separate educational facilities are inherently unequal." The Court had reached the conclusion in the allied case of *Bolling et al v Sharpe et al*, that "segregation in public education is not reasonably related to any proper governmental objective," stating, "We cannot turn the clock back . . . We must consider public education in light of its full development and its present place in American life throughout the Nation."[17]

In yet one other major sphere the Court acted. As late as 1935 it had refused to declare that the action of the Texas Democratic State Convention that barred Negroes from the Democratic primaries was state action and therefore unconstitutional. But in 1944, in *Smith v Allwright*, it reversed itself. Once again the Court went to the substance of the issue and found that in fact it was state rather than private action that governed primary elections in Texas. Pointing to the Fifteenth Amendment, which forbids "the abridgment by a state of a citizen's right to vote," the Court specifically overruled its early decision in *Graney v Townsend*.

A leading student of Southern politics, V. O. Key, Jr., writing in 1949, said that "So few have been Negro voters in the South that to estimate their number seems futile." But, he said, "Negro voting has grown quite rapidly since the decision of the Supreme Court holding the white primary invalid in April 1944."[18] Key presented a summary picture of Negroes held qualified to vote in 1947, three years after the Supreme Court's decision on the Texas convention. In Alabama, Louisiana, and Mississippi less than 3 per cent of the adult Negro population was considered qualified to vote. In Tennessee, with the highest proportion, 26 per cent was qualified. The proportion in the other states varied from about 13 per cent in Virginia and South Carolina to about 19 per cent in Georgia and Texas.

In 1946 there was an intensive campaign to register Negroes in Georgia when Carmichael, who was running against Talmadge for governor, sought their support. Texas, according to Key, accepted the 1944 decision of the Supreme Court with good grace, and the number of Negro votes increased substantially in 1946. But progress in many of the other states was slow because of both white hostility and Negro indifference. The nonvoting pattern of the Negro would not be easily broken, but the Supreme Court's decision of 1944 had brought the day of change much closer.

Thus, in the two decades following the election of President Roosevelt the nation faced a series of major crises that changed the terms of relations between white and Negro. In passing the new economic, social welfare, and labor legislation of the 1930's, Congress not only changed the basic relationship of business to government but also provided a basic minimum of economic security for all citizens. Since Negroes were heavily concentrated in the lower-income range, they were among the major beneficiaries of this new legislation.

When the nation mobilized on the civilian and military front to meet the threat from Germany and Japan, it created an almost insatiable demand for manpower. Negroes who had long been on the periphery of the labor market now had opportunities opened to them. The rate of their occupational and economic gains during the 1940's was without parallel.

Most of the one million Negroes who served in the armed forces during World War II sustained a constructive experience. Moreover, most of them became eligible for valuable GI benefits. The postwar prosperity that helped to keep the labor market taut enabled many Negroes to further improve their occupational, economic, and social status. The American economy needed their labor.

National need also contributed to speeding the desegregation of the armed forces in the early 1950's. The Department of Defense discovered that its problems would be increased if it had to fight in Korea and at the same time maintain segregation. The consequent desegregation of the armed forces provided the Negro with his first opportunity in 335 years to live in an integrated society.

The major challenges that the nation faced and surmounted helped to deepen and broaden its democratic commitment, particularly since it was challenged from without as well as from within. Among the important consequences of this renewed commitment to democratic principles was the new stance of the Supreme Court in matters affecting civil liberties, particularly the rights of the Negro. For the first time in its history, the Court looked closely at the commitment made to the Negro in the post-Civil War amendments and insisted that these commitments be met not only formally but in fact. On every front the federal power was employed to strengthen the nation and in the process the Negro came out ahead. The brief submitted by the United States, *amicus curiae,* in the school desegregation cases stated, "it is in the context of the present world struggle between freedom and tyranny that the problem of racial discrimination must be viewed. . . . Racial discrimination furnishes grist for Communist mills and it raises doubts even among friendly nations as to the intensity of our devotion to the democratic path."[19]

NOTES

1. Franklin, John Hope, *From Slavery to Freedom, A History of American Negroes,* Knopf, New York, 1961, p. 514.

2. *Ibid.,* p. 515.

3. *Inaugural Addresses of the Presidents of the United States from George Washington 1789 to John F. Kennedy 1961,* U.S. Government Printing Office, Washington, D.C., 1961, pp. 235–6.

4. *National Party Platforms, 1840–1960,* compiled by Kirk H. Porter and Donald Bruce Johnson,

University of Illinois Press, Urbana, 1961, p. 333.

5. *Inaugural Addresses, op. cit.,* p. 239.

6. Kifer, Allen, "The New Deal and the Negro," presented at the American Historical Association, December 28, 1961, pp. 1, 3.

7. *Inaugural Addresses, op. cit.,* p. 238.

8. Myrdal, Gunnar, *An American Dilemma, The Negro Problem and Modern Democracy,* Harper, New York, 1944, p. 273.

9. Kifer, *op. cit.,* p. 10.

10. Myrdal, *op. cit.,* p. 354.

11. Dykeman, Wilma, and Stokely, James, *Seeds of Southern Change, The Life of Will Alexander,* University of Chicago Press, Chicago, 1962, p. 249.

12. Ickes, Harold, *Secret Diary,* Simon and Schuster, New York, 1954, Vol. II, p. 115.

13. Franklin, *op. cit.,* p. 565.

14. *To Secure These Rights,* The Report of the President's Committee on Civil Rights, Simon and Schuster, New York, 1947, pp. xi, 173.

15. *Freedom to the Free, 1863–1963, Century of Emancipation,* A Report to the President by the United States Commission on Civil Rights, U.S. Government Printing Office, Washington, D.C., 1963, p. 125.

16. Logan, Rayford W., *The Negro in the United States, A Brief History,* Van Nostrand, Princeton, N.J., 1957, p. 152.

17. Blaustein, Albert P., and Ferguson, Clarence Clyde, Jr., *Desegregation and the Law, The Meaning and Effect of the School Segregation Cases,* Vintage Books, New York, 1962, pp. 303–8.

18. Key, V. O., Jr., *Southern Politics in State and Nation,* Vintage Books, New York, 1949, pp. 517–8.

19. Blaustein and Ferguson, *op. cit.,* p. 12.

12 From Freedom to Equality

For nearly 300 years the Negro in America was without a voice of his own, and except for short periods there was no one else to speak for him. First he was a slave with no rights at all; then he became a citizen with his rights so severely circumscribed that his property, even his life, was in constant jeopardy. For many generations he could do no more than pray and hope and wait. On occasion he was driven to such desperation that in a blind rage he set out to kill the whites who had for so long murdered and tortured the members of his race. He could look neither to the courts for justice nor to the churches for charity. He had the companionship only of his fellow Negroes, who likewise were proscribed from participating in the democracy that the nation had proclaimed.

Shortly after the nadir in this story had been reached, which coincided with the years preceding the outbreak of World War I, there began a slow ascent. Today the Negro finally is at the threshold of the freedom that is his by law but which had long been denied him by the violence and the cupidity of his white neighbors.

The burden of this chapter is to trace the changes during the last half-century that have so radically altered the position of the Negro in America and that foreshadow further changes in the years ahead. As we have seen, events both at home and abroad have radically altered the shape of American society and, in the process, the outlook for Negro equality. For the most part these events had little to do specifically with the

Negro. They were embedded in forces that engulfed the nation, and at times the whole world. The major dynamics lay outside his immediate orbit, but much of what transpired was directly related to him—to his deprivations and to his claims for justice and equality. During these years, the Negro began to play a role in shaping his own destiny—a role which at first was small but which he has steadily enlarged. From active participation in the NAACP and the National Urban League to membership in governmental agencies in World War I, the Negro leadership gained strength to plead its case and demand that its claims be granted. Slowly the Negro's control over the essentials for self-assertion—political and economic power—increased. And slowly, under the battering of court and conscience, some of the barriers erected by the whites began to give way.

But his progress continued to be slow, very slow, for even after the Supreme Court spoke in 1954, most white communities in the South refused to comply with its edict. Here was proof indeed that if he were ever to enjoy the freedom which had been vouchsafed him in the immediate post-World War II years, he would have to fight to attain it. And so in 1956 in Montgomery, Alabama, a new fight began. For the first time, the Negro masses rose up out of their despondency and insisted on their rights. They made it clear that they would fight—if necessary, die—for them. The protest movement, thus born, radically changed the terms of the equation. Thereafter, Negroes would demand and the white community would have to accede. For now the Negroes' demands were backed by the power of the ballot box and of the purse.

The backdrop of this latest phase of the Negro's struggle for equality was the 1948 Democratic National Convention and the subsequent presidential election. By a narrow margin the original platform was amended from the floor in several respects. President Truman was commended for his "courageous stand" on the issue of civil rights, and Congress was called upon to support the President in guaranteeing "these basic and fundamental American principles: (1) the right of full and equal political participation; (2) the right to equal opportunity of employment; (3) the right of security of person, (4) and the right of equal treatment in the service and defense of our nation."[1]

Thirty-five southern delegates walked out of the Convention, and shortly thereafter the "Dixiecrats" nominated Strom Thurmond of South Carolina for President. The states' rights platform on which Thurmond campaigned brimmed with recrimination and anger. It talked of the "rugged loyalty" of the South to the Democratic Party, it accused the Democratic convention of being rigged and seeking to "embarrass and humiliate the South," it called the civil rights plank adopted at Philadelphia an "infamous and iniquitous program," and it came out foursquare in favor of the "segregation of the races and the racial integrity of each race."[2]

The Republican platform was also fairly specific on civil rights. It favored an antilynching bill, a federal fair employment act, the elimination of the poll tax for voting, and the termination of segregation in the Armed Services.

The subsequent election proved to be a milestone in the history of America's race relations. It underlined the fact that henceforth presidential candidates would be more interested in the votes of Negroes in the important northern industrial states than in currying favor with white diehards of the South. Since that election of 1948, no presidential candidate has seen any chance of winning without promising to improve the lot of the Negro. Substantial Negro concentrations in Pennsylvania, New Jersey, New York, Michigan, Illinois, and California have become one cornerstone in the growth of Negro political power.

In 1957 Congress passed the first civil rights legislation since the Civil War. The Republican leadership, which for so long had had a tacit agreement with southern Democrats to prevent the expansion of federal power, finally shifted tactics and joined with northern Democratic liberals to pass a new law, the main thrust of which was to strengthen the right of the Negro to vote. A key role in working out the compromise that cut back the scope of President Eisenhower's original proposals but kept the southern diehards from engaging in an all out filibuster was played by Lyndon Johnson, then Democratic majority leader in the Senate. Johnson appreciated better than most southerners that the day when liberal northern Democrats would be content simply to make promises about civil rights and conservative southern Democrats would be able to prevent the Congress from taking constructive action, however moderate, was over now that the Republicans were willing to go after the Negro vote.

Johnson, who had presidential ambitions, also appreciated that his only chance of winning a future nomination would be to prove himself a moderate, preferably a progressive, in the field of civil rights. Except for Woodrow Wilson, who transformed himself into a northerner before he entered politics, and Harry Truman, who came from a border state, no son of the South had made a successful bid for the presidency since Zachary Taylor was elected in 1848. Lyndon Johnson therefore attempted to transform himself from a southerner into a westerner and to indicate his availability for national leadership by moving perceptibly to a more liberal civil rights stand.

In both the 1952 election and again in 1956 Eisenhower, like Hoover a quarter of a century earlier, had broken the solid South. The Republican Party seemed on the way to destroying the Roosevelt coalition, replacing it with an alliance of its own that united the expanding middle class in the North with the rapidly increasing urban population in the economically advanced southern states. The very success that Eisenhower achieved in his two elections set the stage for the Republican debacle of 1960. Richard Nixon lost by only a very narrow margin, but the defeat was much greater than the figures show, since the nation was prosperous and the Democratic candidate was handicapped by his religion and initial lack of national visibility. Throughout the campaign Nixon was unable to decide whether to make a strong play for the votes of southern white conservatives or to bid for the Negro vote in several crucial Northern states. It was John F. Kennedy who called Mrs. Martin Luther King when her husband was jailed, and it was Kennedy who was elected.

A president who has sought the Negro vote during his campaign must use his very considerable power to fulfill his promises. As the leader of the nation, the President can set directions and seek to persuade the public to move speedily toward a goal. As head of the executive branch of the government, he has a wide array of powers in the determination of administrative policy. He makes innumerable appointments, he is responsible for insuring that the decisions of the federal courts are upheld, he is the principal architect of his party's legislative program. The President is, of course, concerned with the realization of a great many different goals that he can attain only with a legislative majority. He must therefore sacrifice, at times, certain goals for others; nevertheless, he can determine how much national effort should be devoted to achieving any one.

The last several decades have seen a second major increment of Negro power as a result of the actions of the federal government through decisions of the Supreme Court, which in the federal-state system is frequently the final arbiter of conflicts. While most of the civil rights cases in recent years have involved school desegregation, the Supreme Court has handed down a great many decisions that have had the effect of denying to states and localities and also to private persons the use of the law to enforce any aspect of segregation. Moreover, the rural areas are no longer in a position to dominate state politics now that the Supreme Court has decided that gross inequalities in representation must be corrected. The Negro has therefore a much better chance both of exercising his franchise in the South and of having his vote count heavily in the North.

Segregation is a pervasive ordering of the relationships between the races from birth to death. For many years Negro mothers gave birth to their children in segregated hospitals. The children in turn grew up in segregated neighborhoods, attended segregated schools, worshipped in segregated churches, and played in segregated parks. When they grew up, they were examined for military service under segregated conditions, and they were forced to serve their country in segregated units. Transportation facilities were segregated, as were places of amusement and recreation. Negroes could borrow books only from segregated libraries; they could obtain training only under segregated conditions and join only segregated labor unions; they could be hired only for certain types of segregated employment; they could buy homes only in segregated sections of the city; they could use only segregated facilities at their places of employment and in the community at large; they were tried in courts making use of segregated practices. And when they died, they were buried only in segregated cemeteries.

No such detailed ordering of the lives of people was possible unless it had the sanction of law and was backed by political power at the state and local levels. While the Supreme Court helped to undermine the legal foundations of the system, its dissolution has been assisted by changes in the political power of Negroes in the several states and localities where it has been long ensconced.

During the last several decades the Negro has made significant gains in state and local politics, even in the South. The Department of Justice estimated that in 1932 fewer than 100,000 Negroes voted in the twelve southern states. As a result of the elimination of the white primary under the dictate of the Supreme Court, state action to eliminate the poll tax, relocation of the Negro population from farm to city, and various educational campaigns, the number of registered Negro voters had risen to about 650,000 in 1947. By 1962 it exceeded 1 million and today it probably approximates 1.7 million.

The nature of the benefits that have accrued to Negroes as a result of their more active participation in state and local politics is complex. The election of Negroes to local and, more recently, state offices indicates one inherent weakness of any segregated system of race relations, whether legally buttressed or enforced only by tradition, in a republican system of government. Some years ago Eugene Talmadge warned the Georgia electorate that if his opponents, the moderates in race relations, had their way, it would not be long until "you will see negro Mayors, negro School Superintendents, negro Congressmen, negro Judges and negro Sheriffs and negro Jailers in that part of the state where the negroes predominate. . . ."[3] Even if segregation were not falling by the wayside for other reasons, it would not be able to survive in the face of an intensifying competition for the votes of a growing Negro electorate. The coordinated use of governmental power reinforcing the many sources of nongovernmental power used to force Negro acquiescence to second-class citizenship can be effective only in communities where the white majority stands together. But as more and more Negroes are permitted to vote, they will strike bargains with one or another of the white factions to secure their demands.

At the conclusion of his comprehensive study of *Southern Politics,* V. O. Key comments: "Candidates for municipal office are finding it easier and easier to understand the plea of Negro leaders (with a bloc of dependable votes at their command) for improved street lighting, paving or sewerage facilities in the Negro section of town. Demands for improved school and recreational facilities and for Negro policemen are other political objectives for which Negroes rally with a fair degree of unanimity if one candidate will promise them and another is indefinite."[4]

Thus in a Jacksonville, Florida, election in the early 1950's, a local Negro leader pressed the several candidates to state what they had done or would do for the Negro population. The incumbent Commissioner of Health and Sanitation replied, "As Chairman of the Budget Committee . . . , I was largely instrumental in securing the first $40,000 . . . for the construction of the Negro swimming pool. . . . As President of the Council I expended my best efforts in securing an additional $25,000 for the project. . . . As your Health Commissioner, I take pride in the fact that one-third of the nurses of this Department are colored, and that they receive salaries equal to those of the white. While serving on the Police Committee of the Commission . . . I became convinced of the wisdom of having Negro policemen in Jacksonville, and voted accordingly. . . ."[5]

Negroes outside of the South, especially in the states and localities where they are heavily concentrated, are usually able to make a better bargain in return for their support at the polls. In addition to protection from police brutality and justice in the courts, northern Negroes are constantly increasing their demands for appointment to office in proportion to their support. They are also concerned with neighborhood programs, particularly those aimed at improving welfare programs. More recently they have broadened the scope of their demands to insist upon affirmative action by government to overcome many forms of *de facto* segregation, particularly in education, housing, and employment. They have played a key role at both state and local levels in the passage of new legislation aimed in the outlawing of any form of discrimination in public accommodations and employment. New York took the lead in 1945, and thirty-one states now have enforceable fair employment practices laws on their books. Illinois was the last of the major industrial states to pass such legislation. Moreover, a number of major cities have fair employment practices or human relations commissions empowered to investigate charges of discrimination and to take various types of action to eradicate it. Recourse to law to secure equality for minority groups is a new departure. Only as this experience is accumulated and evaluated will the full strength of the law be felt.

The pervasive systems of segregation and discrimination have been breached not only by the gains that Negroes have been able to register on the political front—federal, state, and local—but also by transformations within the white and Negro community in other attitudes and behavior.

During the last several decades there have been significant breaks in the solid white front in the South. The increased mobility of white southerners, which led them to the North and West, to Europe, and to other continents, has contributed to loosening the rigidity with which they held to their singular model of race relations. The inmigration of millions of northern whites has also added a dynamic element to a static environment. The impact of military desegregation has weakened white dedication to the maintenance of the system; by now millions of young white southerners have lived in a desegregated society.

Southerners have also been increasingly exposed to new ideas, to which they as well as others have contributed significantly. While the southern press, as the press everywhere, tends to reflect the views of the leadership sectors of the community that it serves, several papers have been willing to speak out on racial questions. Both radio and television have made important contributions by enabling southerners to confront directly news of dramatic racial episodes that were disturbing to white people whose feelings were not too deeply encrusted with prejudice. The communications industry—press, radio, television, and, to a lesser extent, the movies—deprived the South of much of the luxury of secrecy that had forestalled criticism of segregation and its consequences.

There has long been sporadic criticism of and dissent from the southern way of life, particularly those aspects that result in gross injustices to the Negro. The last decades have seen a burgeoning of this literature. Distinguished southern as well as northern writers have written about not only what is warm and good about the South but also the ugliness and baseness that corrode so many aspects of race relations.

Another crack in the wall of prejudice was made by the white leadership of the academic community and of various professional societies. Negro scholars and scientists are increasingly invited to participate in conferences and conventions held under white auspices. White professors are increasingly willing to lecture at Negro colleges, and there is a lowering of racial barriers among professional groups, particularly physicians, lawyers, and clergymen.

The strongest anomaly in southern life was the gap on the religious front, where the practice of segregation was a screaming denial of the Scriptures and of the Judeo-Christian tradition. Churchmen, clerical and lay, had provided much of the white leadership for the group which worked within the broad framework of segregation for the amelioration of the worst burdens on the Negro minority, especially excesses of exploitation and abuse. But most churchmen spoke in a whisper for fear of losing their pulpits.

The social welfare departments of some of the major denominations had long been concerned with racial matters and through special studies and conferences sought to bring the white leadership to work jointly with the Negro community. After World War II the Catholic Church declared that any manifestation of racism was a sin. The principal Jewish organizations, which had increased the scale and scope of their activities when Hitler rose to power, became ever more aware of the fact that prejudice against any minority was a danger to all. These organizations became directly involved in helping the southern Negro win his rights to full citizenship.

However, Protestantism dominated the South, and for a long time most of the Protestant clergy was silent concerning segregation. The 1954 Supreme Court decision finally elicited a broad response from the Protestant groups. Directly after the decision was handed down, the General Board of the National Council of Churches of Christ hailed the opportunity which it provided for "translating into reality Christian and democratic ideals." The Southern Baptist Convention declared that the decision was "in harmony with the constitutional guarantee of equal freedom to all citizens, and with the Christian principles of equal justice and love for all men." The General Assembly of the Presbyterian Church took a most forthright position by declaring that "segregation of the races is discrimination which is out of harmony with Christian theology and ethics" and went on to stress that it is the responsibility of the church to lead. Some denominations were more outspoken than others, but the clergymen of all denominations have increasingly moved into the foreground of those who insist that segregation must go if Christianity is not to be denied.[6]

Many who are responsible for informing the South, many who love the culture of the South, many who instruct the South and provide it with professional leadership, and many who stand as guardians of its heritage are no longer willing to defend segregation. They are instead actively engaged in preparing the South to reconcile itself—in fact, to welcome—the day when it is freed of the system, originally designed to oppress the Negro, that has also shackled the white man.

The same congruence of forces that has altered white leadership opinion in the South has been manifested in the North, where segregation has been long imbedded but without legal sanction. The combined weight and influence of the press and other communications instrumentalities, universities, academic and other professional groups, religious leaders, as well as special groups organized for the explicit purpose of speeding integration represent a powerful and increasing force aimed at closing the very wide gap between pretention and fact that has long prevailed north of the Mason-Dixon line.

Perhaps the single greatest change in recent years has been that the Negro himself has assumed leadership in the struggle for his full emancipation and equality. This has been possible because of the recent enhancement of his power from two sources, the improvement in his economic circumstances and his organized determination to secure his rights.

Since 1940 the Negro has substantially improved his occupation status and his income. He has become much less vulnerable to economic reprisals when he becomes active in drives to enhance his political and civic rights. He has been able to use his dollars and his patronage to exert pressure against white groups who insist on the maintenance of the status quo.

The relatively persistent high level of employment that characterized the economy between 1940 and 1960 was one source of the Negro's great gains. During these two decades the total Negro labor force grew from about 5.6 million to 7.7 million, or by more than 37 per cent. Since the unemployment rate was considerably higher in 1940 than in 1960, the growth in the labor force understates the number of Negroes who have secured paid employment during those twenty years. Not only did many more Negroes obtain jobs, but there were marked improvements in the type of jobs available to them. In 1940 there were approximately 180,000 Negro males in a total of 3.1 million in the white-collar sector, or roughly one out of every sixteen. The comparable data for 1960 were about 560,000 Negroes out of 4.1 million, or about one out of every nine.

Negro women also scored important employment gains. In

1940 about 100,000 were white-collar workers; in 1960 there were 500,000. The white-collar sector accounted for about one in sixteen of the total Negro female labor force in 1940 and one in five and a half in 1960.

Those decades also saw the very rapid withdrawal of Negroes from agriculture, where earnings were lowest. The number of males was cut in half and the number of females by one-third. By 1960 less than 800,000 Negro men and women out of 6.8 million total in the labor force were still attached to agriculture.

During these two decades the income of the Negro population advanced substantially as a result of their improved employment status and the substantial advances in real income that characterized the economy at large. In addition, during these years, those in the lower wage brackets enjoyed the most rapid gains.

At the outbreak of World War II, the median annual income of Negro families was about $490, roughly 40 per cent of the $1,230 for white families. Shortly after the end of the war (1947) the respective median incomes for Negro and white families were about $1,615 and $3,160; the ratio was then 51 per cent. At the time of the Korean War (1954) the figures were, respectively, $2,340 for Negroes and $4,410 for whites; the ratio had further improved to 57 per cent. During the last decade there has been some contrary movement: both Negroes and whites earned considerably more income, but the gap between the two began to widen. In 1962 the median earnings for Negroes was $3,300, that of whites $6,240, and the ratio stood at 53 per cent.

Increased purchasing power provides leverage not only in the market place but in the community at large. Many white merchants depend on Negro patronage, as do many white manufacturers and distributors. As the Negro community, South and North, acquired more purchasing power, it began to insist on rights and privileges previously denied it. Sales personnel in white department stores were instructed to be civil and polite to Negro customers. Banks no longer served white customers first. In fact, all who wanted the Negroes' dollars had to demonstrate this by their actions.

In Tuskegee, Montgomery, Nashville, Birmingham, and a great many other cities, small and large, an unbending attitude on the part of whites with respect to Negroes has been met by boycott. Many of the ensuing compromises were worked out because of the power of the Negro dollar, which is enhanced when it is backed by a strong community organization. The bankruptcy of the Montgomery busline was a lesson that all of the South learned.

Rising Negro incomes serve as leverage for improving the circumstance of Negroes in another way. One concomitant of segregation has been the dual market, with many businesses and services—from proprietary hospitals to funeral parlors—depending almost exclusively on meeting the needs of the Negro community. Increased Negro incomes during the past two decades have opened up many new opportunities for enterprising Negroes in business, the professions, journalism, and other sectors of the economy. Most of the economically successful Negroes achieved their new positions by capitalizing on their ability and skill in meeting the needs of the members of the Negro community, including insurance, education, medical service, housing, recreation, and merchandising. The dual market has also led to the employment of many Negroes by white businessmen for the explicit purpose of helping them to penetrate the minority market.

But other factors have been more important than increased purchasing power in achieving political and social change. The rapid inroads recently made in the South to unravel the system of segregation and the increasingly rapid strides to further effective integration, particularly in education and in housing, reflect, first, the marked improvement in Negro organization and leadership and, secondly, the rising intensity of Negro protest accompanied by courage, discipline, and determination.

Self-help and protest organizations have long been a part of the efforts of the Negro to secure his full rights of citizenship and to enjoy equally with the white members of the community the full range of available opportunities. But during the last two decades vastly greater efforts have been expended by these organizations. The National Association for the Advancement of the Colored People has been particularly active in developing challenges in the courts, which spurred the Supreme Court to hand down its many far-reaching decisions. Since 1941 the attorneys for the National Association for the Advancement of Colored People have won forty-three of the forty-seven cases that they argued in the Supreme Court. The National Urban League has concentrated its efforts on working with large employers, including the federal government, to take steps to eliminate all forms of discrimination and particularly to alter the employment policies of organizations that had previously denied equal opportunity to the Negro. The National Urban League, together with other Negro organizations, played an important part in eliminating segregation from the armed services.

During the past few years unique protest and action groups have been organized. Their membership is composed primarily of southern Negroes; southern Negro youth has played a key role in their development, and their leadership, in contrast to the older protest organizations that had a biracial structure, more typically is exclusively Negro. The Southern Leadership Conference was organized in 1957 in Atlanta as a direct consequence of the success that the Montgomery Negro community had achieved through the use of nonviolent protest to eliminate segregation on the Montgomery buses. The Reverend Martin Luther King, who had led the Montgomery effort, was elected president of the new organization. The Congress on Racial Equality (CORE), which had been established in 1943 and was also dedicated to nonviolent protest, expanded considerably after the Negro victory in Montgomery. After the spectacular sit-in action undertaken by four Negro students at the Agricultural and Technical College at Greensboro, North Carolina, in February, 1960, a Student Nonviolent Coordinating Committee was organized in Atlanta, again with financial help from Dr. King's organization.

The boycotts, the "sit-ins," the "kneel-downs," "the freedom riders," the voting registration classes, and the many other evidences of the rising level of Negro protest and action depended in the first instance on the individual commitment of a large number of Negroes who were willing to risk expulsion from college, loss of employment, denial of credit on which their businesses depended, jail sentences, bodily injury, and even death. The middle-aged working woman who set off the Montgomery bus episode, the four students who initiated the "sit-in" in Greensboro, and the many others who precipitated action were responding to the accumulation of discontent growing out of the continued denial of their rights as citizens and as individuals. They were in the vanguard, but large numbers—in fact, the overwhelming majority of all Negroes—were close behind.

The real change in the last few years has been the frontal attack on segregation unleashed by the Negroes themselves. No longer will they accept it. Segregation has cost the South dearly, and its *de facto* counterpart has extorted a heavy price from the North. But South and North seemed to be largely unaware of the costs involved in this division of American democracy.

However, the value of a system that required constant tests of strength—involving even the use of federal troops— could not be taken for granted once the Negroes, with their substantial increases in power, set out to demolish segregation. But its rapid demise involves more than the accretion of Negro power. Substantial as that power has been, it was still not enough to win over the much greater power of the whites. By insisting and continuing to insist that he is entitled to his rights and will not cease his agitation until he receives them, the Negro has confronted the white community with a challenge it cannot avoid or deflect. The Negroes' determination to put an end to exploitation and degradation tipped the scales in their favor. The white community can continue to deny the Negro his rights only at the cost of jeopardizing its own and placing the future of American democracy in jeopardy. The cost of maintaining segregation and flaunting judicial opinion is public disturbance, economic disruption, and social chaos. This is a price that the great majority of white citizens, South and North, will not pay for maintaining a system of race relations that they know is neither sound nor equitable—and one that has no future.

It is clear that, except in the rural areas of the South, Negroes will soon have their freedom. But, though freedom is a precondition of equality, they are not the same. Even when the Negro finally achieves his political and civil rights, he will still be severely handicapped. Centuries of slavery and segregation have resulted in retarding his educational achievement, in restricting his occupational status and income, and in impeding his development of a strong family and community structure. Education, income, and values are the keys to the achievements of individuals and groups in a competitive society—even if the element of color is finally neutralized. The Negro leadership and masses have been, naturally, so concerned with winning the battle of civil rights that only a few perceive the wide gap that will remain between the freedom that is won and the equality that is desired. Many in the white community who are convinced that the Negro is entitled to his freedom also see that far and no farther.

There are currently about 20 million Negroes in the population, and because of a rapidly rising birth rate, the number of Negroes will approximate 25 million by the end of the 1960's. So pervasive has been the element of race in the attitudes of whites and Negroes alike that each tends to think of the entire Negro population as a homogeneous group. But most of the characteristics of such a large group are of course not homogeneous. To appraise each of the three major determinants of equality—education, income, and values—the Negro population of over two-score million must be considered as several subgroups.

In 1960 the Negro population had a level of educational achievement, measured in terms of school years completed, and without allowance for the important element of quality, that was the approximate equal of that of the white population during the 1930–1940 decade. In 1960 about 40 per cent of the Negro population between twenty-five and twenty-nine years of age had completed four years of high school or more; 5.4 per cent had attended college for four years or more. Of the white population in 1960, 64 per cent had four years or more of high school and 11.8 per cent had had four years or more of college. But the figures indicate, that despite this lag, roughly two out of every five younger Negroes are achieving a level of education that will enable them to compete successfully for jobs, even though only a relatively small percentage have the educational prerequisites to compete successfully for top jobs.

A great many other figures about the relative educational achievements of Negroes and whites could be adduced, but they would not alter the basic picture. The rate of gain among the Negroes has been faster than among the whites, because, among other reasons, they had so much farther to go. However, a sizable gap continues to exist in favor of the whites. The quality of Negro education, particularly in the South, where approximately half of the Negroes still reside, is so distinctly inferior that even the discrepancies noted above underestimate the true situation. Probably no more than one of every five Negroes has the desirable educational preparation to compete for skilled or white-collar jobs, while among whites the rate is likely to be more than one in two.

Two conclusions can be ventured. A significant and growing minority of Negroes have achieved the educational qualifications required for competing successfully in our complex technological society. But a majority—in fact, a large majority—are still educationally deprived and have little prospect of attaining more than an unskilled or semiskilled job at the lower end of the income scale.

With regard to occupational achievement and income, seven out of eight of the Negroes between the ages of twenty-five and twenty-nine who succeeded in graduating from college also succeeded in becoming professional, managerial, or clerical workers. The corresponding ratio among white males was over nine out of ten. Moreover, three times as many whites as Negroes became managers, officials, or proprietors. Even more revealing is the fact that the median income of this group for whites was about $5,400, while for Negroes $3,700, or roughly only 70 per cent as much.

For high school graduates, the occupational and income picture is less favorable. Only slightly more than one of every three of such young Negro males secured a skilled or white-collar job, while two of every three white high school graduates obtained employment in this sector. The average Negro high school graduate earned $3,300, or 68 per cent of the white graduates' income of $4,900.

The foregoing comparisons have presented data about a younger age group in order to minimize the influence of the seriously adverse conditions that so long characterized the Negro population. But it is the occupational status and income of the adult Negro population that will strongly influence if not completely determine the opportunities available to their children.

In 1962 about three out of every five Negro families earned less than $4,000 annually; in the South the income of over three of every four families was less than this amount. On the West Coast, however, only one in three Negro families earned so little. For the country as a whole slightly over one in four Negro families earned between $4,000 and $7,000 annually, a sum barely sufficient to give their children a reasonable start in life. Only one out of seven Negro families earned in excess of $7,000 annually, and one in twenty earned in excess of $10,000.

But once again the pattern in the South is noticeably different from that of the West. Only 5 per cent of Negro families in the South earned more than $7,000, while on the West Coast the corresponding figure was 71 per cent. (The latter figure is somewhat inflated by the relatively large number of nonwhites other than Negroes who are included in the Census category.) The pattern in the Northeast and the North Central states resembled that of the West much more than that of the South.

The situation in the West is indeed more favorable. Only one-third of the nonwhite population earned less than $4,000, and roughly the same proportion earned over $7,000. In fact, the distribution of income of nonwhites, most of whom are Negroes, on the West Coast was exactly parallel to that of the white population in the South. It also compared relatively favorably with that of the white population in the West; one-third of the nonwhites earned more than did over half of all white families.

The occupational and income data reinforce the educational data given earlier. While many Negroes, especially in the South, are in a poor position to advance themselves or even to afford their children a start in life that would enable them to compete successfully, a significant minority has passed the threshold. Approximately one in four or one in five families outside the South belongs to the middle class, and a small minority even belong to the upper middle class.

The type of education and jobs to which children aspire and the type of preparation for work and life they acquire depends in the first instance on the circumstances of their home. The foregoing data have called attention to the deprivations in many Negro homes because of the limited education, income, and occupational competence of the parents. In the quality of Negro family and community the past weighs most heavily.

Since the mothers of a relatively high percentage of Negro children are not married or have been deserted by their husbands, they must divide their energies and efforts between earning a living and raising their children. Many are unable to cope adequately with these burdens, and their children grow up deprived. When inadequate parental supervision is added to poverty, slum living, sexual promiscuity, and racial prejudice, it is not surprising that so many Negro children grow up poorly prepared. Approximately one out of every five Negro births is illegitimate, compared to a ratio of one in fifty among the white population. Family disorganization is compounded among Negroes by the fact that the head of the household is a woman in somewhat more than one out of five Negro families, compared with a ratio of one in eleven for white families. A great many young Negro males are growing up without a male parent or proper substitute.

Broken families represent one dimension of the larger social setting. But there are some social components which help to mitigate and compensate for their weaknesses. To some extent Negroes have an opportunity to rely on what the sociologists call the extended family. Children are frequently cared for by grandmothers, sisters, or aunts, particularly in the small communities of the South. Unlike the earlier generations of immigrants who were assisted by various ethnic organizations led by their countrymen who sought to give them a helping hand, the minority of Negroes who rose to middle class status were determined to live and act like their white counterparts. In their drive for respectability and acceptance, they sought to widen the gulf between themselves and their poverty-stricken brothers, leaving the latter to their own resources. Carrying the burdens of prejudice, poverty, and ignorance, the poor Negroes have been bereft of any substantial assistance from their more fortunate fellows.

Though Negroes account for a disproportionately large number of the poorly educated, the unemployed and those in unskilled jobs, those with family incomes below $4,000, and those from broken homes, they do not stand alone. There are many more disadvantaged white citizens, but they account for a smaller percentage of the total white population.

It is right and proper for the Negro to insist that his acquisition of first-class citizenship is a racial matter and should be treated accordingly. The freedom that he seeks has for so long been denied him because of his color. The remedy, to paraphrase Justice Harlan's formulation, must be to make this nation color-blind. But is his search for equality also a racial matter? Some among the Negro leadership believe that it is—or at least should become so. They argue that the United States should make retribution to the Negro for the centuries during which it has exploited and oppressed him. Their analogy is reparations made by the Federal Republic of Germany to the victims of Hitlerism. Certainly, a great many Negroes will never be able to achieve through their own efforts alone the rewards that come to those who can compete successfully. Affirmative action can be taken by individuals, churches, social organizations, professional societies, employers, foundations, universities, and other bodies deliberately to reduce and eliminate the roadblocks that interfere with the Negro's development of his full potential. Much can be done for the Negro without violating commitments to a society predicated on equality of opportunity.

The more difficult question involves the actions of government—federal, state, and local. Should government seek to treat the Negro differentially in order to enable him to enjoy the benefits that should flow from his gaining his freedom? Attractive as the doctrine of differential treatment might at first appear to be—and the ease with which it could be supported by the theory of compensation for past wrongs—it runs counter to the inner momentum of American democracy, to the Negro's own desire to eliminate color from the body politic, and to his present realities and future prospects.

America's democratic tradition does not justify singling out one group of disadvantaged people to the neglect of others. As we have noted above, there are many handicapped Negroes and many more handicapped whites. This country faces the urgent task of a direct and indirect attack on poverty and the conditions that help to increase or maintain it. A great many children, in every part of the country, need improved opportunities for further education, training, and retraining. As the nation faces and meets this challenge, more and more Negroes and more and more white people will be able to undertake the educational preparation that they require for life in an advanced technological society.

Similarly, with respect to jobs and income: the Employment Act of 1946 places a major responsibility on the federal government to take all possible actions to establish, maintain, and, if necessary, re-establish a high level of employment. Since the end of the Korean conflict the number of jobs has increased, but the number of persons seeking employment has increased even more. Many jobs in automobile, steel, meat packing, rubber, and other basic industries have been eliminated as a result of automation; many white workers and relatively even more Negro workers have lost preferred jobs. Currently the rate of Negro unemployment is more than twice that of the white population. The plight of Negro youth entering the labor market for the first time is particularly acute. Not one net additional Negro has obtained employment in the private sector of the economy since 1957.

Such gains as he has made have been solely in the government and nonprofit sectors. The outlook for more and better jobs for the Negroes, especially for those who enter the labor market with little in the way of specialized education or skill, depends on a much more rapid growth of employment. The rate of job creation must expand by at least 50 per cent above the level of this past decade if unemployment is not to worsen. If it is to improve, an even higher rate of job creation will be required.

In the face of this imbalance between jobs and job seekers, even the eradication of all vestiges of racial discrimination, reinforced by effective action by employers and trade unions to ease the employment and promotion of Negroes, would be of limited value. To insure his advance, the Negro needs a rapidly expanding job market like that which characterized the United States between 1940 and 1953. Only then would many Negroes now living in the South be able to move to other regions where they would have greater access to better paying jobs; only then would the handicapped Negro youth from the northern urban slum find a toe-hold in the economy. The poor Negro, like the poor white, must look to the federal government to act to quicken the economy's pace and to expand employment. No other instrumentality is capable of such a task.

Much as private groups can do for the Negro, and much as government must do for those whites and Negroes alike who are deprived of a proper education, a job, and a minimum income, the Negro has a crucial role to play in transmuting his freedom into equality. He alone makes choices about his time, his energy, and his money. He alone can stimulate the interests, cultivate the capacities, and inculcate the values that will give meaning and direction to the lives of his children and his children's children. Much of this is the task of the individual family, but some of it remains the task of the Negro community.

Among the important by-products of the intensified drive for first-class citizenship has been the broadening and the deepening of the Negro community. For the first time, the gulf between the "talented tenth" and the Negro masses is being narrowed, and in some instances it has even been eliminated. The Negro has come to realize, to paraphrase Lincoln, that in seeking freedom for himself, he must assure freedom to all Negroes. The Negro has come down a long road. No longer need he aspire to emulate white life and culture;

no longer need he feel ashamed and apologetic for his past. He is building a tradition that is unique and valuable and on which he can base a community of strength and dignity within the larger context of American society. In the process he can help himself and he can enrich the society that has finally come to make a place for him as an equal.

It has been a very long struggle, congruent with the whole of American history. The first Negro arrived in Jamestown a year before the Pilgrims reached Plymouth. The Negro was a stranger in the world of the white man, and a stranger he long remained as colonist and citizen held him at arm's length. The leaders of Virginia fashioned the system of slavery in order to regulate the relations between white and Negro. In time, colonists in both the South and the North had to improvise a new system, for some Negroes had become free in the eyes of the law. Many of the leaders of the country, fearful that white and Negro could not live peacefully together within or without the context of a slave society, attempted to establish a colonization movement in the hope that the Negro might be sent back to Africa. This effort had only limited success and Negroes soon found themselves on the periphery of the society.

At the end of a bloody Civil War, which was rooted in conflicts over the extension of slavery, the basic relations between white and Negro were permanently altered. Northern victory on the battlefield reinforced by constitutional amendments gave to all Negroes a promise of freedom, and slavery was proscribed. When the white South refused to abide by the new imperatives, federal soldiers protected the newly gained rights of the freedmen. But southern opposition was so fierce and northern preoccupation with other matters so great that the troops were shortly withdrawn, and the southern leaders were left with the task of evolving a new modus vivendi with their former slaves. For several decades the South resorted to violence and intimidation, even to lynching, to prevent the extension of Negro rights. So successful was this policy—and so little opposition did it engender in the North—that in the 1890's the southern leadership decided to relegate the Negro permanently to second-class citizenship in a minutely elaborated and legally reinforced system of segregation. This was maintained for a half century, while in the North *de facto* segregation was the order of the day.

But in time these systems too proved unsatisfactory. Slowly but surely the walls of segregation, first in the North and then in the South, began to fall. In many instances informal discrimination replaced legal segregation. Even that proved untenable. For finally the Negro himself, with the knowledge that the President, the Supreme Court, and eventually even the Congress would support him, struck out to realize the freedom so long denied him. Inevitably his determination to win immediately led to conflict, even bloody conflict on occasion. But the outcome has never been in doubt.

America, having experimented with every possible alternative except genocide—slavery, restrictions on free Negroes, colonization, emancipation, constitutional freedom protected by federal soldiers, violence and intimidation as instruments of policy, segregation *de jure* and *de facto*, discrimination—and having found each in turn unsatisfactory, has slowly but surely expanded the framework of its democratic structure and is now establishing the first biracial democracy in the world. America is finally acting on the Biblical injunction:

Withhold not good from them to whom it is due,
When it is the power of thy hand to do it.
Say not unto thy neighbor: 'Go, and come again,
And tomorrow I will give'; when thou hast it by thee.

NOTES

1. *National Party Platforms, 1840–1960*, compiled by Kirk H. Porter and Donald Bruce Johnson, University of Illinois Press, Urbana, 1961, p. 435.

2. *Ibid.*, pp. 467–8.

3. Key, V. O., Jr., *Southern Politics in State and Nation*, Vintage Books, New York, 1949, p. 650.

4. *Ibid.*, p. 648.

5. Price, H. D., *The Negro and Southern Politics*, New York University Press, New York, 1957, pp. 66–7.

6. *Freedom to the Free, 1863–1963, Century of Emancipation*, A Report to the President by the United States Commission on Civil Rights, U.S. Government Printing Office, Washington, D.C., 1963, pp. 169–70.

Postscript: The Promise Still Delayed, 1993

In Studs Terkel's evocative interviews about white-black relationships in the United States in the last decade of the twentieth century, focused on southern black migrants in Chicago in search of freedom and jobs, one finds the phrase the "Second Betrayal." Almost a century after Reconstruction, when blacks had been promised forty acres and a mule, the significant advances of the Civil Rights movement marked by the desegregation of the public schools, access to the ballot box and other civic rights, and affirmative action in the job market, the assassination in 1968 of Martin Luther King, Jr. resulted in a new turn in the road. The Second Reconstruction had held out the promise for the early completion of the long delayed emancipation of all blacks by enabling them to enjoy not only the freedoms vouchsafed all Americans by the Declaration of Independence but also equality of opportunity, the other basic commitment of our democracy.

There is no agreement among the leaders, scholars, or members of either the white or black groups about how to interpret the post-King era, but most of them would probably agree that the high hopes for the proximate achievement of the long-delayed full emancipation of blacks were undermined by intent, accident, or some combination of both. Not everybody accepts the phrase, the "Second Betrayal," which sees the further delays in the full emancipation of the blacks as the direct and ineluctable consequences of white power groups working to maintain their privileges, but few observers could fail to acknowledge that the promise of blacks' full progress from freedom to equality has been delayed. Since almost all of the power in America resides with the white majority, it should come as no surprise that many blacks read the last quarter century as the era of the Second Betrayal.

We must pause and consider at least briefly the alternative explanations of what happened between 1968 and 1992, for in the absence of broad agreement about the recent past, we will find it very difficult to pursue a dialogue about the opportunities and constraints that will continue to bound the changes in white-black relations in the years ahead. Meaningful action depends upon entering and pursuing meaningful dialogues, both within each group and between groups. The fact that such dialogues are difficult to initiate and to maintain does not mean that the effort can be shortcircuited, since dialogue and action are the twin supports of a virile democracy. Without dialogue, action is likely to be blind, but without action, dialogue will lead to despair and destruction. Let us consider the post-King era in two parts: the first focuses on generalizations that can be supported and substantiated by data and analysis. The second concerns the more speculative interpretations about which even well-informed and involved persons can differ, often considerably.

The almost four decades that have passed since a unanimous Supreme Court outlawed segregation in the public schools epitomize both the strength and weaknesses of our democracy in its efforts to right the wrongs so long visited on blacks. In a large number of small and even large communities, principally in the south, but also in other regions, the educational authorities complied willingly or resentfully with court orders to desegregate their public schools. But forty years later a high proportion of all blacks are enrolled in public schools in which they account for at least 75 percent of the total student body.

Although many courts resorted to enforced bussing to speed desegregation, they were unable to prevent or even slow various counterstrategies by white parents, such as their relocating to the suburbs where the schools were predominantly or totally white, or to the transfer of their children from public schools to private schools. Since this latter decision would involve them in substantial expenditures, some pursued a third alternative: they were able to enroll their children in special public schools with strong curricula and good teachers that had been in place earlier, or had recently been put in place to provide improved educational opportunities for talented blacks, but where most students continued to be white, because their parents knew better how to negotiate the newly reformed system. Thus, the school desegregation decision did not result in all, or even most, black youths having access to schooling equal to that available to most white children. While many middle-class black families also moved out of the inner city, for the same reasons that motivated whites, most blacks continued to live in the city proper. The evidence is overwhelming that many, though not all, inner-city public schools with a large black student body are characterized by high dropout rates, low skill acquisition, and fewer graduates who continue with their education.

Over the intervening three decades, however, the gaps between black and white educational achievement narrowed perceptibly, particularly in the case of black females, although the gaps continue to be substantial, particularly in the case of the ratio of blacks to whites who graduate from college or who acquire postgraduate degrees. The favorite recommendations for improving the education of blacks include: more parental involvement; more minority leadership and teaching staff; more equal allocation of funding, more preschool (Headstart) programs; more support programs (counselling, health, tutoring) for children and young people at risk; an elongated school day, week, year, and still other sensible and reasonable reforms most of which have been easier to formulate than to implement.

The most vexatious aspect of black school experience concerns the large numbers of young black males who get "turned off" early on, because they have come to view the classroom as an oppressive environment, and who drop out as soon as they can since they see no point of continuing. In a study that I carried out with two black graduate students at Columbia University in 1978, entitled *Tell Me About Your School* (National Commission for Employment Policy, Washington, D.C.) we asked a group of forteen to fifteen year olds still in Harlem schools whether they knew of anyone who had obtained a regular job as a result of having completed high school. The overwhelming replies were negative.

Many of the young male dropouts are drawn to the streets, join a gang, participate in the off-the-record economy, get involved in petty or not so petty crime, deal in stolen goods or sell drugs. They see no future for themselves if they remain on the educational track. A significant number of the young women who have had difficult lives, and have little or no hope that their future will be different, respond to the importunings of their boyfriends and become sexually active without use of birth control. Many carry their babies to term in the hope that becoming a mother, going on welfare, and being the head of a household will change their lives for the better. They, too, see no point in staying in school.

The simple and overwhelming fact is that young people, growing up under the most disadvantaged circumstances at home, in the community, and at school, see little or no point in schooling which they have found difficult and unrewarding, particularly since they have been unable to make a linkage between their staying in school and, later on, getting a regular job and improving their lives. The young alienated black men mock and ridicule their peers who continue to take school seriously as imitating "whitey." As we will find to be the case with each dimension of black experience during the past several decades, the great expectations engendered by the Supreme Court's *Brown* decision were not realized. On the other hand, sizable numbers of blacks have acquired the educational preparation and credentials that have provided them with a bridge into the regular labor market and a decent income.

Before leaving the school environment we need to look more closely at the early alienation and subsequent aggression that many young black males in particular develop toward all established societal values and institutions. A significant number of young black men by their early adolescence have concluded that the larger society has little interest in their development and well-being and is rigged against them. Accordingly they see little or no point in playing by society's rules. They cut classes; if they come to school they act up. Before long they join a street gang that engages in petty theft, violence, and other forms of destructive behavior. The larger society has dealt them a bad hand and their response is to repay the society in kind by not abiding by its rules and regulations. In adopting and acting in a defiant mode they go a long way to assuring the dismal outcomes, the prospects of which led them in the first instance to turn their backs on the status quo.

But not all who are alienated engage in such self-destructive behavior. A significant number are attracted to the Nation of Islam or other Afro-American separatist ideologies and patterns of life which see gains for blacks who separate themselves from whites and define and pursue their own goals. But impressive as some of these separatist efforts have been they have limited attractiveness. Most blacks want to make it as part of a diverse American public.

Turning from the schools to the voting booth, what have been the consequences of the belated right of blacks to exercise voting privileges and enjoy other civic rights? Equality of treatment on the street, in the courtroom, in the voting booth, in restaurants and hotels, in stores, in the real estate market, is still not available for many blacks. But the inequalities that they continue to experience have less to do with the direct attempt by whites to use political power to deprive blacks of their rights, and more with the historical fact that most of the nation's resources, both property and income, is in the hands of whites who have every intention to hold on to what they own.

But we cannot assume that black advances at the polls have resulted in no benefits for them. Political power has always been associated with economic advantage and the fact that blacks are now the mayors of many of the nation's leading metropolises has been reflected in increased access by blacks to public employment, public contracts, public licenses and a growing voice in local political decision-making. While the election of thousands of black political officials has not led to an equal sharing of political power with whites, it has led to some accommodation. Moreover, the weakening of white hegemonic control over the instruments of political power—local, state, and national—is a portent that in times to come the present division of the spoils will move more to the benefit of blacks, as their successes in the polling booths multiply.

The widespread belief on the part of many blacks that a "second betrayal" occurred with the assassination of Martin Luther King is grounded in their perspective of what has occurred on the job front, particularly with respect to affirmative action. Instead of a friendly federal government continuing to take the lead through the courts and via administrative agencies to widen opportunities for blacks to be hired and promoted, putting in place diverse mechanisms to assure that these objectives are speeded, the federal government turned neutral, if not hostile. No sooner did employers, large, medium, and small, become aware of the diminished interest of the federal government in affirmative action, than most of them responded in similar fashion.

For the last two decades there has been a great deal of roiling of the U.S. labor market, including the substantial shrinkage in the number and proportion of well-paying manufacturing jobs previously available to modestly educated whites and blacks. The more recent repeated reduction of the work forces of service sector corporations has intensified this trend. The third disturbing factor has been the relocation of many firms from urban centers to outlying areas and to overseas which left large numbers of young black males with limited educational credentials with little or no access to the unskilled entrance jobs in the suburbs or to the increasingly sophisticated advanced business services jobs in the central city.

As the opportunities diminished for many whites to be hired or promoted, their opposition to affirmative action intensified, a signal that most politicians were quick to recognize and respond to, none more quickly than recent Republican presidents. The disappointment of many blacks in this major turnaround in federal policy was one more proof of the unwillingness of most white Americans to address and remove the heavy hand of racism from where it counted most—in the job market. A slack job market, on the other hand, has never been conducive to expanding the opportunities for those who have been on the periphery.

But once again, the evidence is not quite so simple. The data leave no doubt that many more blacks than whites are mired in poverty, about one-third of the blacks compared to 10 percent of the whites. The fact remains, however, that during the last decades a significant proportion of blacks, particularly those in two-worker families, have moved up the income scale. And this is true not only for the small minority of two-worker families where both members are college graduates, but for the much larger numbers who have more modest educational credentials and who are in lower-paying jobs.

There are both black and white analysts who would find the foregoing interpretations both too general and too benign. They argue that our white-dominated industrial system is constructed to keep blacks in their place; that the so-called victory of political emancipation is largely illusory; that the hegemony of white power in all legislative, executive and judicial branches continues, and that the bifurcated income distribution patterns between whites and blacks are the direct outcome of these differentials in power. There are however conflicting interpretations of the black condition.

These include black family structure, black violence and crime and black leadership. With regard to the black family, there is widespread concern among both black and white leaders about the disturbing fact that 43 percent of all black children are being raised in one-parent homes and that the majority (57 percent) of all black children are born to mothers who are not married or who have never been married. Since the emotional and economic support that most single parents, especially those with limited educational and occupational experience, are able to offer their offspring are severely limited, many of these children face no future or, at best, an impoverished future.

The question raised by the finding that a growing predominance of black children are born out-of-wedlock, invites a consideration of the societal forces that may be responsible for such an aberrant situation. Earlier attention was called to the considerable number of black female teenagers who, confronting a bleak future, become mothers overwhelmingly outside of marriage. But the vast majority of black children of single mothers are born to women in their twenties, not in their teens. In these cases, a large part of the explanation for the high proportion born out-of-wedlock reflects the shortage of young black males of marriageable age who are capable and willing to assume the obligations of fatherhood. The young men, however, have had their ranks diminished by premature death or imprisonment as well as by the growing shortage of regular jobs with regular incomes to which they have access. The data tell us that if black women want to be mothers, they can delay having a child until they are in their twenties, or even longer, but their prospect of finding a stable husband to share the joys and responsibilities of parenthood are not likely to improve.

What are the specifics of this shortage of marriageable males? First, if not foremost, is the high death rate of young black males from homicide, suicide, and accidents. More important by far is the high proportion of young blacks who are confined to prison. The United States has more people in confinement than any other advanced country and although blacks account for only about 12 percent of the total population, they account for almost half of all prison inmates. When they are released after serving their term, a significant proportion become recidivists and many others face great difficulties in finding a regular job at which they can earn enough to support themselves; it is very difficult for blacks with prison records to find jobs that will enable them to support a wife and children.

But even those blacks who are able to stay out of serious trouble with the law, are often unable to find and keep a regular job; without a job they are not good prospects for a woman who seeks a husband and a father for the child or children that she looks forward to raising. It is easier for the white majority to build more prisons in which to lock up more young criminals; to legislate changes in the welfare system aimed at forcing unwed mothers off the rolls; to take more fathers to court to force them to pay child support, than to pursue the more difficult alternatives of righting the conditions that have resulted in the shortage of eligible young black males able to play a constructive role in society via education, jobs, marriage, and parenthood.

The post-King era has revealed serious lacunae in the black leadership structure. The NAACP and the National Urban League are finding it increasingly difficult to respond to the new challenges they confront as the century draws to an end. Their greatest difficulty has been to build bridges to the two generation and more of young blacks who have come of age since King's assassination.

Many of these young people have lost patience with the unfilled promises of the white leadership; they have decided to turn inward, to seek their roots, to draw strength from their African-American background, to isolate themselves increasingly from mainline America. While this stance is attractive to many, especially during their college years when they experience considerable isolation on the nation's campuses, it is not a propitious long-run strategy. Blacks surely do not have to accommodate to white America, but they cannot stop fighting for their full emancipation. To win that fight, they must continue to confront the white majority and not toy with the unrealistic option of withdrawing from the fray. One major challenge the black minority confronts is to develop a successor to King who can engage the energy and commitment of blacks in a renewed struggle for their full emancipation. This struggle must elicit renewed support from the white majority, leading to the joint support that attested to King's genius. The long-delayed full emancipation of the blacks requires joint action by both blacks and whites, a challenge that the leadership of both groups must confront and resolve if the United States is to avoid the chaos of civil disorder and fulfill its promise to itself and to the world.

The second major challenge that the black minority confronts is to do its utmost to instill in its young people that, however unfair the legacy of racism is and continues to be, every individual must see himself or herself primarily in control of his or her own future. Whether they will be able to surmount the many dangerous challenges that they are likely to encounter, how to avoid dropping out of school prematurely, how to avoid becoming parents prematurely, how to avoid becoming entangled in the criminal justice system, how to say no to drugs and the many more "temptations" that they will encounter during their formative years—depends in the first place on themselves, not on the members of the dominant white community. It is surely more comfortable for many young blacks to hold the white community responsible for the aberrations in their own behaviors and actions. But that is a dangerous and false posture. Even in a society characterized by discrimination, gross inequalities, and widespread poverty, each younger and older person must be responsible for his or her actions.

There are at least several persuasive reasons that the deep-seated unresolved, if lessening, oppression of blacks by whites during the extended period of U.S. development is probably drawing toward an end. How quickly the end will come remains shrouded by events that still lie ahead but it is unlikely that racism, qua racism, will prevail indefinitely.

The first and, in my view, the overwhelming reason to look forward to the relatively early demise of racism is rooted in the shifting realities of the American demographic structure that will relatively soon (by 2010 or shortly thereafter) displace blacks as the top-ranking minority group is already far advanced in several large states and metropolitan centers in the West, South, and on the East Coast including, but not limited to, such key urban centers as Los Angeles and San Diego, Dallas, Houston, San Antonio, Miami and New York City.

A further demographic consideration relates to the inclusivity of the term "blacks." In point of fact there are several distinctive subgroups of blacks—U.S. blacks, black immigrants from the British-speaking Caribbean countries; black Haitians whose mother tongue is Creole; and small numbers of recent black immigrants from Africa. They differ on a great many critical dimensions from level of education to entrepreneurial experience and occupational objectives.

Aside from the black-Latino prospective inversion, further demographic changes appear to have substantial momentum, the most important of which is the substantial and continuing growth of Asians, particularly from East and Southeast Asia, but also from other parts of the continent. In the face of such steadily growing diversity of peoples of different nationalities, ethnicity, language, culture, educational background and still other differentiating characteristics, the long-standing simplistic division of the U .S. between whites and blacks will be overwhelmed by the new and greater diversity of the emerging U.S. population. While the strength of U.S. racism will be undermined by the changing arithmetic that lies ahead, its proximate demise will be speeded by other factors. These include various incongruities, crosscurrents and new departures that are certain to gain strength in the decades ahead.

Aside from how to "classify" Puerto Ricans who are black, often blacker than Southern blacks whose ancestors were in the U.S. since before the Revolutionary War, what possible sense does it make to continue to consider blacks as an undifferentiated socioeconomic group of 30 million persons, many of whom have made outstanding contributions to literature, music, religion, politics and sports, while large numbers of others have been trapped in poverty, living on our society's fringes, characterized by violence, drugs and crime.

The argument that the foundations of racial divisiveness are being eroded by accelerating demographic and political-economic changes does not imply that all dimensions of white-black racism will be eradicated soon, but that differentiations among the ever-more diversified American population will be reflected in language, ethnicity, education, occupation, and income and above all, by class, rather than by race. This is already apparent: native-born Asian-Americans in California have, on average, much more education and higher income than white Americans. This finding does not imply that most Chinese who own or work in restaurants, or most Laotians and Vietnamese who are struggling to make the transition to an American life-style, have succeeded in their efforts or that success is right around the corner for them. Nevertheless, the highest median family income is found among native-born Asian-Americans.

While it will not be easy for political alliances to be forged among some, or all, of the fast-growing diverse groups in our major metropolitan centers and more populous states, it is inevitable that local and state politics and, to a lesser extent, national politics will be reconfigured along the lines of emerging if unstable coalitions. Sooner or later, given the nature of interest-group politics, the groups which have been on the outside will realize that the only way they will be able to make progress is through alliances with other groups.

This focus on the political process leads to two related points: the first relates to the actions that the federal government initiated in the 1960s to speed desegregation so as to integrate blacks into the job market. Aside from the recent resistance by whites to affirmative action in the face of a less buoyant labor market, the rapidly growing numbers of other "minorities" that have also sought preference—women, the elderly, the handicapped, Latinos, Asian-Americans, the gay and lesbian communities, and many other groups—have made it more difficult to continue to use affirmative action as a major rebalancing device to provide delayed justice for blacks alone.

The role of government in broadening opportunities for formerly excluded minorities must, however, remain on the nation's agenda. Without the active participation of government, it will not be possible to develop human resources effectively, and to reduce the losses from the underutilization of the potential and competencies of its black and other minorities. Nor will the costs of the current policies of dealing with group tensions—more police, more prisons, more whites fleeing the city to suburban enclaves—remain manageable. Fleeing the city is not the answer either for those who relocate and surely not for those who are left behind.

While the challenge is formidable and the answers will not come easily, the U.S. has an historic commitment—not to equality of outcome—but to equality of *opportunity*. While government alone cannot do the job, there is no possibility of the nation delivering on this promise without the continued active role of government at all levels.

There are many who continue to proclaim that financial responsibility, hard work, and family values have been and must continue to be the foundations for this nation's commitment to itself and to its future. While there is much in our history to support this contention, it does not provide the whole answer.

A state that cannot assure the security of person and property for large numbers of its citizens, that cannot assure that its young people are prepared to enter the workforce at the end of their years of compulsory education, that is unable to provide employment opportunities for all adults who want and need to work and fails to provide sustenance and support for those who are unable to support themselves, is a state inviting turmoil and conflict. Admittedly the state, qua state, cannot assure solely by its own actions that parents rear their children properly; that students apply themselves to their studies; that those who work for a wage are able and willing to give good measure for the wages that they receive. But unless a society can meet its basic responsibilities to assure public order, have its schools perform effectively, enable parents to work to support themselves and their dependents, it is at a serious risk.

The case of racism in the United States has long manifested itself in a societal indifference to the conditions of life confronting the black minority. But in neglecting and ignoring the needs of the blacks, our society has also failed to respond effectively to the needs of a great many disadvantaged and handicapped whites, Hispanics, and increasingly, the members of other diverse groups. The primary engine of social reform, government, has been underutilized, stunted, and misdirected because it was unwilling to look four-square at its obligations to respond to the primary needs of all of its citizens. In avoiding its responsibilities to its black citizens, it has also failed large numbers of its nonblack citizenry and because of both failures it has placed the future well-being of the nation at serious risk.

What then can be done? The question is more important now when so many whites and blacks alike realize that "affirmative action" cannot be relied upon as the principal tool to open what remains of a still largely closed white society. There are some among the black leadership who, convinced that the hostility of the whites is so great and so deep that the blacks must refocus their energies and their efforts and build and strengthen their own institutions—church, school, businesses—instead of seeking acceptance from whites which they see as a doomed undertaking. Separatism is an ideology whose dynamism is easy to appreciate, but, at least to this outsider, it does not appear that its rationale and prospects have much more to offer in the 1990s than when Marcus Garvey first put forward an earlier version of the same doctrine in the early decades of this century.

In the early 1960s Whitney Young, the newly elected head
of the National Urban League, put forward a proposal for a
Marshall Plan for black Americans, reparations for the
centuries of neglect and exploitation which they had suffered
at the hands of the dominant whites. But the steady erosion
of affirmative action in the intervening decades is a potent
reminder of the unbridgeable gap between what Young
proposed and what the white political leadership has been
willing to consider. It is questionable whether one out of
every ten politically engaged whites has ever heard of
Young's proposal and that more than one in a hundred
would think it worthwhile to discuss it today. During the Civil
Rights movement of the 1960s King and his colleagues were
able to organize the blacks and at the same time elicit broad
support from diverse groups of whites, from college students
to Lyndon Baines Johnson. There is no telling if, and when,
some variant of the 1960s will reemerge with equally
salubrious effects. But movements that depend on inspired
leadership cannot be created without a leader, however
compelling the conditions and the challenges.

What then is there to do? The sensible answer is to use
whatever mechanisms are in place to which blacks have
access and which the white majority will support. This
suggests that blacks with their considerably expanded
political leverage in local governments, particularly in a great
many large cities led by black mayors, should focus the
government apparatus to improve public security in minority
neighborhoods. Adults, young people, and children cannot
function effectively if their person and property are at
constant risk. A first obligation of government towards all its
citizens, blacks and whites, is to establish and maintain a safe
environment. As is so often the case, an involvement of the
local community in neighborhood policing might reduce the
resource cost of enhanced security and also add to its
effectiveness.

The next step is the improvement of the local schools.
Once again the growing influence of blacks in many local
governments, places them in a preferred position to gain

more leverage than they have enjoyed in the past over the leadership and direction of their local public schools. While more tax revenue would make the task of reform easier, the major challenge has less to do with additional funding and is more closely linked to the improved use and accountability of existing funds. Most black children and young people should anticipate that if they perform effectively in school they will be able to earn their high school diplomas and make a satisfactory transition into the world of work.

A few adjustments are called for, but none are costly or complex. The United States is behind almost all of Western Europe in having pre-kindergarten programs such as Headstart in place for all young children. More attention needs to be paid to children in grades one to six to insure that they master the fundamentals and that slow learners receive special help. Moreover, we know that the academic preparatory program is not suitable for all high school students. Many need the opportunity to be part of a more occupational-oriented curriculum, more closely linked to the world of adult work, from health to media. The models exist. The supplemental budgetary costs are small.

Parents in low income neighborhoods, blacks and others, must press for these minimum reforms, and responsible whites must assist them in achieving the goal that all young people leave school able and ready to enter the world of work. The shortage of dollars is less to blame than the shortage of political commitment and drive on the part of blacks, whites, and persons of other backgrounds.

The more complicated challenge is having sufficient jobs available for all who are able and willing to work. Ours is a society in which we look in the first instance to private employers to create and maintain a demand for labor. Since 1946 the federal government has had the obligation under the Employment Act to establish and maintain an optimal level of employment and income. As the longtime chair of successive federal committees and commissions with oversight over $85 billion of federal appropriations for employment and training programs between 1962 and 1981,

I have had a unique opportunity to learn at first hand about the difficulties that the federal government has faced in responding to these obligations.

But one thing is clear: we cannot insist that people who are able to work do so unless jobs are available to them. The only and last time that sufficient jobs were available for all who wanted to work was in 1943-44 at the height of World War II. In the mid-1970s after many months of intense discussion, I persuaded my friend, Arthur F. Burns, at the time Chairman of the Federal Reserve Board, to announce his support for the federal government to institute a program whereby it would become the employer of last resort, with a proviso that anybody able and willing to work could get a public sector job at 10 percent below the minimum wage. I do not believe that the establishment of such a governmental program would solve all of the job problems facing unemployed and underemployed blacks and other low income persons, but I believe that until such a program is in place together with an expanded system of earned income credits and income supplements that we will not know what it can contribute and how it should be modified and strengthened.

Finally, I find much of the criticism of our welfare system to be unjust. I do not question that we made a number of mistakes in facilitating the explosive growth of the welfare system in the 1960s, but our unwillingness to pursue aggressive initiatives in family planning for young men and young women makes our distress over the number of single parent families more than a little hypocritical.

After years of so-called welfare reform, we are using assorted kinds of pressure on young mothers on welfare to go back to school and/or seek training and a job without providing the funding that would make such a program both realistic and promising. Recently, federal and state governments have increased their efforts to identify the fathers of many children being reared by mothers on welfare who have made no contribution to child support because of lack of income or lack of commitment to mother or child. It would be difficult to argue against strengthening the child support system including obligatory payments by fathers in a position to assist. But it is not difficult to question the contribution that a strengthened child support system can make to the stabilization of poor black communities in the face of the violence that pervades these neighborhoods, the ineffectiveness of the schools, the flight into pregnancy of many young women who see no better future for themselves, the absence of jobs for young men, and many other ghetto pathologies.

What is my conclusion? No one who has read with care, as I did, Studs Terkel's more than four hundred pages of insightful interviews on *Race* can believe that after the problem has been on the nation's agenda for 373 years, that it will shortly be resolved. But it is not unrealistic to believe that the intensity of the racism that has long dominated white-black relationships in the United States has entered an era that holds promise of its continuing weakening, if not early disappearance. The major reasons for cautious optimism are these: the growing diversity of the United States will inevitably moderate the sharp confrontations between whites and blacks but we must take care to avoid new conflicts among the many new minority groups. The only way that a multiracial, multiethnic society will be able to function effectively is through coalitions among the outsiders against the insiders, with political coalitions expanding opportunities for those on the outside.

There is no possibility that the U.S. will maintain its leadership role in the world's economic and political affairs unless it makes full use of the capabilities and potentials of all its people, whatever their color or ethnic origin. The costs of the racism that we have practiced are no longer sustainable because they will henceforth be paid for not only by blacks but also by whites.

Finally, the instruments for progress and resolution are in place. They do not have to be developed de novo. The great legacy from the Civil Rights movement has placed the vote in the hands of all blacks and the same is true for all the

Hispanics and other non-Anglos who are or will shortly become citizens. And as they learn to use the vote more effectively through organization and alliances, they will be able to make government more responsive to their needs and goals.

The major challenges to government are old, not new: to assure the safety of persons and property; to operate the schools effectively; to help the economy sustain a high level of employment; to care for the needy.

The more that blacks and other ethnic groups succeed in spurring government to discharge its appropriate missions effectively, the better it will be not only for them but for whites. The future of the nation is inscribed in its motto: *E Pluribus Unum.*

SOURCES AND READING LIST

OVER AND ABOVE the books listed at the end of each chapter, we relied for factual information on the following, particularly in regard to Chapters 10, 11, and 12.

From Slavery to Freedom, John Hope Franklin, Knopf, 1961.

Historical Statistics of the United States, U.S. Government Printing Office, Washington, D.C., 1960.

An American Dilemma, Gunnar Myrdal, Harper, 1944.

The Negro Potential, Eli Ginzberg, Columbia University Press, 1956.

Economic Growth and Employment Opportunities for Minorities, Dale L. Hiestand, Columbia University Press, 1964.

Consumer Income, Series P60, No. 37, Current Population Report, January 17, 1962, U.S. Government Printing Office, Washington, D.C.

The following readily accessible books will enable the reader to pursue further the major theme of the confrontation between American democracy and the Negro.

Frank Tannenbaum, *Slave and Citizen,* Knopf, New York, 1948.

Stanley M. Elkins, *Slavery,* University of Chicago Press, Chicago, 1959.

Life and Times of Frederick Douglass, Collier Books, New York, 1962.

Eric L. McKitrick, *Andrew Johnson and Reconstruction,* University of Chicago Press, Chicago, 1960.

W. S. Cash, *The Mind of the South,* Doubleday Anchor (A27), New York, 1941.

George W. Cable, *The Negro Question,* Doubleday Anchor (A144), New York, 1958.

C. Vann Woodward, *Reunion and Reaction,* Doubleday Anchor (A83), New York, 1956.

C. Vann Woodward, *The Strange Career of Jim Crow,* Oxford, New York, 1957.

W. E. Burghardt Du Bois, *The Souls of Black Folk,* Fawcett, Greenwich, Conn., 1961.

Gunnar Myrdal, *An American Dilemma,* Harper, New York, 1944.

Saunders Redding, *The Lonesome Road,* Doubleday, New York, 1958.

Freedom to the Free, 1863–1963, Century of Emancipation, A Report to the President by the U.S. Commission on Civil Rights, Washington, D.C., 1963.

The two best histories of the Negro are *From Slavery to Freedom, A History of American Negroes,* by John Hope Franklin, Knopf, 1961; and *The Negro in the United States, A Brief History,* by Rayford W. Logan, Van Nostrand (Anvil Book 19), Princeton, N.J., 1957.